ALSO AVAILABLE FROM TOKYOPOP

PSYCHIC ACADEMY
QUEEN'S KNIGHT, THE
RAGNAROK
RAVE MASTER
REALITY CHECK
REBIRTH
REBOUND
REMOTE
RISING STARS OF MANGA™, THE
SABER MARIONETTE J
SAILOR MOON
SAINT TAIL
SAIYUKI
SAMURAI DEEPER KYO
SAMURAI GIRL™ REAL BOUT HIGH SCHOOL
SCRYED
SEIKAI TRILOGY, THE
SGT. FROG
SHAOLIN SISTERS
SHIRAHIME-SYO: SNOW GODDESS TALES
SHUTTERBOX
SKULL MAN, THE
SNOW DROP
SORCERER HUNTERS
SOUL TO SEOUL
STONE
SUIKODEN III
SUKI
TAROT CAFÉ, THE
THREADS OF TIME
TOKYO BABYLON
TOKYO MEW MEW
TOKYO TRIBES
TRAMPS LIKE US
UNDER THE GLASS MOON
VAMPIRE GAME
VISION OF ESCAFLOWNE, THE
WARCRAFT
WARRIORS OF TAO
WILD ACT
WISH
WORLD OF HARTZ
X-DAY
ZODIAC P.I.

NOVELS

CLAMP SCHOOL PARANORMAL INVESTIGATORS
SAILOR MOON
SLAYERS

ART BOOKS

ART OF CARDCAPTOR SAKURA
ART OF MAGIC KNIGHT RAYEARTH, THE
PEACH: MIWA UEDA ILLUSTRATIONS
CLAMP NORTH SIDE
CLAMP SOUTH SIDE

ANIME GUIDES

COWBOY BEBOP
GUNDAM TECHNICAL MANUALS
SAILOR MOON SCOUT GUIDES

TOKYOPOP KIDS

STRAY SHEEP

CINE-MANGA®

ALADDIN
CARDCAPTORS
DUEL MASTERS
FAIRLY ODDPARENTS, THE
FAMILY GUY
FINDING NEMO
G.I. JOE SPY TROOPS
GREATEST STARS OF THE NBA
JACKIE CHAN ADVENTURES
JIMMY NEUTRON: BOY GENIUS, THE ADVENTURES OF
KIM POSSIBLE
LILO & STITCH: THE SERIES
LIZZIE MCGUIRE
LIZZIE MCGUIRE MOVIE, THE
MALCOLM IN THE MIDDLE
POWER RANGERS: DINO THUNDER
POWER RANGERS: NINJA STORM
PRINCESS DIARIES 2, THE
RAVE MASTER
SHREK 2
SIMPLE LIFE, THE
SPONGEBOB SQUAREPANTS
SPY KIDS 2
SPY KIDS 3-D: GAME OVER
TEENAGE MUTANT NINJA TURTLES
THAT'S SO RAVEN
TOTALLY SPIES
TRANSFORMERS: ARMADA
TRANSFORMERS: ENERGON

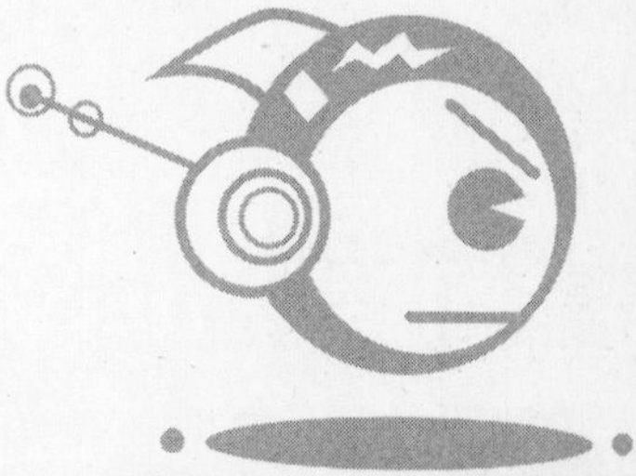

You want it? We got it!
A full range of TOKYOPOP products are available now at:
www.TOKYOPOP.com/shop

10.19.04T

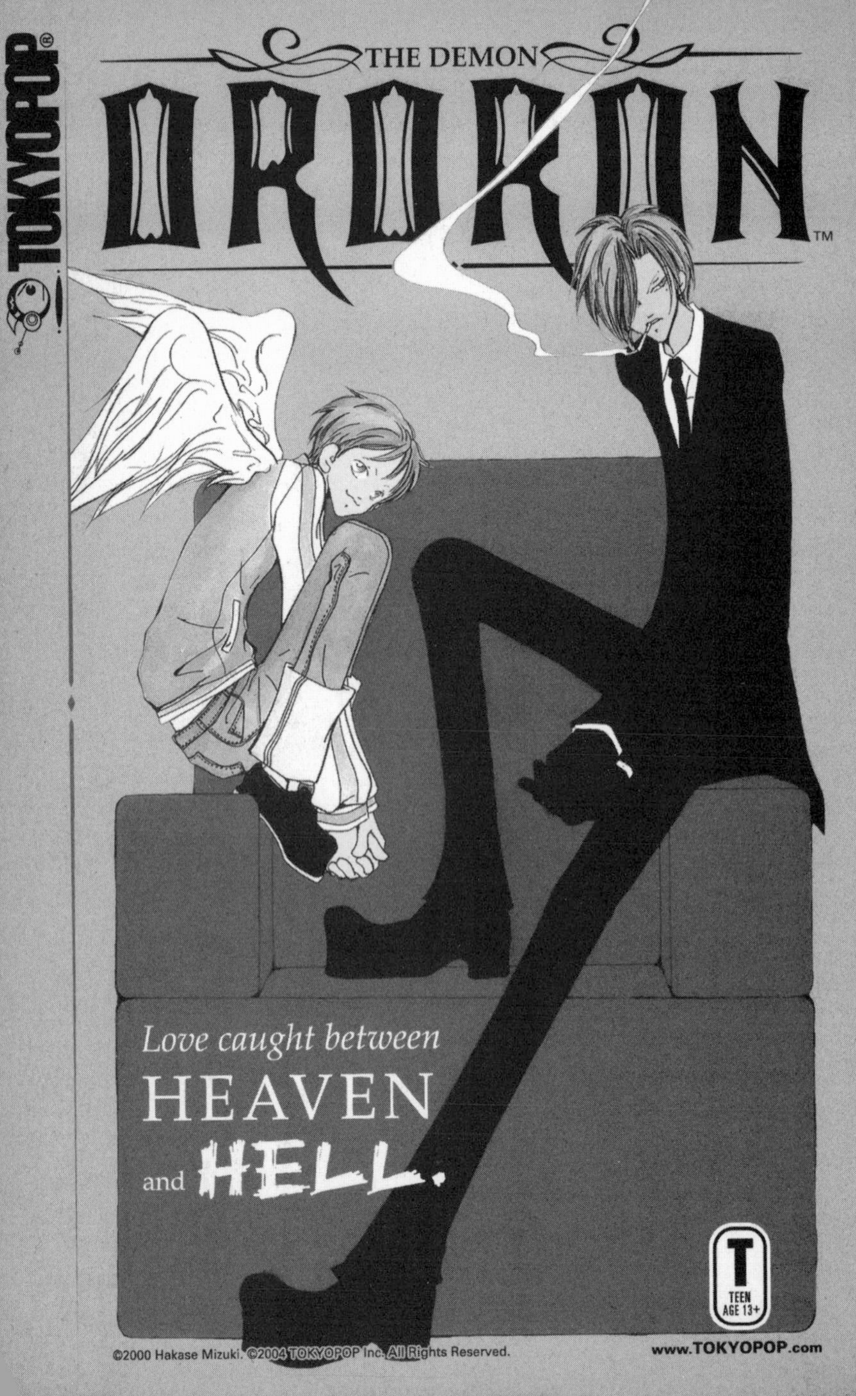
TOKYOPOP
THE DEMON
ORORON™
Love caught between
HEAVEN
and HELL.
T
TEEN
AGE 13+
©2000 Hakase Mizuki. ©2004 TOKYOPOP Inc. All Rights Reserved.
www.TOKYOPOP.com

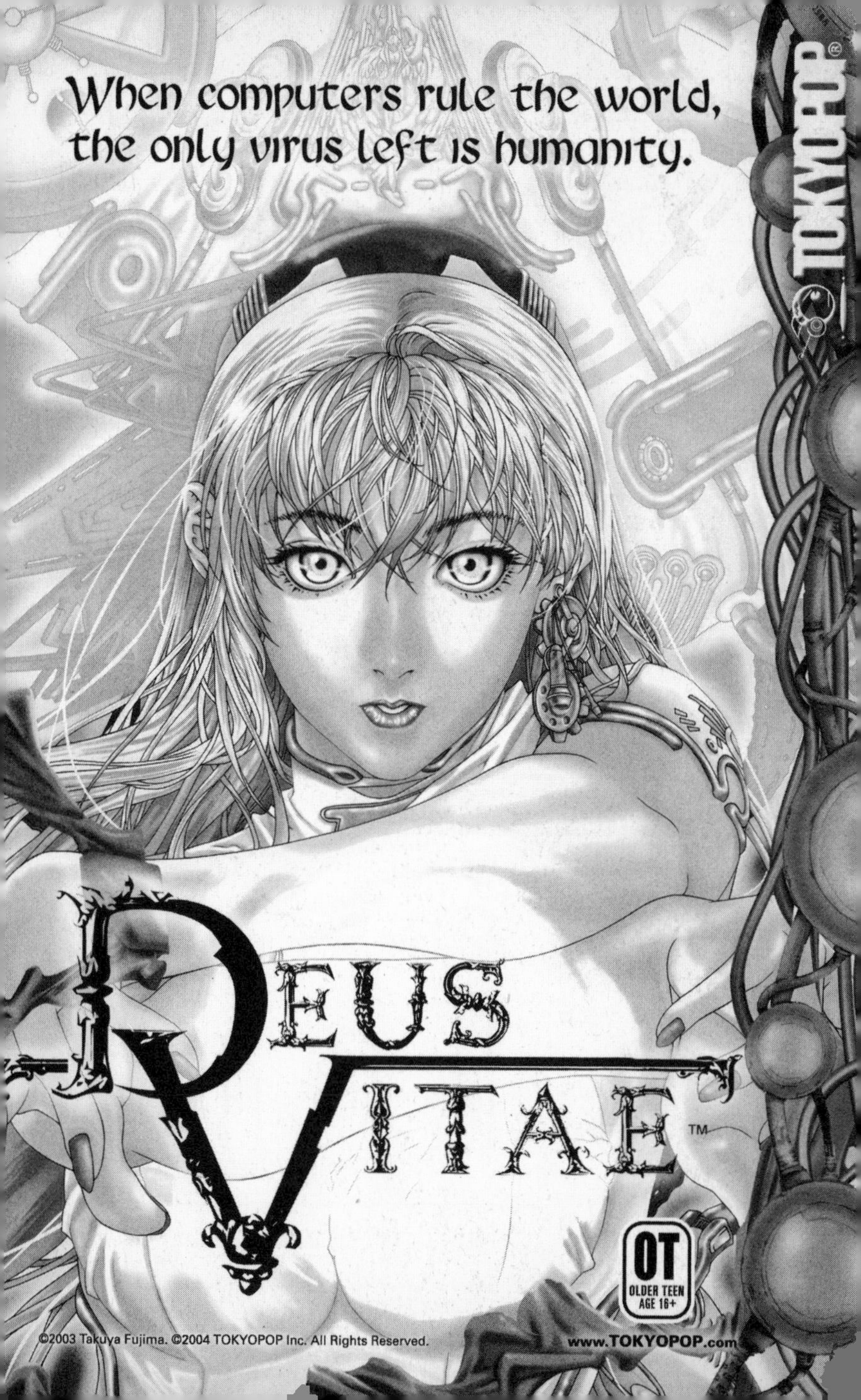
When computers rule the world,
the only virus left is humanity.
TOKYOPOP
DEUS VITAE™
OT
OLDER TEEN
AGE 16+
©2003 Takuya Fujima. ©2004 TOKYOPOP Inc. All Rights Reserved.
www.TOKYOPOP.com

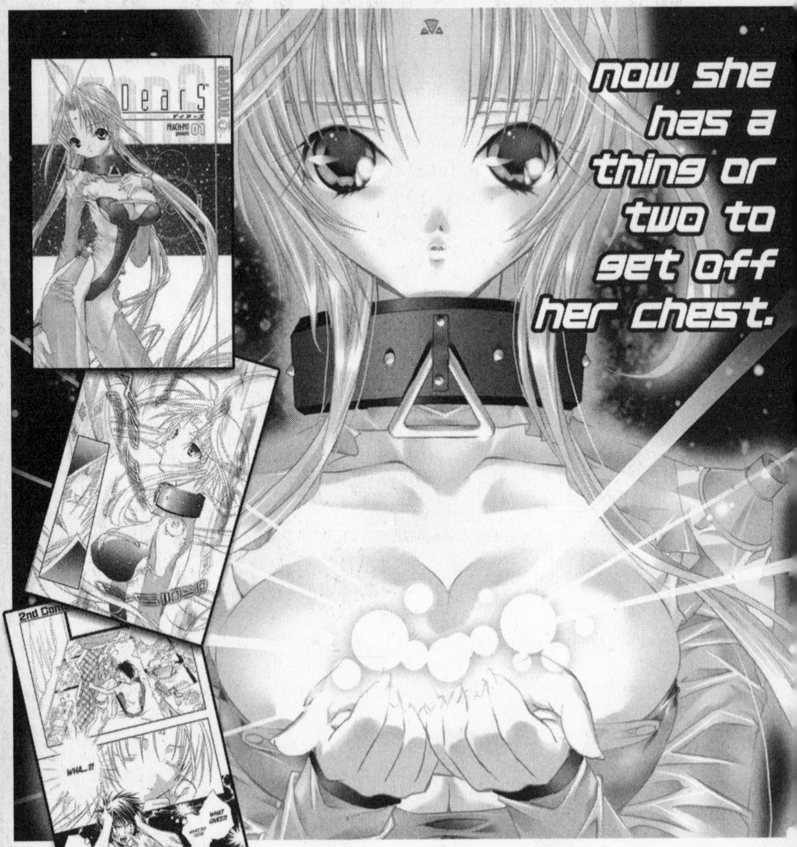
now she has a thing or two to get off her chest.
Dears
PEACH-PIT
01
2nd Con
WHA...?!
WHAT GIVES?!

IN THE NEXT VOLUME OF

IMMORTAL RAIN

A year has passed, and Machika's desperate
search for Rain is looking increasingly like
a fool's errand. Stowing away on a plane,
Machika's goal is to get to the city of
Raimei, home of the Calvaria Corporation,
and hopefully uncover the secret of Rain's
whereabouts. But there are detours and
distractions along the way, not to mention a
helping hand from one of the most unlikely
allies imaginable.
The adventure continues in Immortal Rain
volume 5!

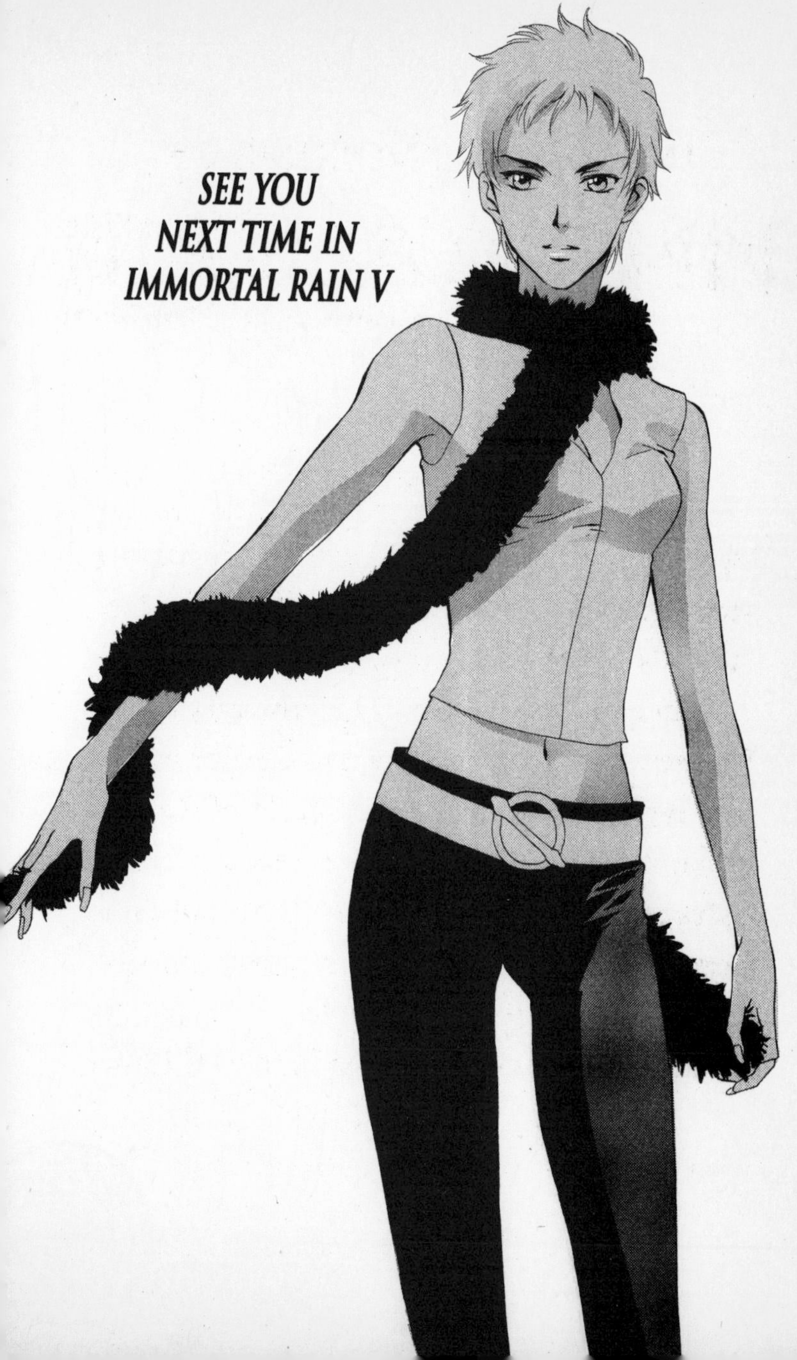
SEE YOU
NEXT TIME IN
IMMORTAL RAIN V

I have one more
announcement.
At the same time these
four volumes of Immortal
Rain are out, there is also a
short publication featuring my debut
work from nine years ago. It's pretty
old and embarrassing, but if you're
interested, pick up a copy.
I will use the royalties to buy a
car since I finally got my license.
Did you hear that?
Can you believe her?

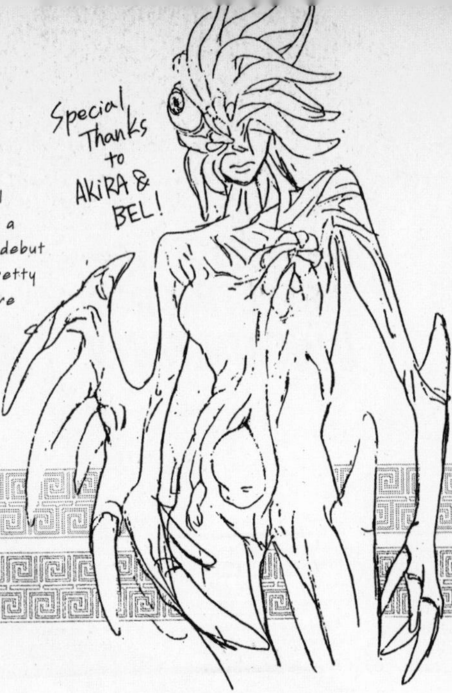
Special Thanks to AKIRA & BEL!

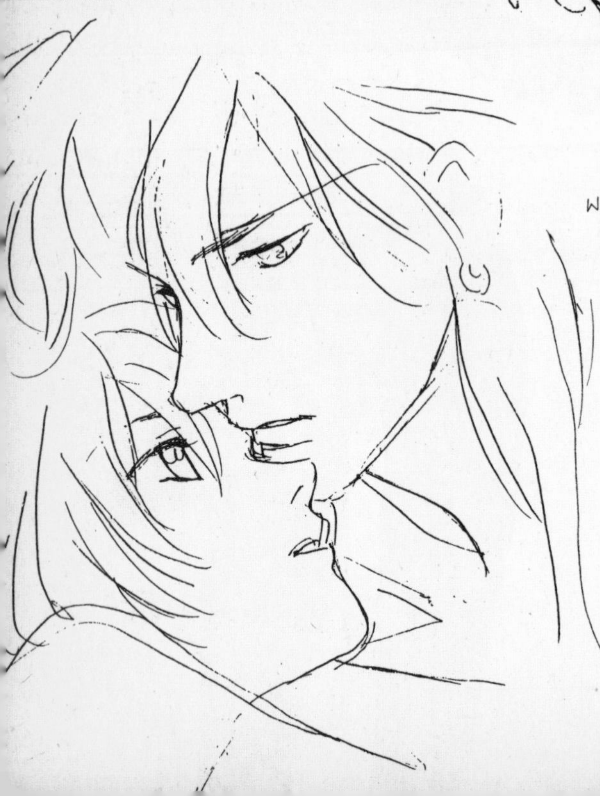

What kind of cruel word is "live"?

But I had to write it.
So that I could keep living.

Ozaki Kaori
May 2002

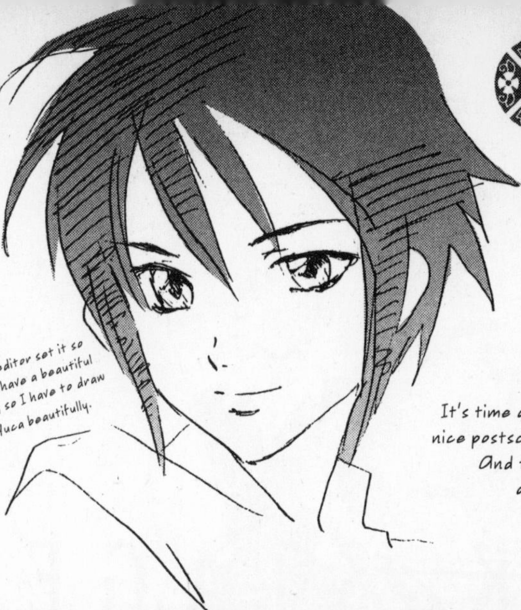

The editor set it so he'd have a beautiful face, so I have to draw Yuca beautifully.

Hello again.
This book came out a little sooner than the others.
I'm on the brink of death and madness.

It's time again for me to try to write a nice postscript but I'm no good at these.
And today I burned my hands and they really hurt.

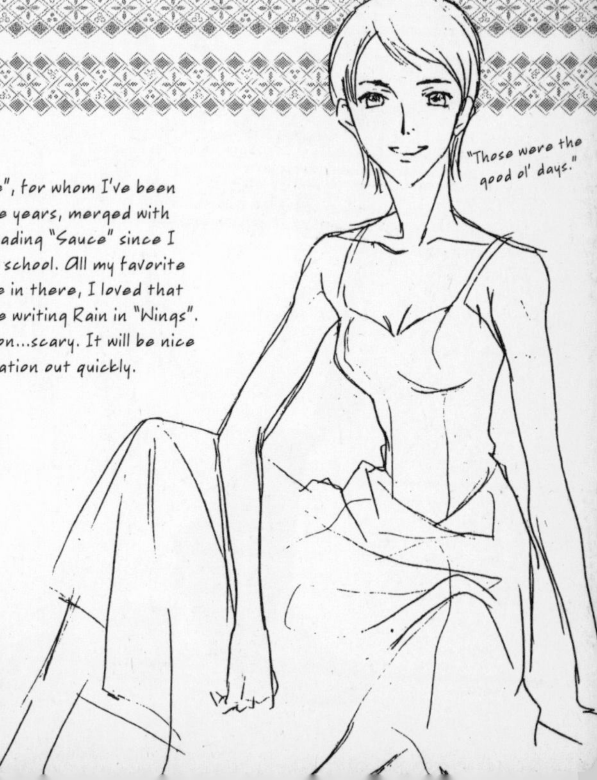
"Those were the good ol' days."

The magazine "Sauce", for whom I've been drawing the last nine years, merged with "Wings". I've been reading "Sauce" since I was probably in middle school. All my favorite teacher's manga were in there, I loved that magazine. I will continue writing Rain in "Wings". It's a monthly publication...scary. It will be nice to get my publication out quickly.

Immortal Rain
IV

BACKSTAGE

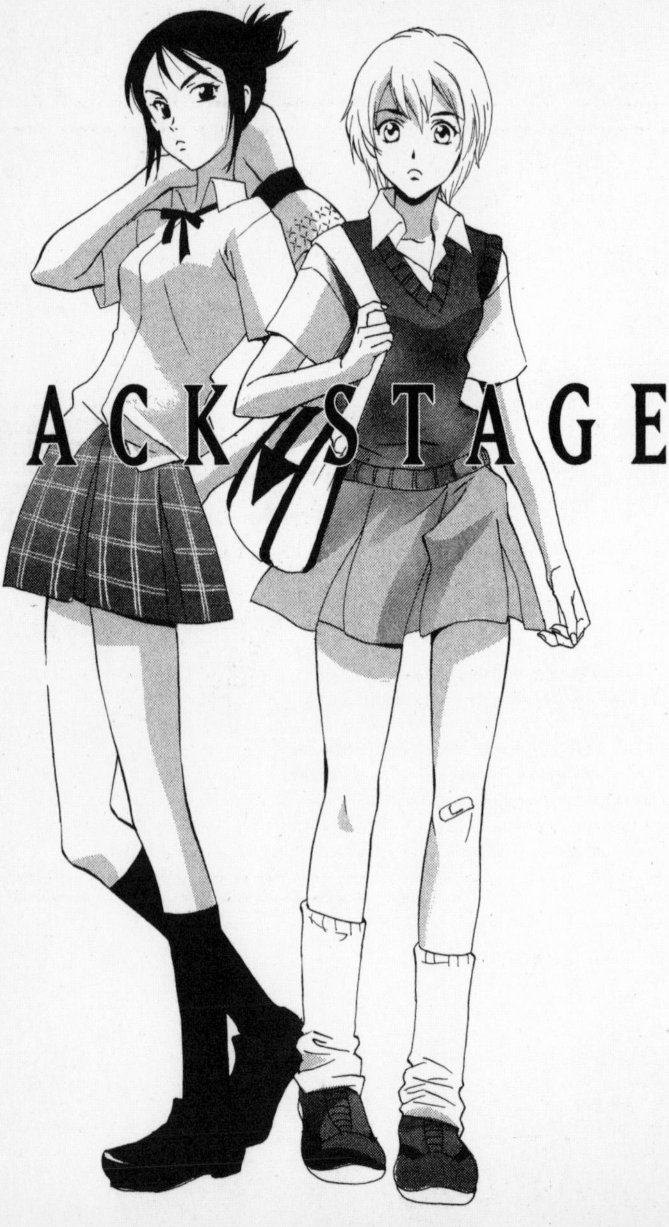

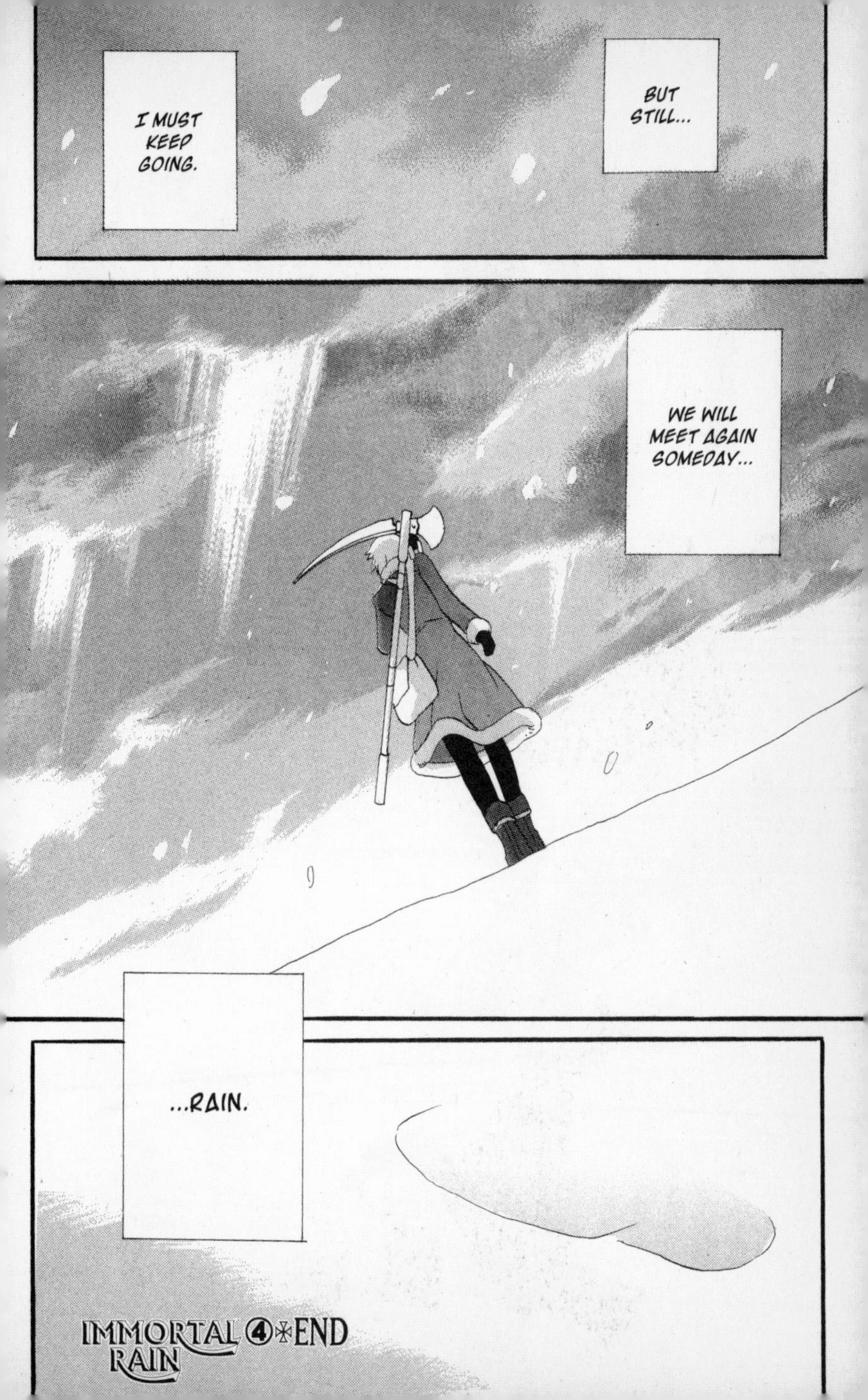
I MUST KEEP GOING.
BUT STILL...
WE WILL MEET AGAIN SOMEDAY...
...RAIN.
IMMORTAL RAIN 4 END

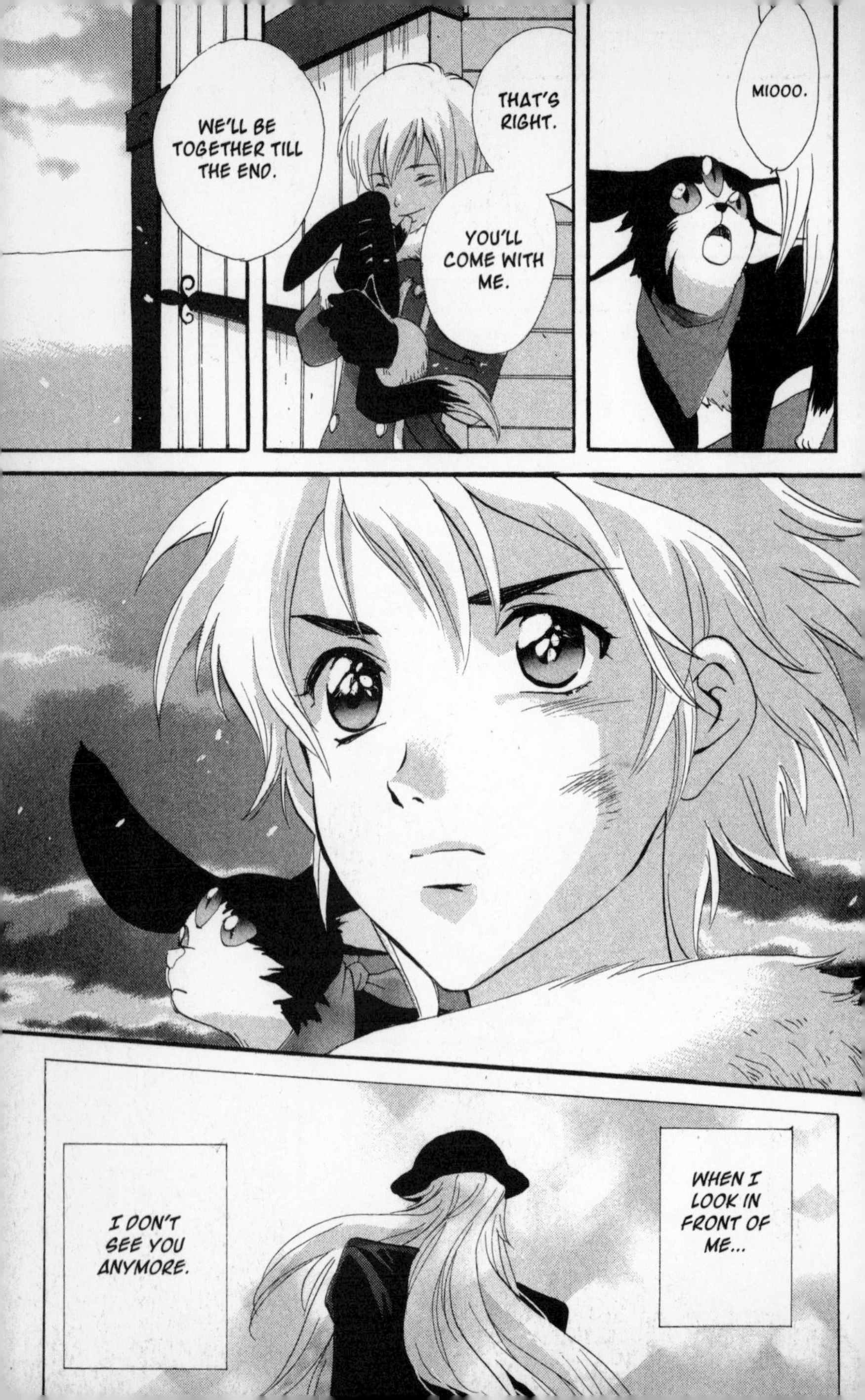
MIOOO.
THAT'S RIGHT.
YOU'LL COME WITH ME.
WE'LL BE TOGETHER TILL THE END.
WHEN I LOOK IN FRONT OF ME...
I DON'T SEE YOU ANYMORE.

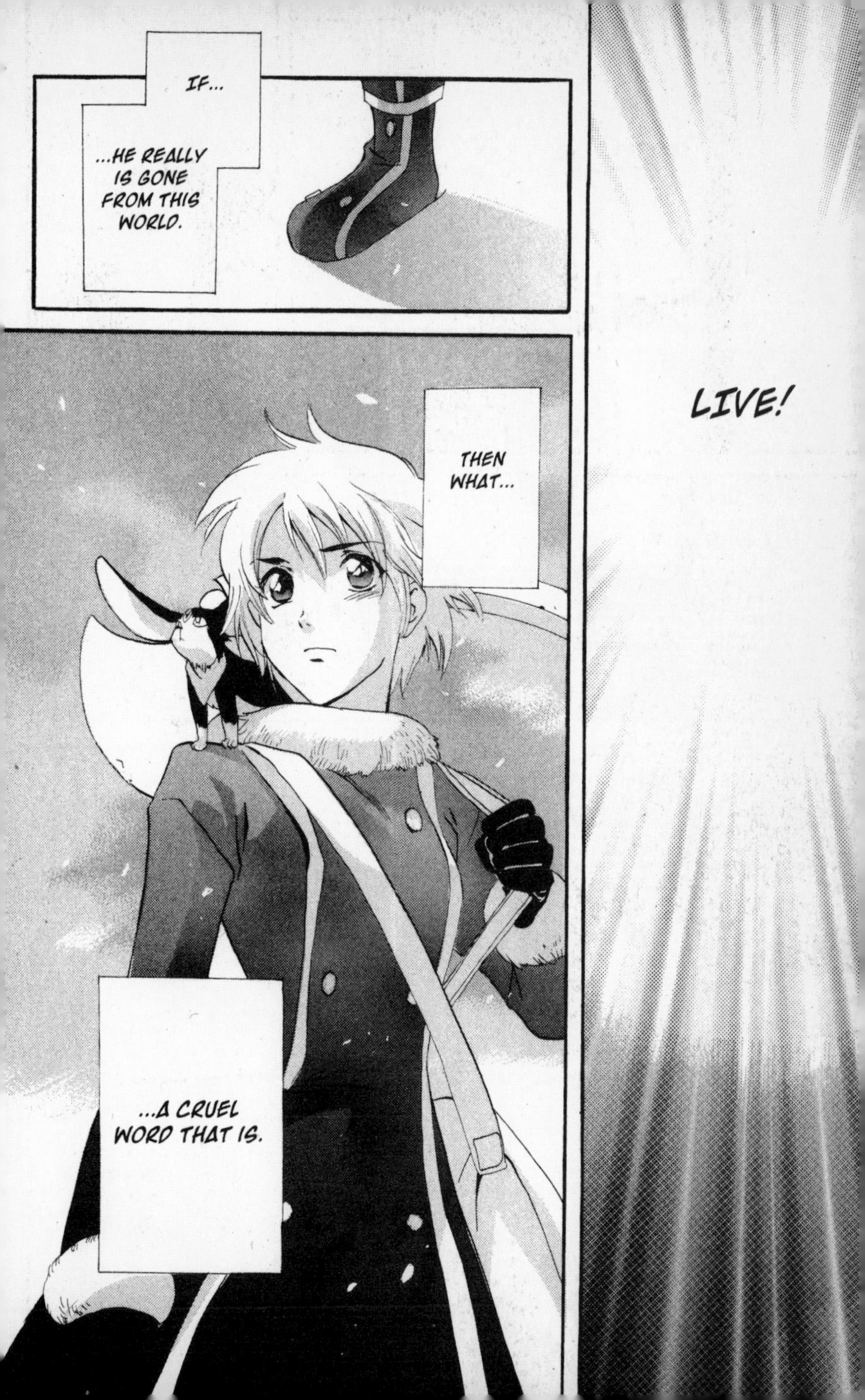
LIVE!
IF...
...HE REALLY IS GONE FROM THIS WORLD.
THEN WHAT...
...A CRUEL WORD THAT IS.

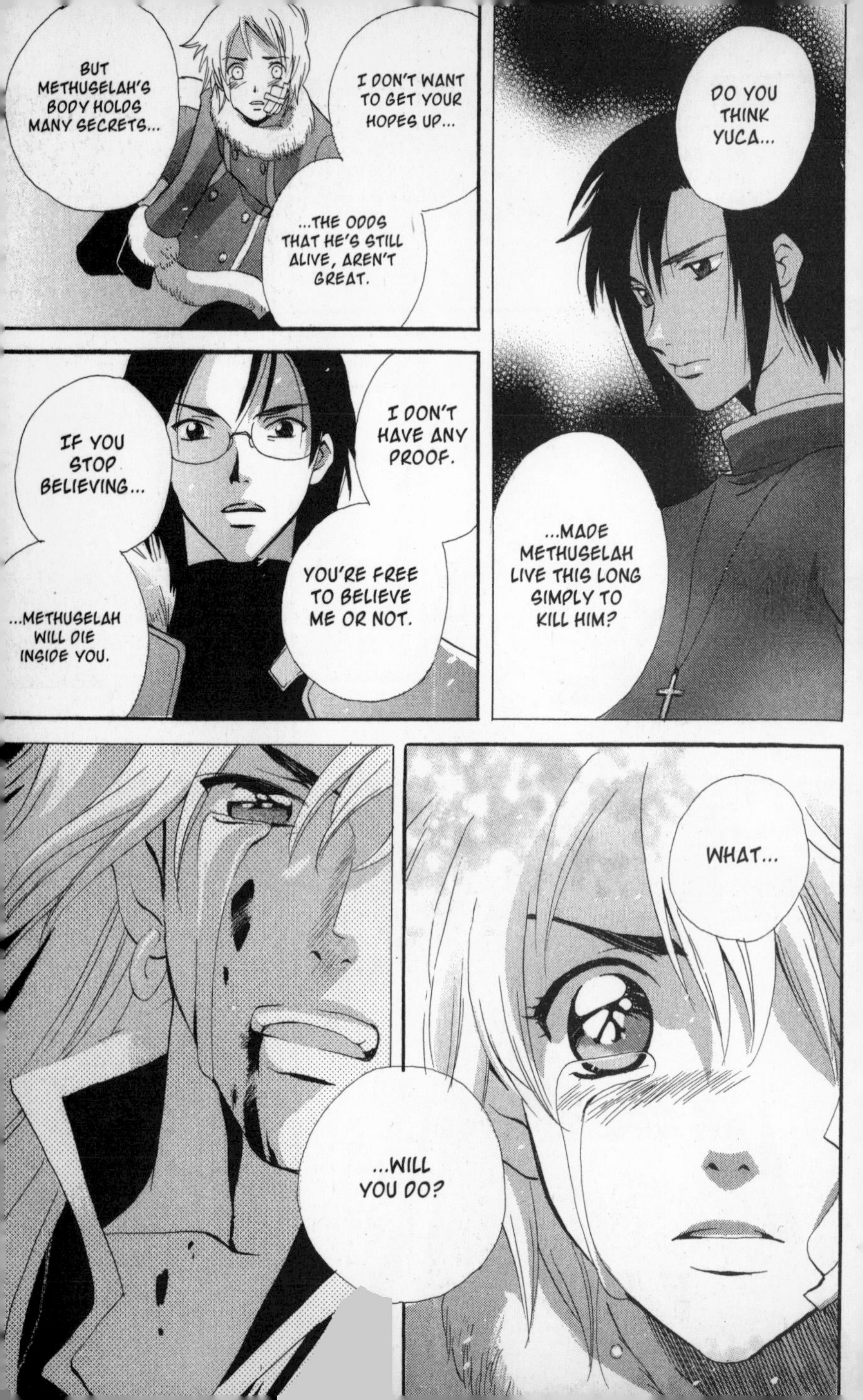
DO YOU THINK YUCA...
...MADE METHUSELAH LIVE THIS LONG SIMPLY TO KILL HIM?
I DON'T WANT TO GET YOUR HOPES UP...
...THE ODDS THAT HE'S STILL ALIVE, AREN'T GREAT.
BUT METHUSELAH'S BODY HOLDS MANY SECRETS...
I DON'T HAVE ANY PROOF.
YOU'RE FREE TO BELIEVE ME OR NOT.
IF YOU STOP BELIEVING...
...METHUSELAH WILL DIE INSIDE YOU.
WHAT...
...WILL YOU DO?

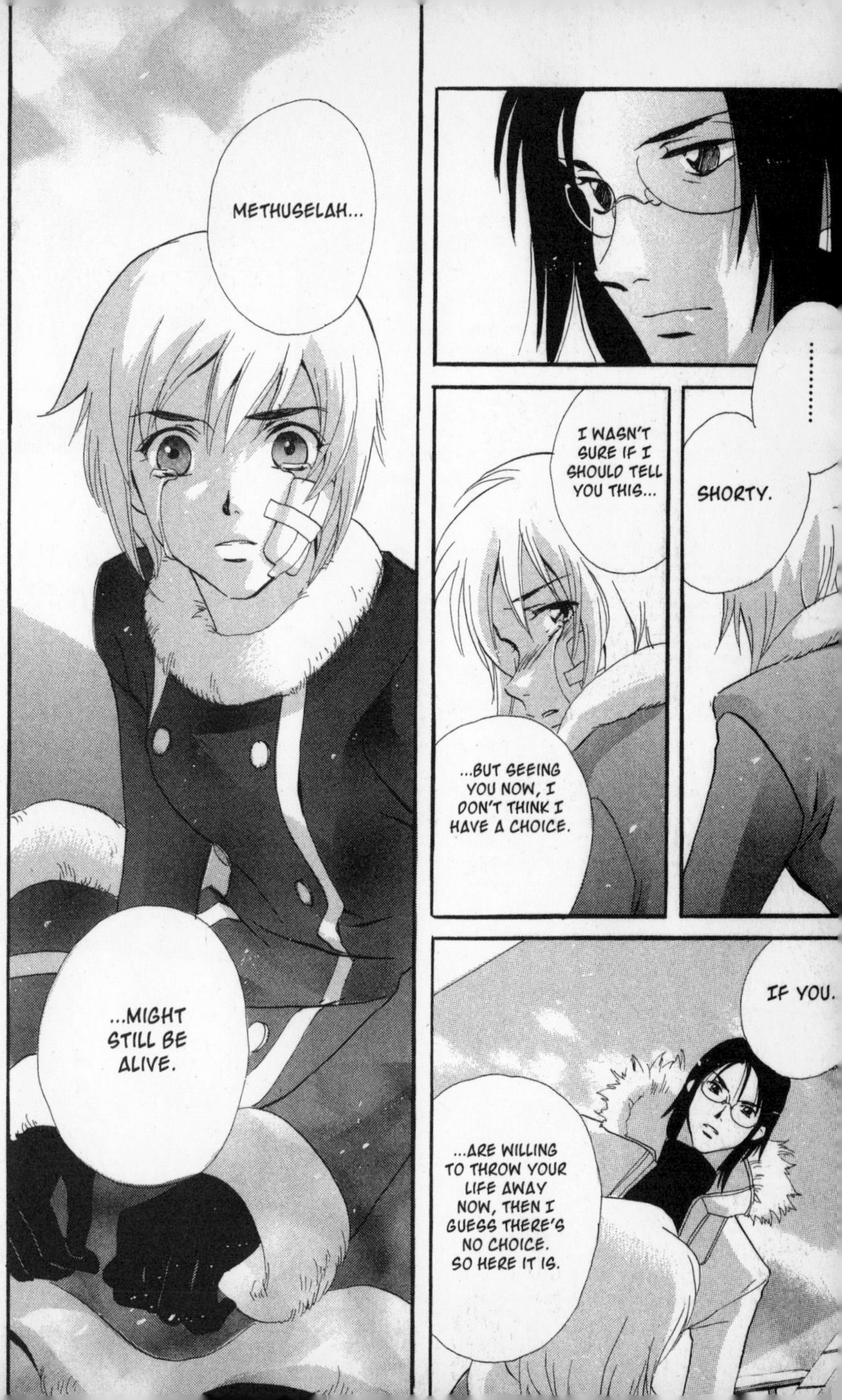
......
SHORTY.
I WASN'T SURE IF I SHOULD TELL YOU THIS...
...BUT SEEING YOU NOW, I DON'T THINK I HAVE A CHOICE.
IF YOU.
...ARE WILLING TO THROW YOUR LIFE AWAY NOW, THEN I GUESS THERE'S NO CHOICE. SO HERE IT IS.
METHUSELAH...
...MIGHT STILL BE ALIVE.

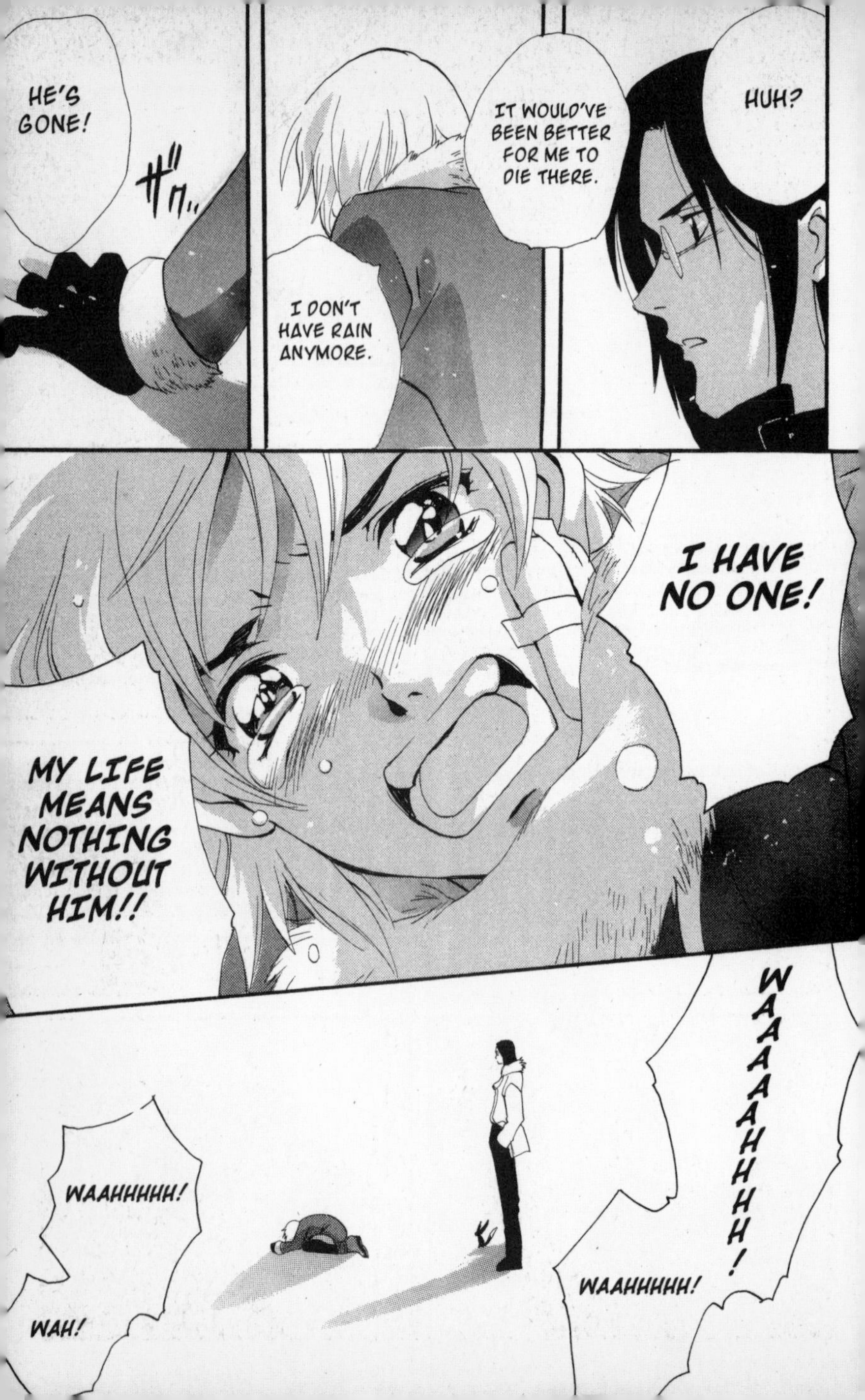
HUH?
IT WOULD'VE BEEN BETTER FOR ME TO DIE THERE.
I DON'T HAVE RAIN ANYMORE.
HE'S GONE!
I HAVE NO ONE!
MY LIFE MEANS NOTHING WITHOUT HIM!!
WAAAAAHHHH!
WAAHHHHH!
WAAHHHHH!
WAH!

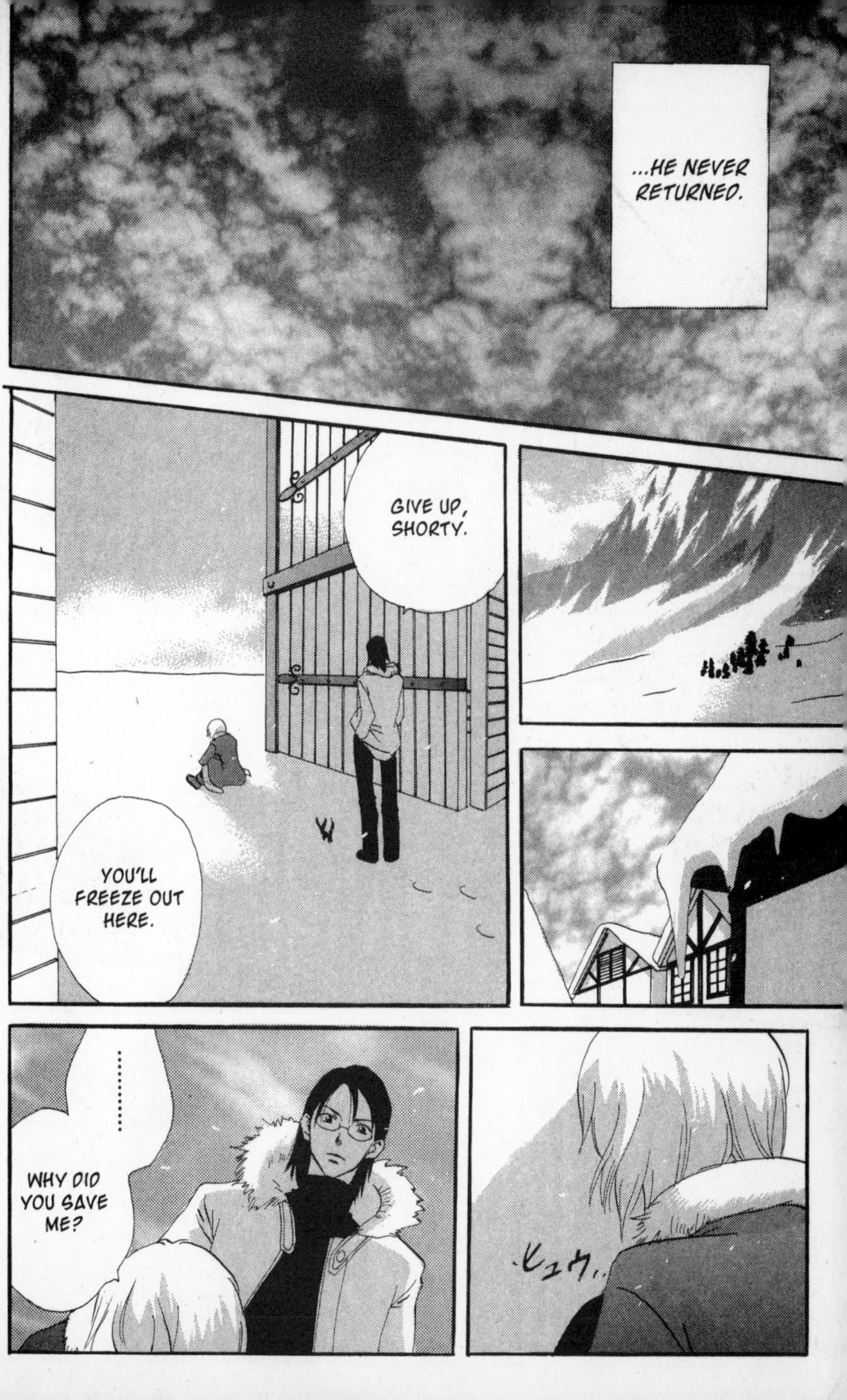
...HE NEVER RETURNED.
GIVE UP, SHORTY.
YOU'LL FREEZE OUT HERE.
......
WHY DID YOU SAVE ME?
ヒュウ

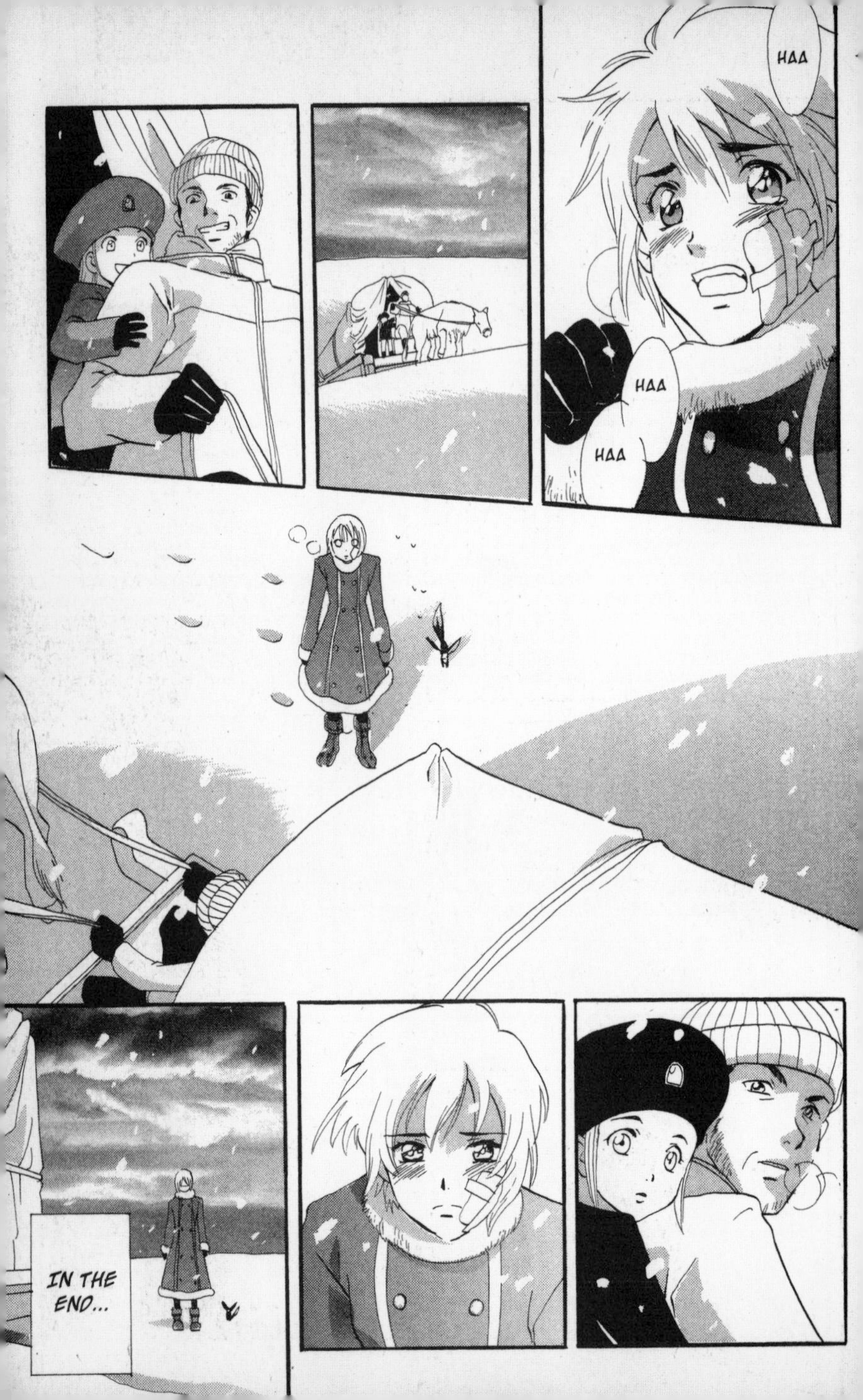
HAA
HAA
HAA
IN THE END...

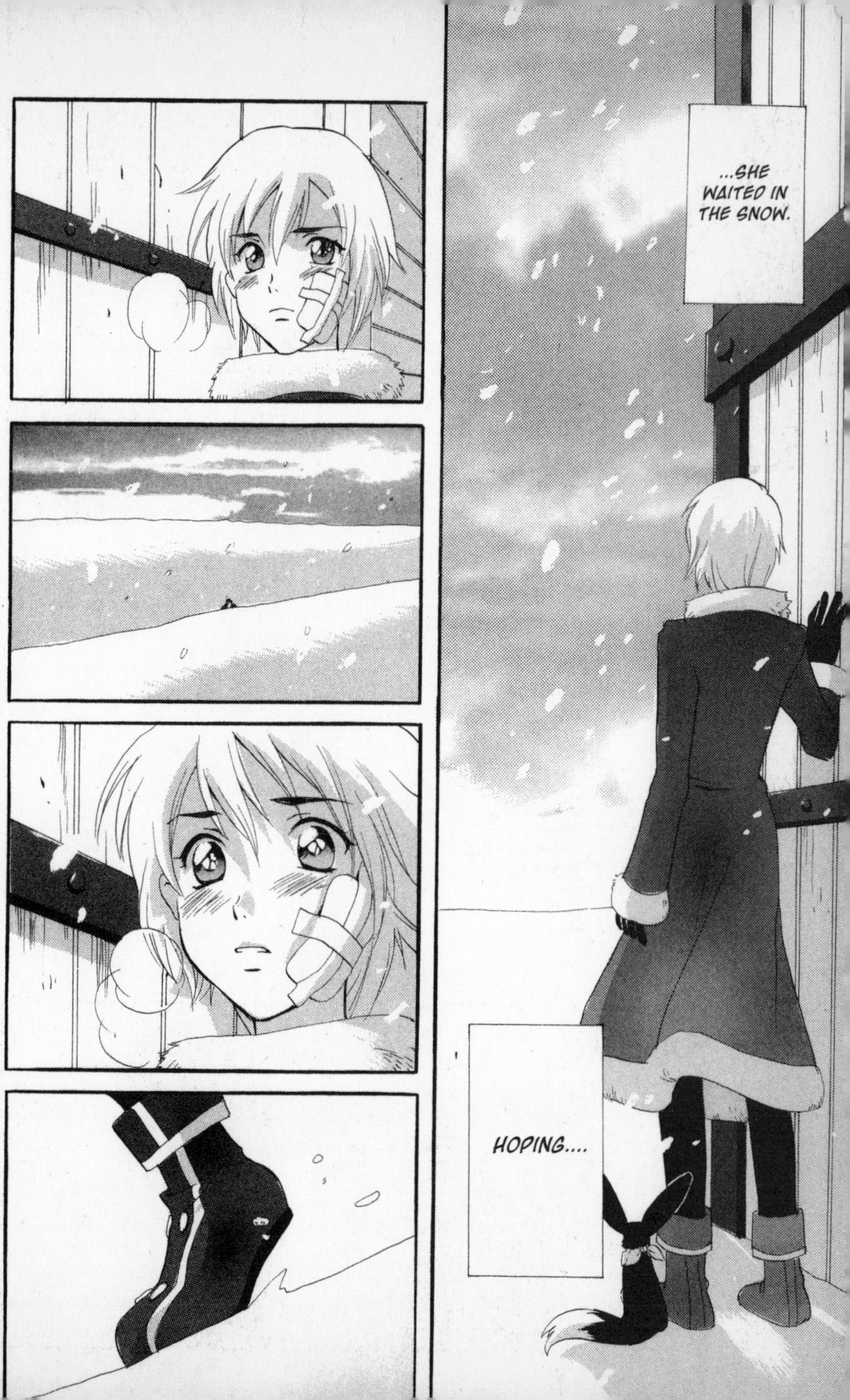
...SHE WAITED IN THE SNOW.
HOPING....

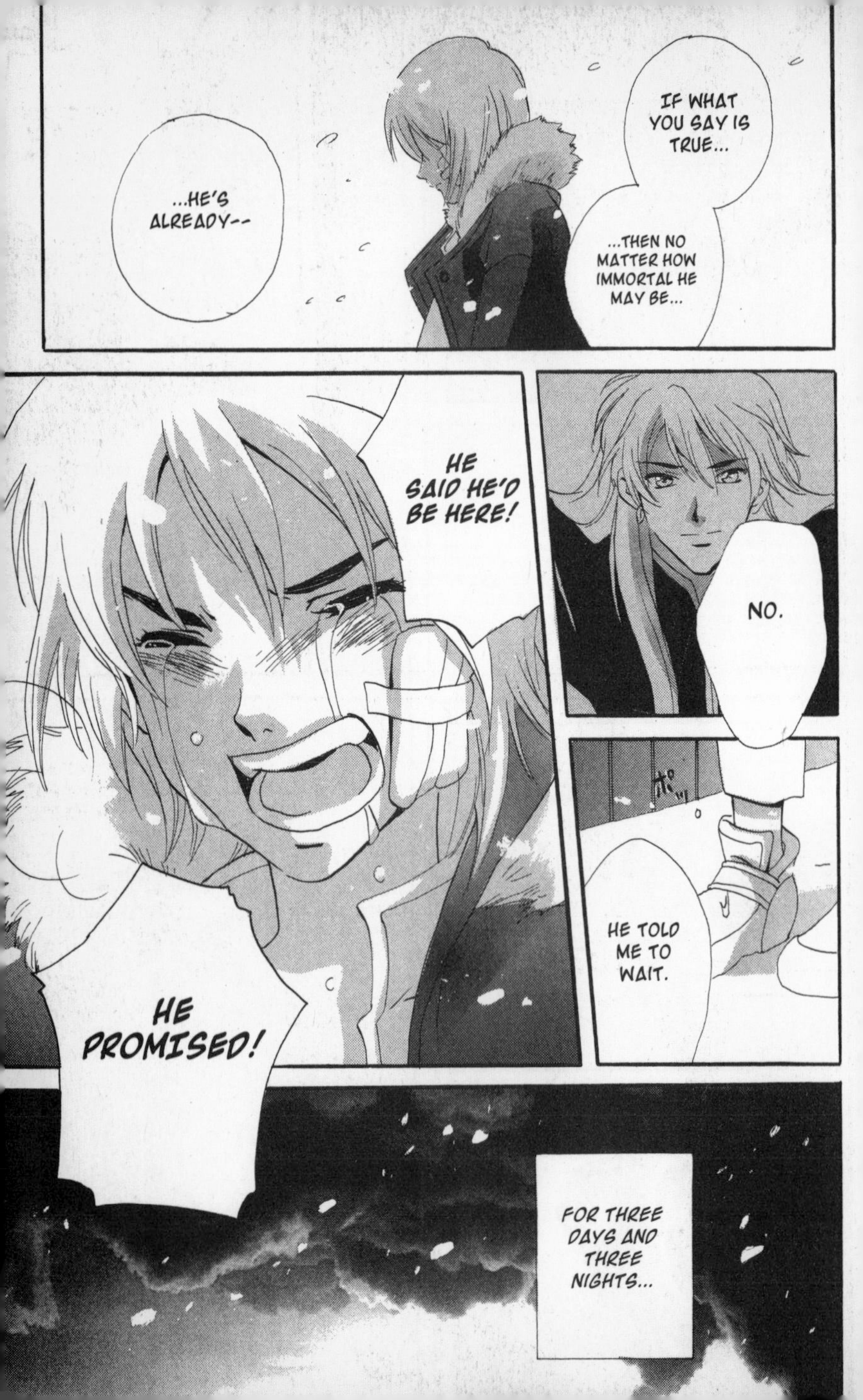
IF WHAT YOU SAY IS TRUE...
...THEN NO MATTER HOW IMMORTAL HE MAY BE...
...HE'S ALREADY--
NO.
HE TOLD ME TO WAIT.
HE SAID HE'D BE HERE!
HE PROMISED!
FOR THREE DAYS AND THREE NIGHTS...

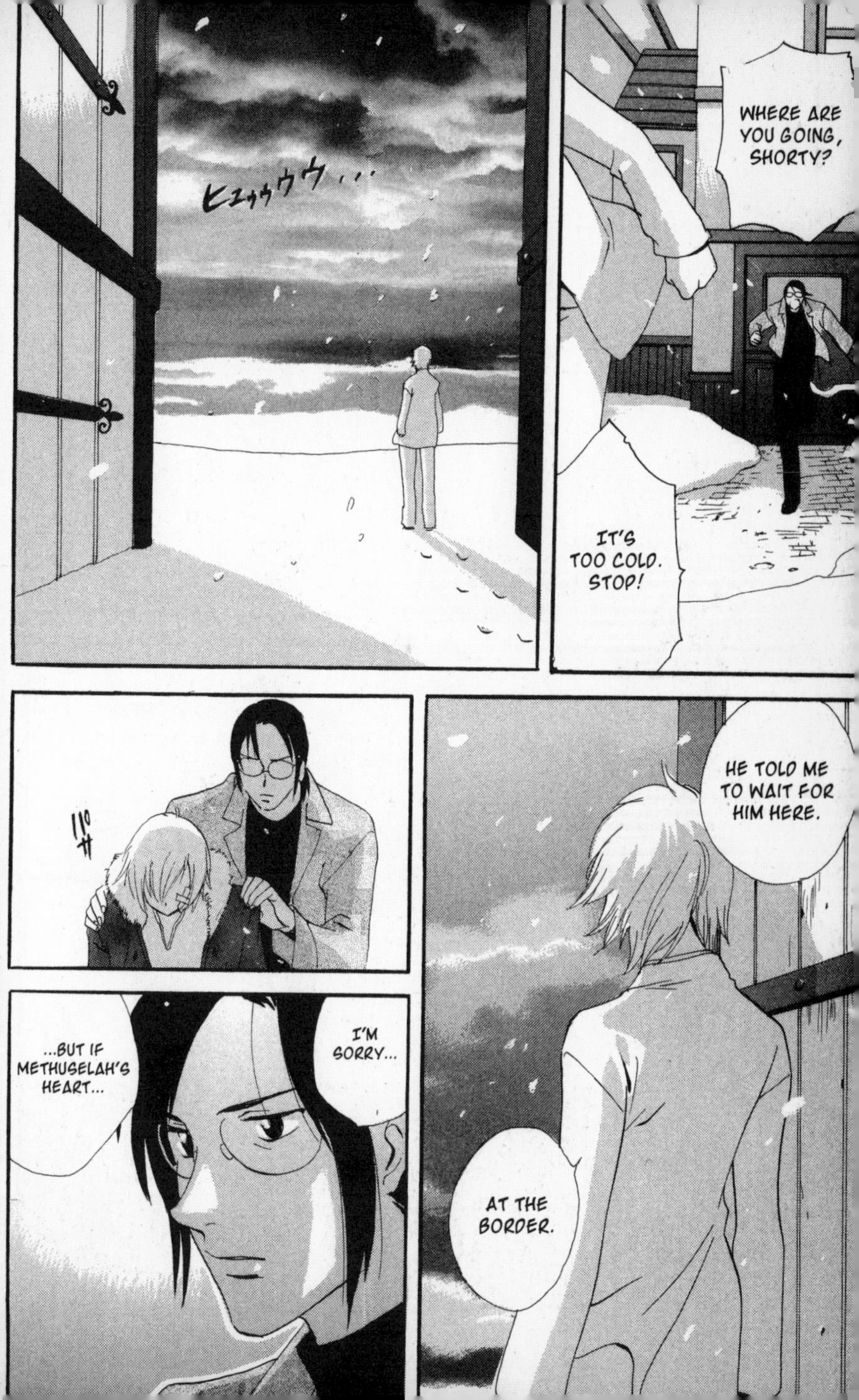
WHERE ARE YOU GOING, SHORTY?
IT'S TOO COLD. STOP!
ヒュゥゥウ…
HE TOLD ME TO WAIT FOR HIM HERE.
AT THE BORDER.
ハッ
I'M SORRY...
...BUT IF METHUSELAH'S HEART...

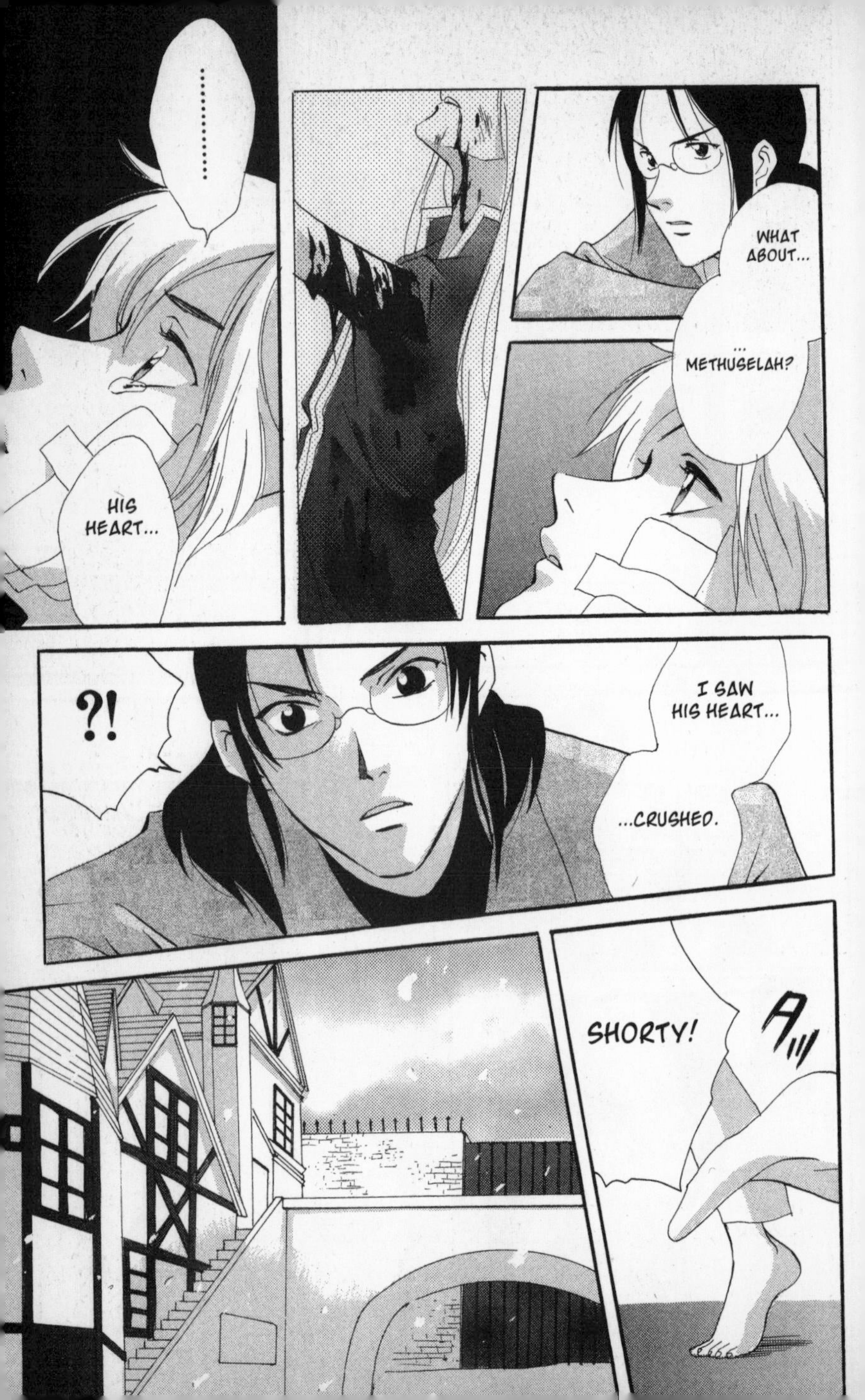
WHAT ABOUT...
... METHUSELAH?
....
HIS HEART...
I SAW HIS HEART...
...CRUSHED.
?!
A
SHORTY!

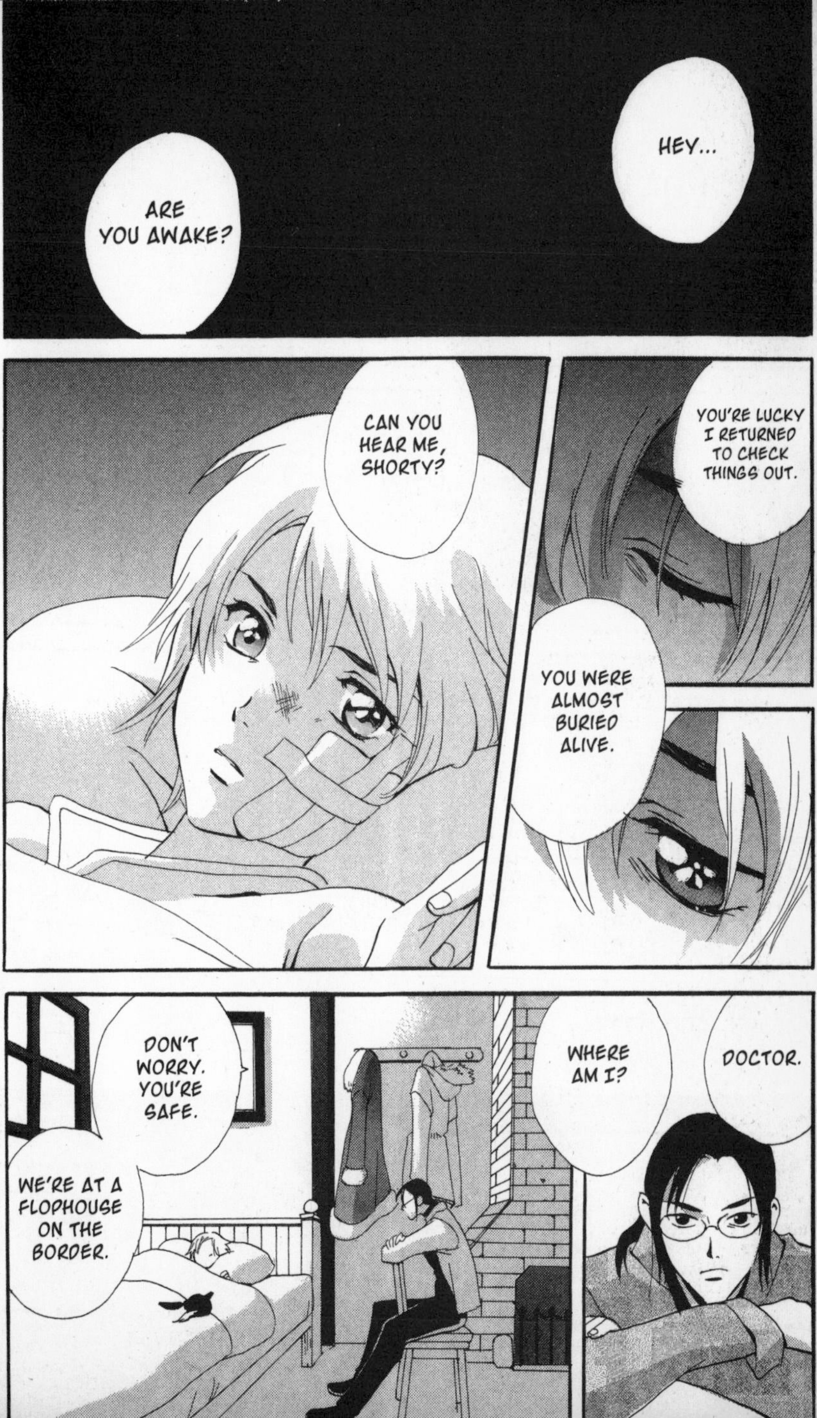
HEY...
ARE YOU AWAKE?
CAN YOU HEAR ME, SHORTY?
YOU'RE LUCKY I RETURNED TO CHECK THINGS OUT.
YOU WERE ALMOST BURIED ALIVE.
DOCTOR.
WHERE AM I?
DON'T WORRY. YOU'RE SAFE.
WE'RE AT A FLOPHOUSE ON THE BORDER.

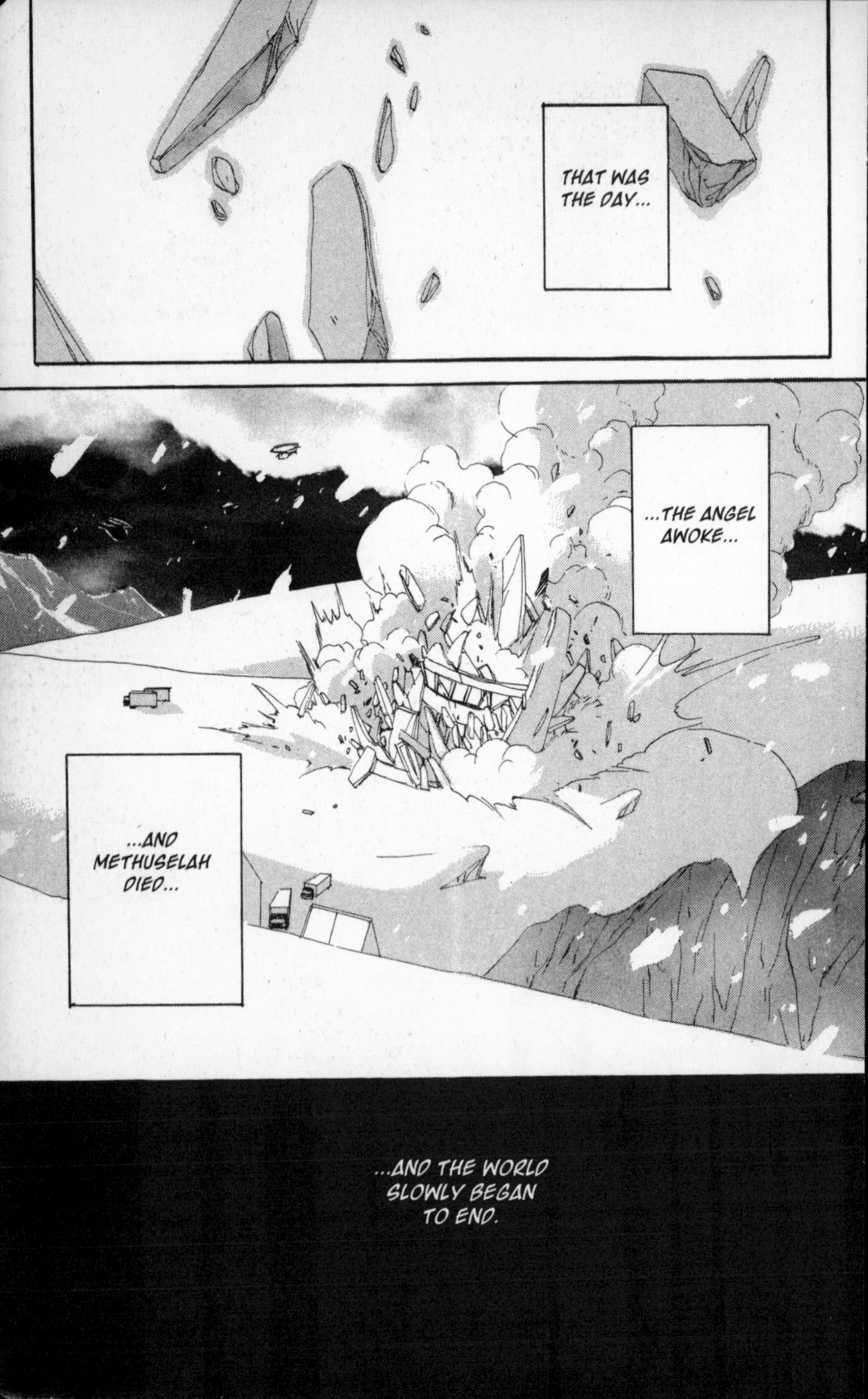
THAT WAS THE DAY...
...THE ANGEL AWOKE...
...AND METHUSELAH DIED...
...AND THE WORLD SLOWLY BEGAN TO END.

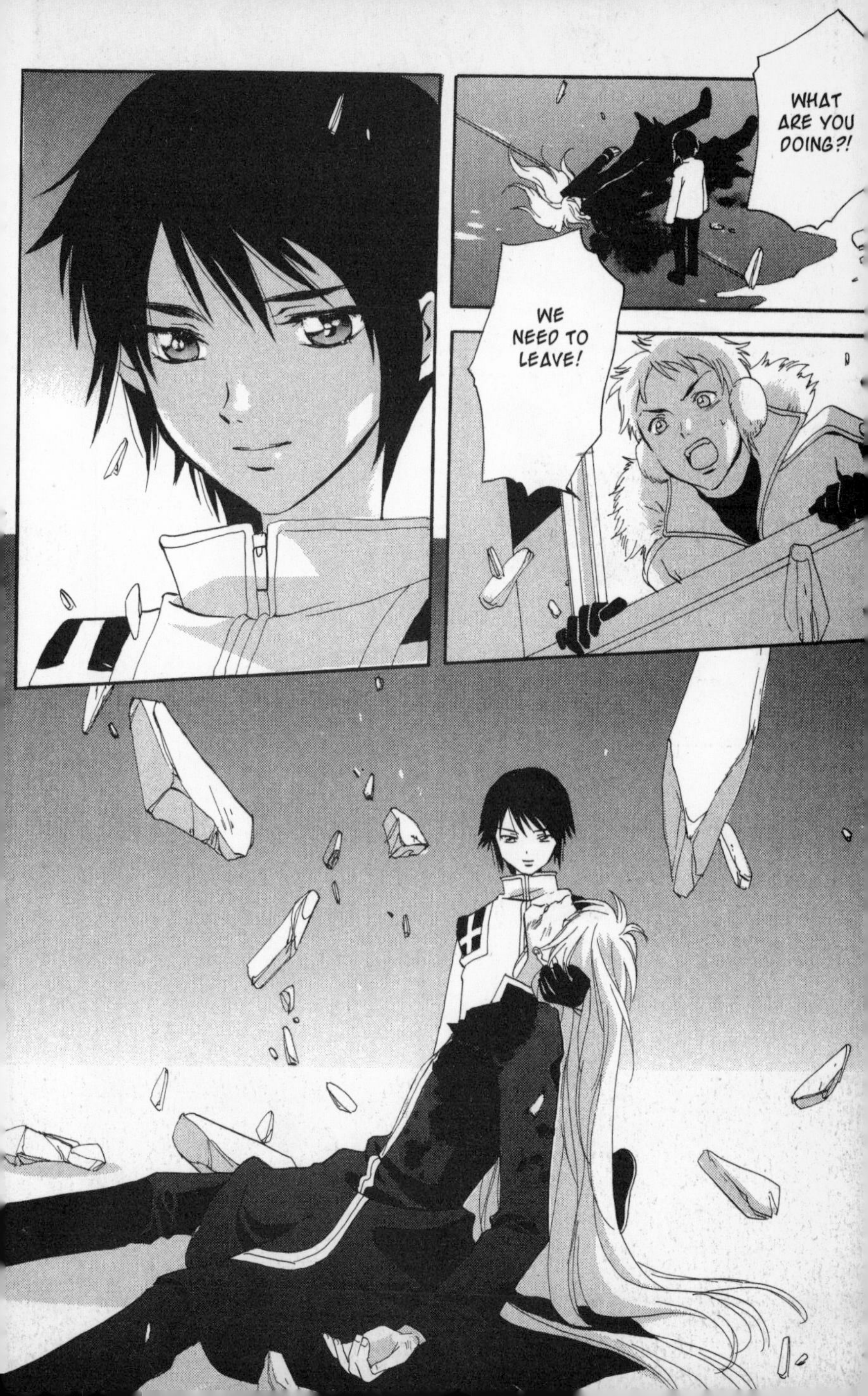
WHAT ARE YOU DOING?!
WE NEED TO LEAVE!

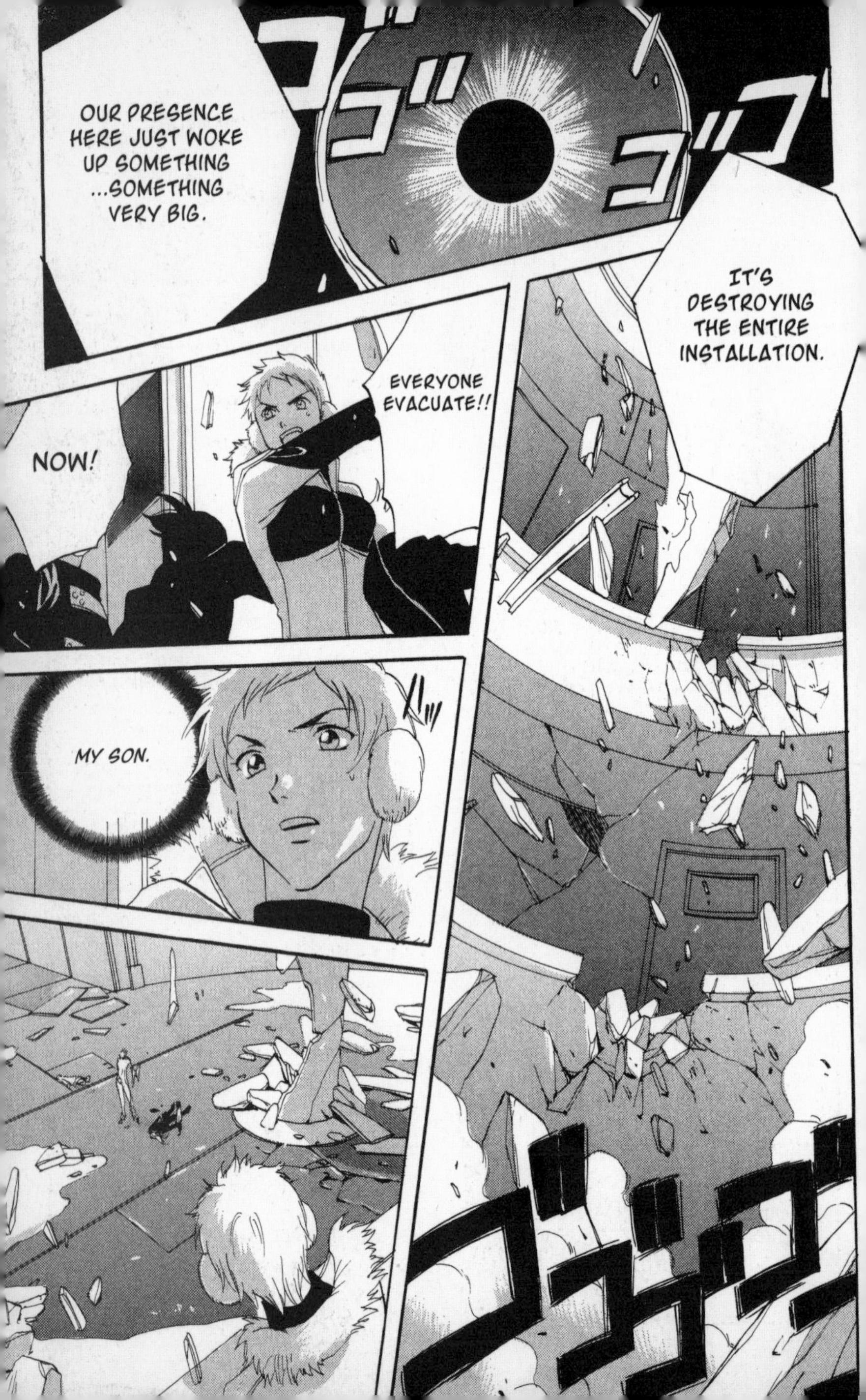

OUR PRESENCE HERE JUST WOKE UP SOMETHING ...SOMETHING VERY BIG.
IT'S DESTROYING THE ENTIRE INSTALLATION.
EVERYONE EVACUATE!!
NOW!
MY SON.

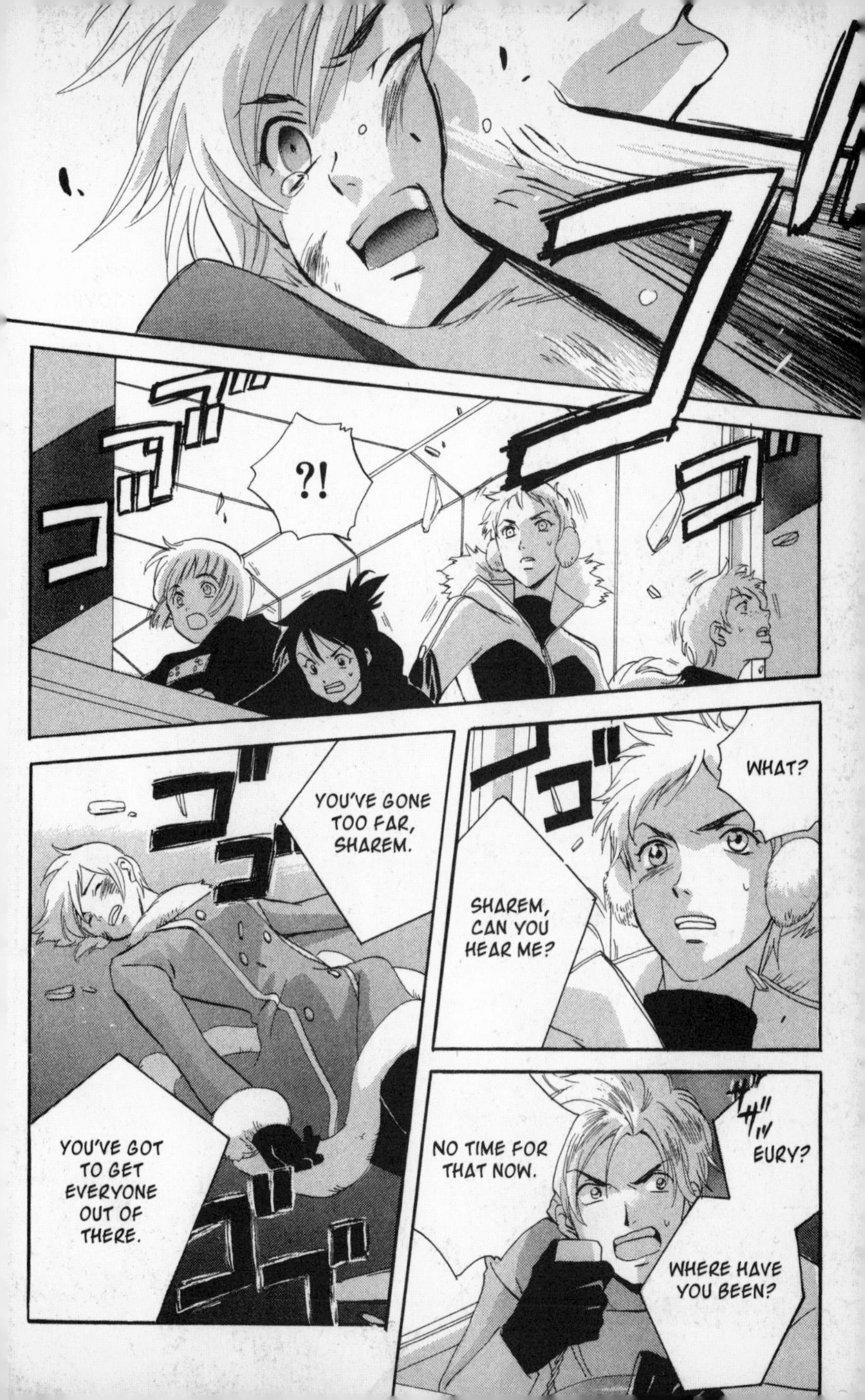
?!
WHAT?
YOU'VE GONE TOO FAR, SHAREM.
SHAREM, CAN YOU HEAR ME?
EURY?
WHERE HAVE YOU BEEN?
NO TIME FOR THAT NOW.
YOU'VE GOT TO GET EVERYONE OUT OF THERE.

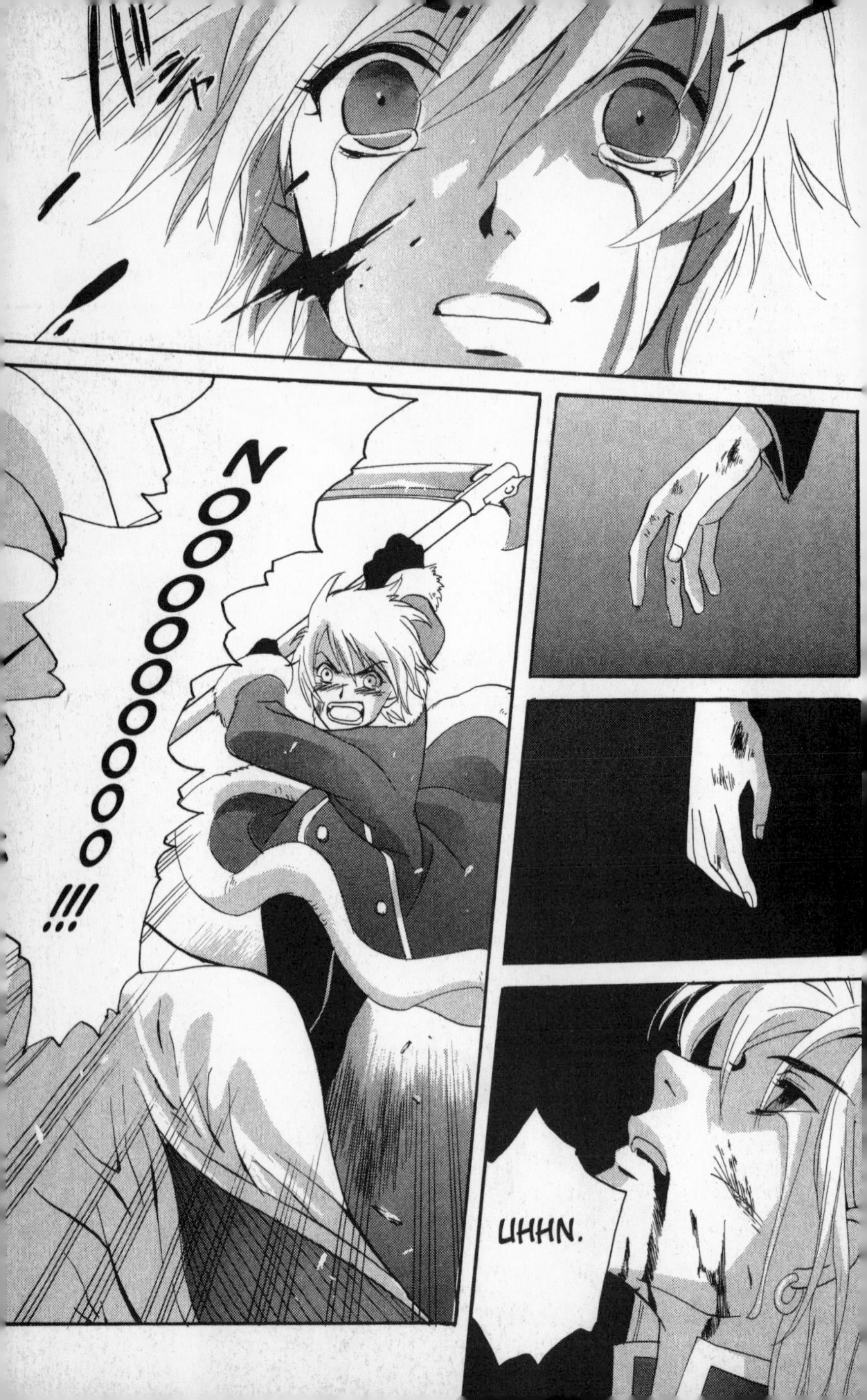
バシャ
NOOOOOOOOO!!!
UHHN.

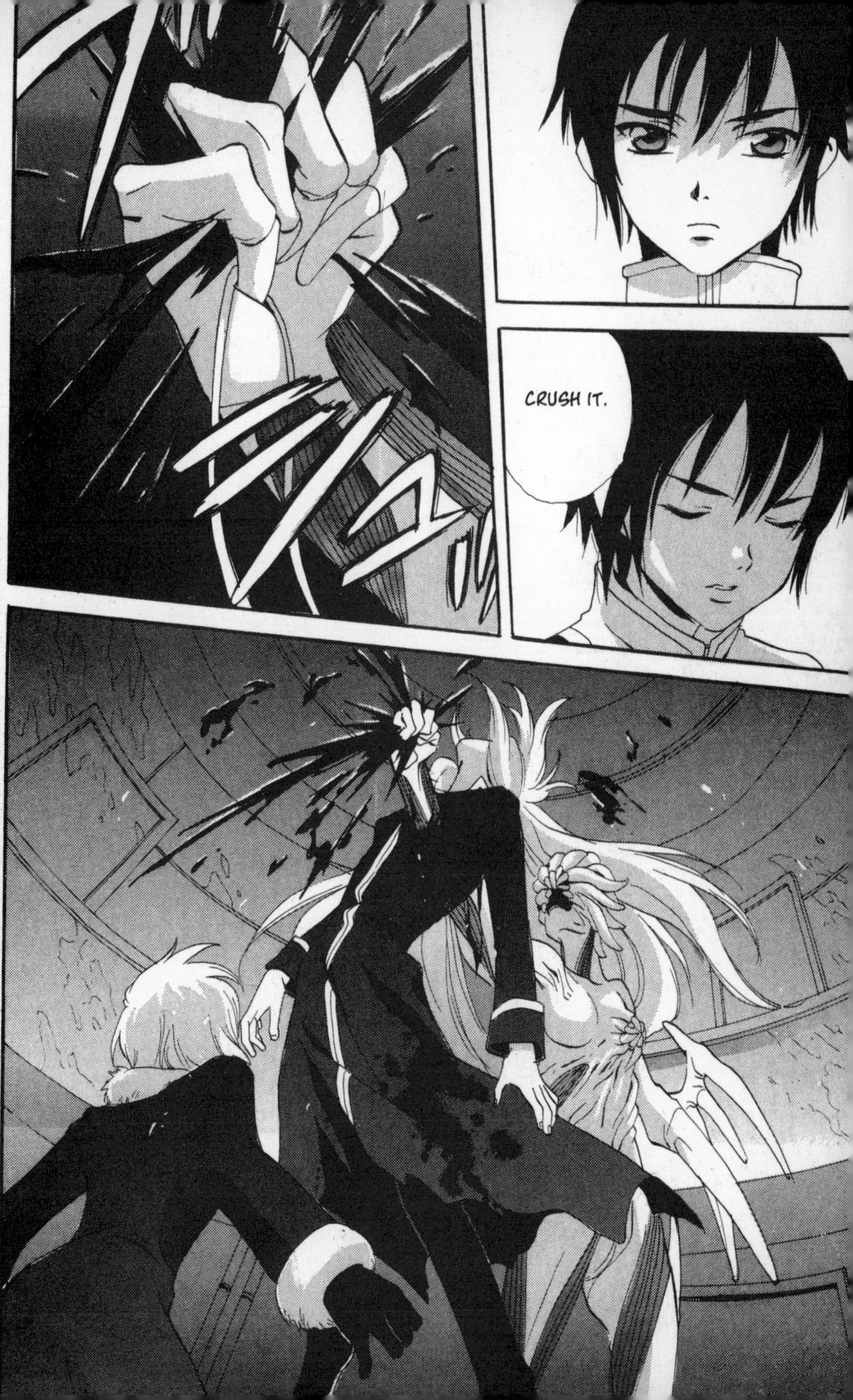
CRUSH IT.

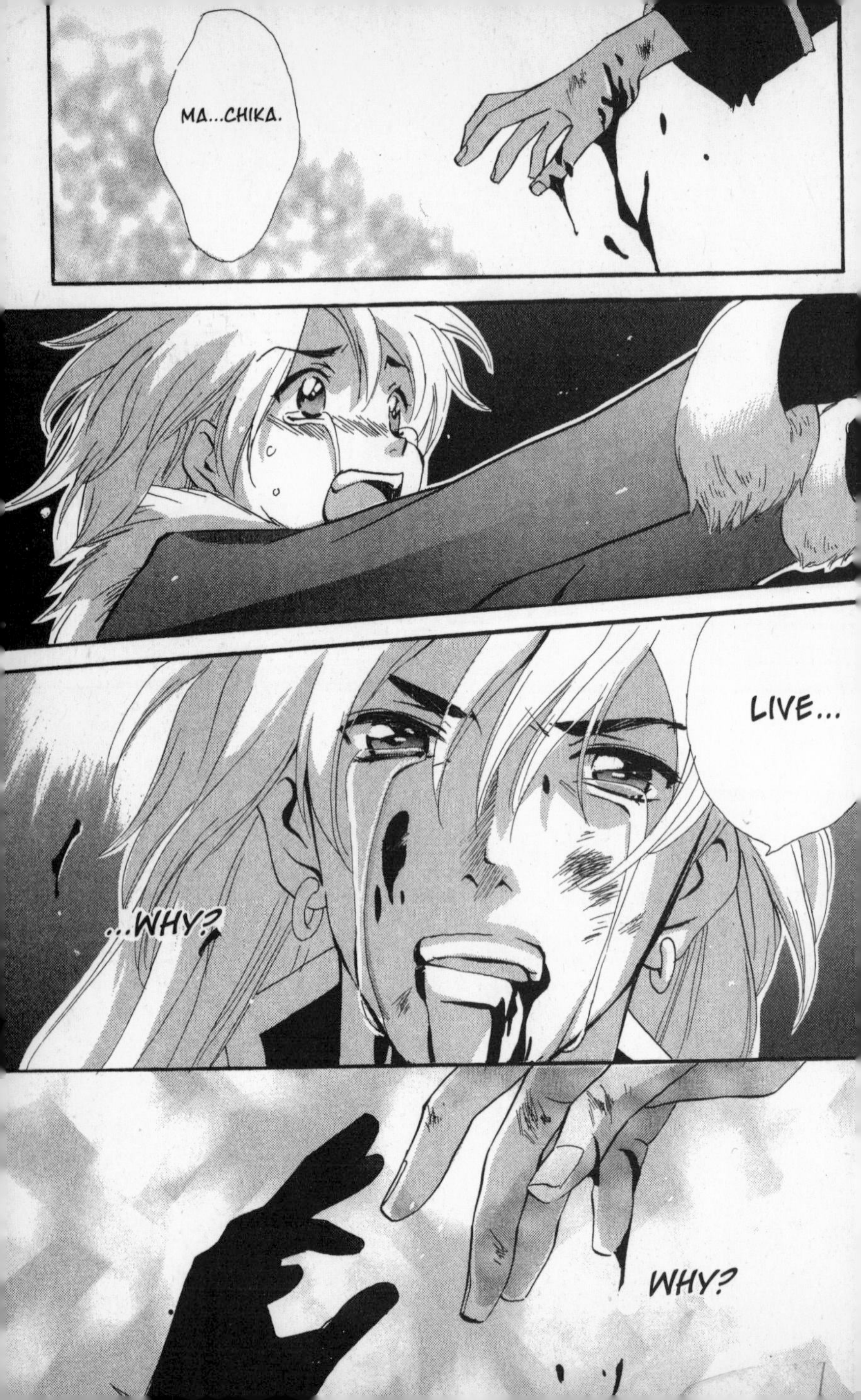
MA...CHIKA.
LIVE...
...WHY?
WHY?

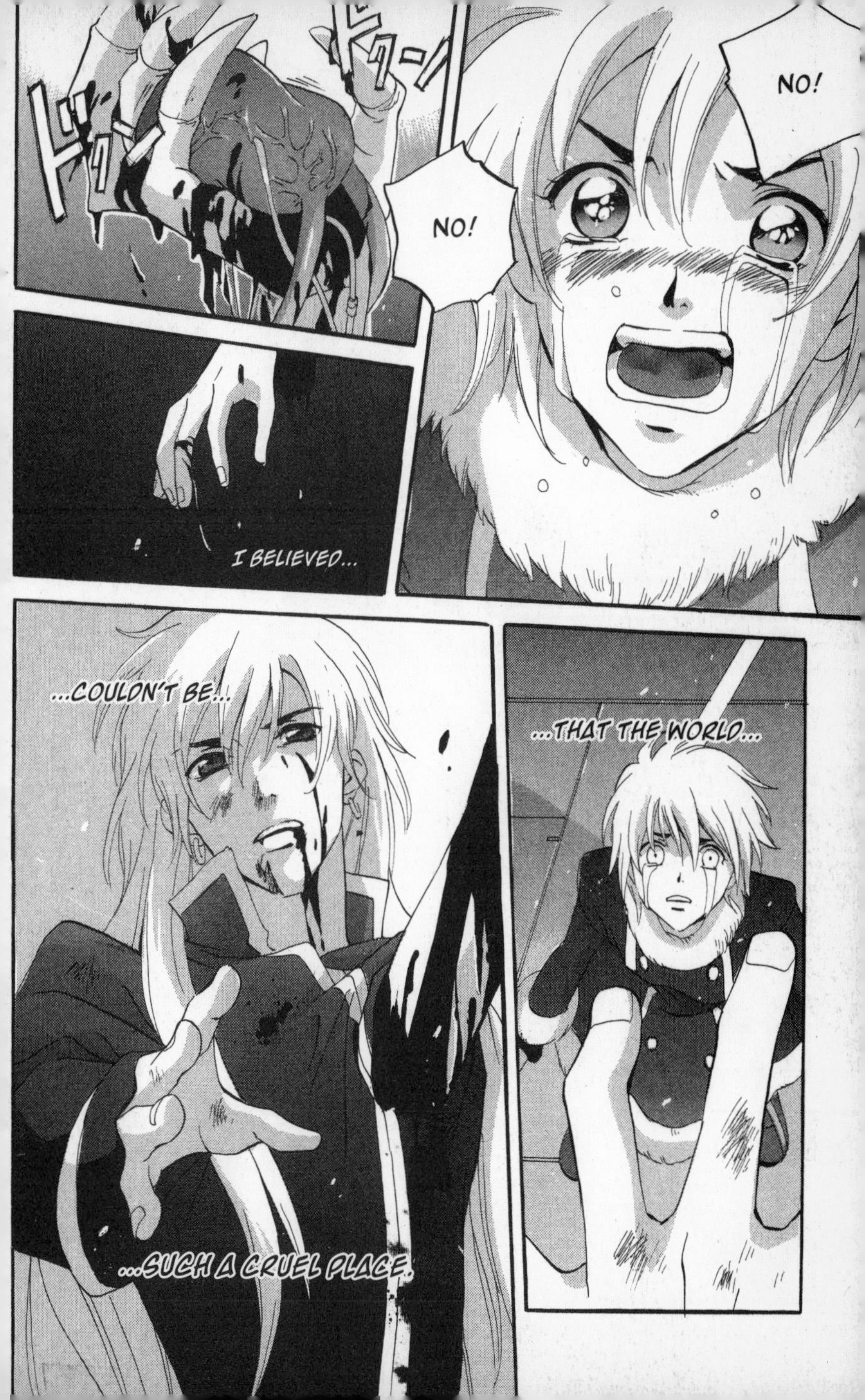
NO!
NO!
I BELIEVED...
...THAT THE WORLD...
...COULDN'T BE...
...SUCH A CRUEL PLACE.

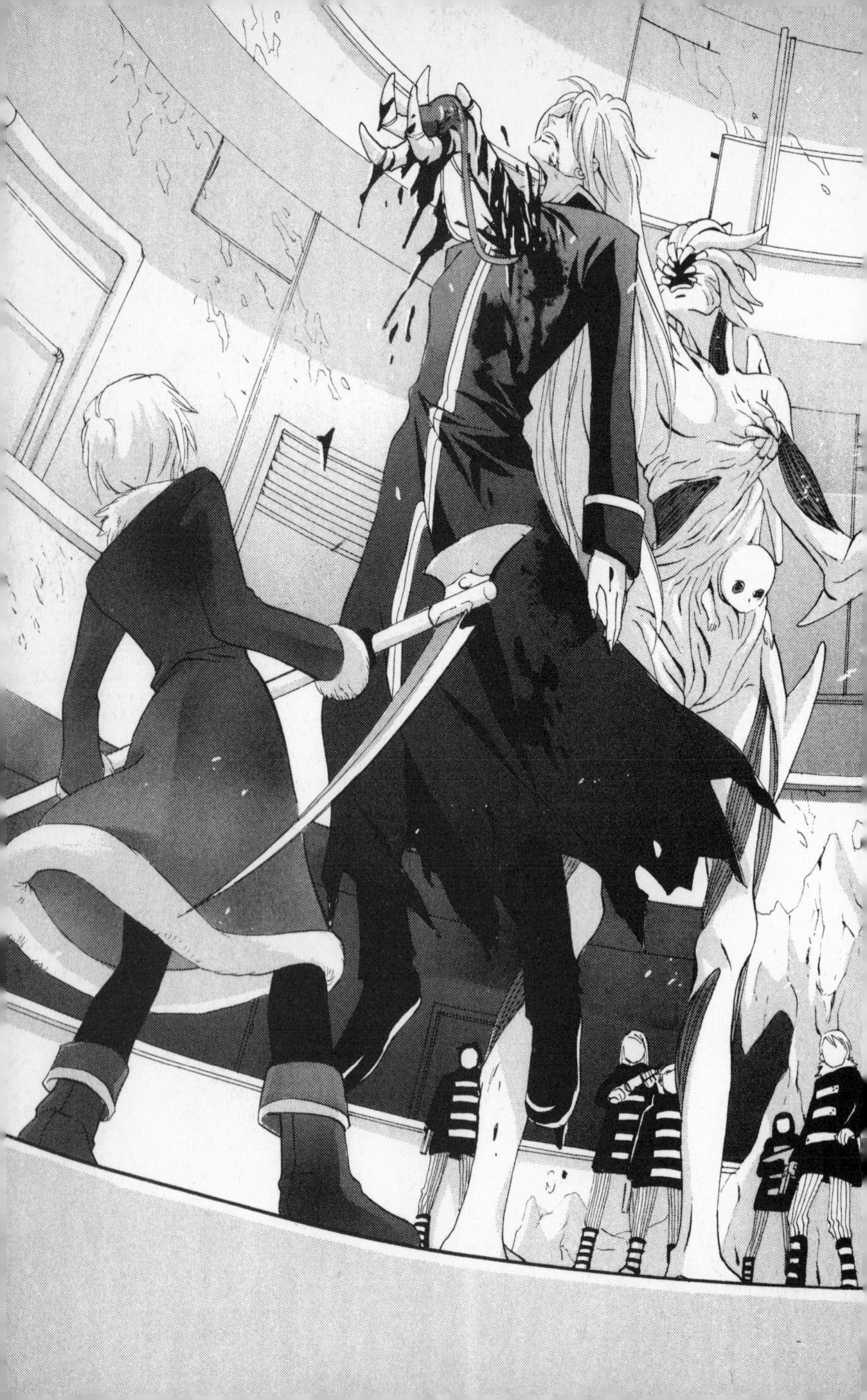

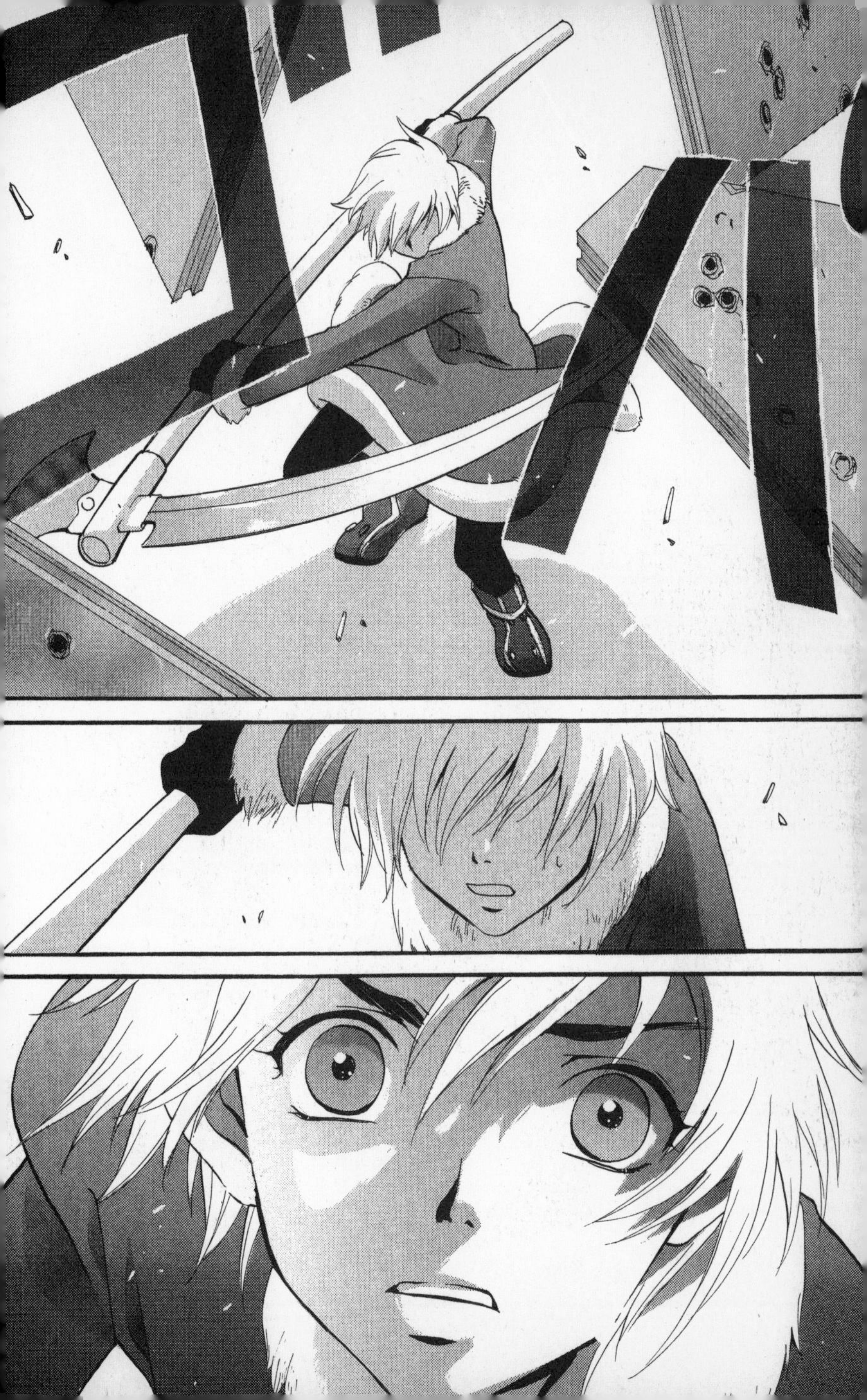

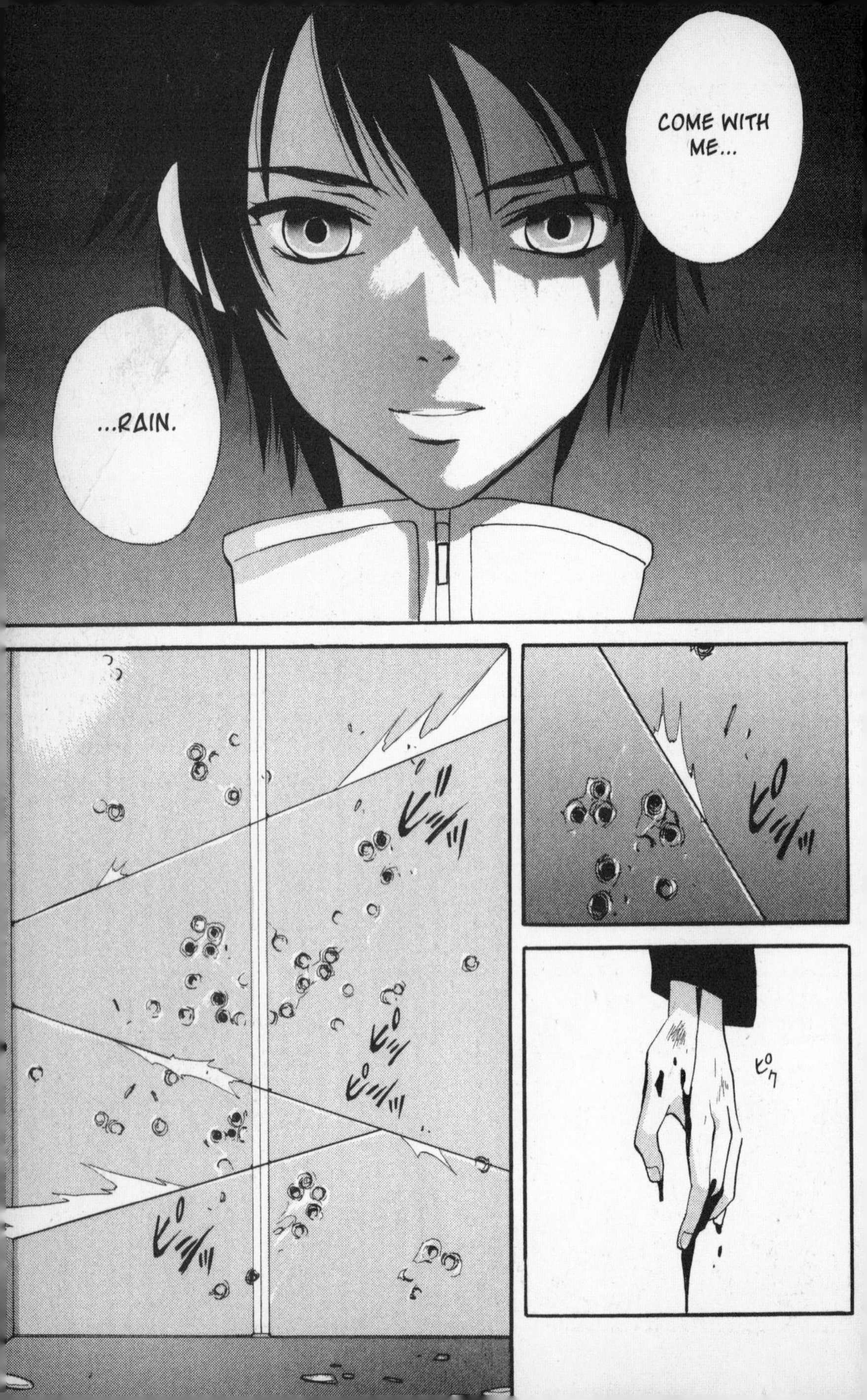
COME WITH ME...
...RAIN.
ビッ
ビッ
ピク

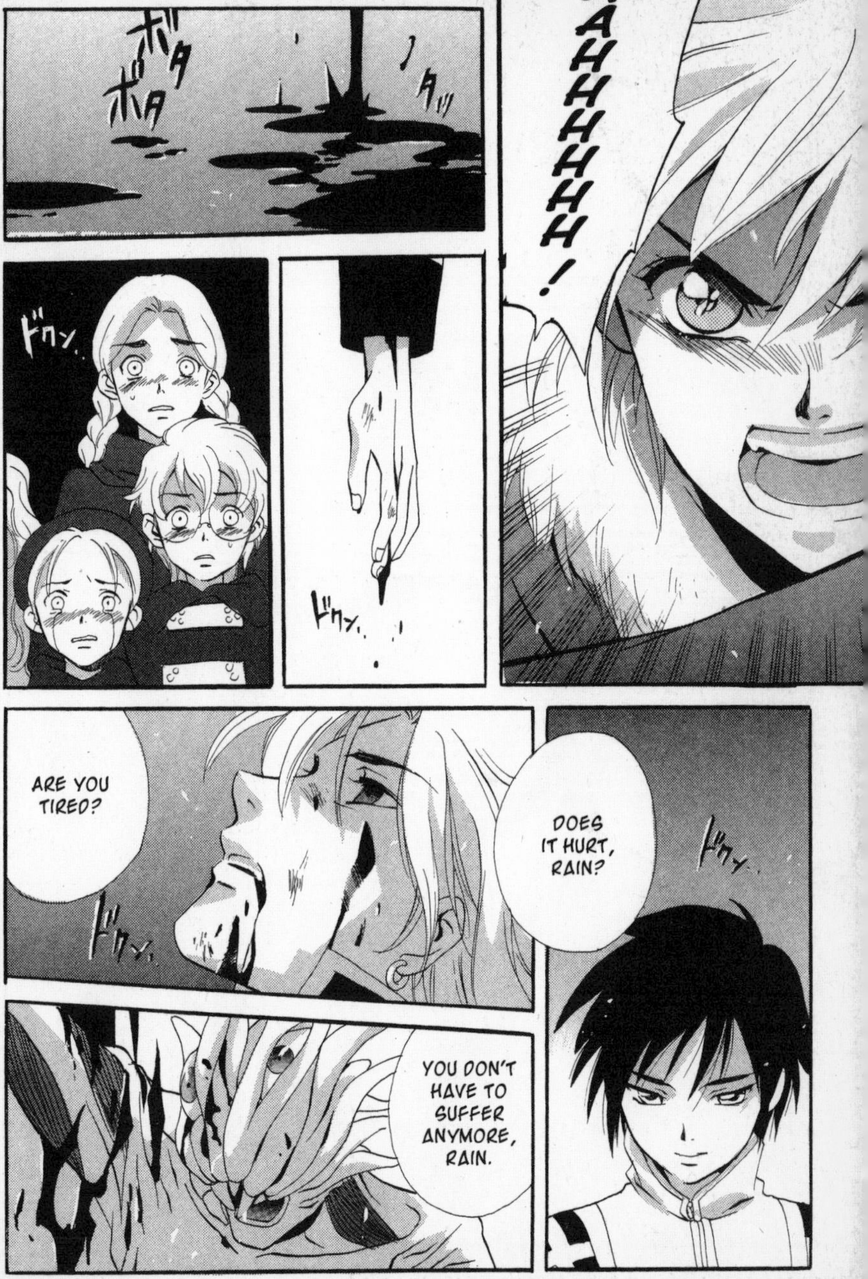
AAHHHHHHHH!
ボタボタ
ドクン..
ドクン..
DOES IT HURT, RAIN?
ドクン..
ARE YOU TIRED?
ドクン..
YOU DON'T HAVE TO SUFFER ANYMORE, RAIN.

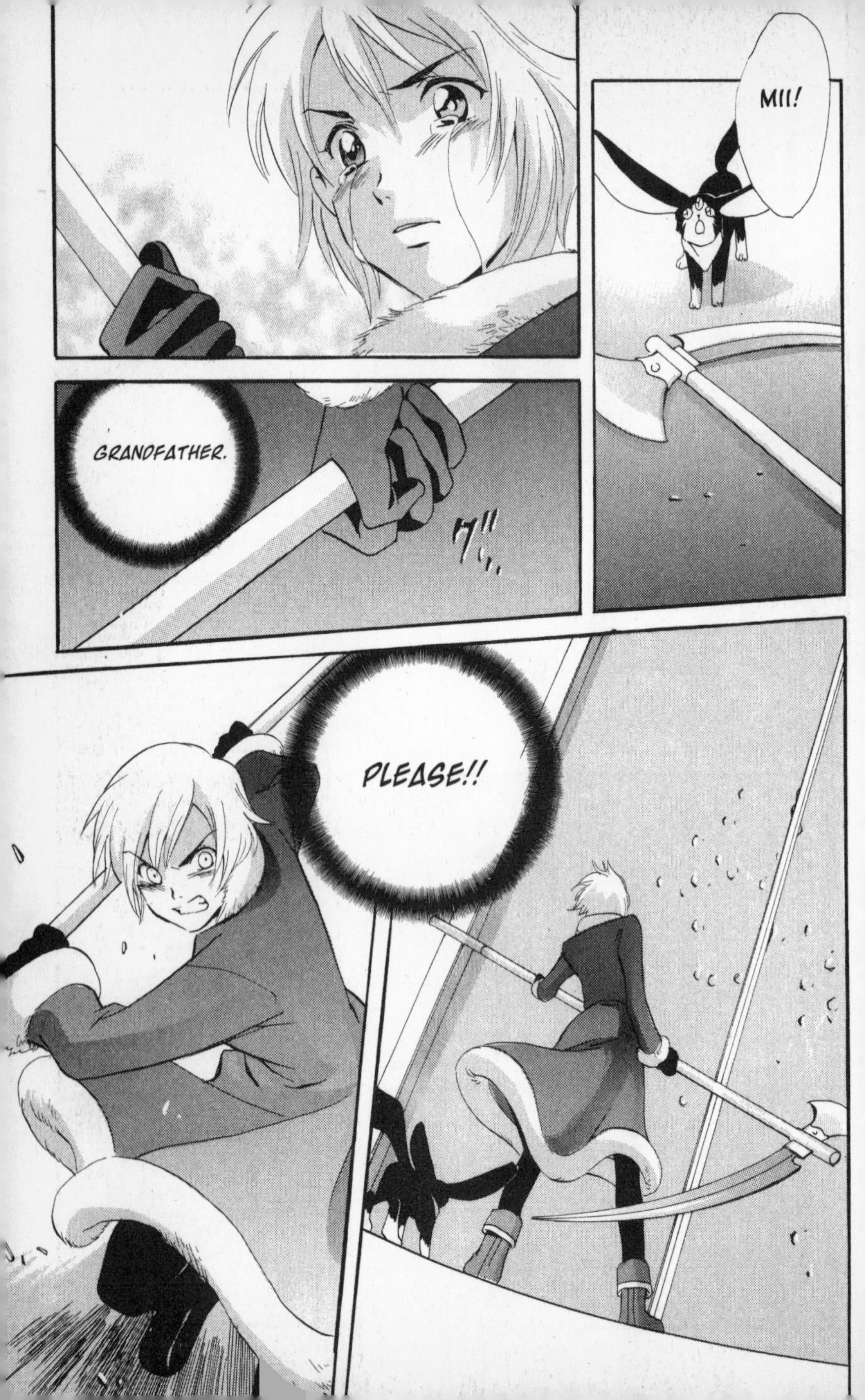
MII!
GRANDFATHER.
PLEASE!!

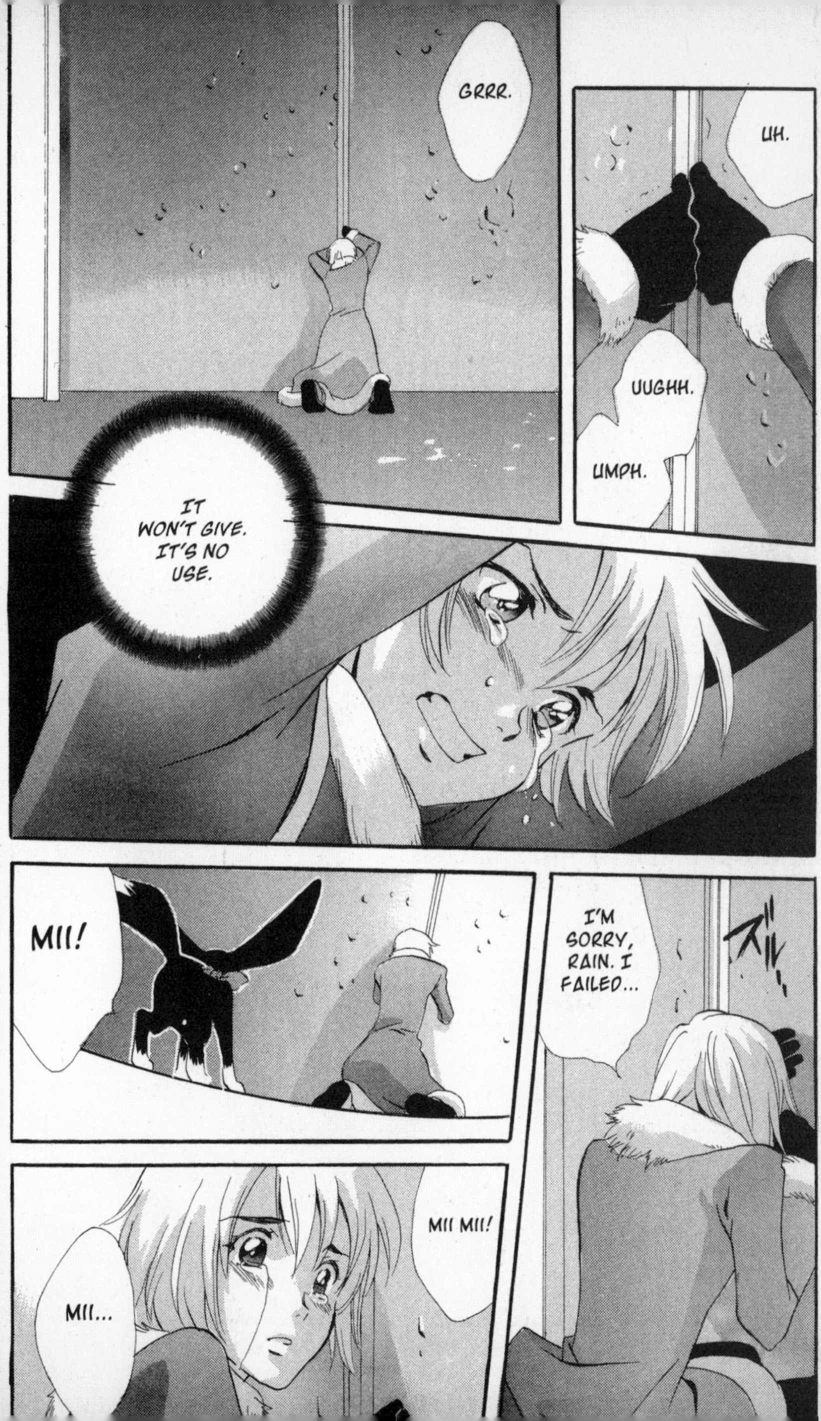
UH.
UUGHH.
UMPH.
GRRR.
IT WON'T GIVE. IT'S NO USE.
I'M SORRY, RAIN. I FAILED...
ズル
MII!
MII MII!
MII...

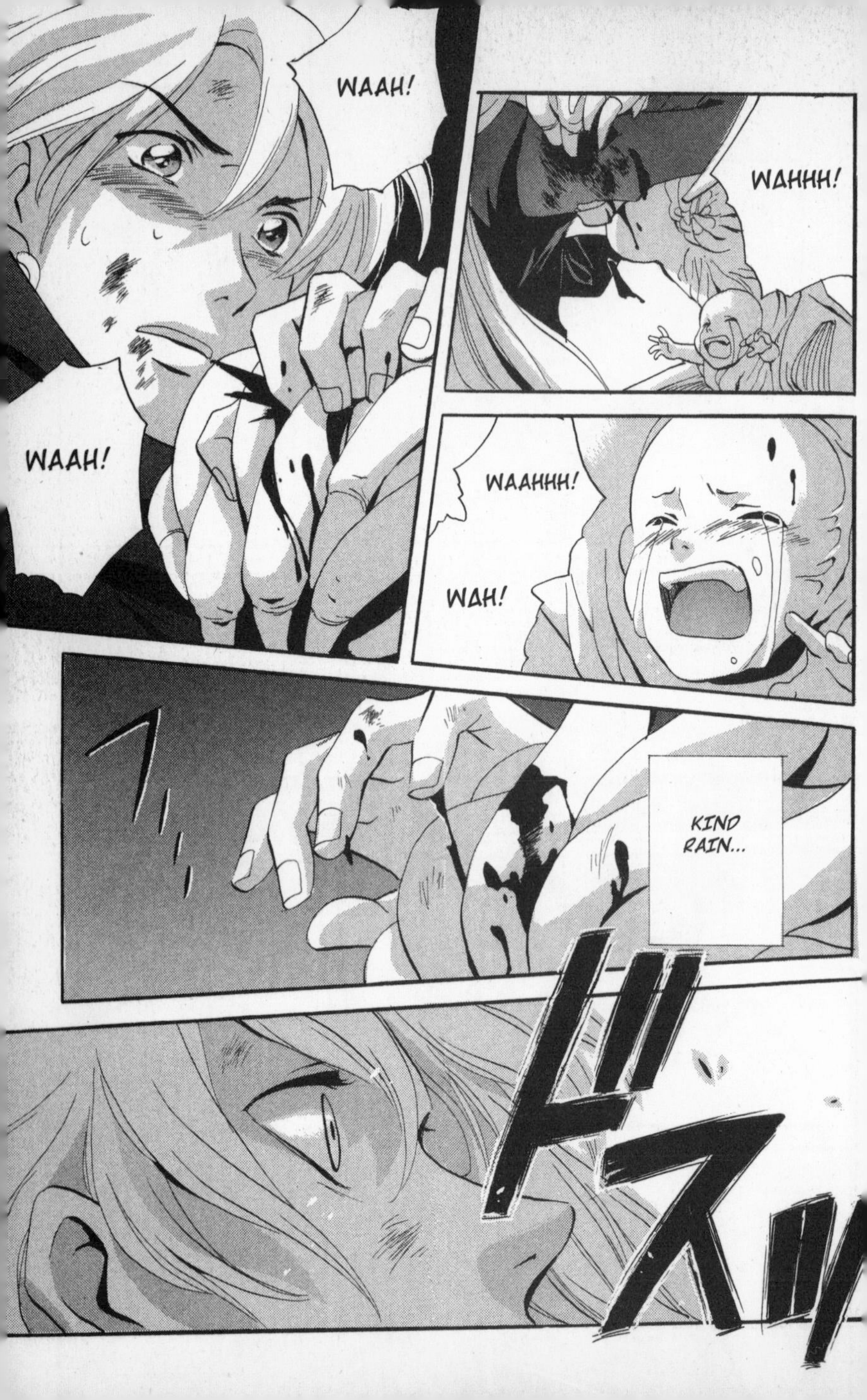
WAHHH!
WAAHHH!
WAH!
WAAH!
WAAH!
KIND RAIN...
ドスッ

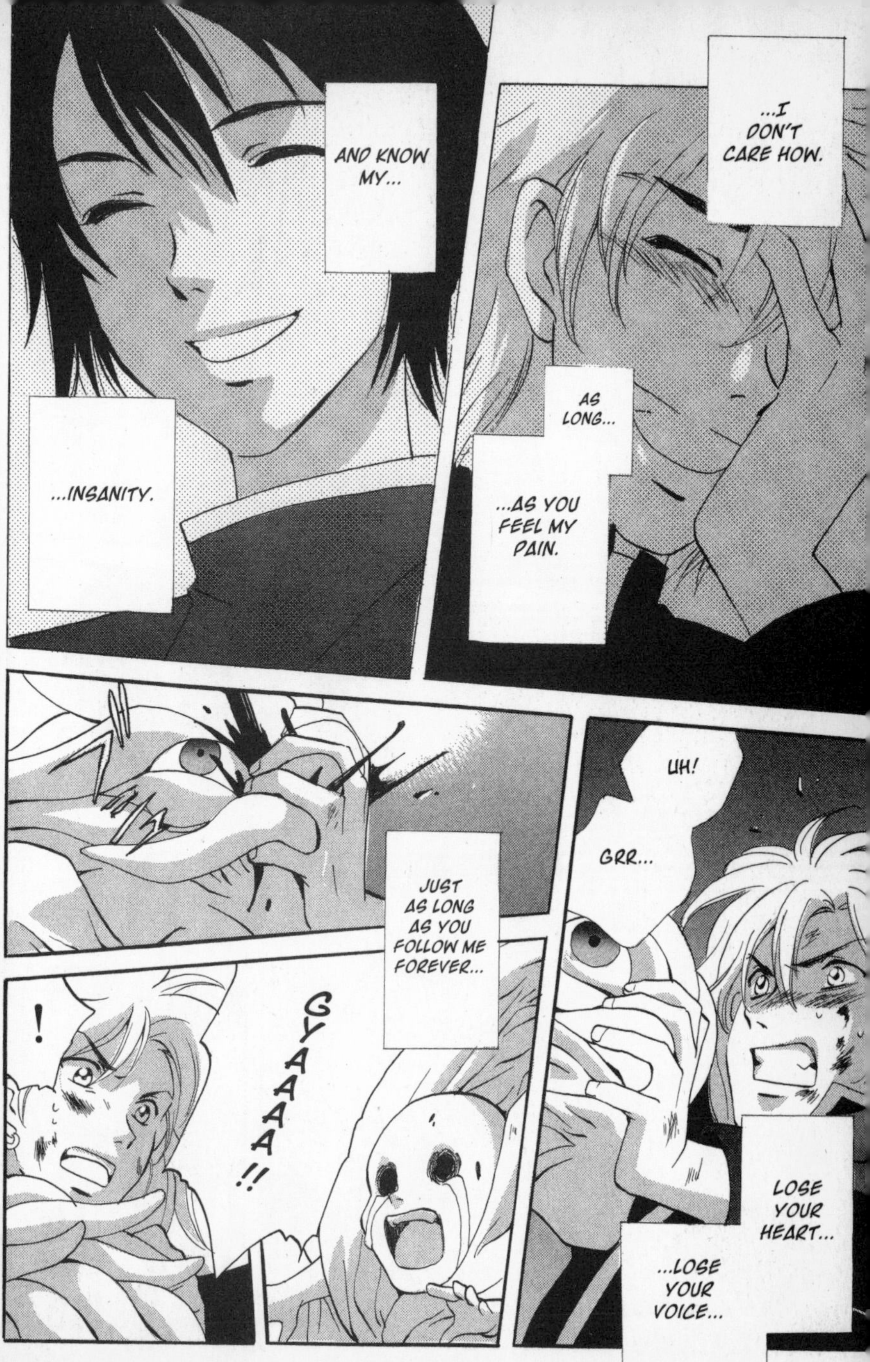
...I DON'T CARE HOW.
AS LONG...
...AS YOU FEEL MY PAIN.
AND KNOW MY...
...INSANITY.
UH!
GRR...
LOSE YOUR HEART...
...LOSE YOUR VOICE...
JUST AS LONG AS YOU FOLLOW ME FOREVER...
!
GYAAAAA!!

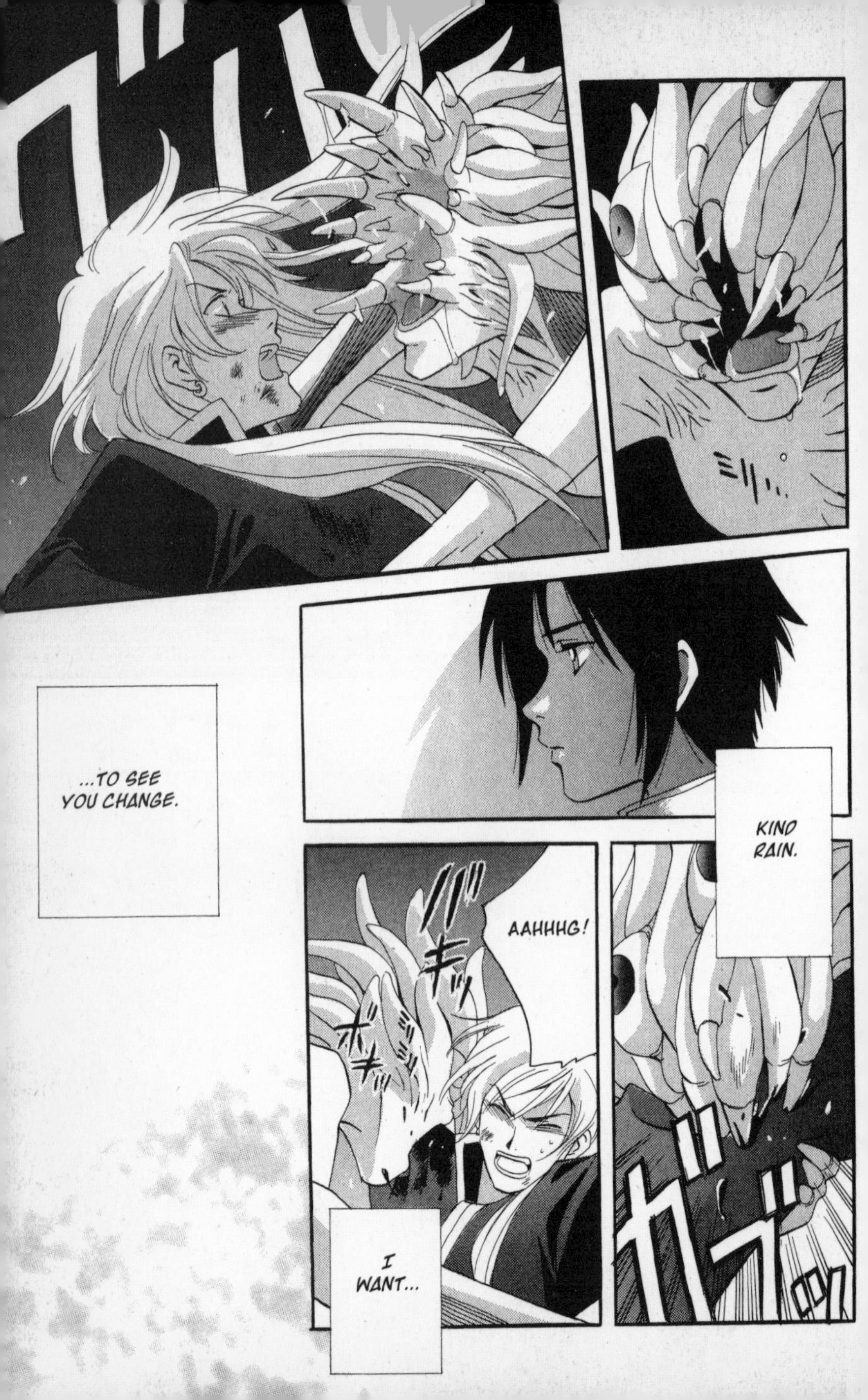
KIND RAIN.
AAHHHG!
I WANT...
...TO SEE YOU CHANGE.

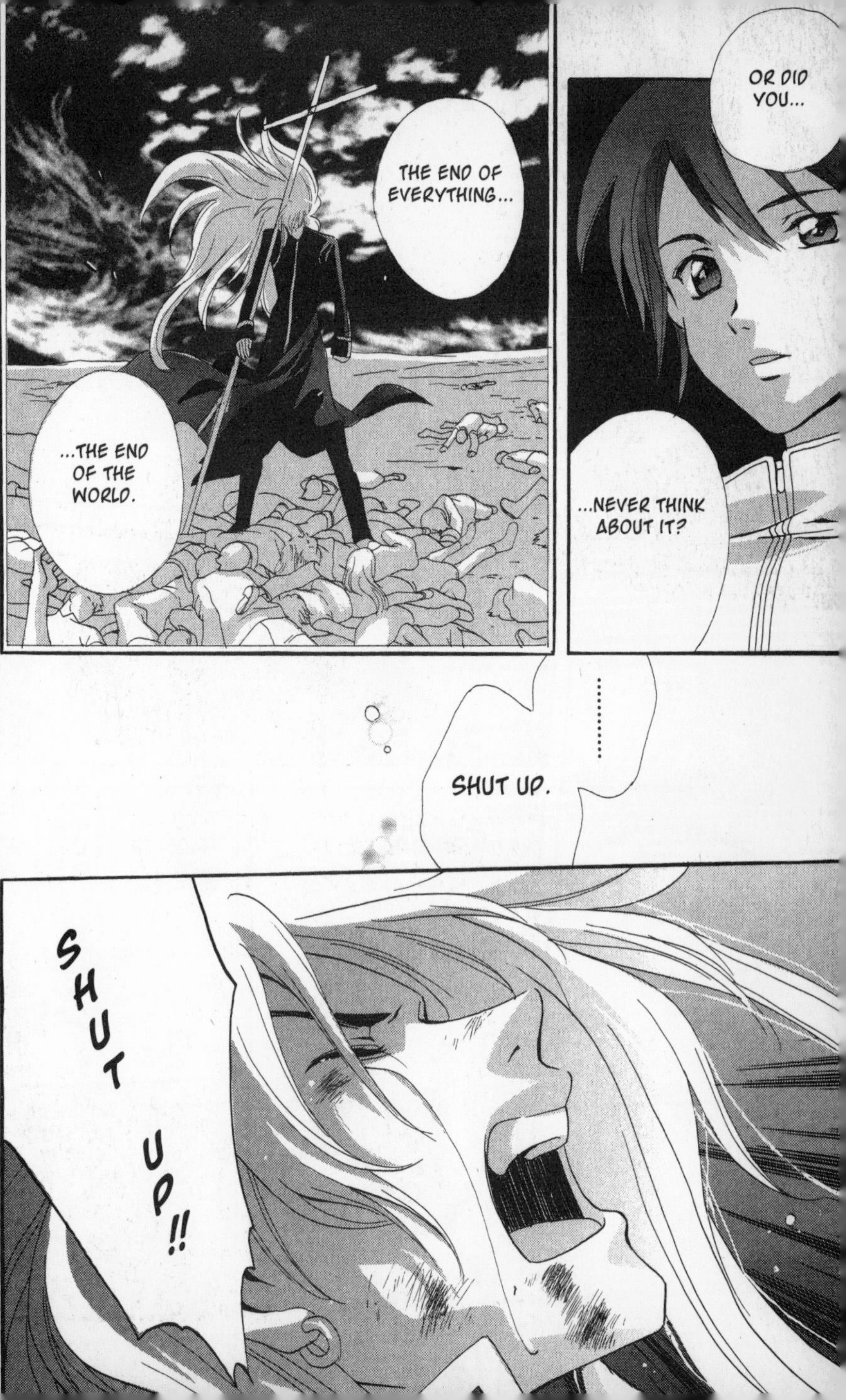
THE END OF EVERYTHING...
...THE END OF THE WORLD.
OR DID YOU...
...NEVER THINK ABOUT IT?
......
SHUT UP.
SHUT UP!!

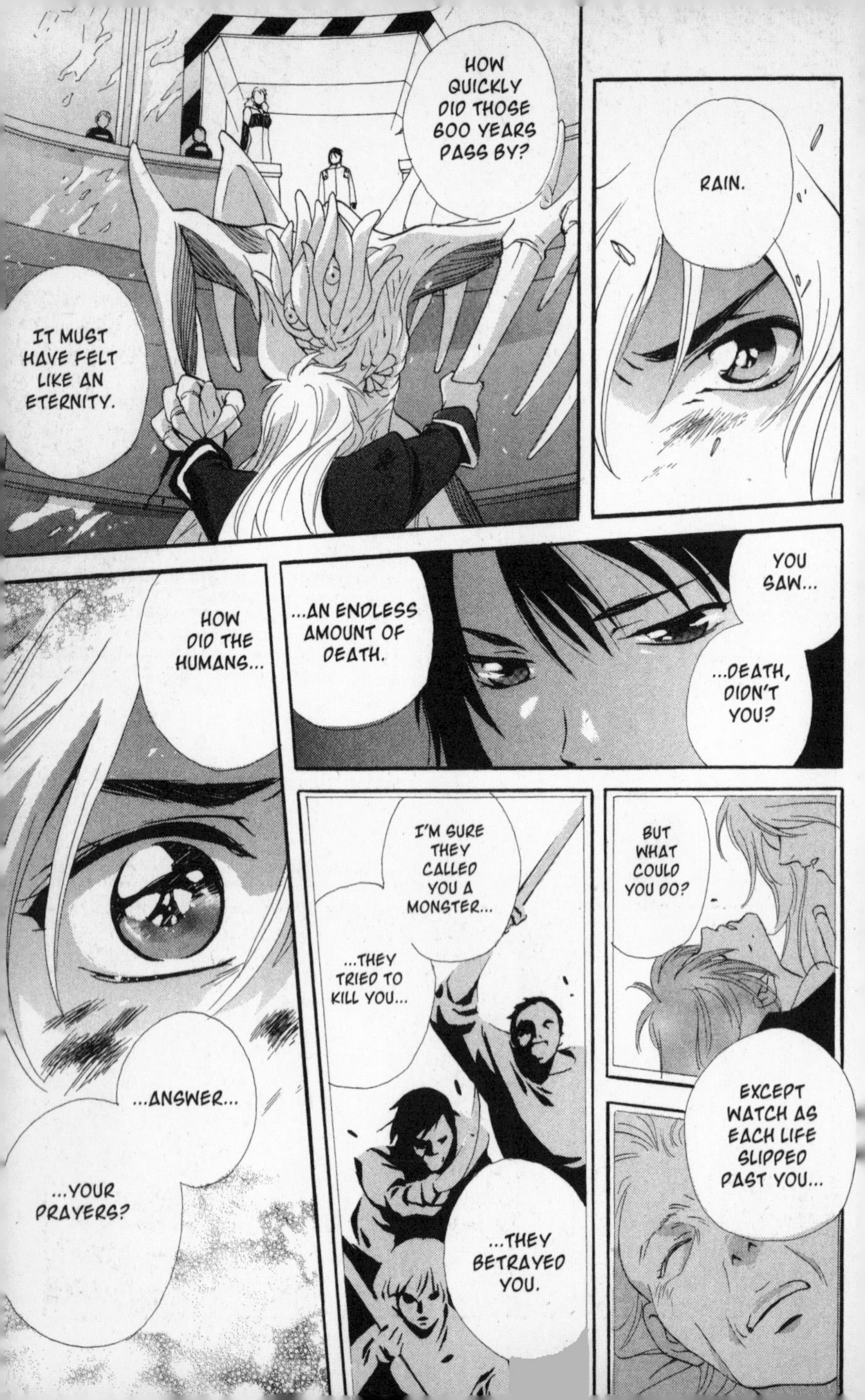
RAIN.
HOW QUICKLY DID THOSE 600 YEARS PASS BY?
IT MUST HAVE FELT LIKE AN ETERNITY.
YOU SAW...
...DEATH, DIDN'T YOU?
...AN ENDLESS AMOUNT OF DEATH.
BUT WHAT COULD YOU DO?
EXCEPT WATCH AS EACH LIFE SLIPPED PAST YOU...
I'M SURE THEY CALLED YOU A MONSTER...
...THEY TRIED TO KILL YOU...
...THEY BETRAYED YOU.
HOW DID THE HUMANS...
...ANSWER...
...YOUR PRAYERS?

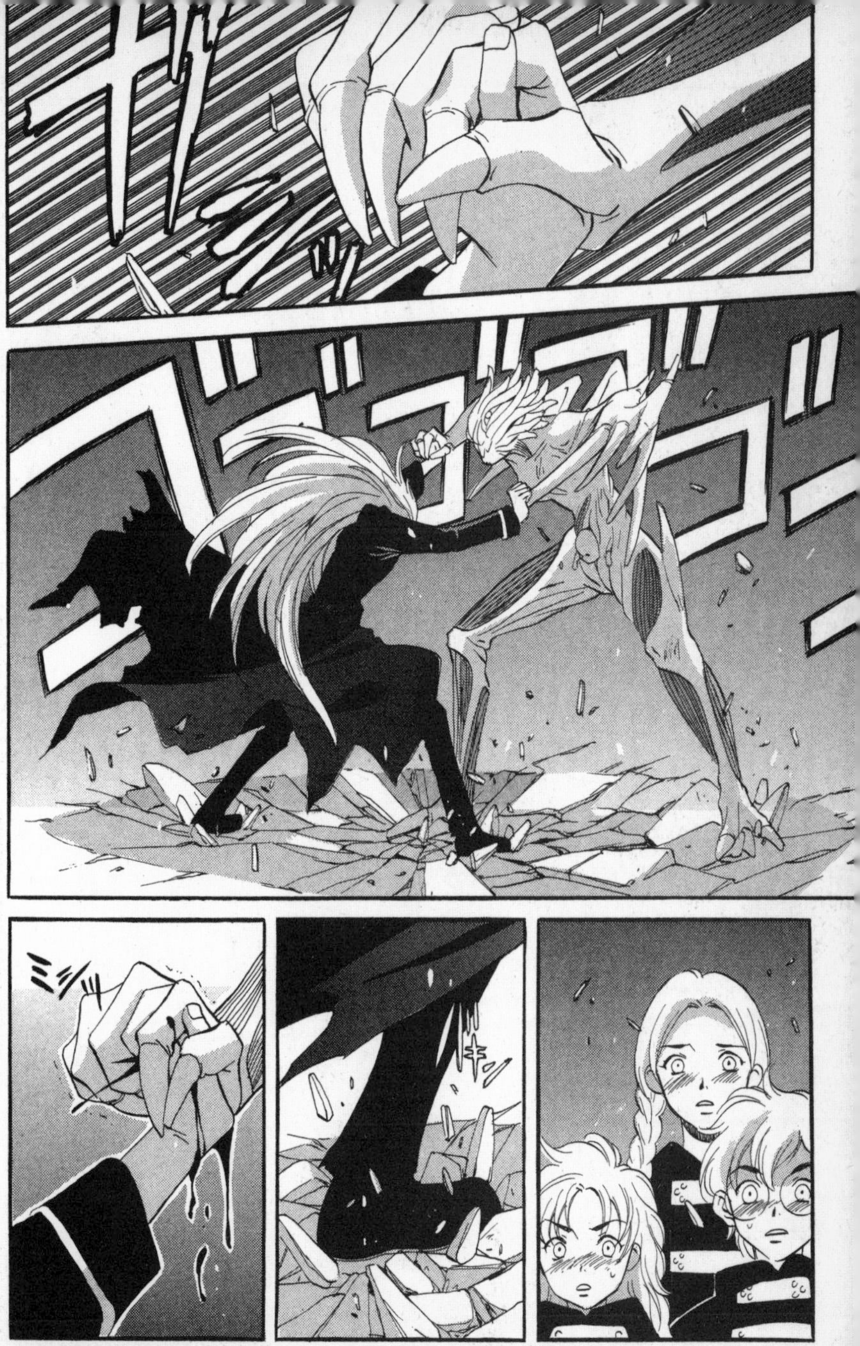
ギシッ
ゴゴゴゴ
キン
ミシッ

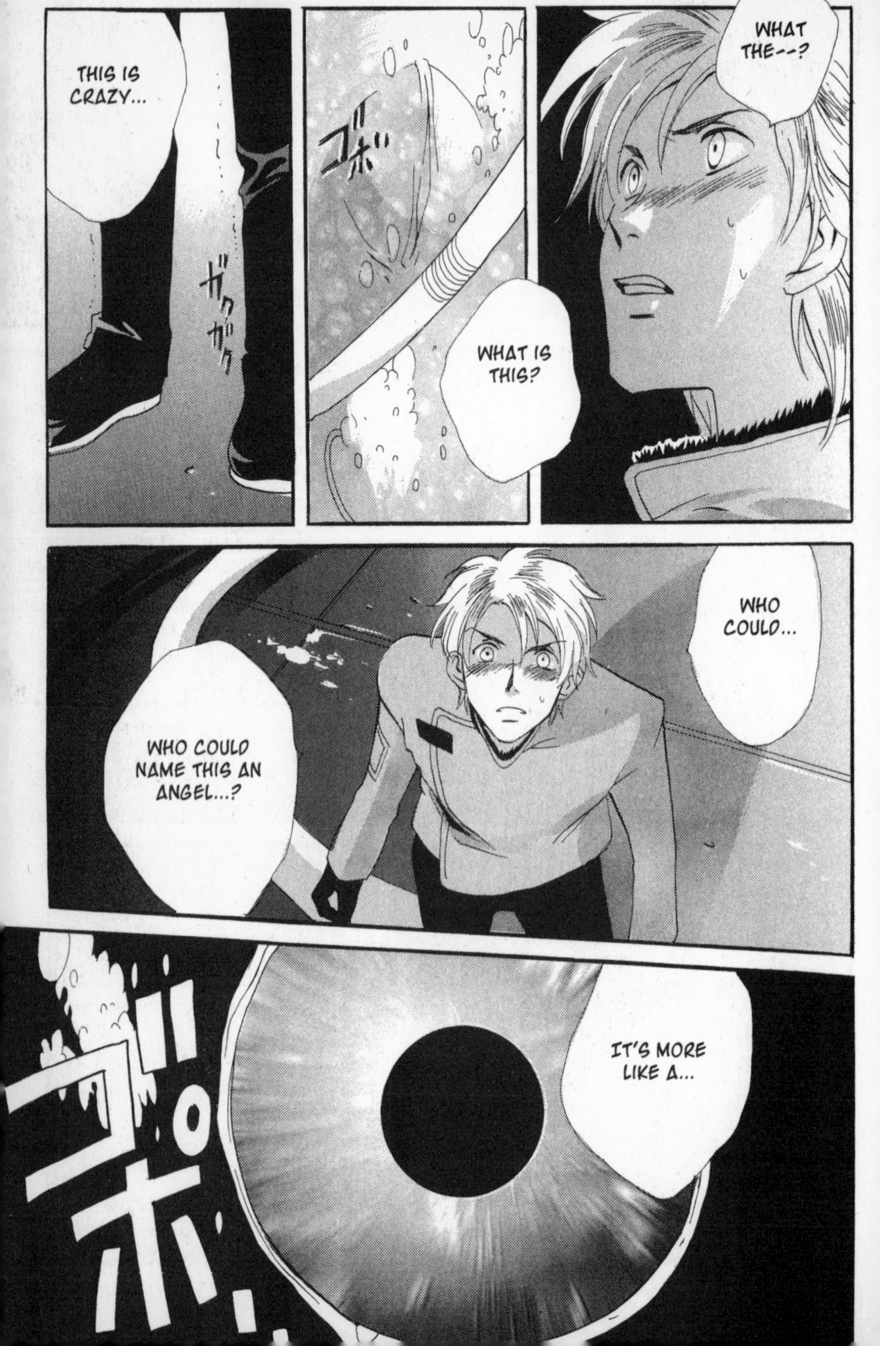
WHAT THE--?
WHAT IS THIS?
ゴボ
THIS IS CRAZY...
ガクガク
WHO COULD...
WHO COULD NAME THIS AN ANGEL...?
IT'S MORE LIKE A...
ゴポ

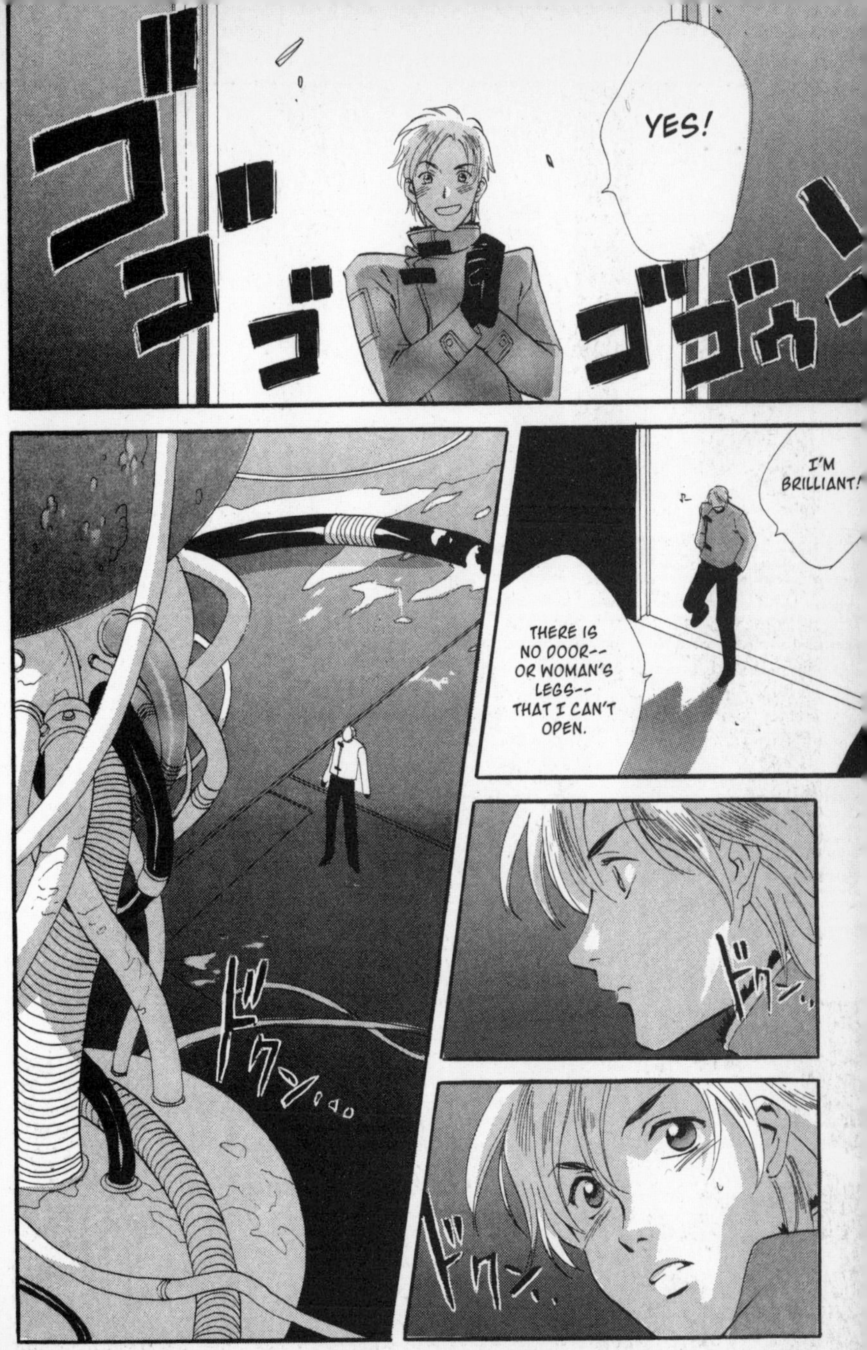
YES!
I'M BRILLIANT!
THERE IS NO DOOR-- OR WOMAN'S LEGS-- THAT I CAN'T OPEN.

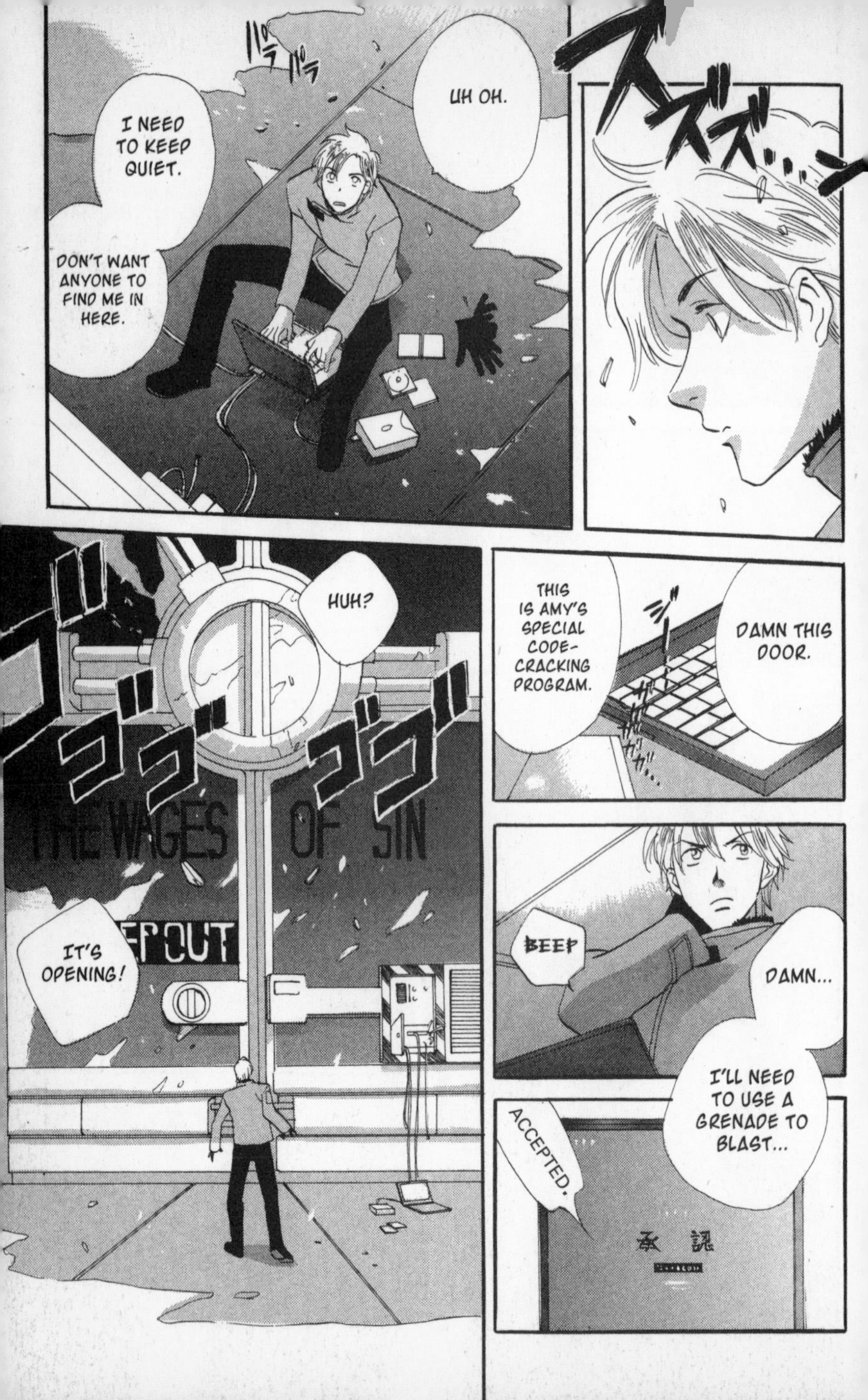
UH OH.
I NEED TO KEEP QUIET.
DON'T WANT ANYONE TO FIND ME IN HERE.
DAMN THIS DOOR.
THIS IS AMY'S SPECIAL CODE-CRACKING PROGRAM.
BEEP
DAMN...
I'LL NEED TO USE A GRENADE TO BLAST...
ACCEPTED.
承認
HUH?
THE WAGES OF SIN
IT'S OPENING!

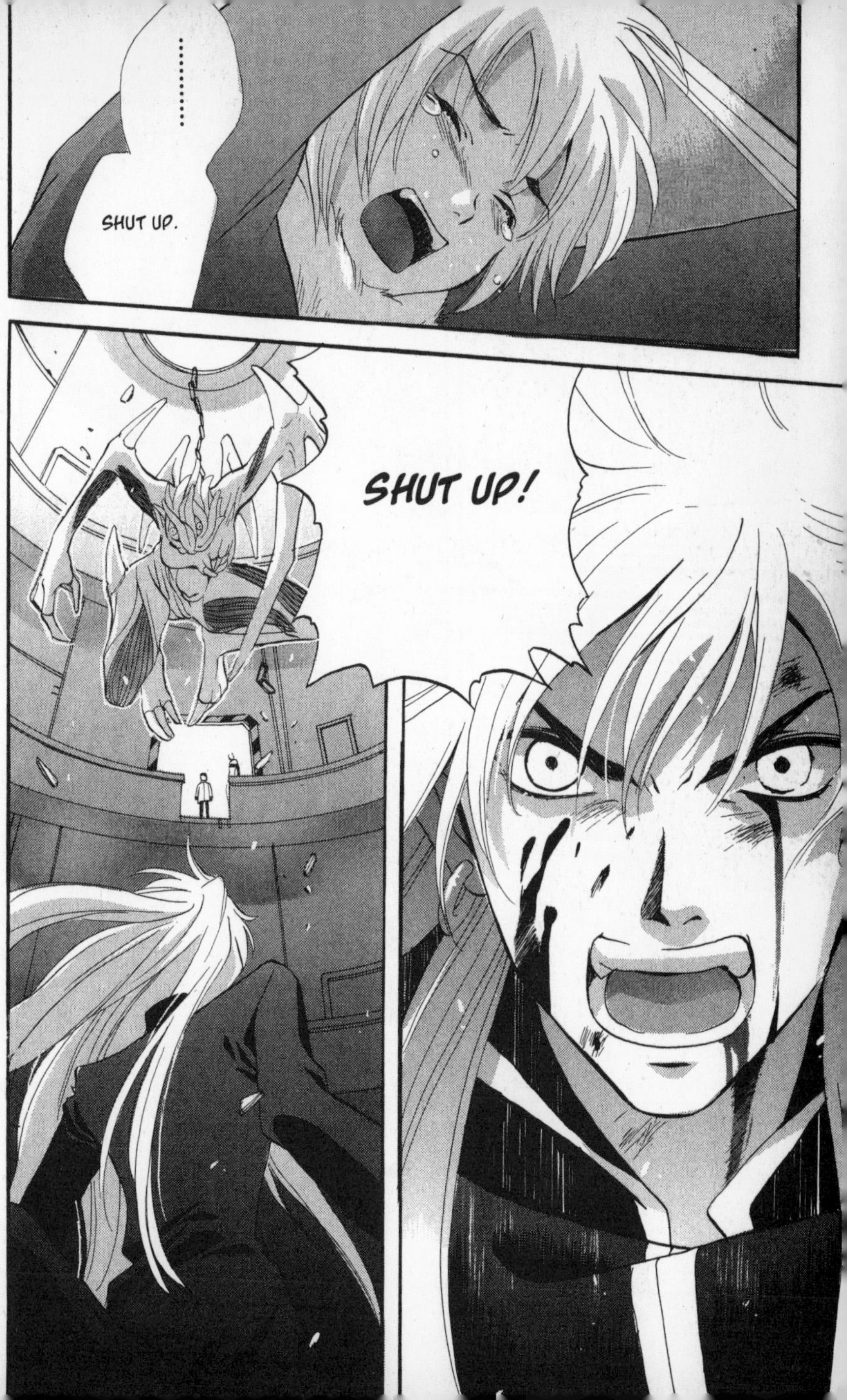
......
SHUT UP.
SHUT UP!

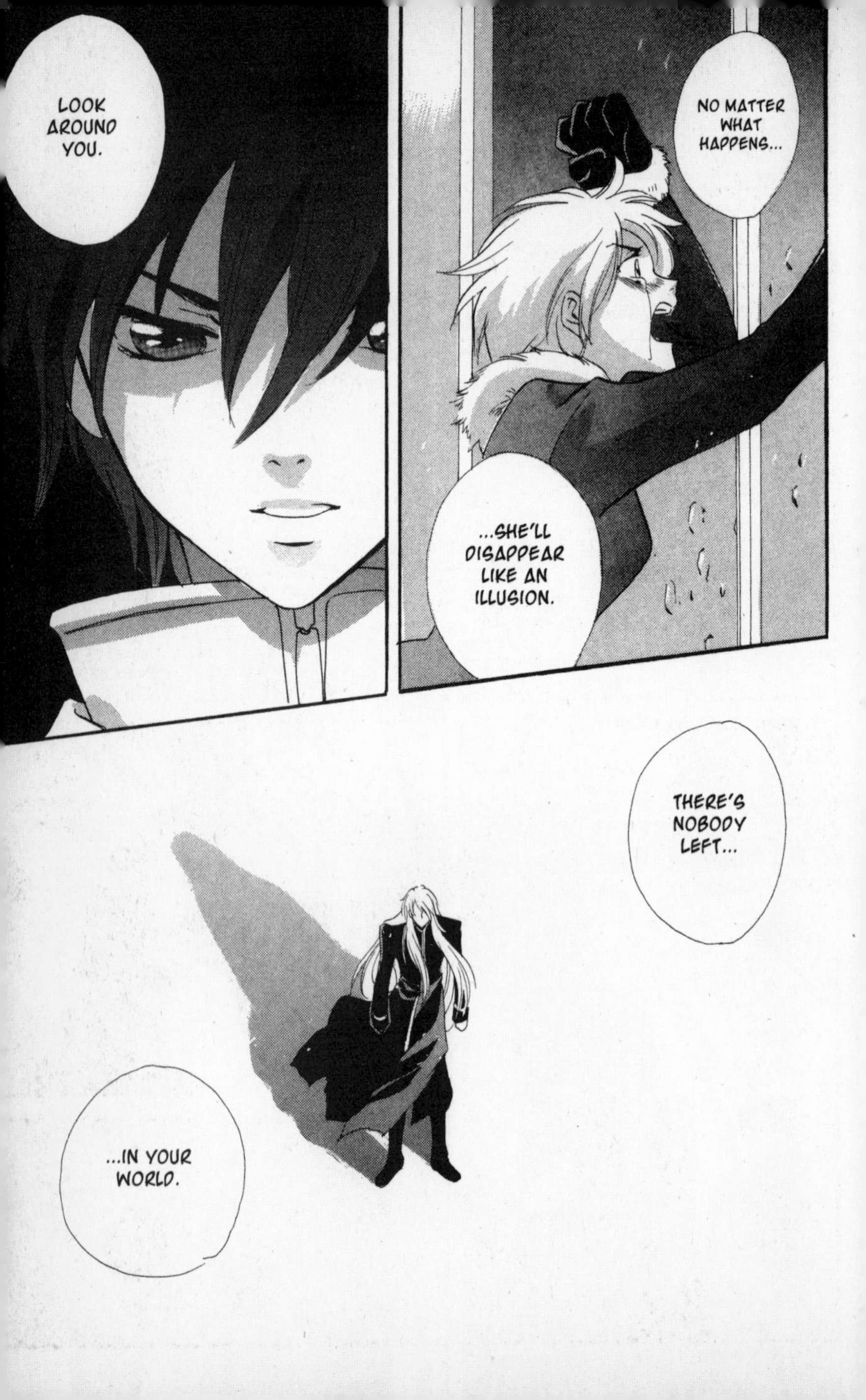
NO MATTER WHAT HAPPENS...
...SHE'LL DISAPPEAR LIKE AN ILLUSION.
LOOK AROUND YOU.
THERE'S NOBODY LEFT...
...IN YOUR WORLD.

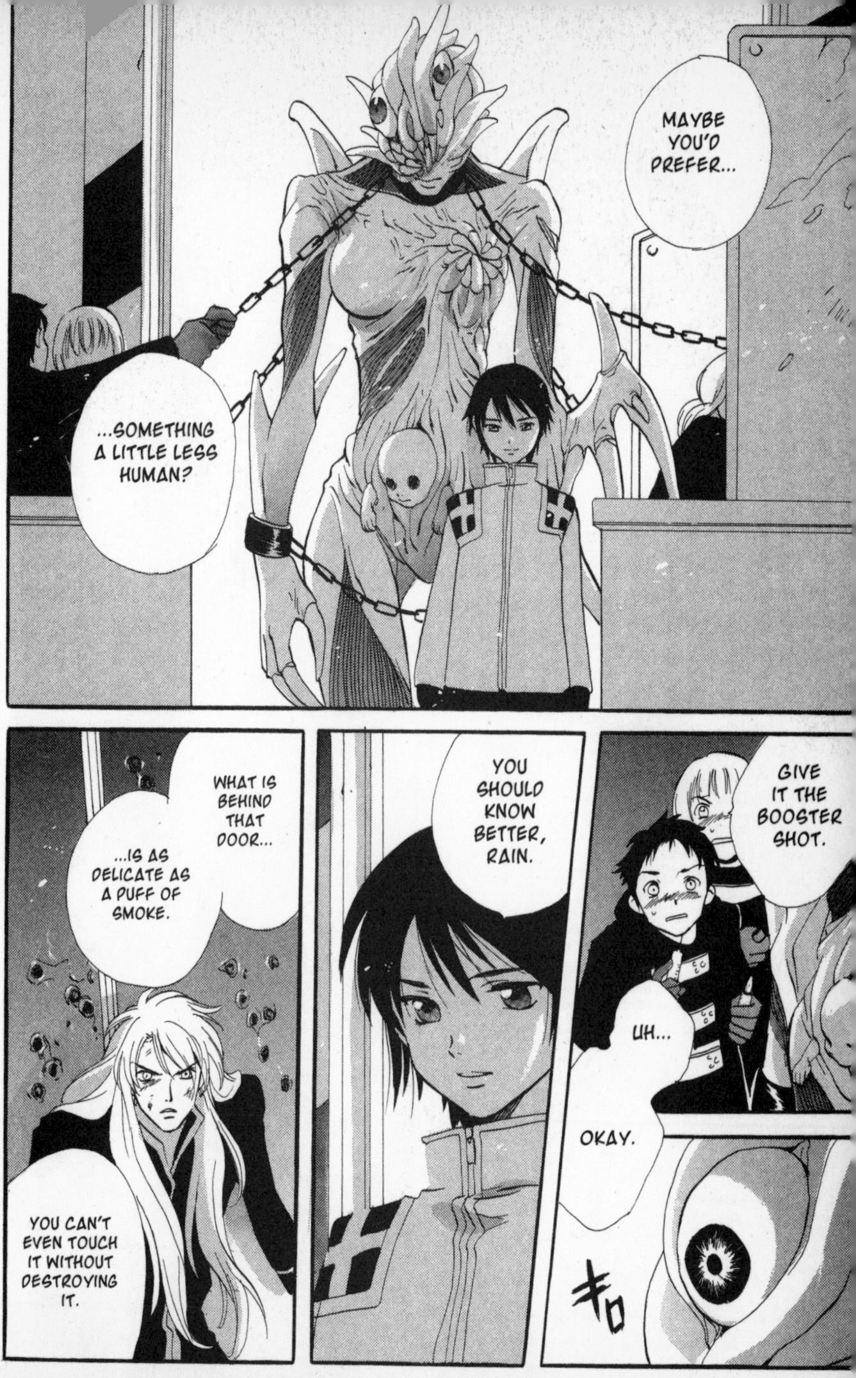
MAYBE YOU'D PREFER...
...SOMETHING A LITTLE LESS HUMAN?
GIVE IT THE BOOSTER SHOT.
UH...
OKAY.
YOU SHOULD KNOW BETTER, RAIN.
WHAT IS BEHIND THAT DOOR...
...IS AS DELICATE AS A PUFF OF SMOKE.
YOU CAN'T EVEN TOUCH IT WITHOUT DESTROYING IT.

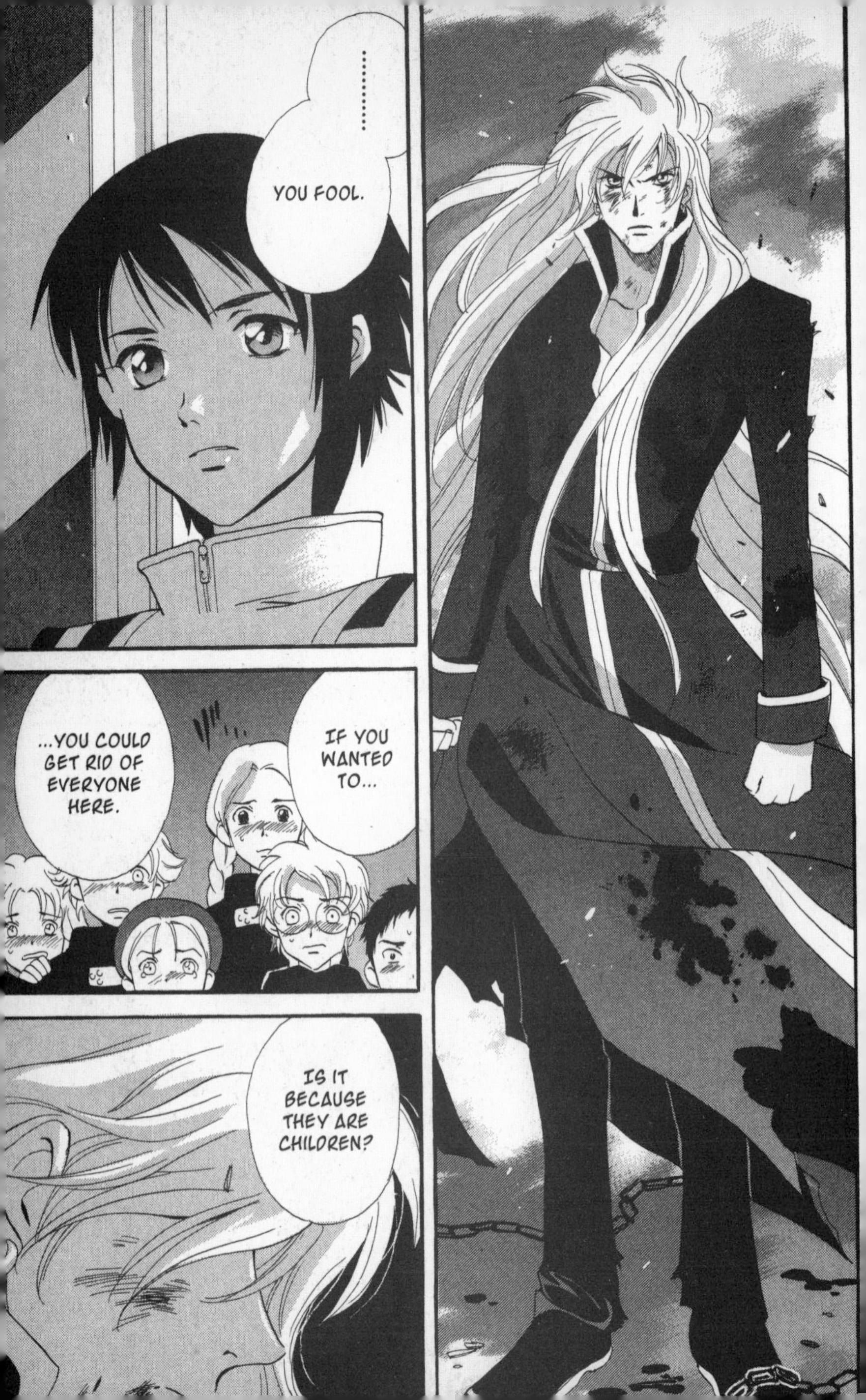
......
YOU FOOL.
IF YOU WANTED TO...
...YOU COULD GET RID OF EVERYONE HERE.
IS IT BECAUSE THEY ARE CHILDREN?

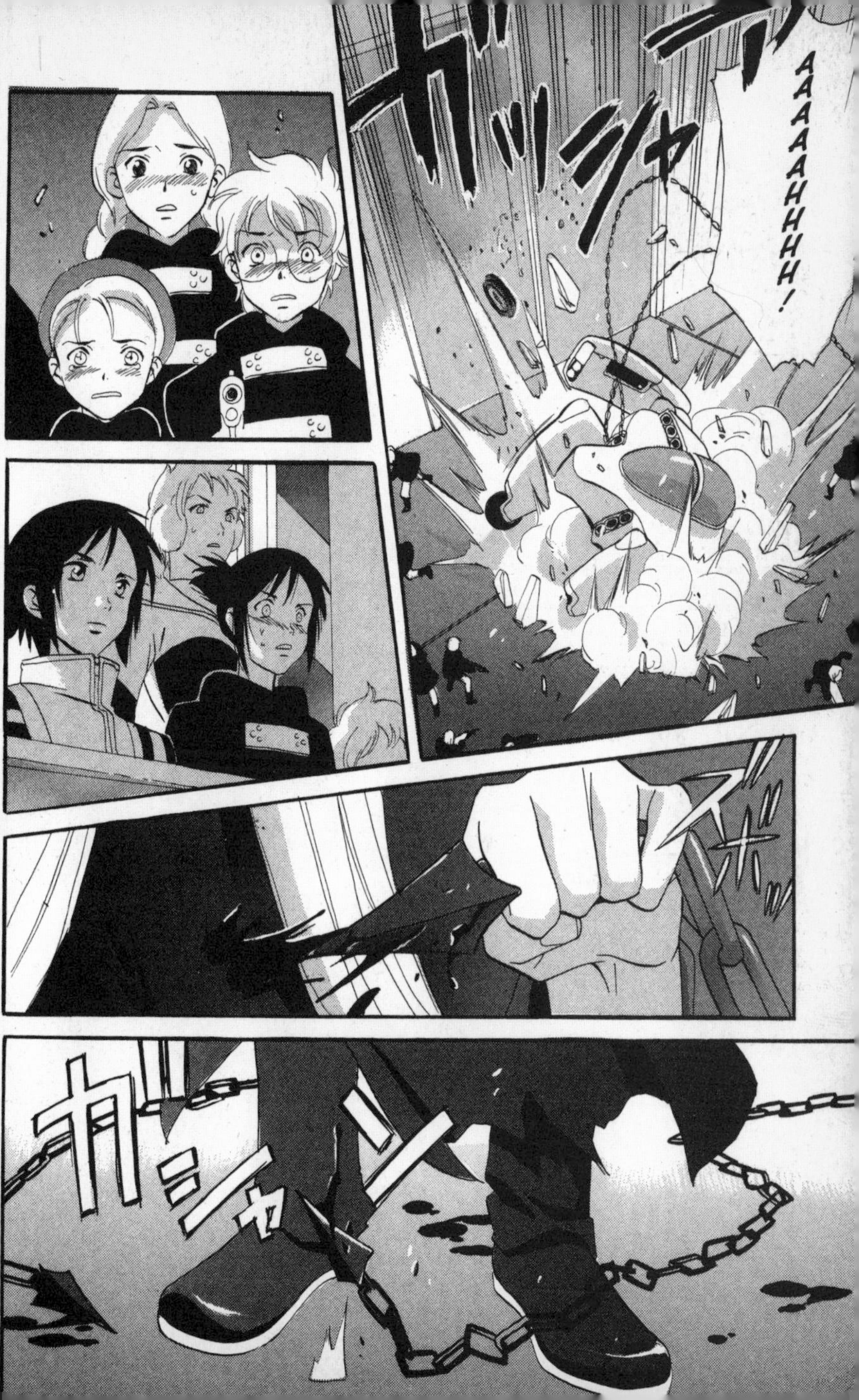
AAAAAAHHHHH!

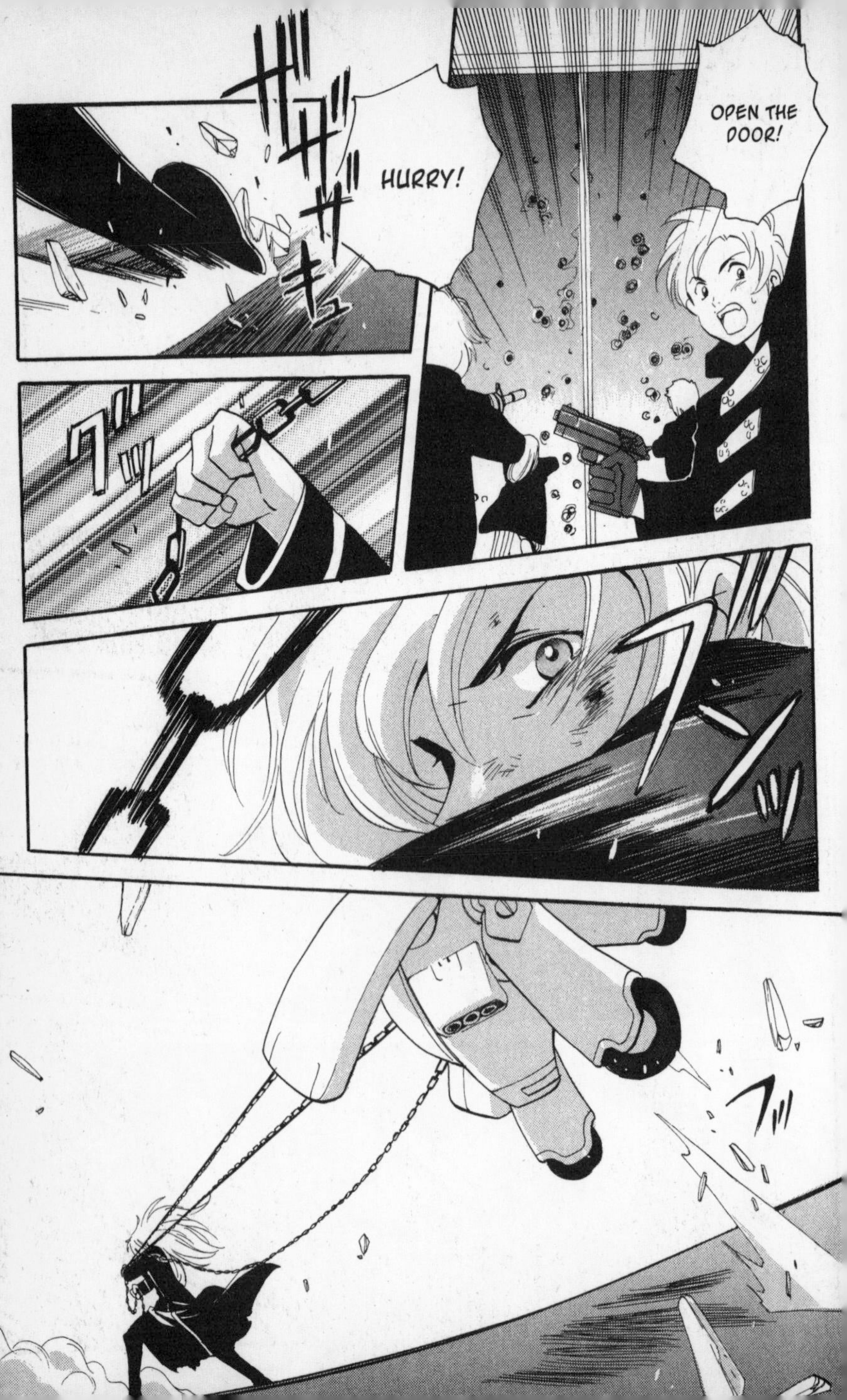
OPEN THE DOOR!
HURRY!

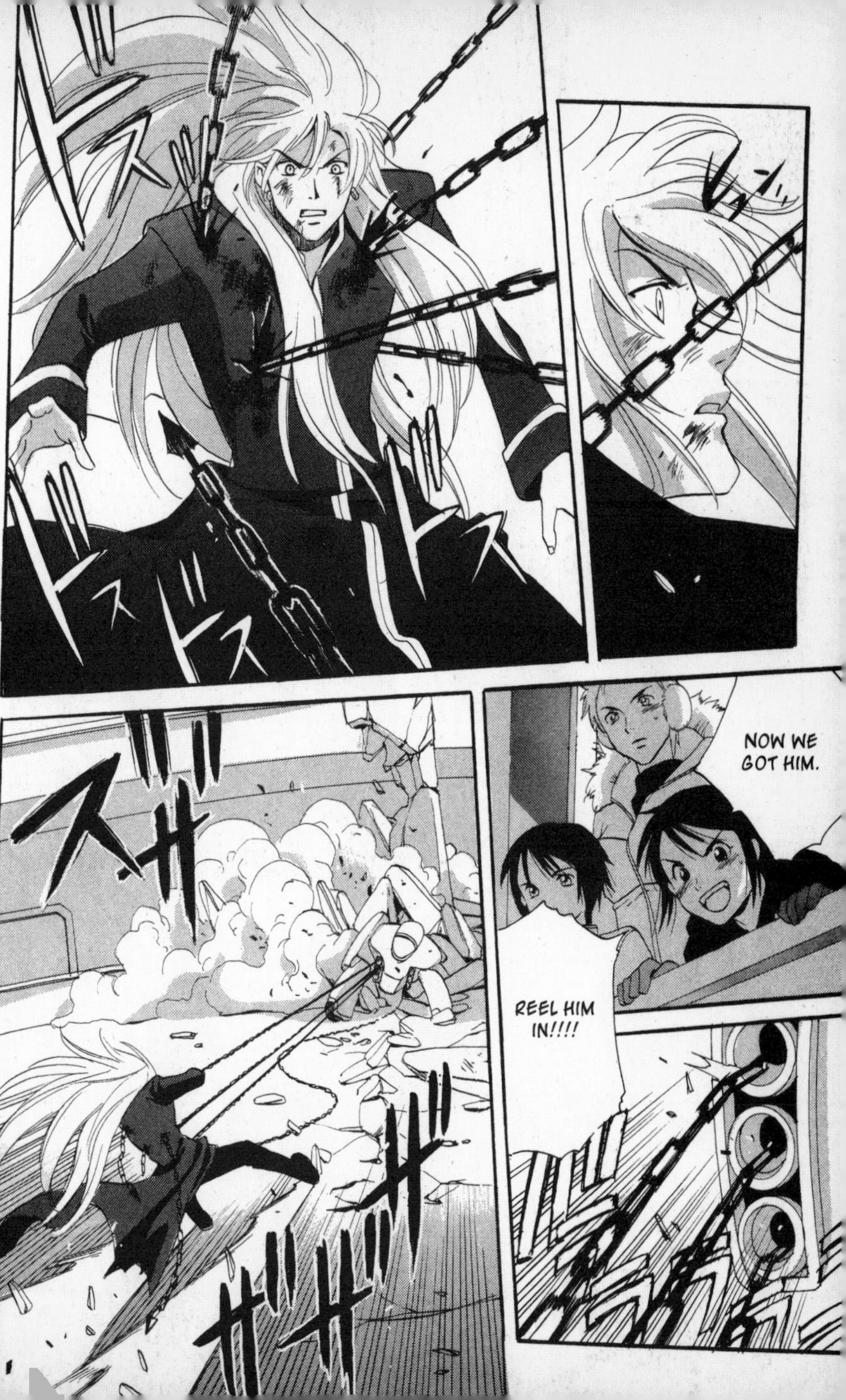
NOW WE GOT HIM.
REEL HIM IN!!!!

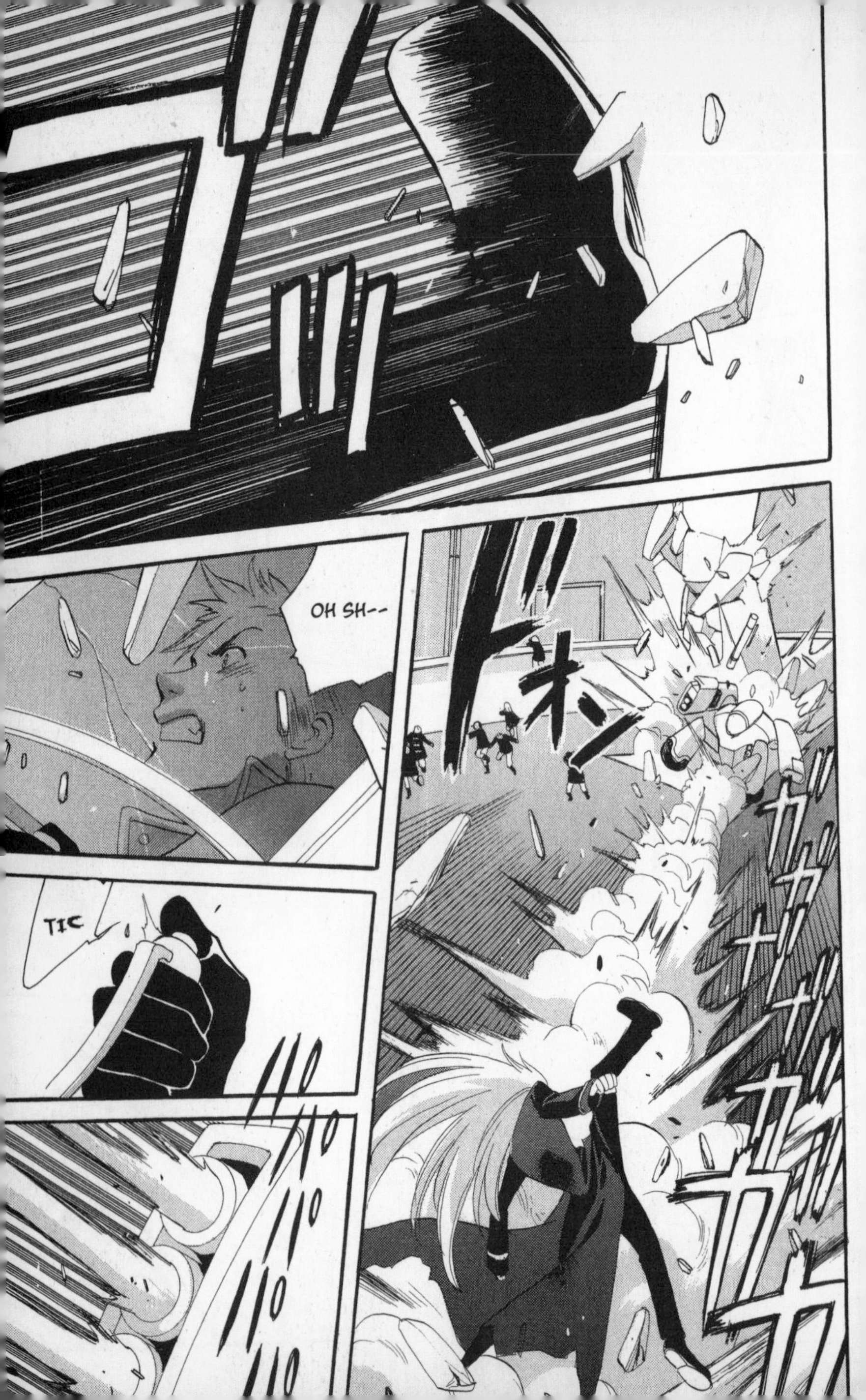
OH SH--
TIC

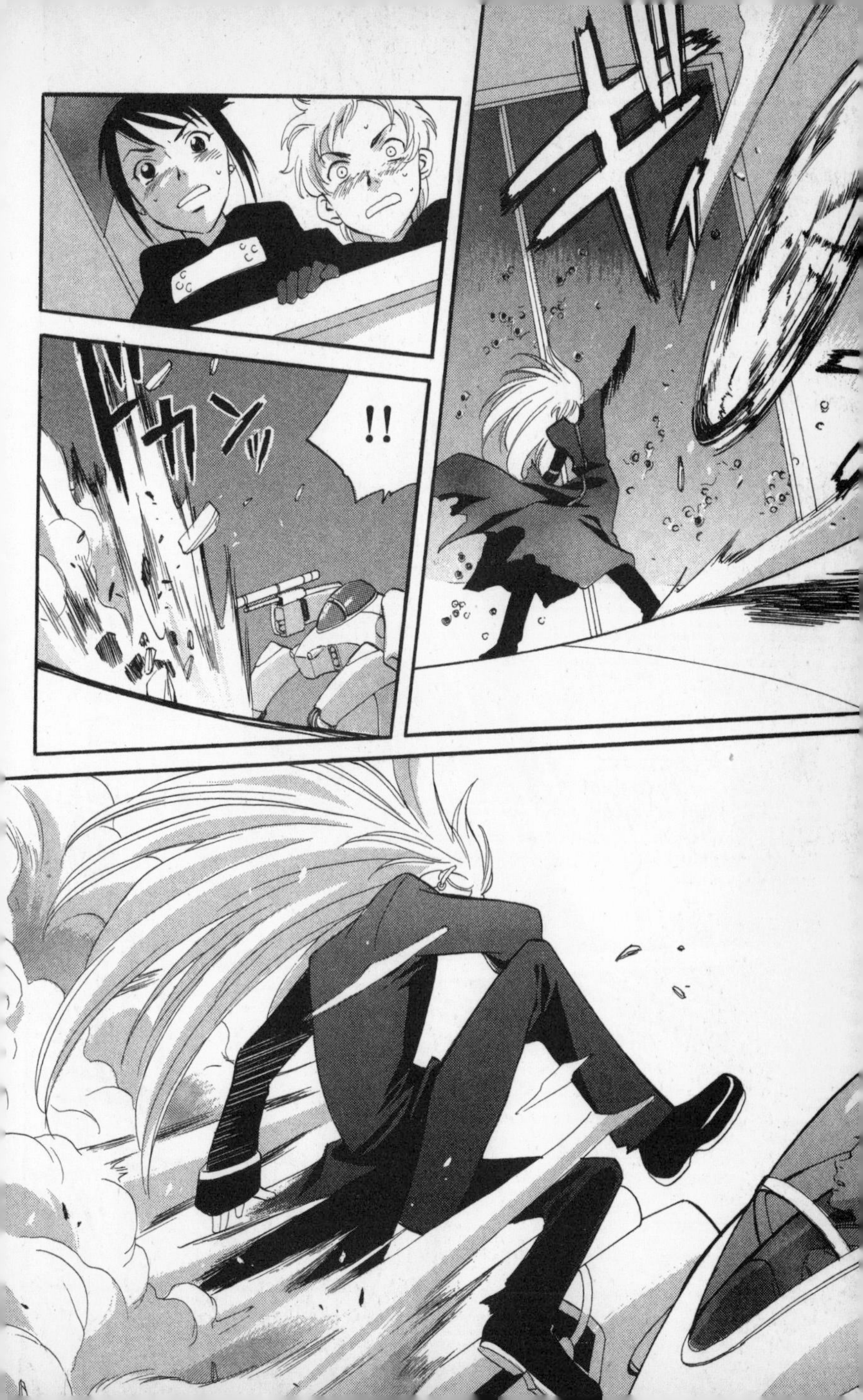
ドカンッ
!!

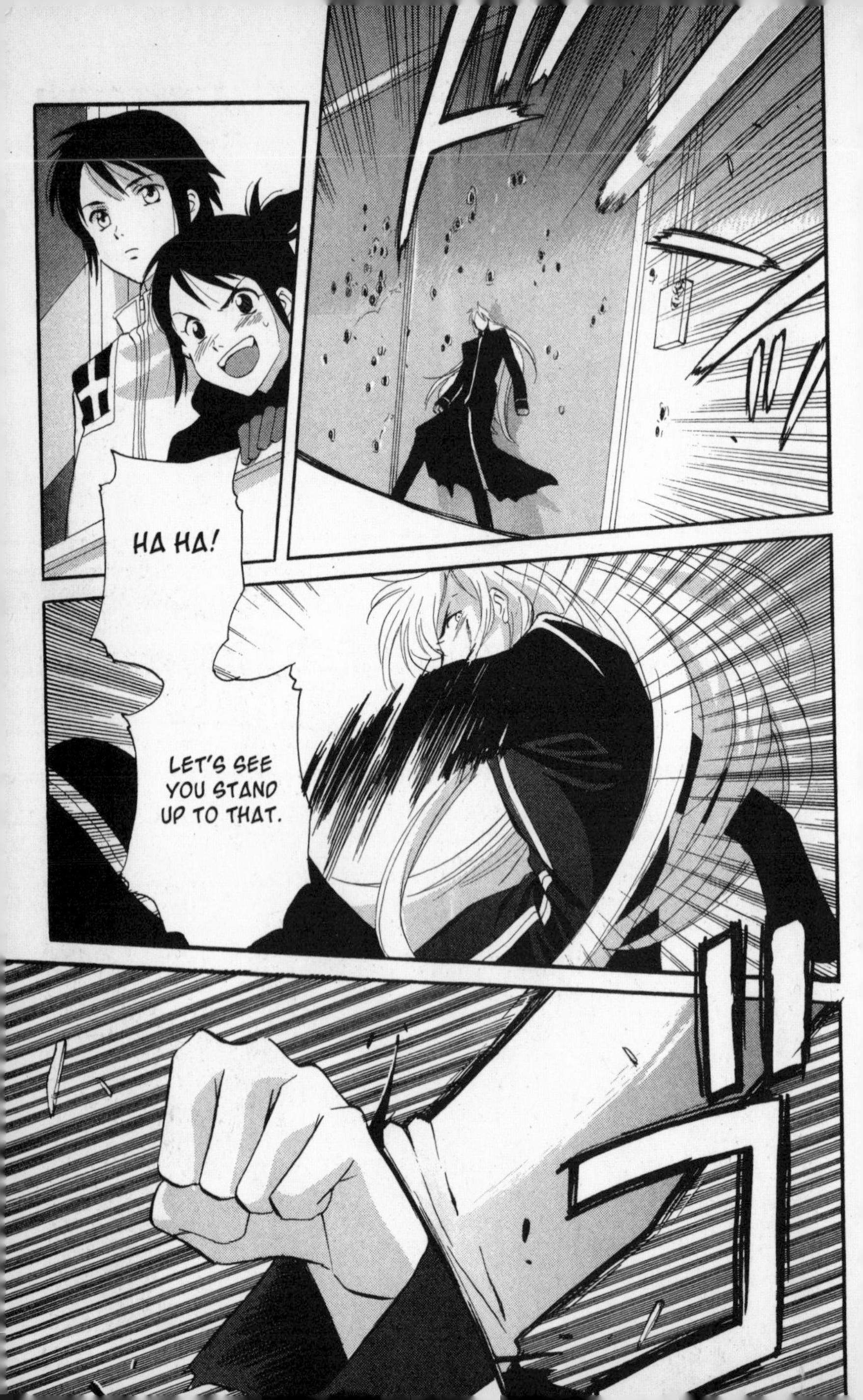
HA HA!
LET'S SEE YOU STAND UP TO THAT.

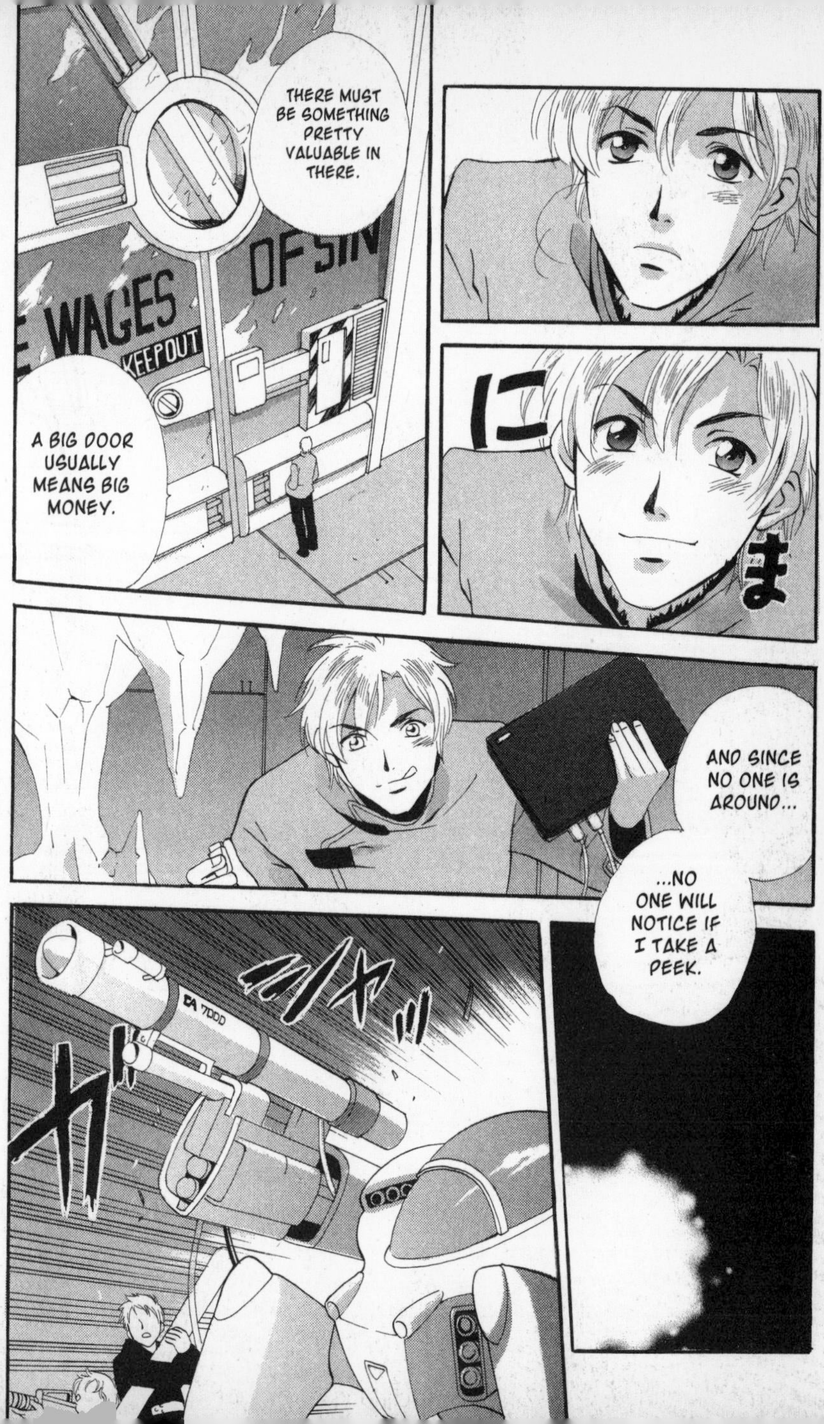
にま
THERE MUST BE SOMETHING PRETTY VALUABLE IN THERE.
THE WAGES OF SIN
KEEP OUT
A BIG DOOR USUALLY MEANS BIG MONEY.
AND SINCE NO ONE IS AROUND...
...NO ONE WILL NOTICE IF I TAKE A PEEK.
EA 7000
ガ

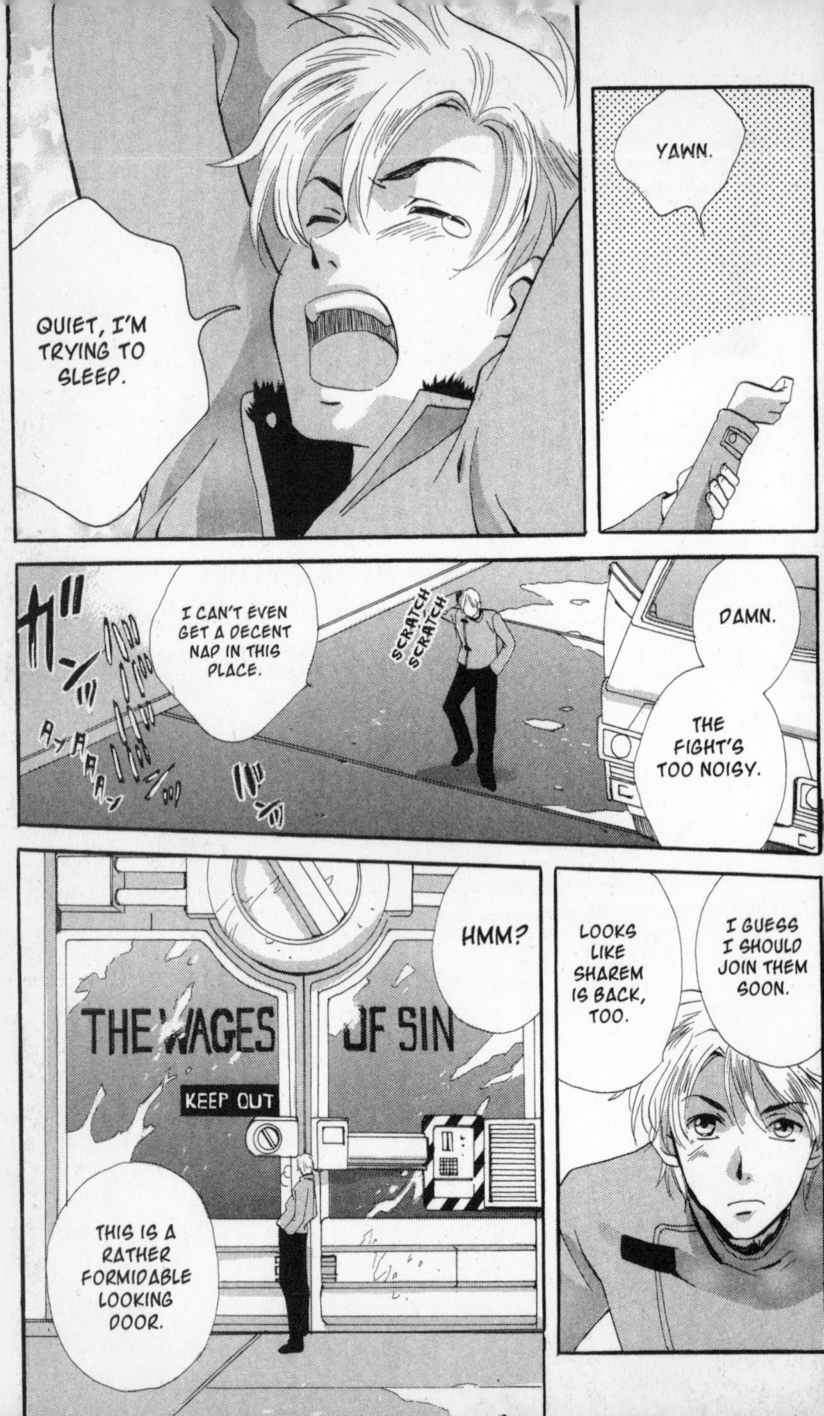
YAWN.
QUIET, I'M TRYING TO SLEEP.
DAMN.
THE FIGHT'S TOO NOISY.
SCRATCH SCRATCH
I CAN'T EVEN GET A DECENT NAP IN THIS PLACE.
I GUESS I SHOULD JOIN THEM SOON.
LOOKS LIKE SHAREM IS BACK, TOO.
HMM?
THE WAGES OF SIN
KEEP OUT
THIS IS A RATHER FORMIDABLE LOOKING DOOR.

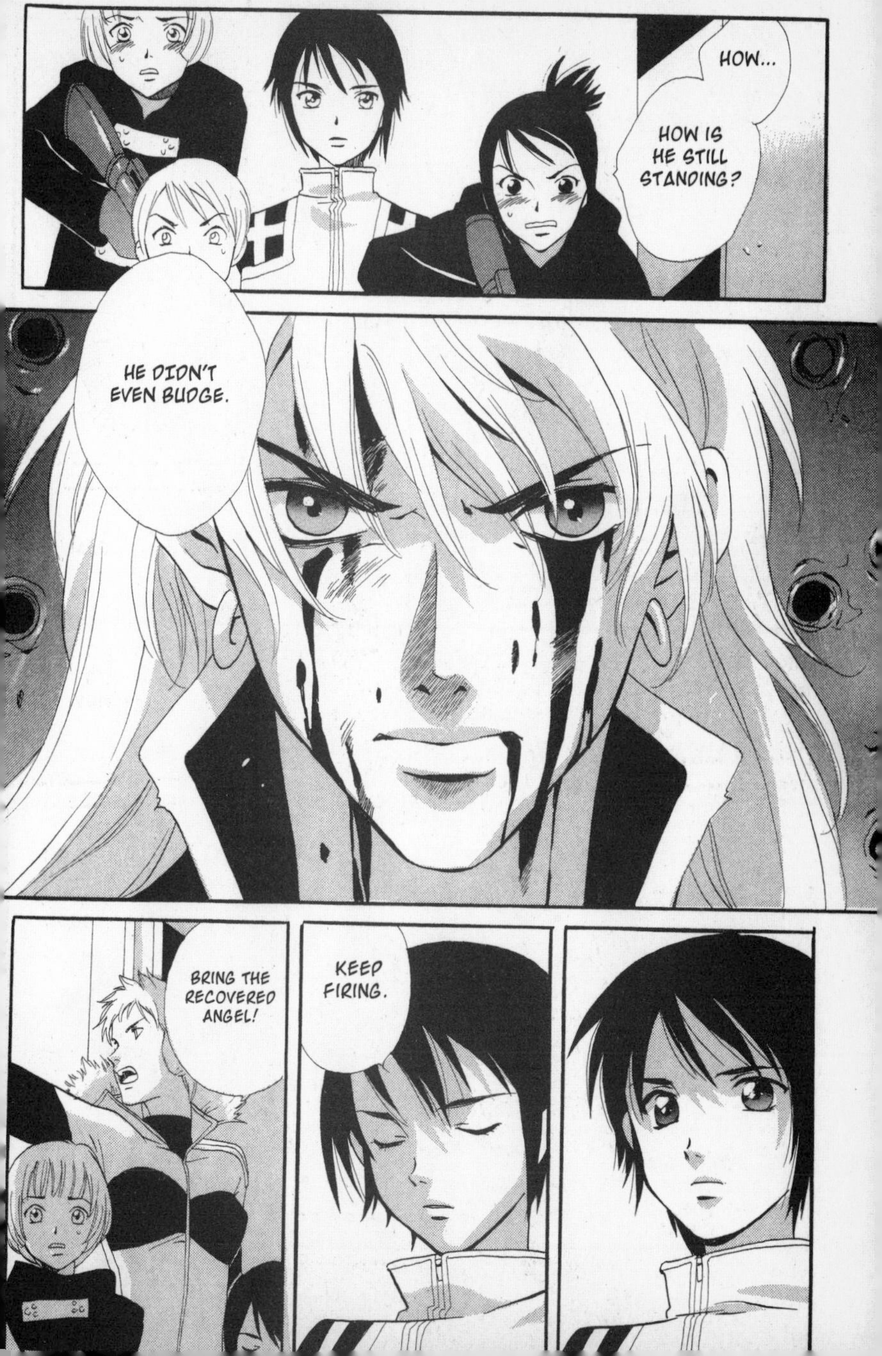
HOW...
HOW IS HE STILL STANDING?
HE DIDN'T EVEN BUDGE.
BRING THE RECOVERED ANGEL!
KEEP FIRING.

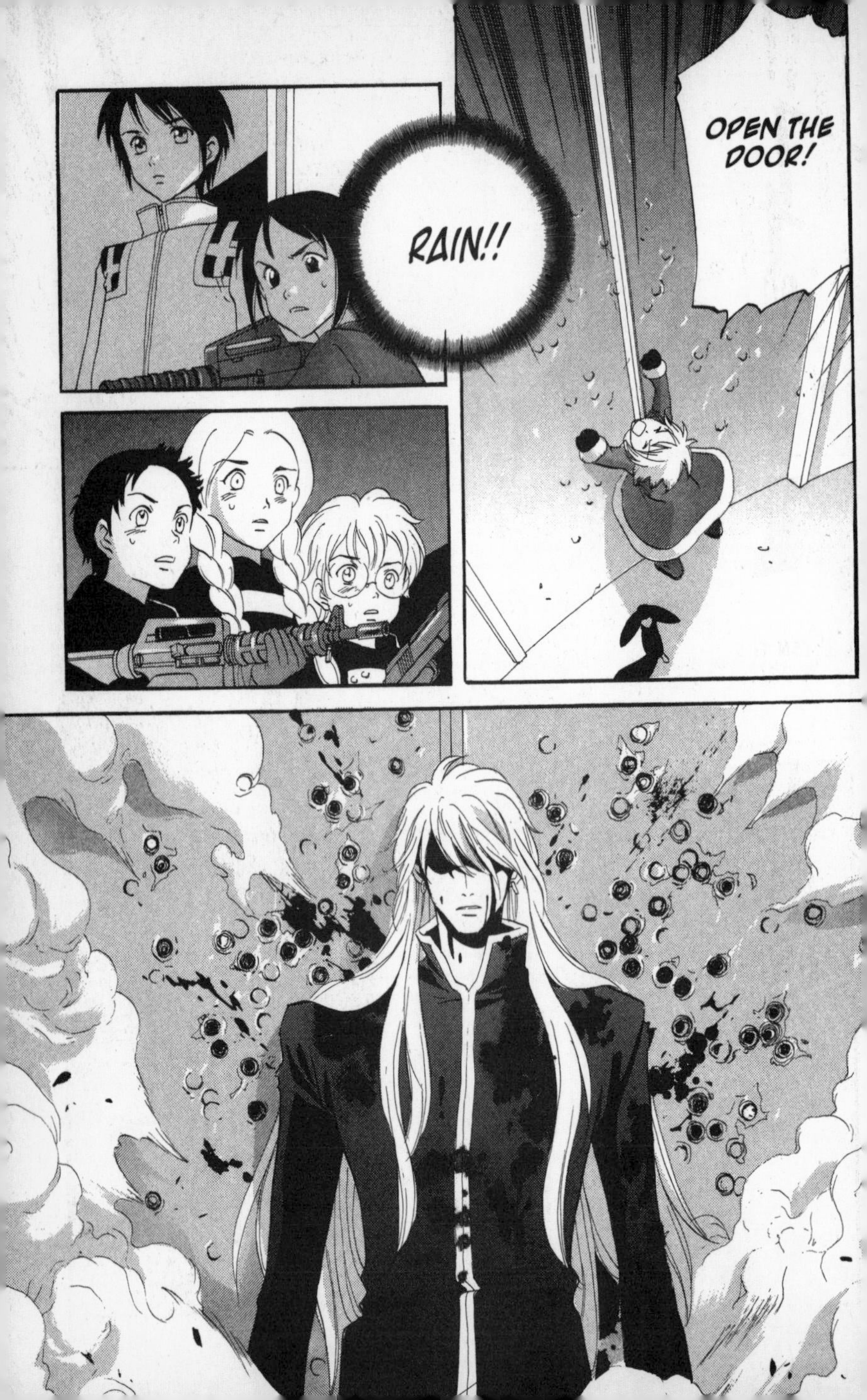
OPEN THE DOOR!
RAIN!!

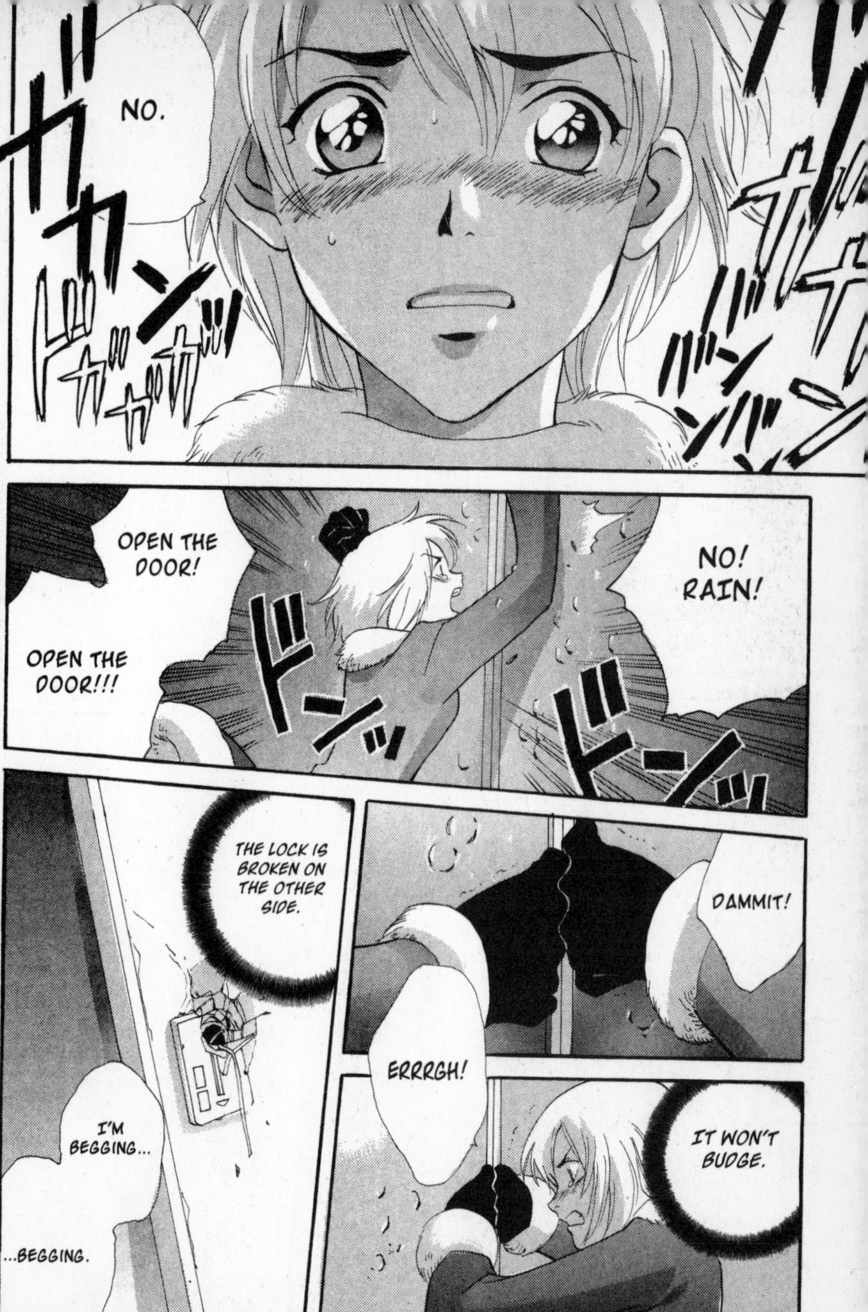
NO.
NO! RAIN!
OPEN THE DOOR!
OPEN THE DOOR!!!
DAMMIT!
THE LOCK IS BROKEN ON THE OTHER SIDE.
IT WON'T BUDGE.
ERRRGH!
I'M BEGGING...
...BEGGING.

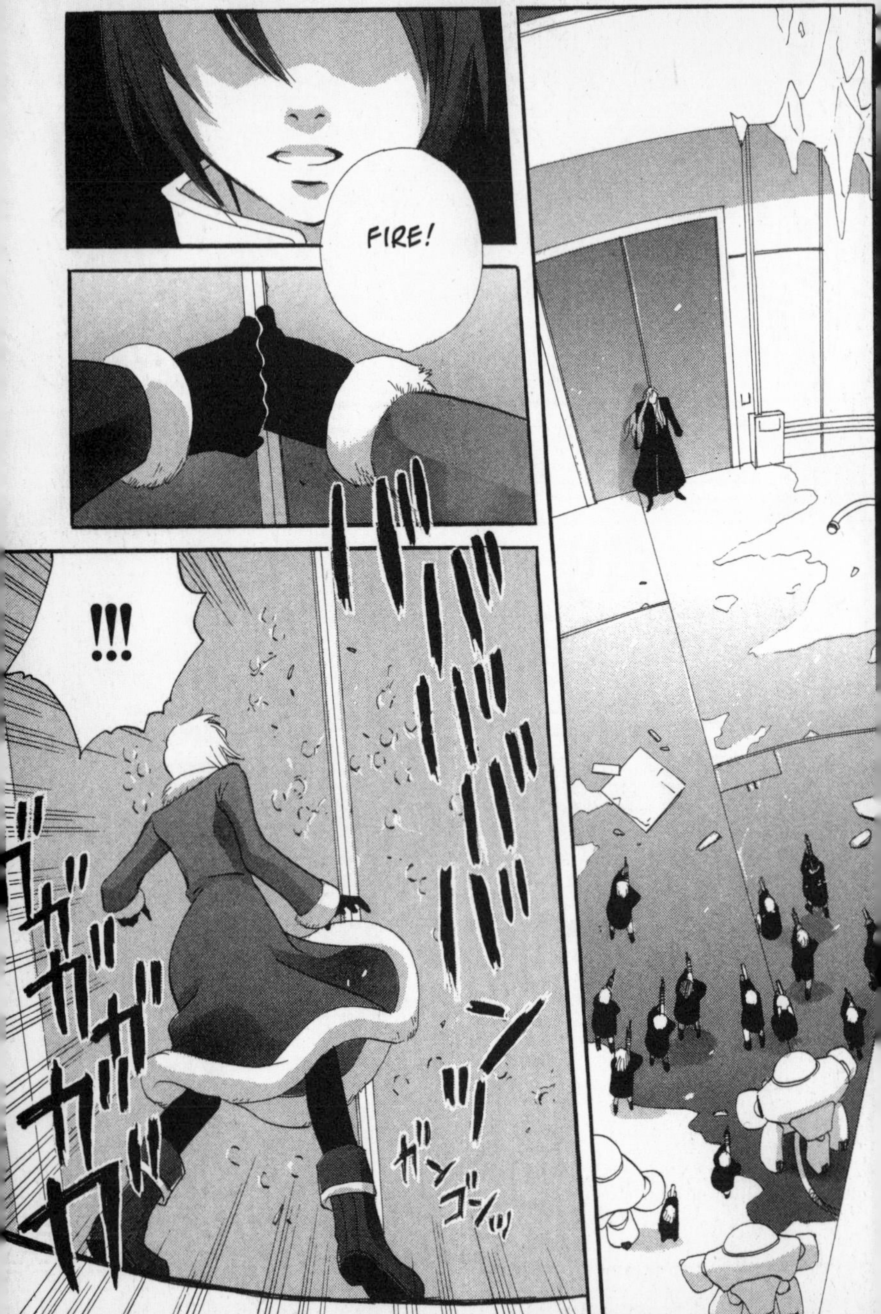
FIRE!
!!!
ガンゴンッ

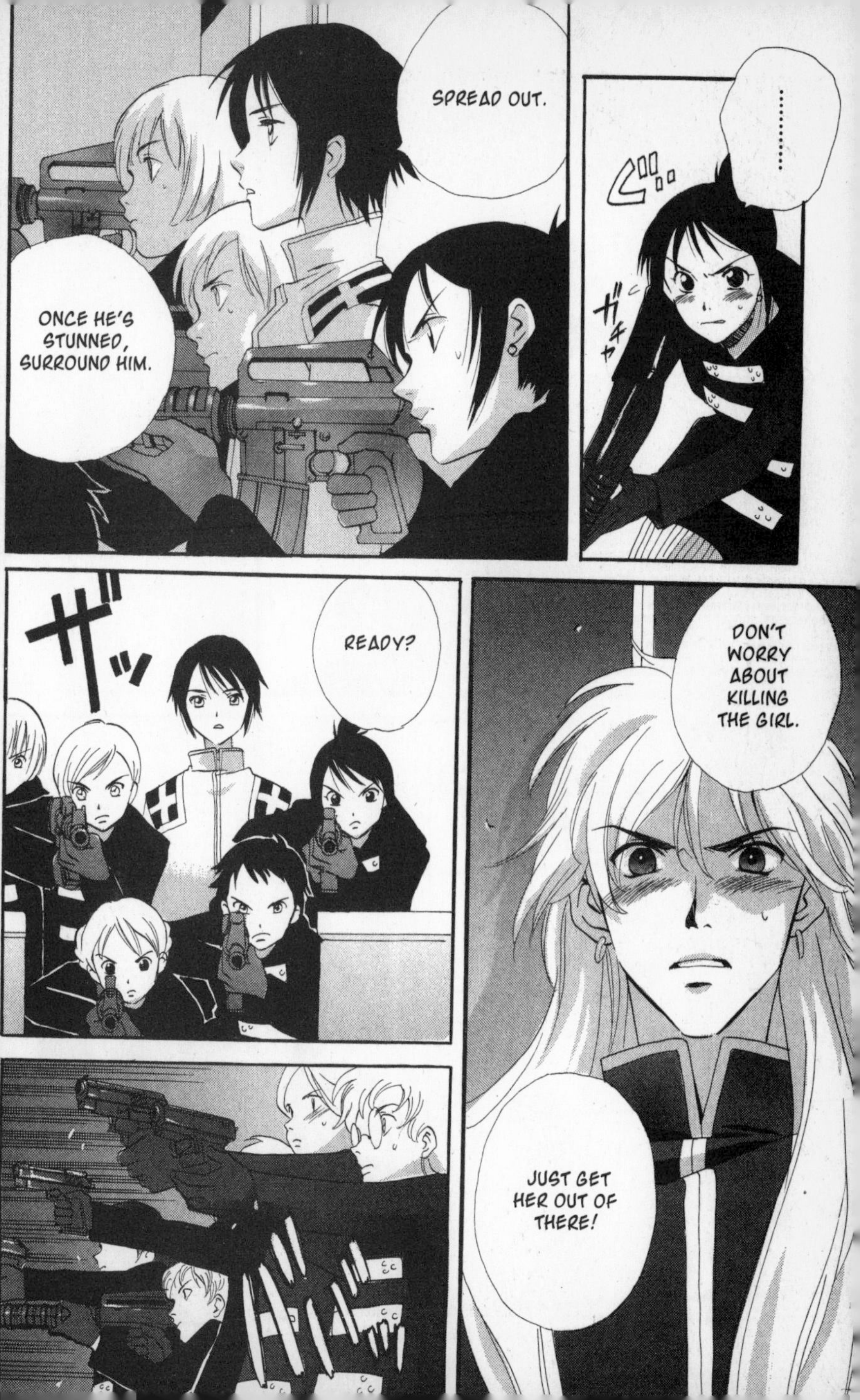
......
SPREAD OUT.
ONCE HE'S STUNNED, SURROUND HIM.
DON'T WORRY ABOUT KILLING THE GIRL.
JUST GET HER OUT OF THERE!
ザッ
READY?

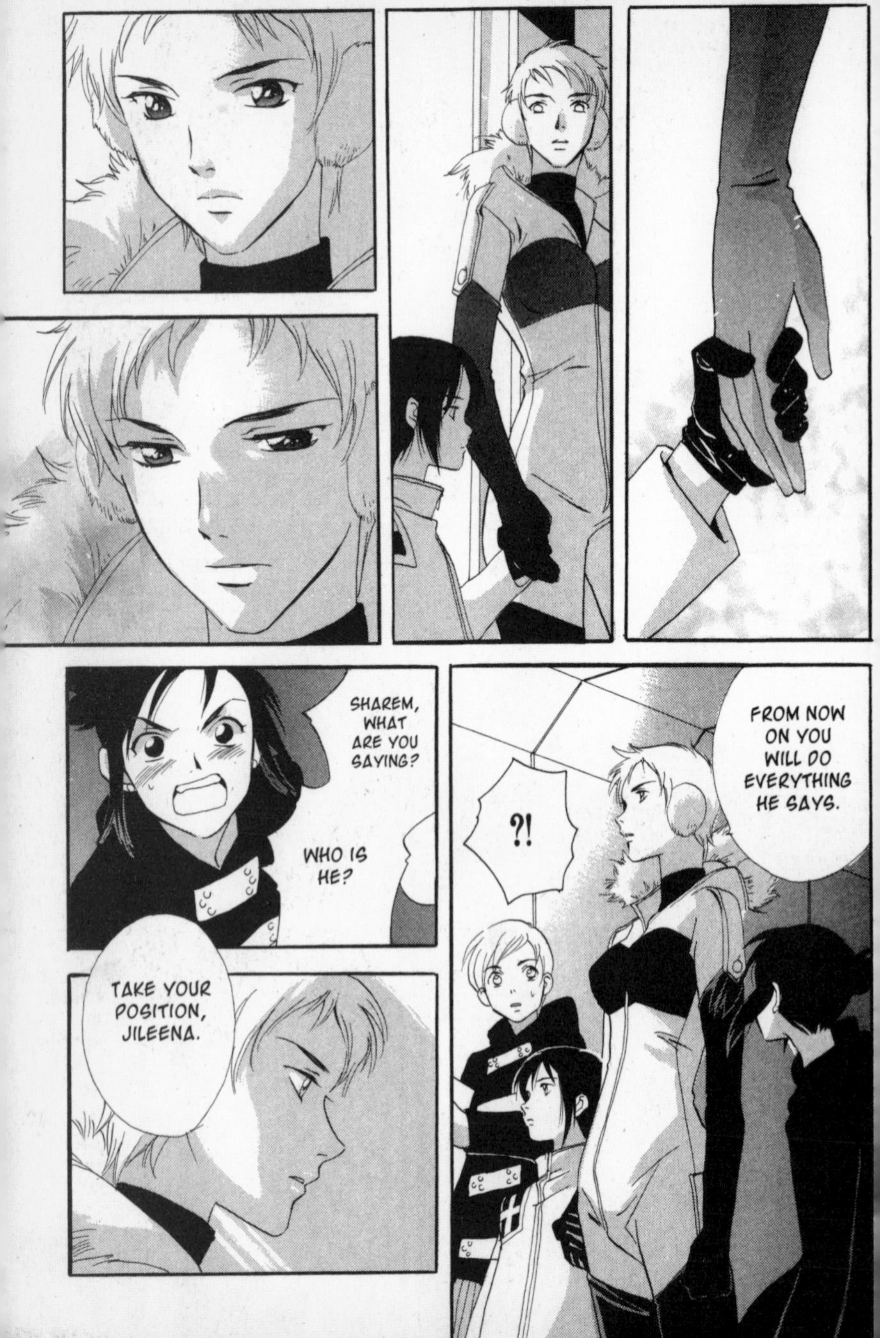
FROM NOW ON YOU WILL DO EVERYTHING HE SAYS.
?!
SHAREM, WHAT ARE YOU SAYING?
WHO IS HE?
TAKE YOUR POSITION, JILEENA.

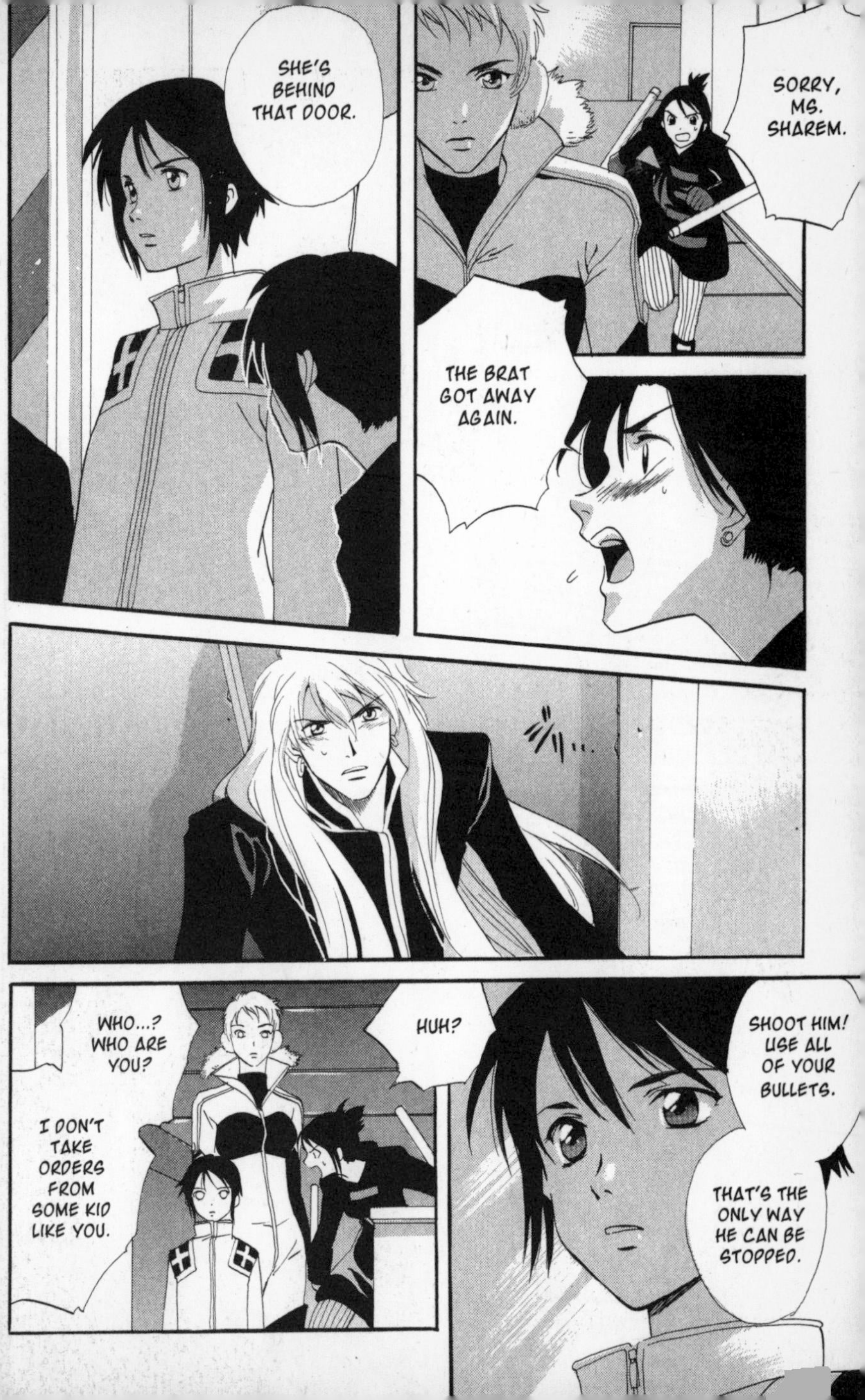
SORRY, MS. SHAREM.
SHE'S BEHIND THAT DOOR.
THE BRAT GOT AWAY AGAIN.
SHOOT HIM! USE ALL OF YOUR BULLETS.
THAT'S THE ONLY WAY HE CAN BE STOPPED.
HUH?
WHO...? WHO ARE YOU?
I DON'T TAKE ORDERS FROM SOME KID LIKE YOU.

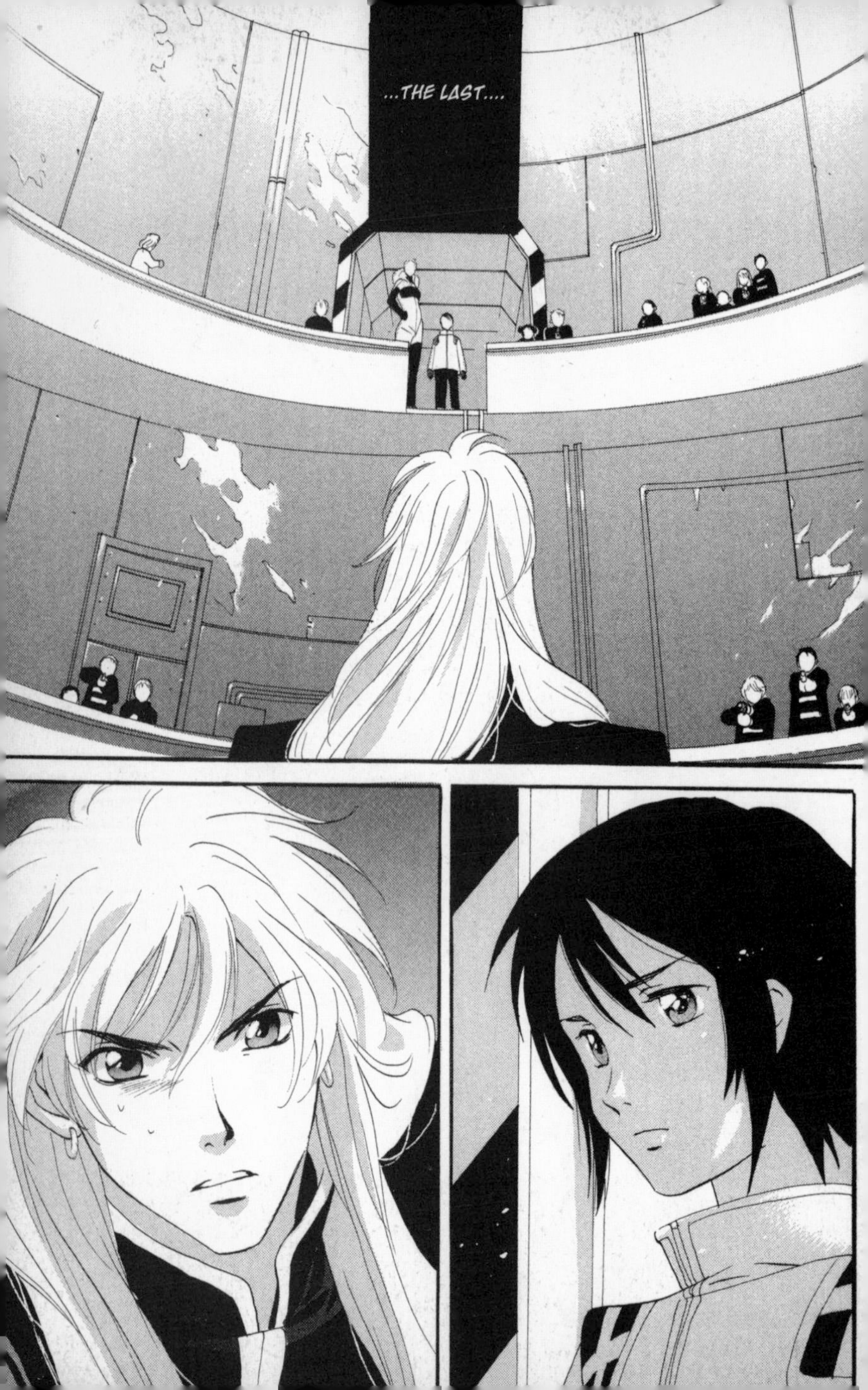
...THE LAST....

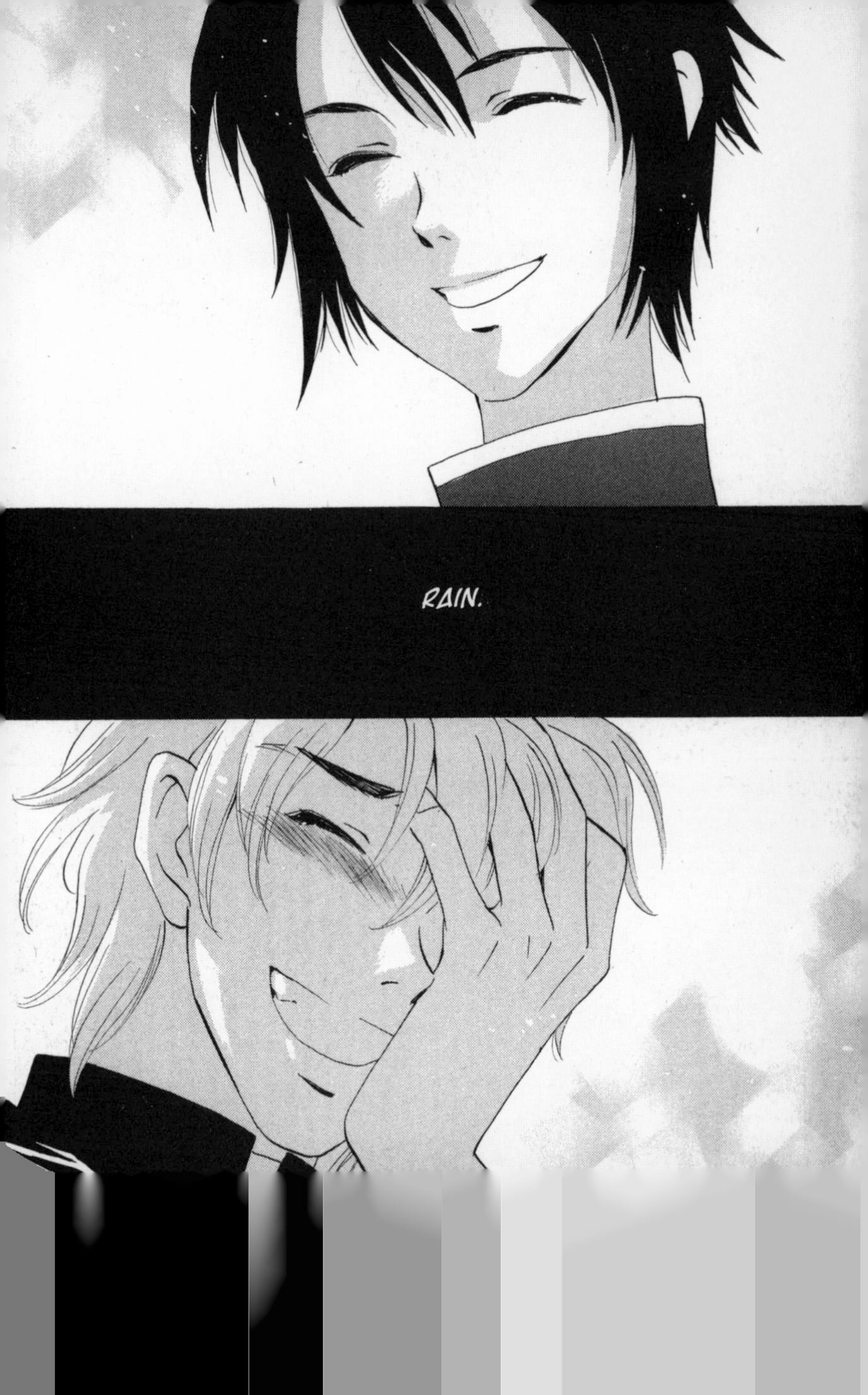
RAIN.

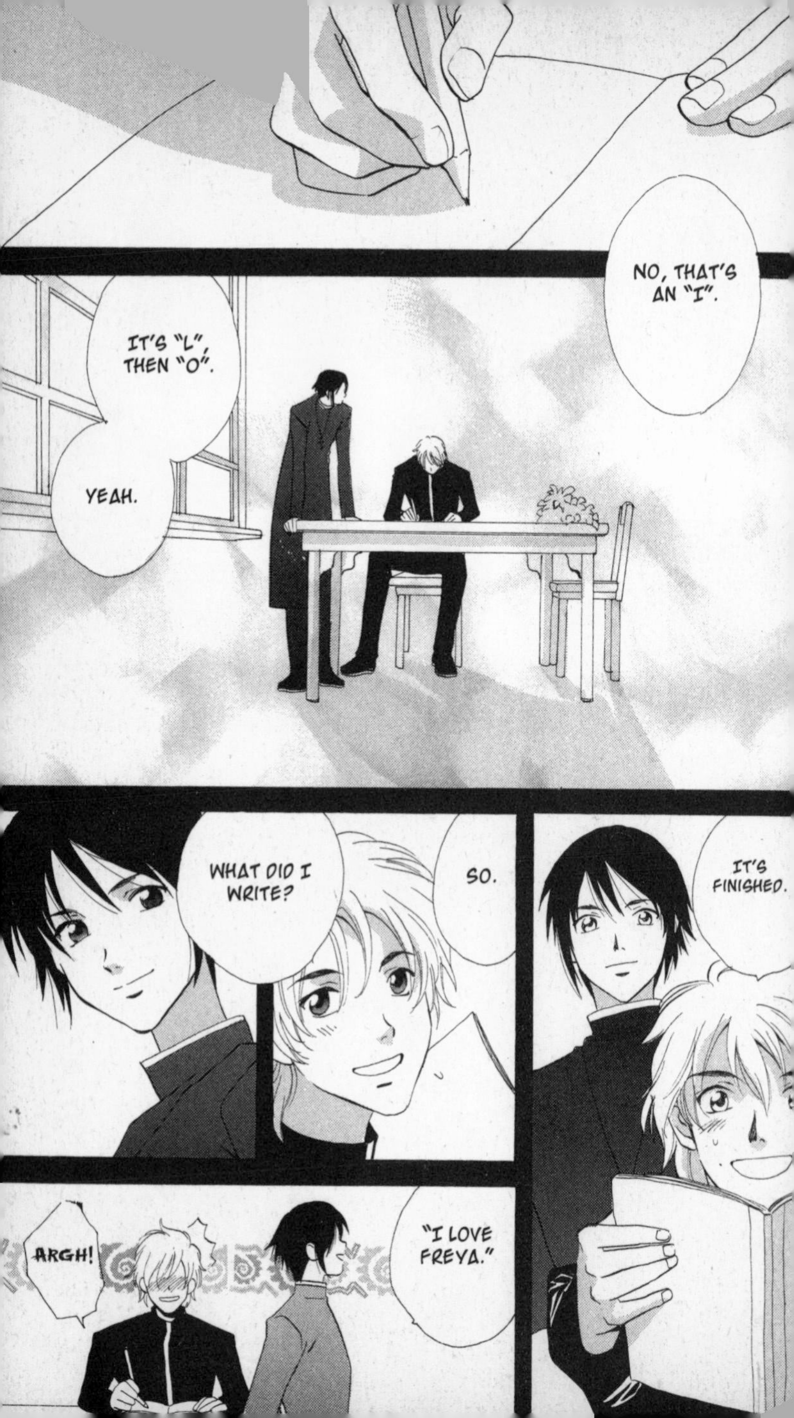
NO, THAT'S AN "I".
IT'S "L", THEN "O".
YEAH.
IT'S FINISHED.
SO.
WHAT DID I WRITE?
"I LOVE FREYA."
ARGH!

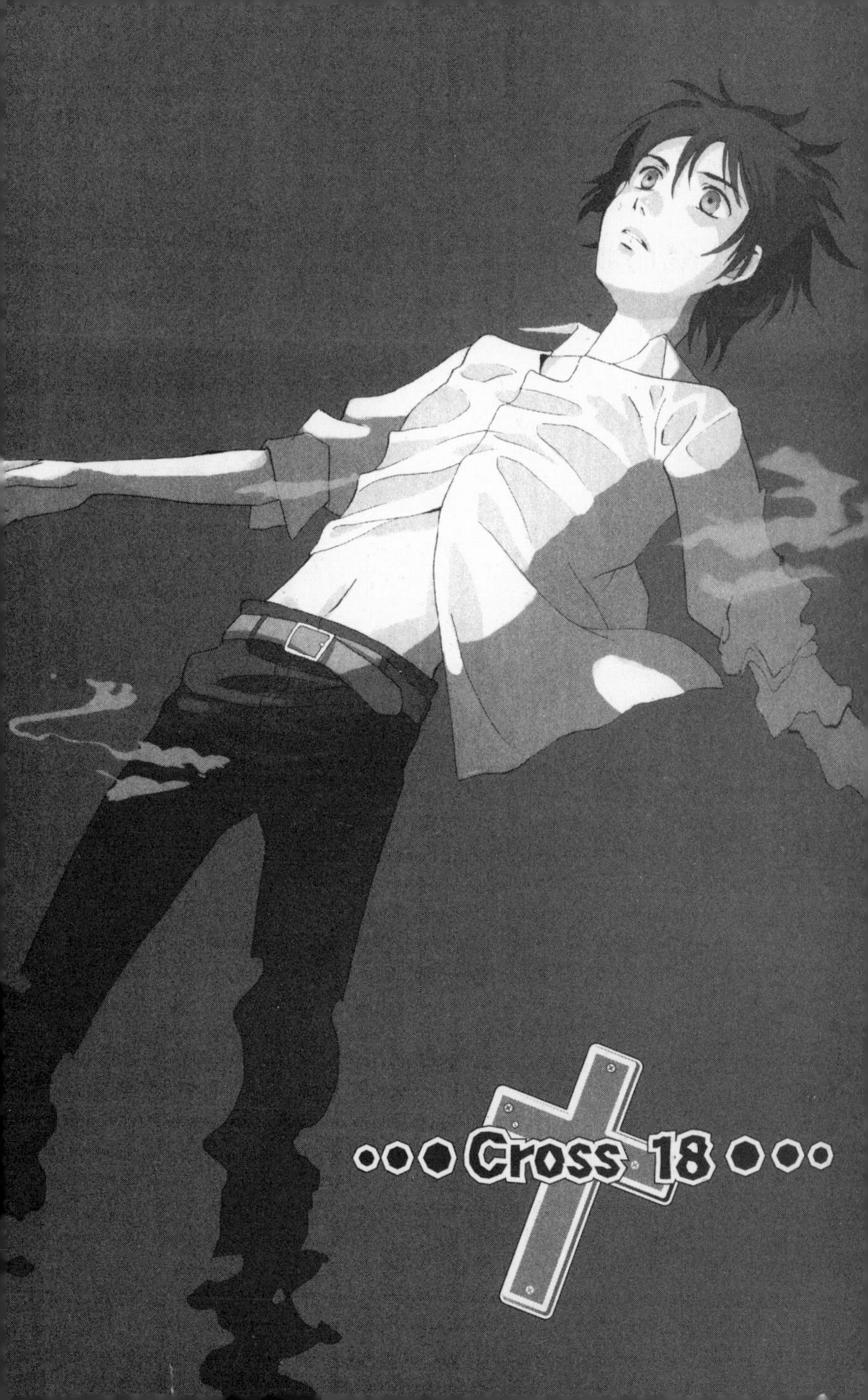
Cross 18

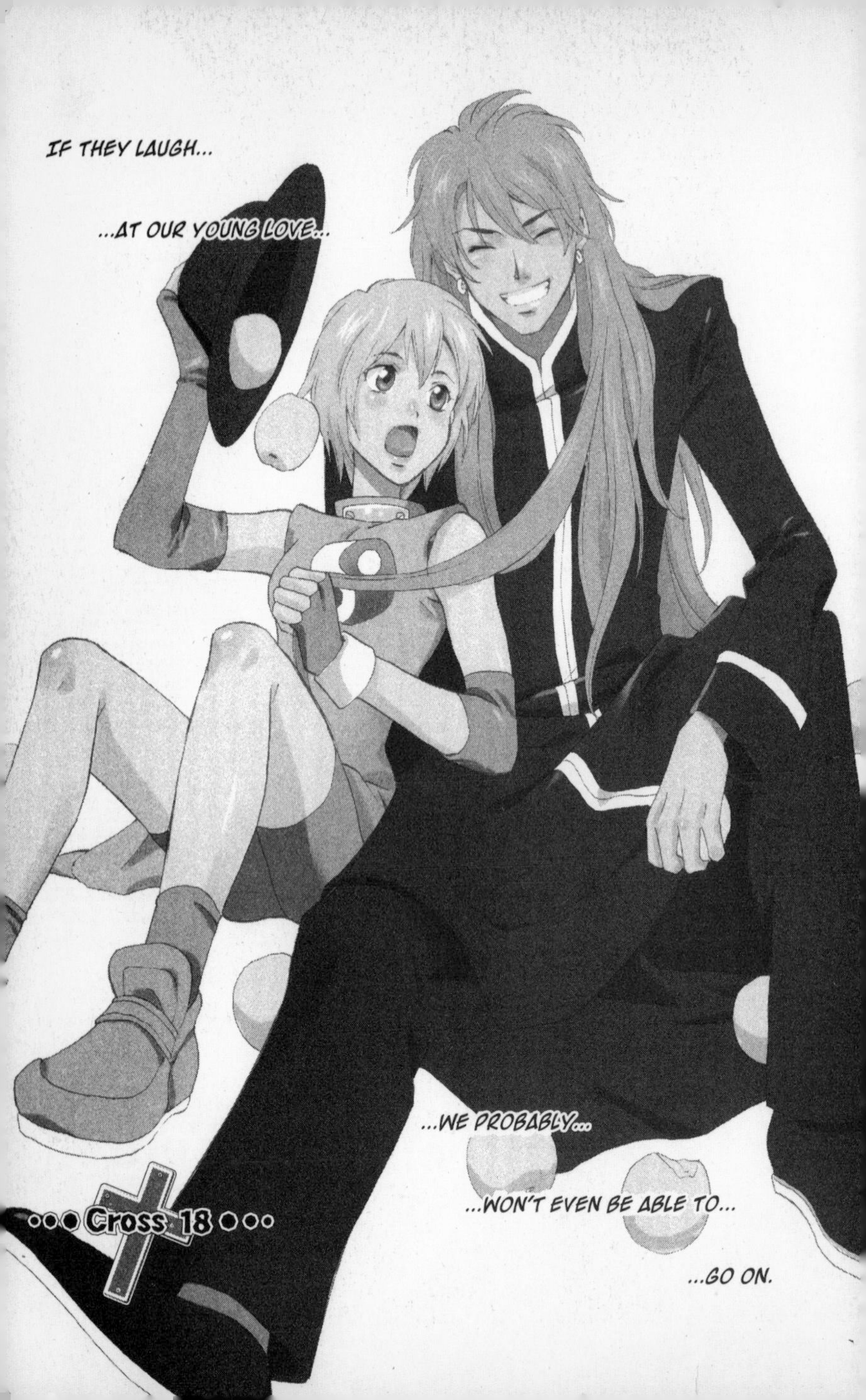
IF THEY LAUGH...
...AT OUR YOUNG LOVE...
...WE PROBABLY...
...WON'T EVEN BE ABLE TO...
...GO ON.
Cross 18

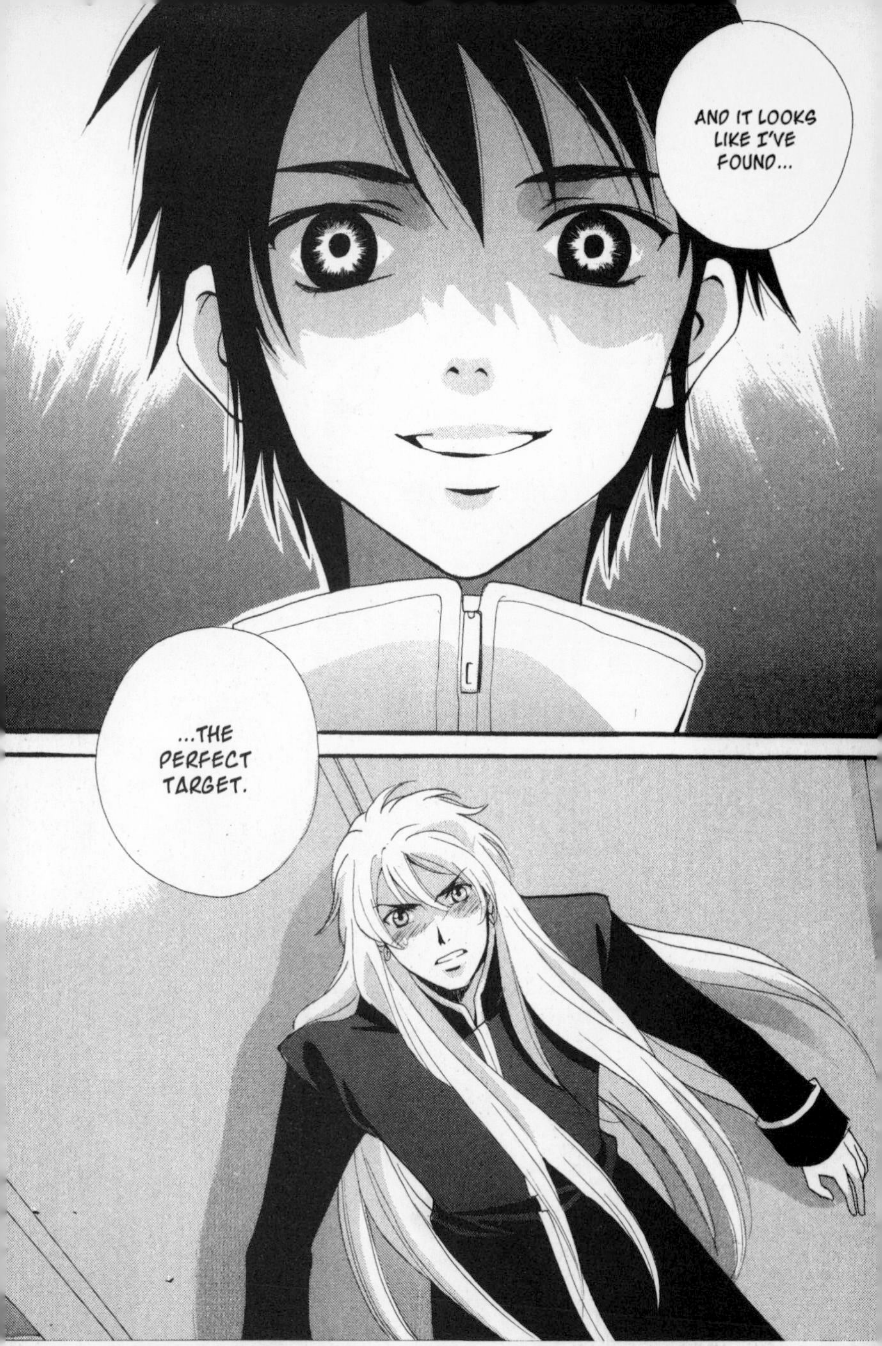
AND IT LOOKS LIKE I'VE FOUND...
...THE PERFECT TARGET.

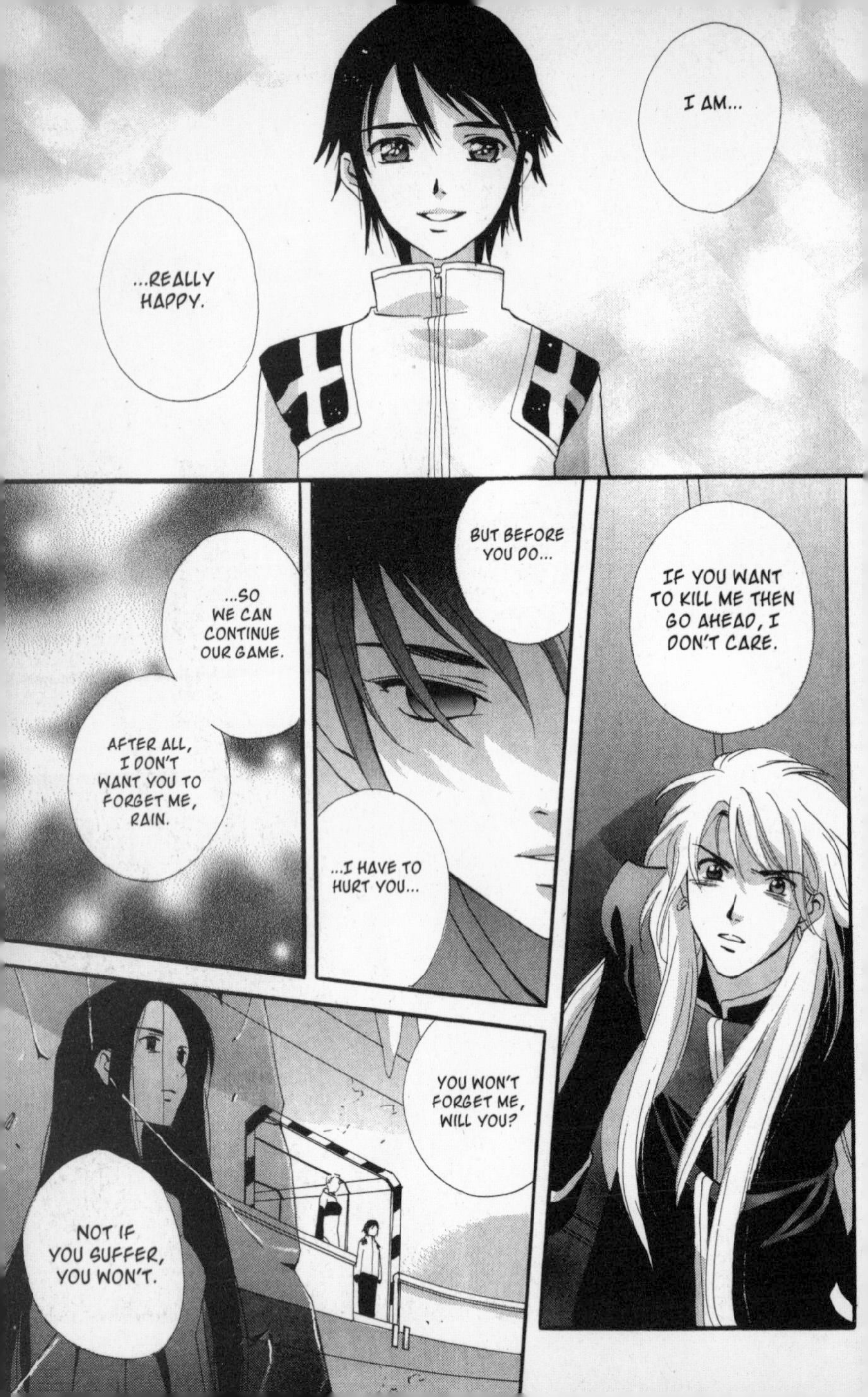
I AM...
...REALLY HAPPY.
IF YOU WANT TO KILL ME THEN GO AHEAD, I DON'T CARE.
BUT BEFORE YOU DO...
...I HAVE TO HURT YOU...
...SO WE CAN CONTINUE OUR GAME.
AFTER ALL, I DON'T WANT YOU TO FORGET ME, RAIN.
YOU WON'T FORGET ME, WILL YOU?
NOT IF YOU SUFFER, YOU WON'T.

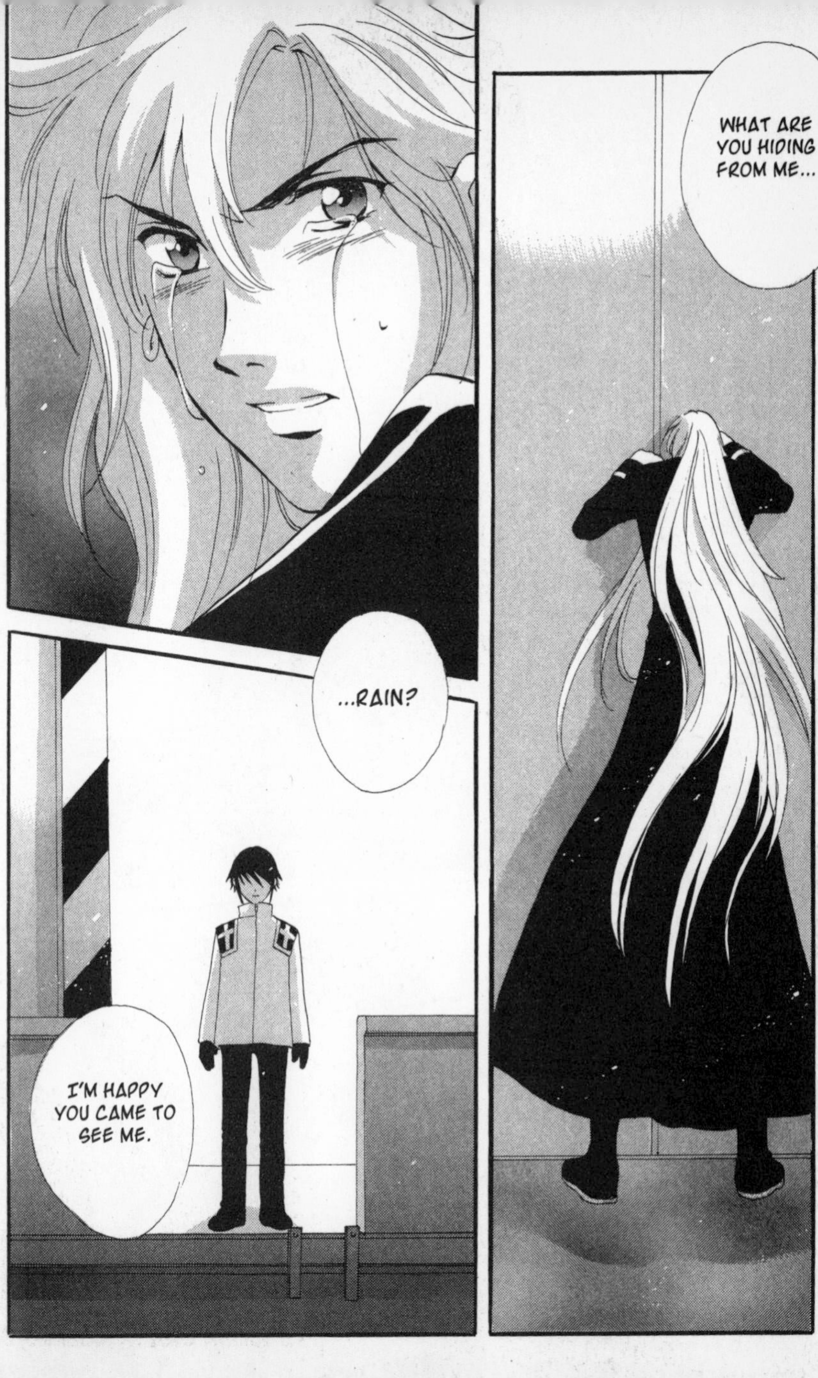
WHAT ARE YOU HIDING FROM ME...
...RAIN?
I'M HAPPY YOU CAME TO SEE ME.

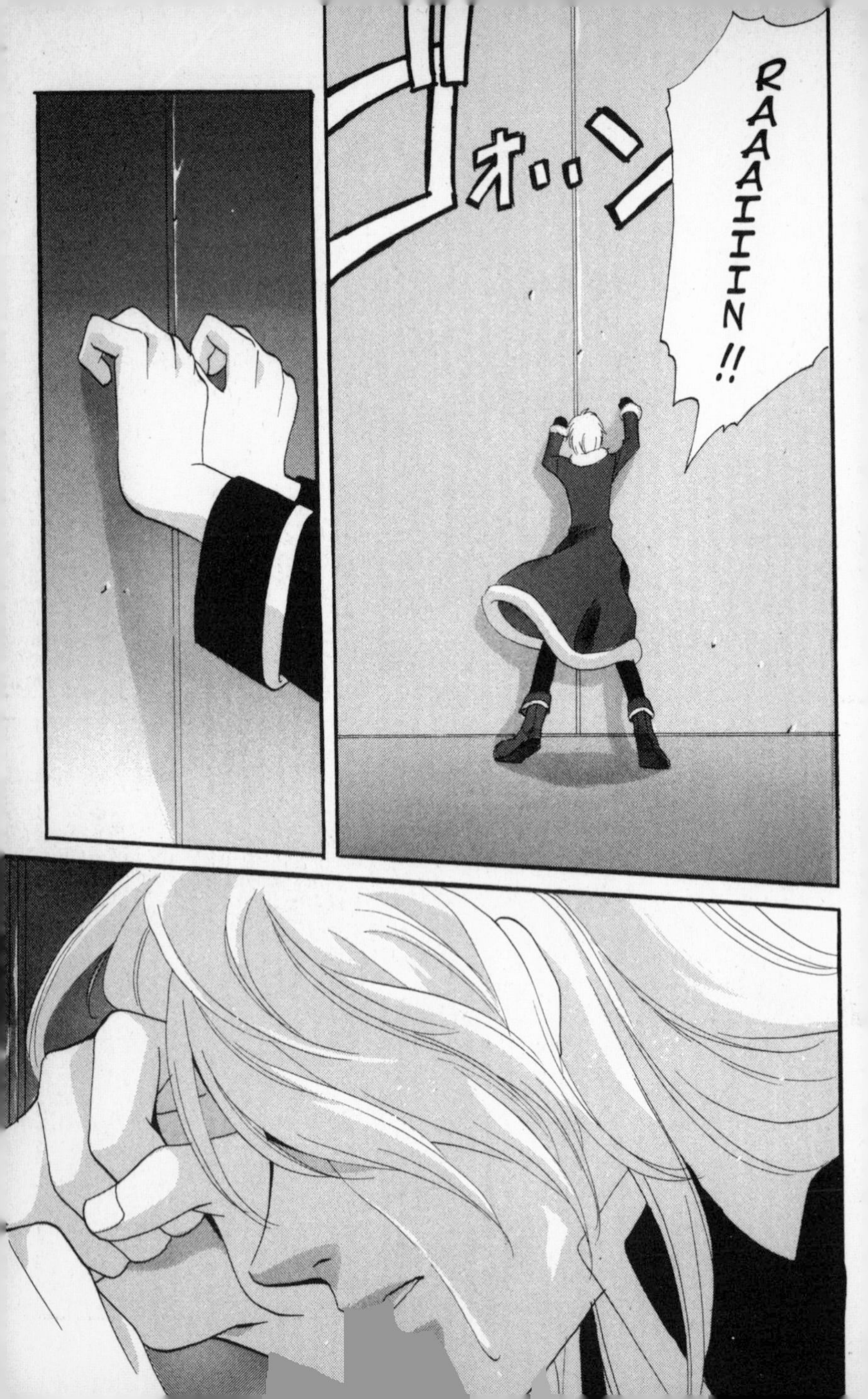
オ・・ン
RAAAIIIIN!!

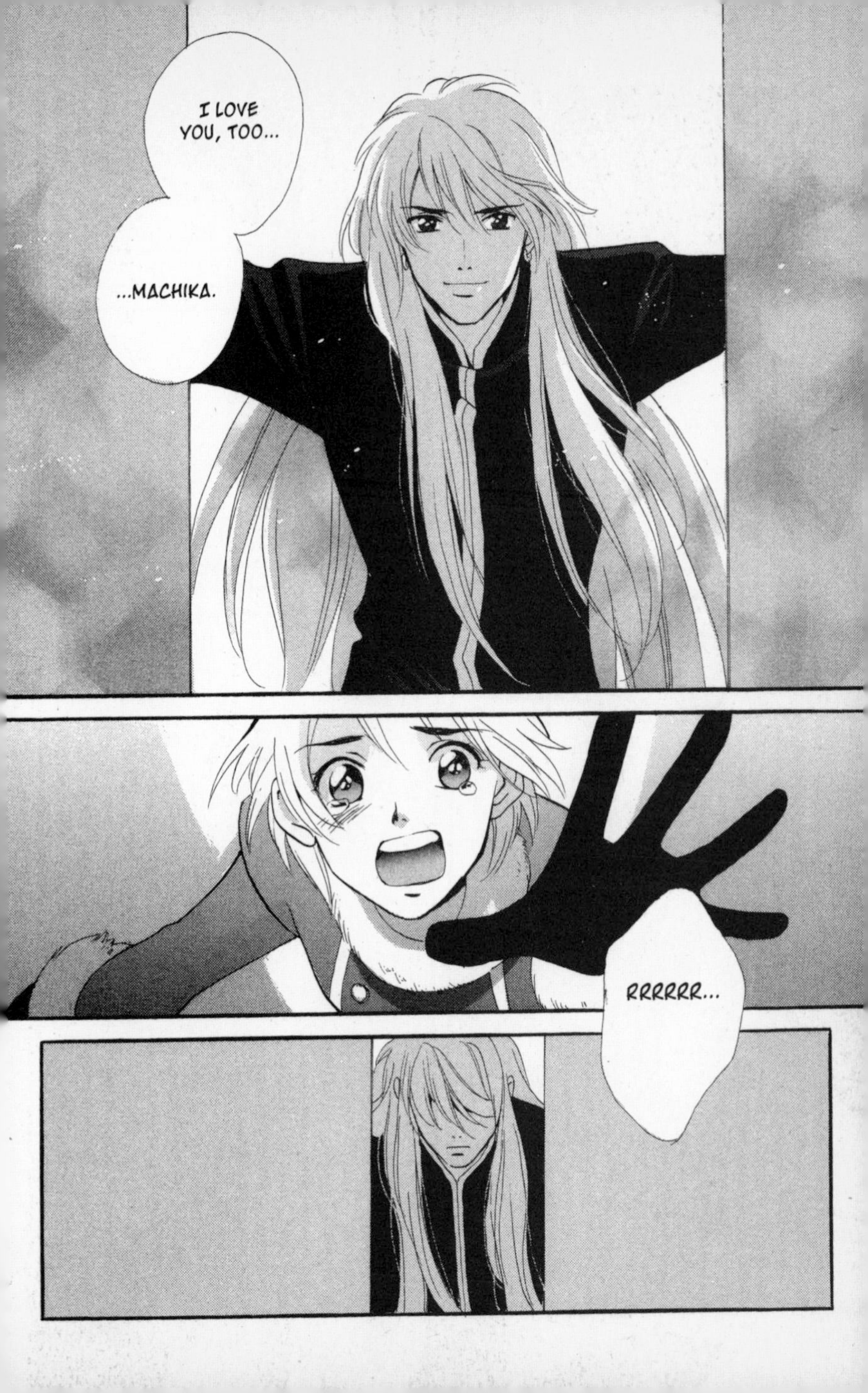
I LOVE YOU, TOO...
...MACHIKA.
RRRRRR...

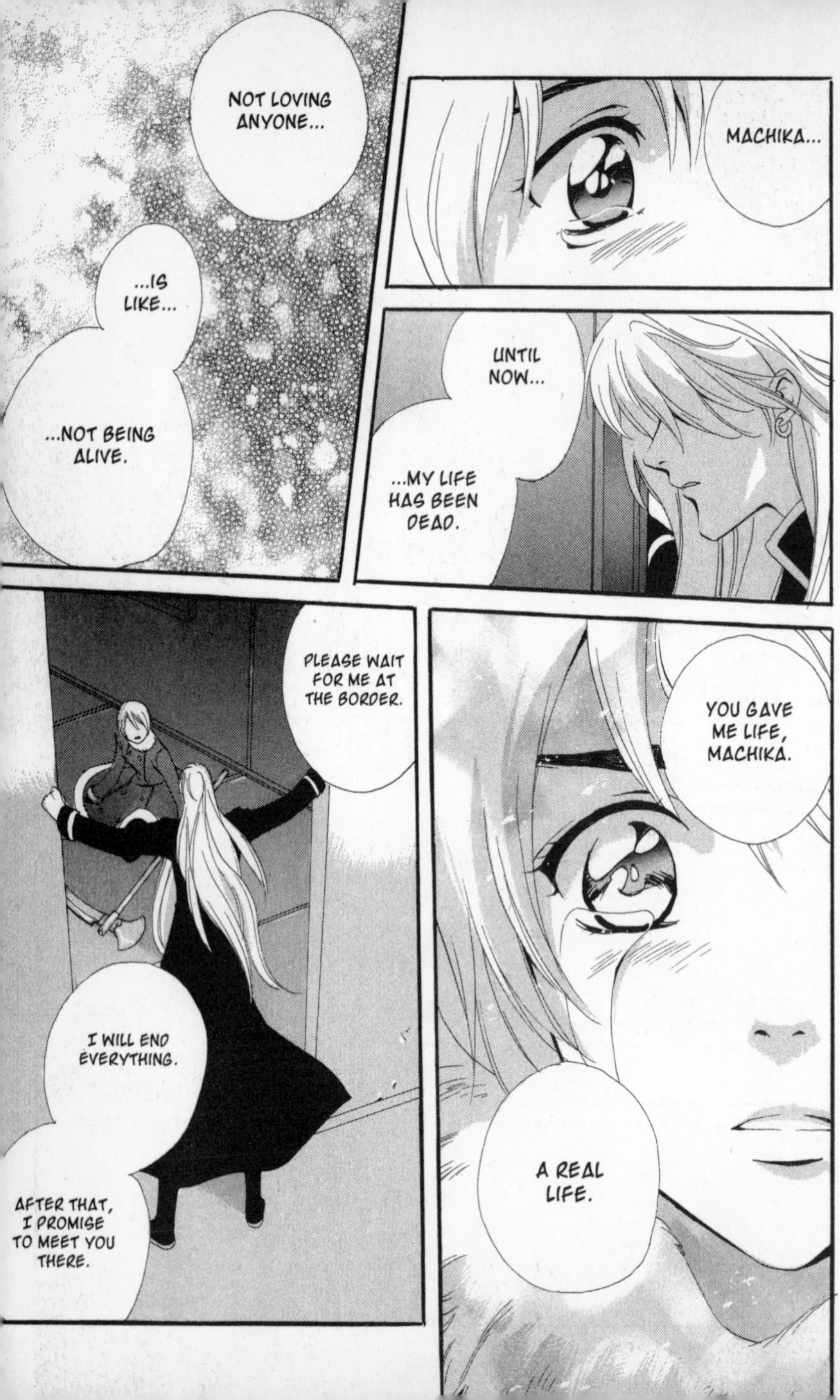
MACHIKA...
UNTIL NOW...
...MY LIFE HAS BEEN DEAD.
NOT LOVING ANYONE...
...IS LIKE...
...NOT BEING ALIVE.
YOU GAVE ME LIFE, MACHIKA.
A REAL LIFE.
PLEASE WAIT FOR ME AT THE BORDER.
I WILL END EVERYTHING.
AFTER THAT, I PROMISE TO MEET YOU THERE.

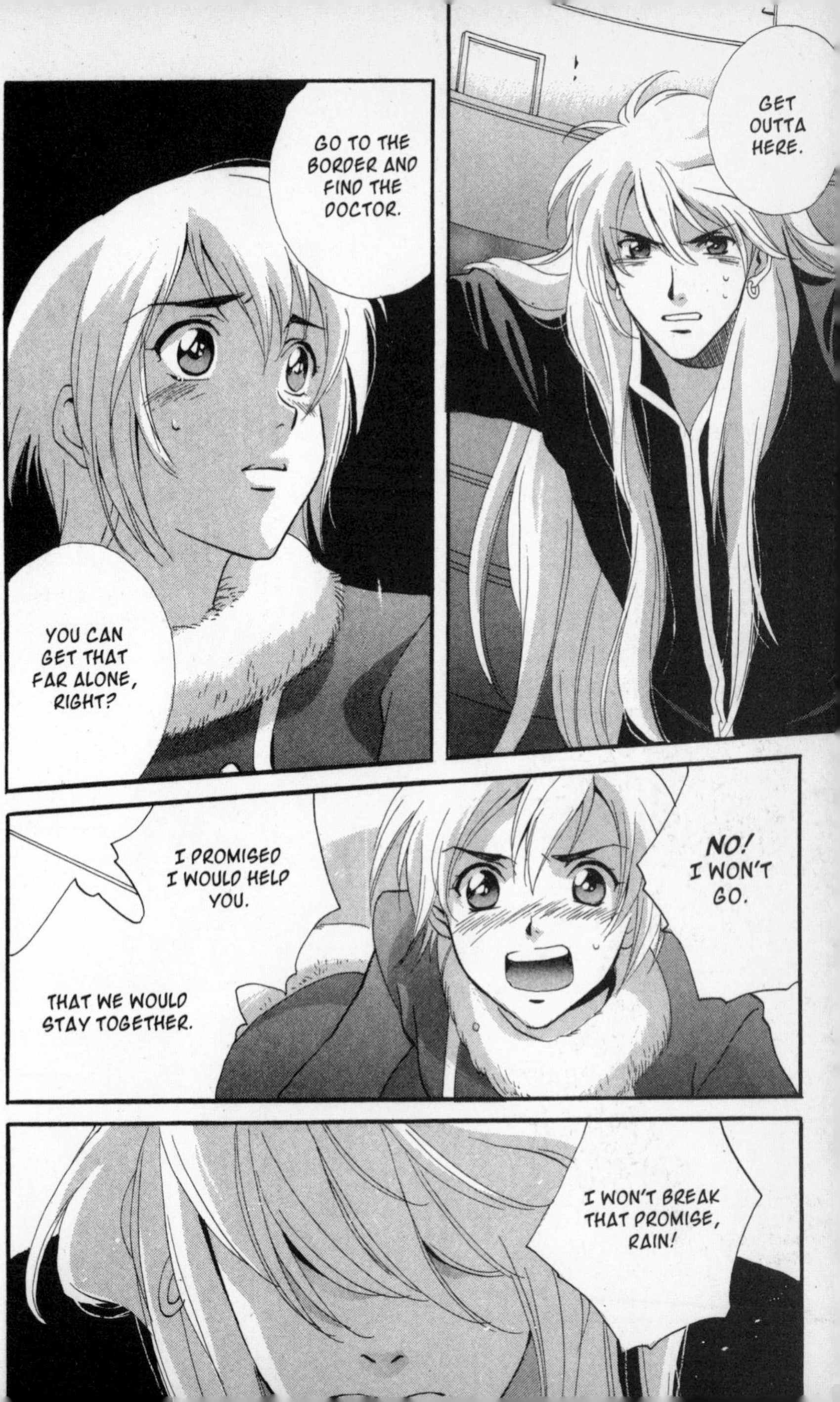
GET OUTTA HERE.
GO TO THE BORDER AND FIND THE DOCTOR.
YOU CAN GET THAT FAR ALONE, RIGHT?
NO! I WON'T GO.
I PROMISED I WOULD HELP YOU.
THAT WE WOULD STAY TOGETHER.
I WON'T BREAK THAT PROMISE, RAIN!

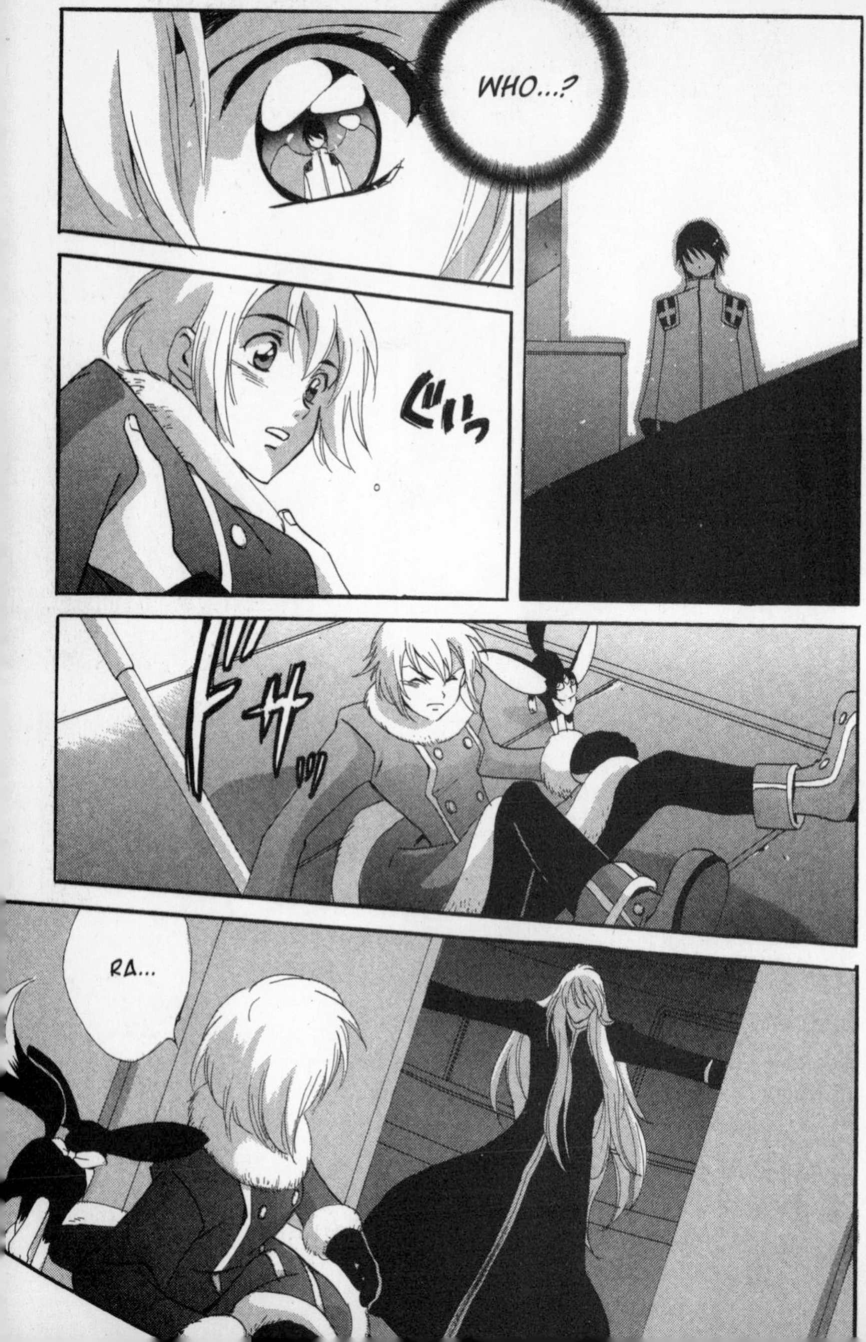
WHO...?
ぐいっ
ドサッ
RA...

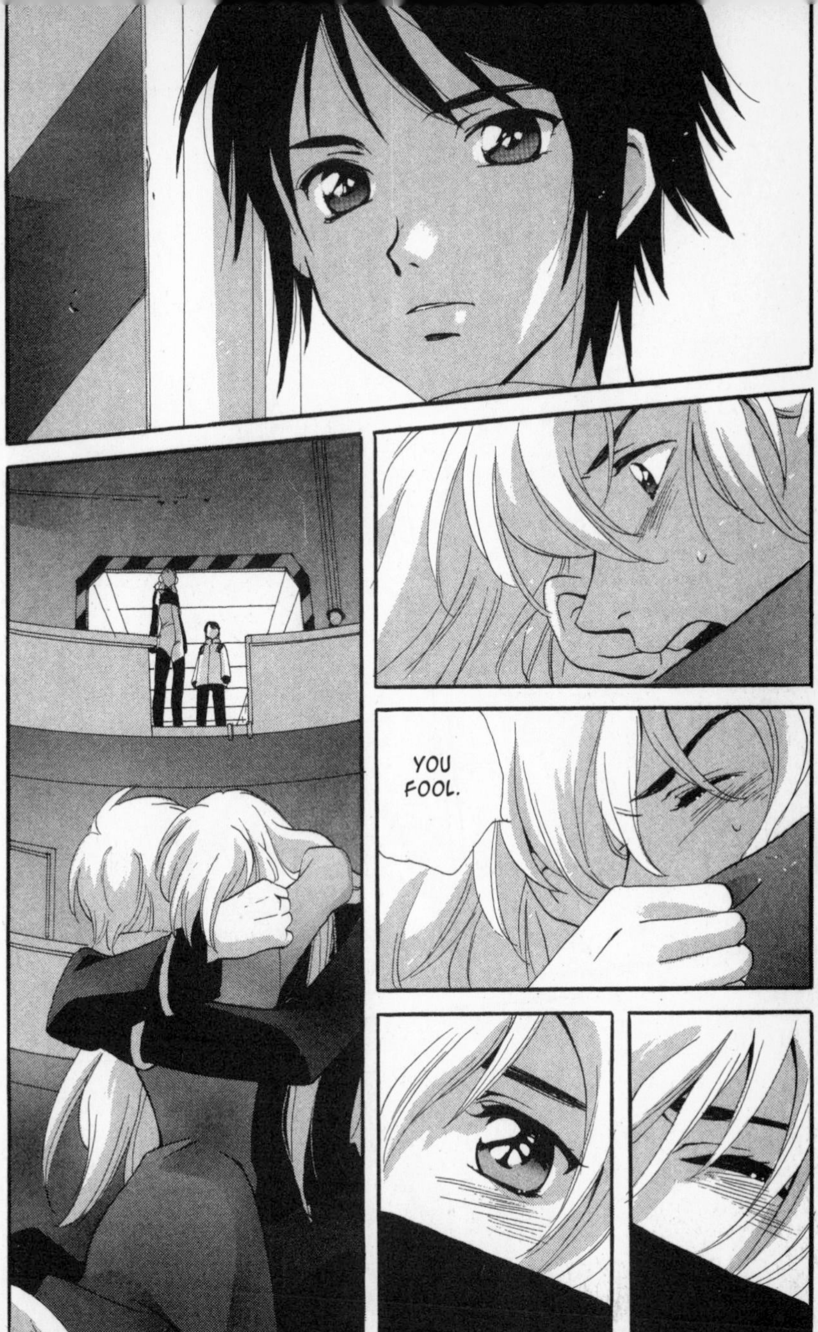
YOU
FOOL.

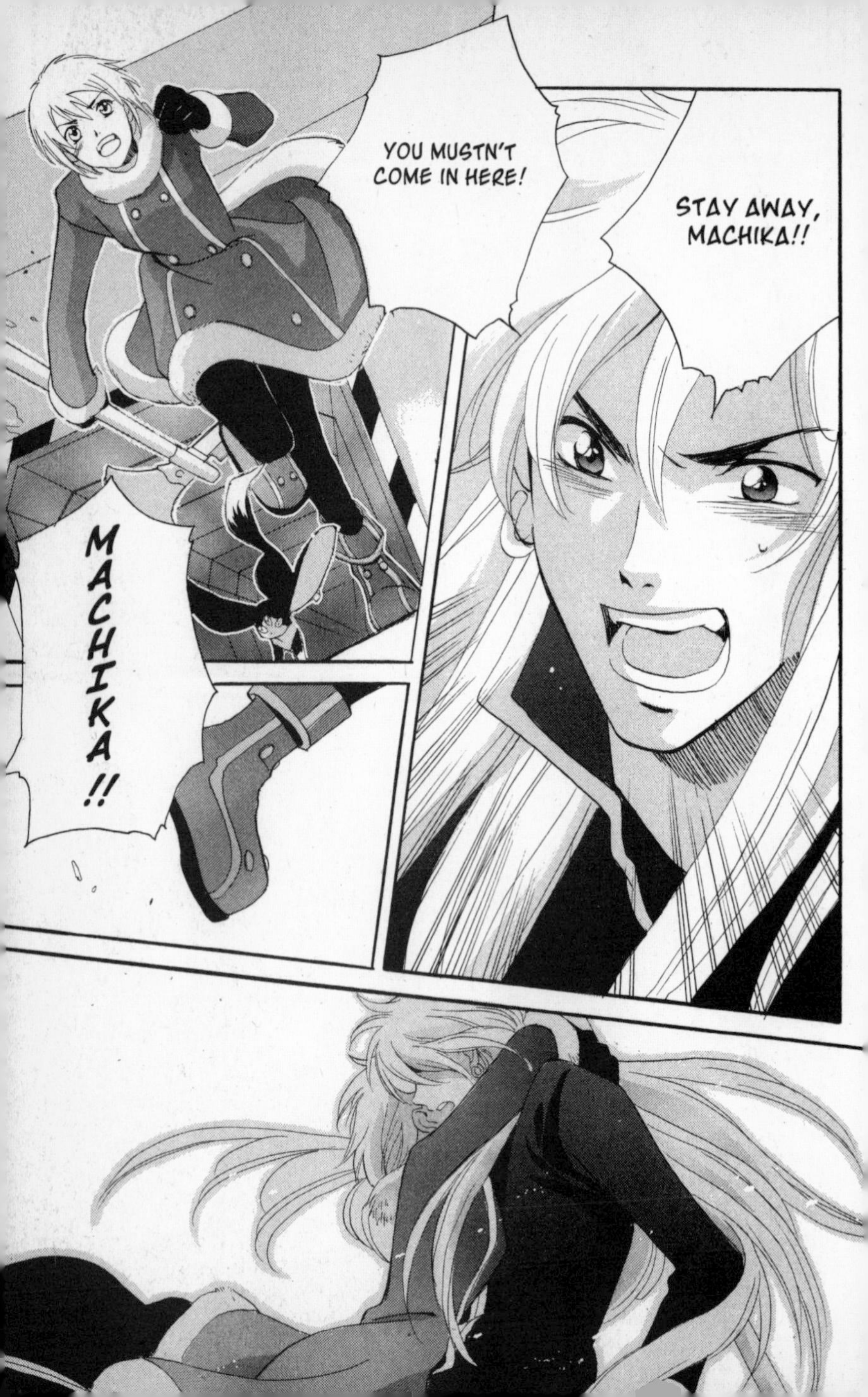
STAY AWAY, MACHIKA!!
YOU MUSTN'T COME IN HERE!
MACHIKA!!

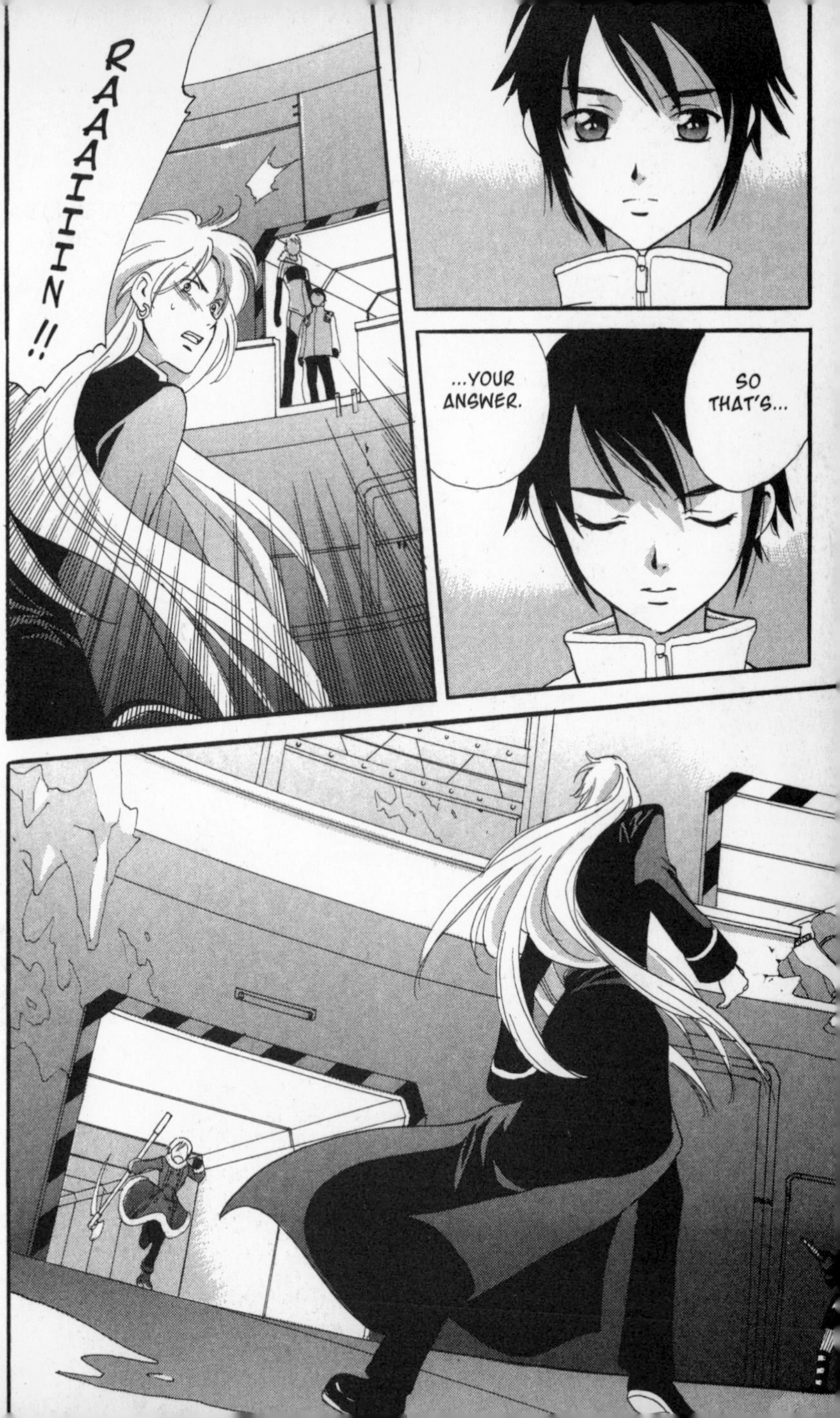
SO THAT'S...
...YOUR ANSWER.
RAAAIIIIN!!

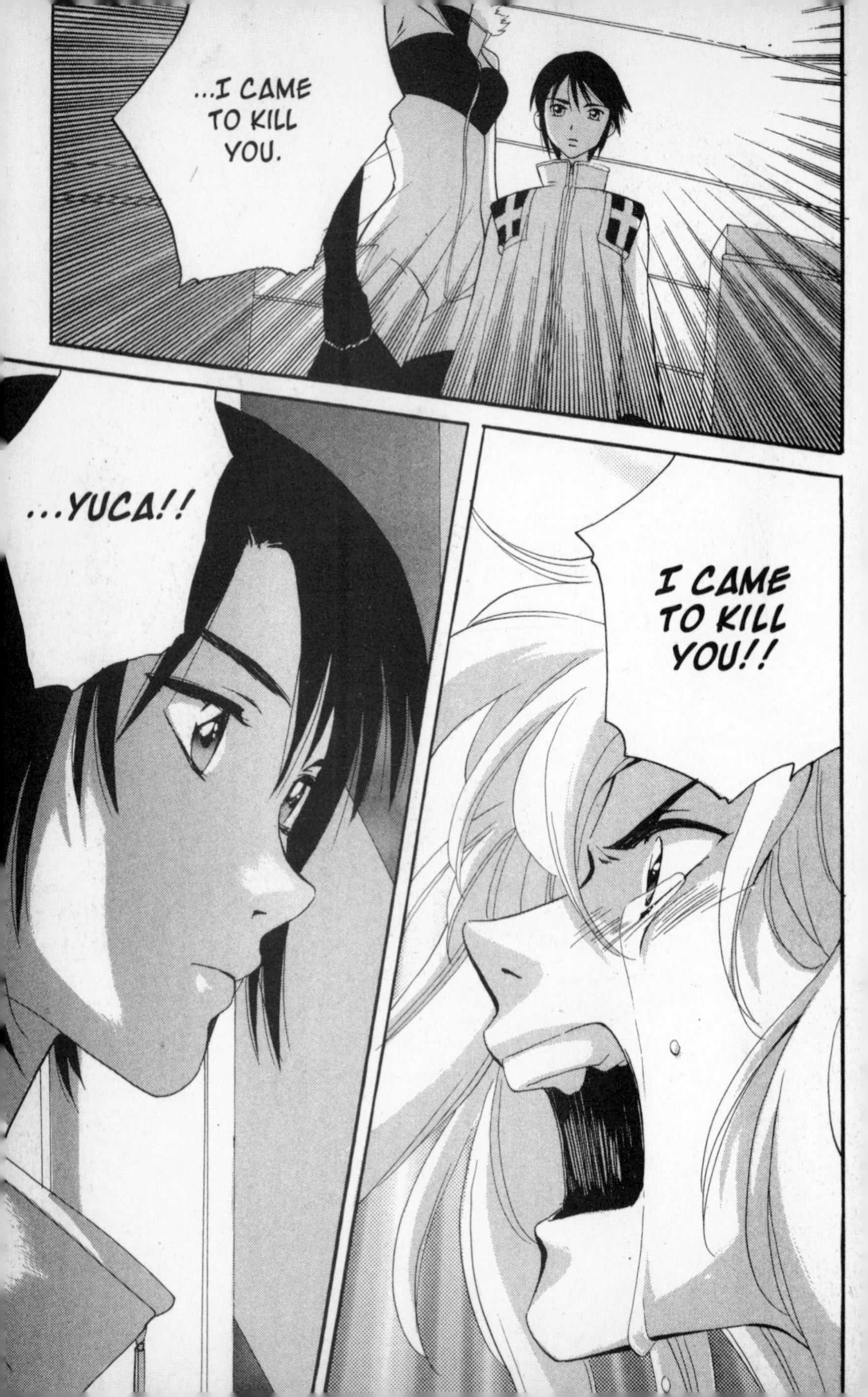
...I CAME TO KILL YOU.
...YUCA!!
I CAME TO KILL YOU!!

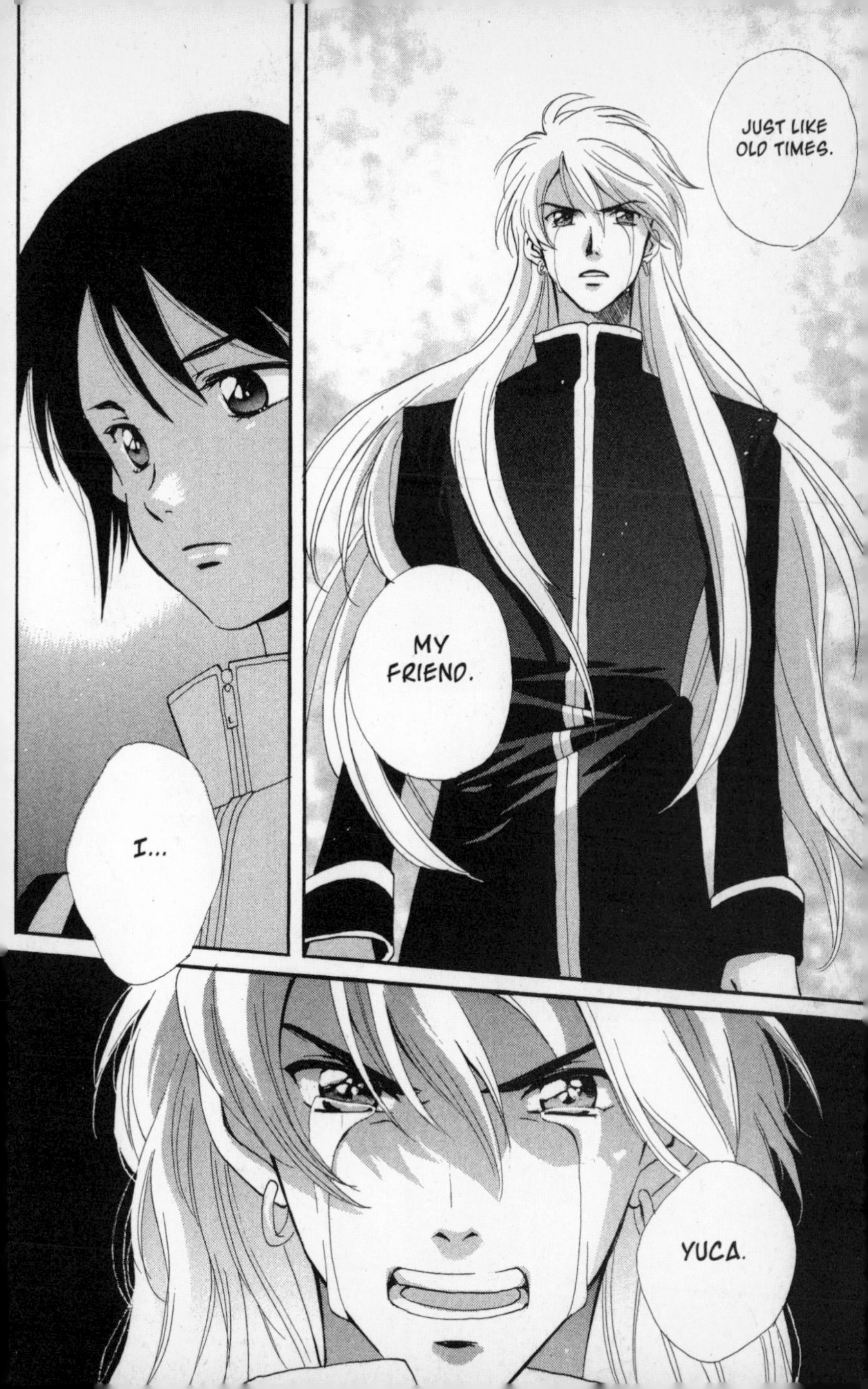
JUST LIKE OLD TIMES.
MY FRIEND.
I...
YUCA.

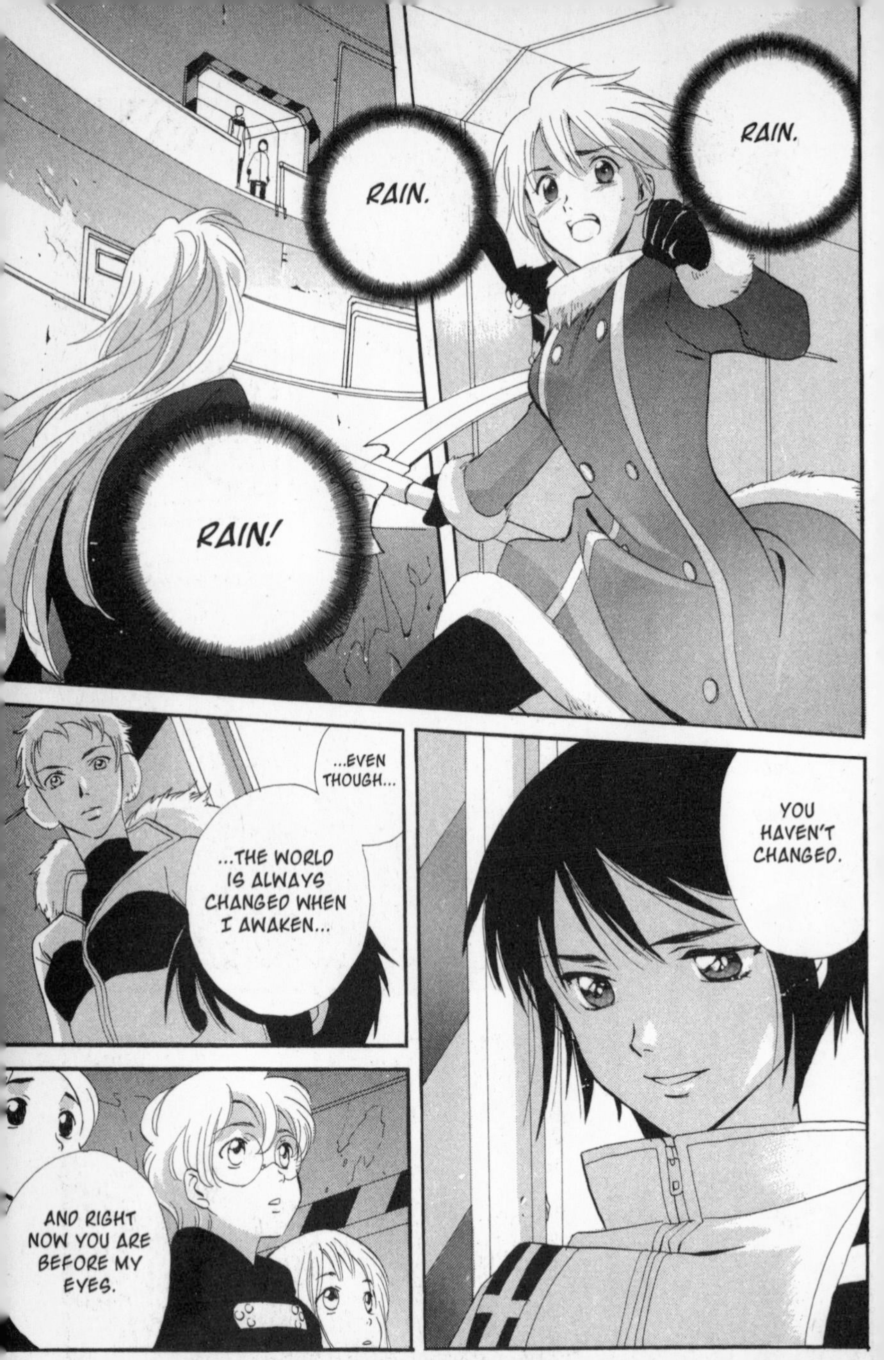
RAIN.
RAIN.
RAIN!
YOU HAVEN'T CHANGED.
...EVEN THOUGH...
...THE WORLD IS ALWAYS CHANGED WHEN I AWAKEN...
AND RIGHT NOW YOU ARE BEFORE MY EYES.

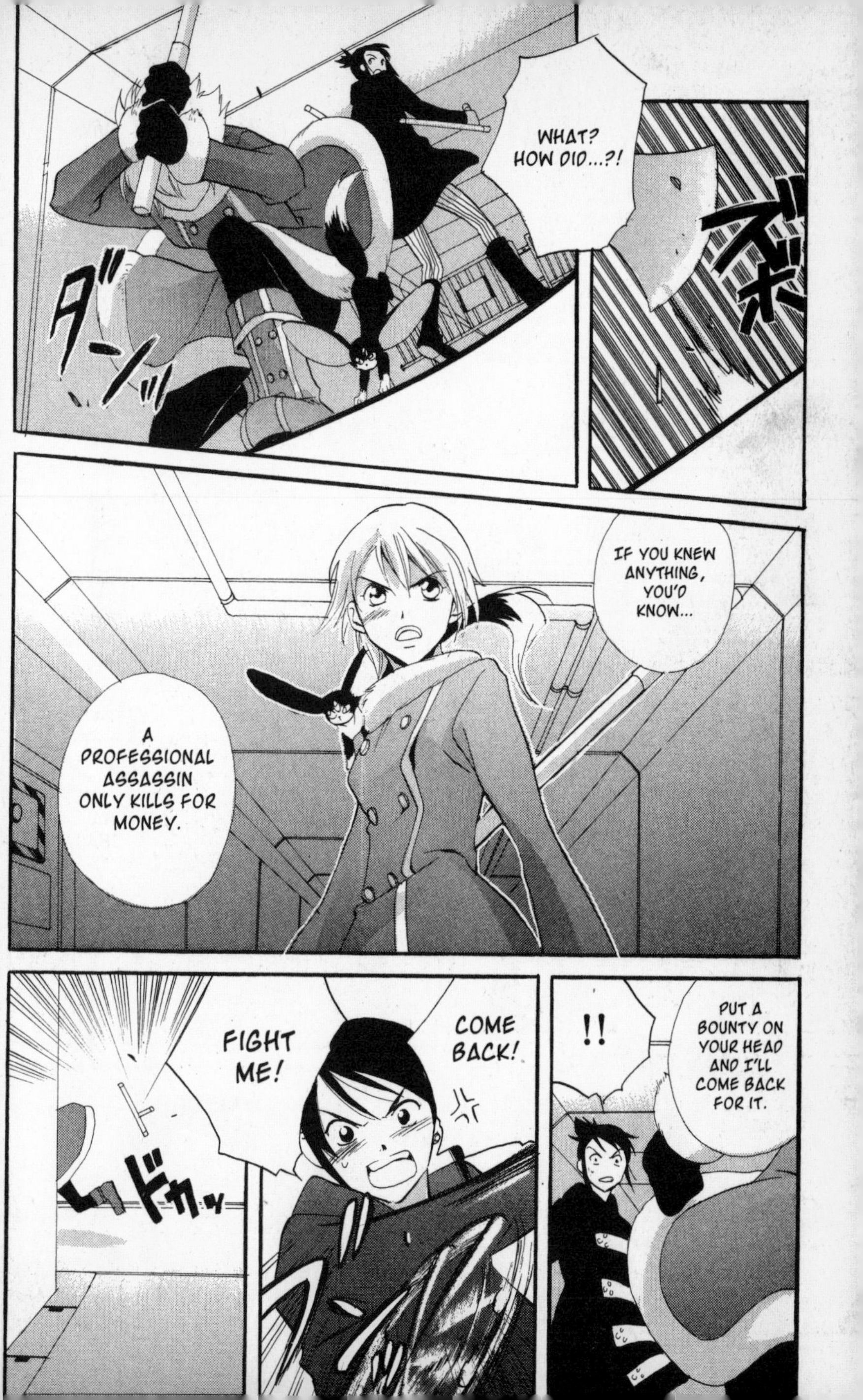

WHAT? HOW DID...?!
IF YOU KNEW ANYTHING, YOU'D KNOW...
A PROFESSIONAL ASSASSIN ONLY KILLS FOR MONEY.
!!
PUT A BOUNTY ON YOUR HEAD AND I'LL COME BACK FOR IT.
COME BACK!
FIGHT ME!

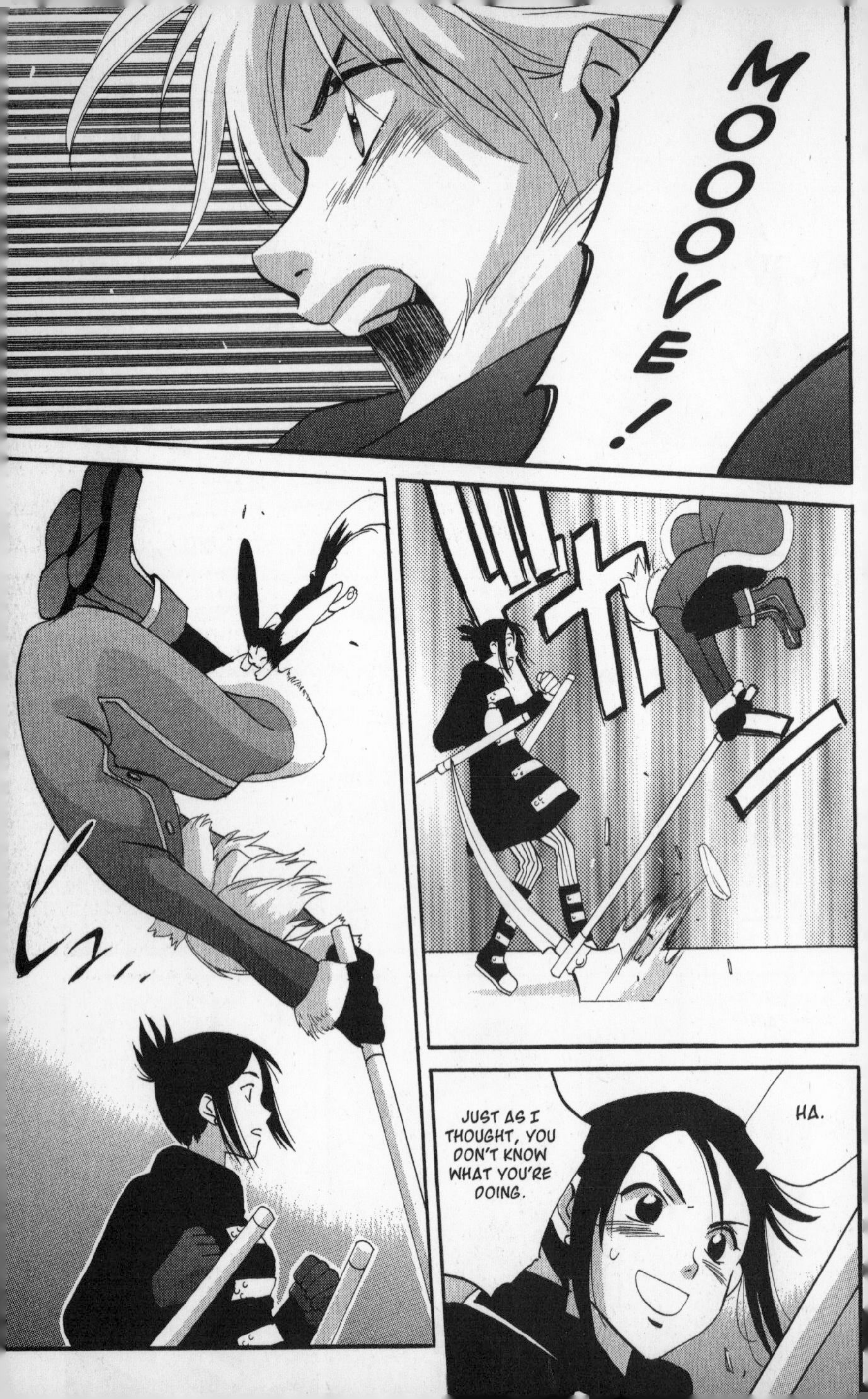
MOOOOVE!!
JUST AS I THOUGHT, YOU DON'T KNOW WHAT YOU'RE DOING.
HA.

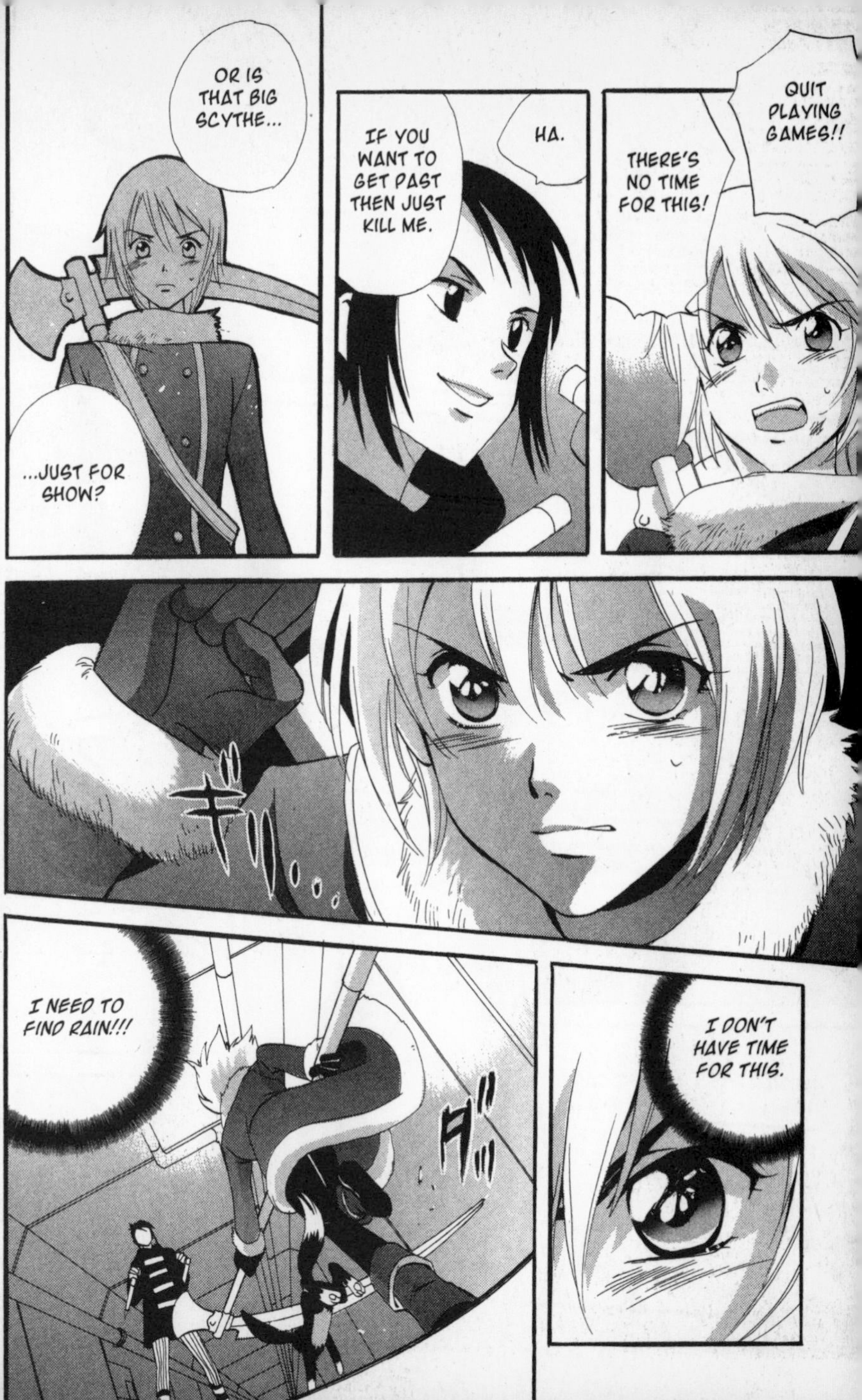
OR IS THAT BIG SCYTHE...
...JUST FOR SHOW?
HA.
IF YOU WANT TO GET PAST THEN JUST KILL ME.
QUIT PLAYING GAMES!!
THERE'S NO TIME FOR THIS!
I NEED TO FIND RAIN!!!
I DON'T HAVE TIME FOR THIS.

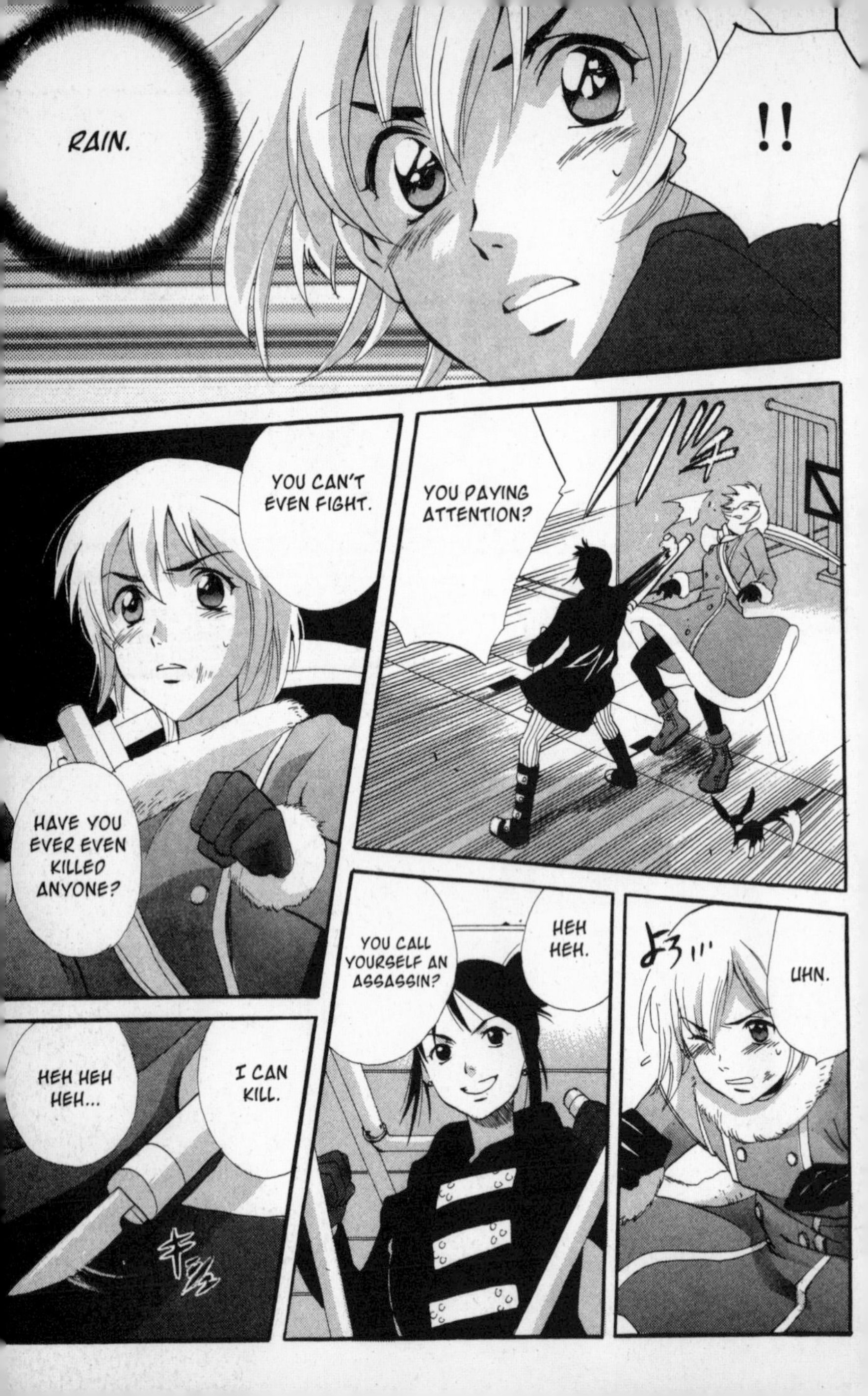
RAIN.
!!
YOU PAYING ATTENTION?
YOU CAN'T EVEN FIGHT.
HAVE YOU EVER EVEN KILLED ANYONE?
UHN.
よろ
HEH HEH.
YOU CALL YOURSELF AN ASSASSIN?
I CAN KILL.
HEH HEH HEH...

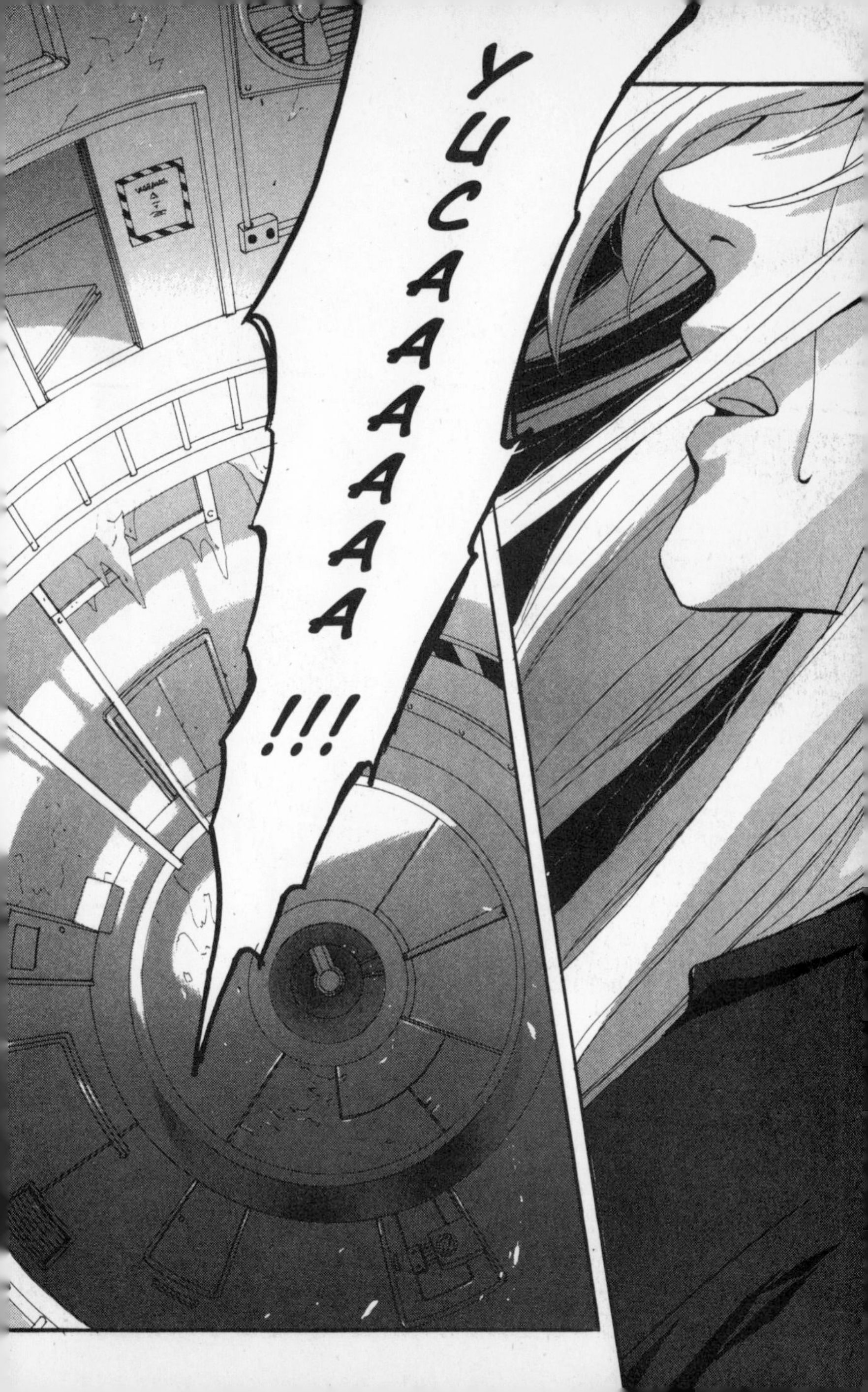
YUCAAAAAAA
!!!

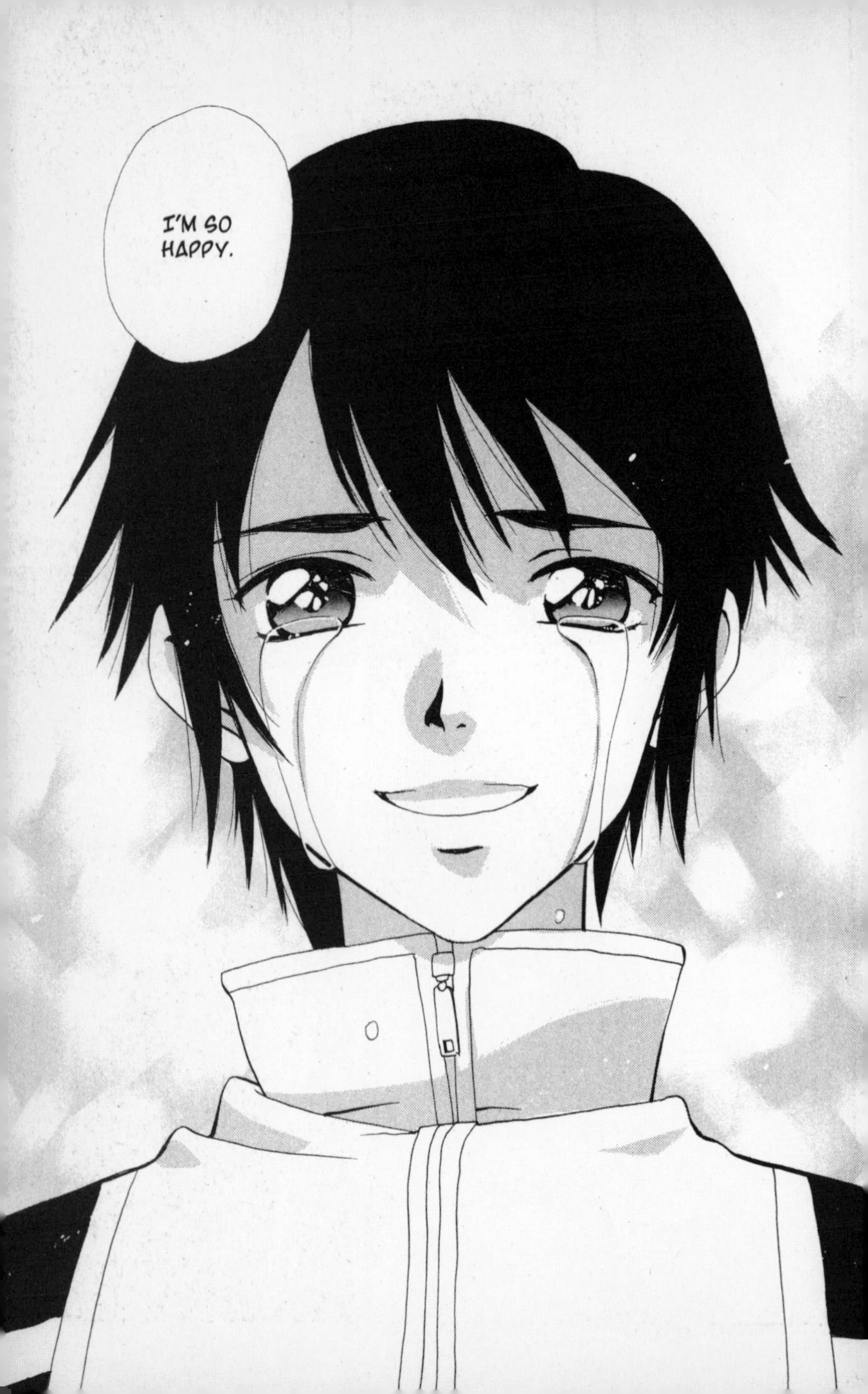
I'M SO HAPPY.

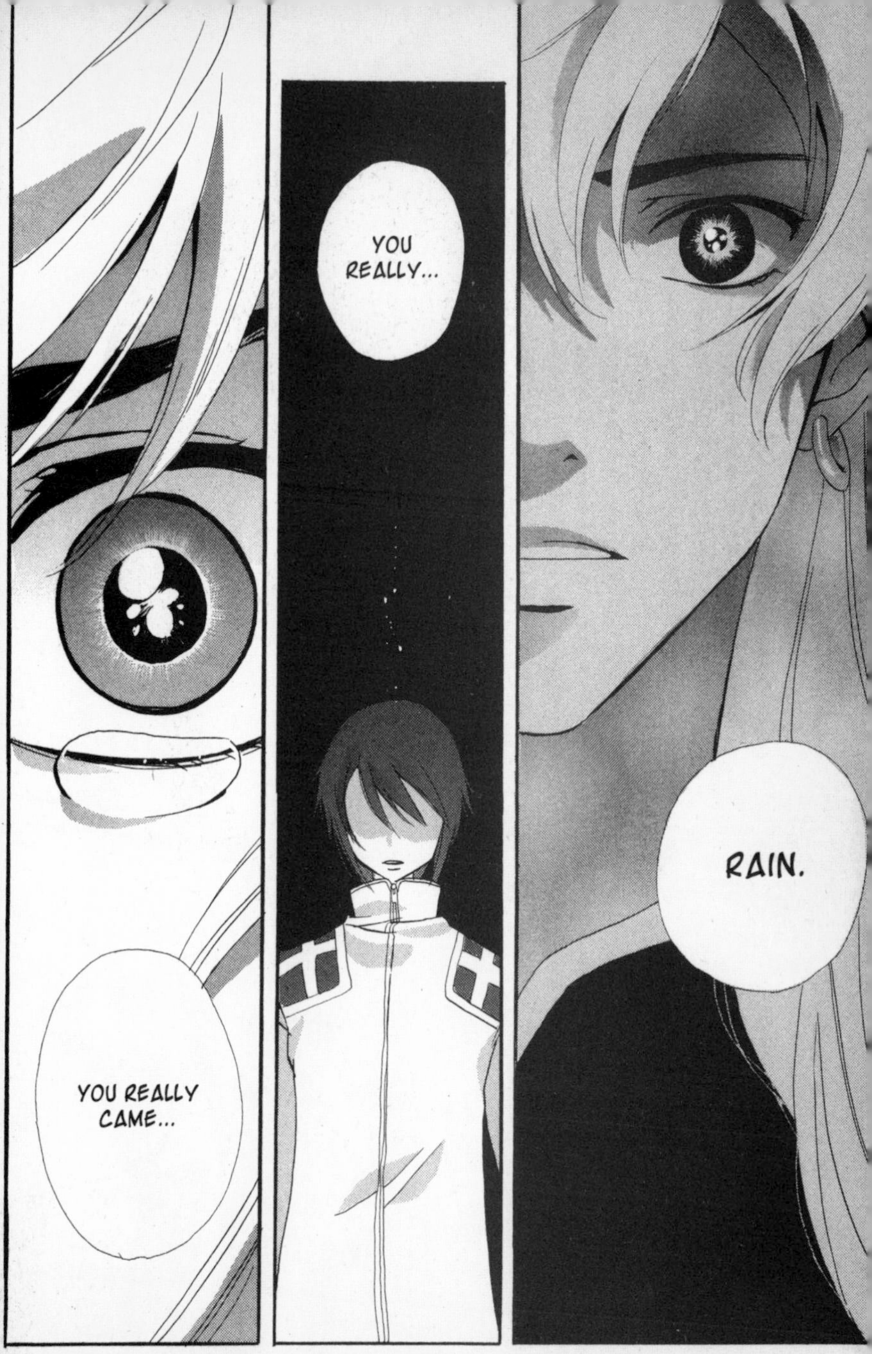
RAIN.
YOU REALLY...
YOU REALLY CAME...

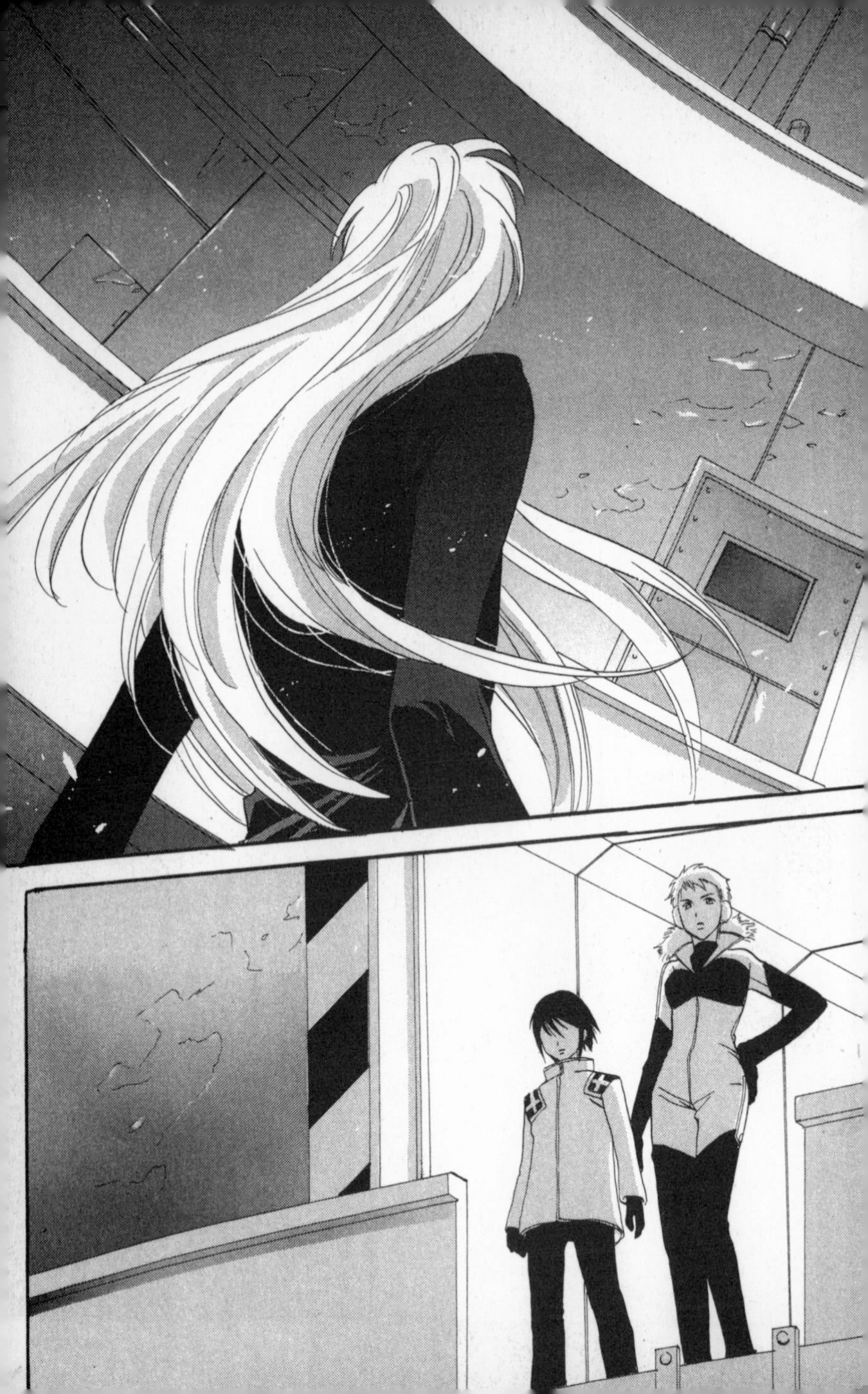

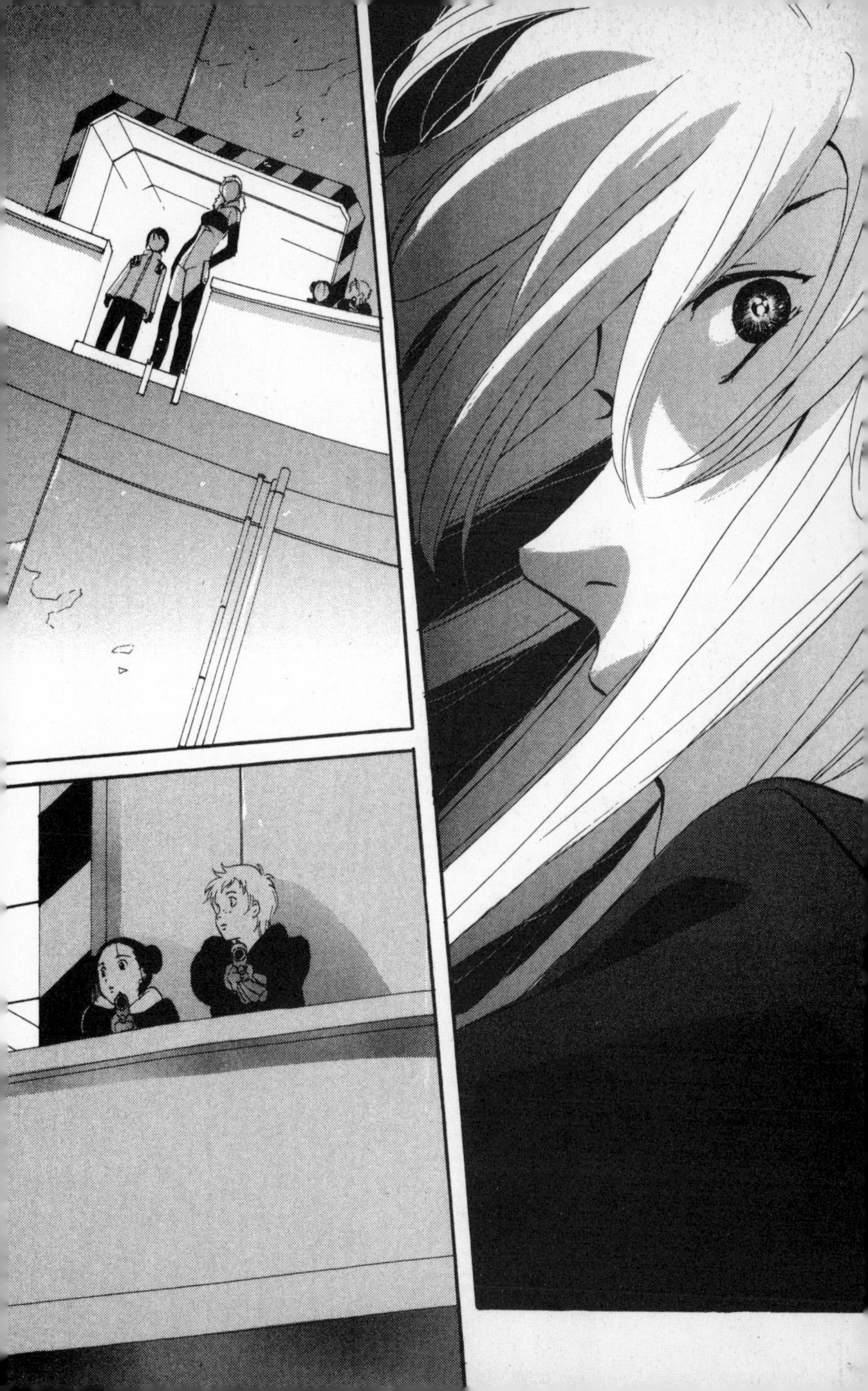

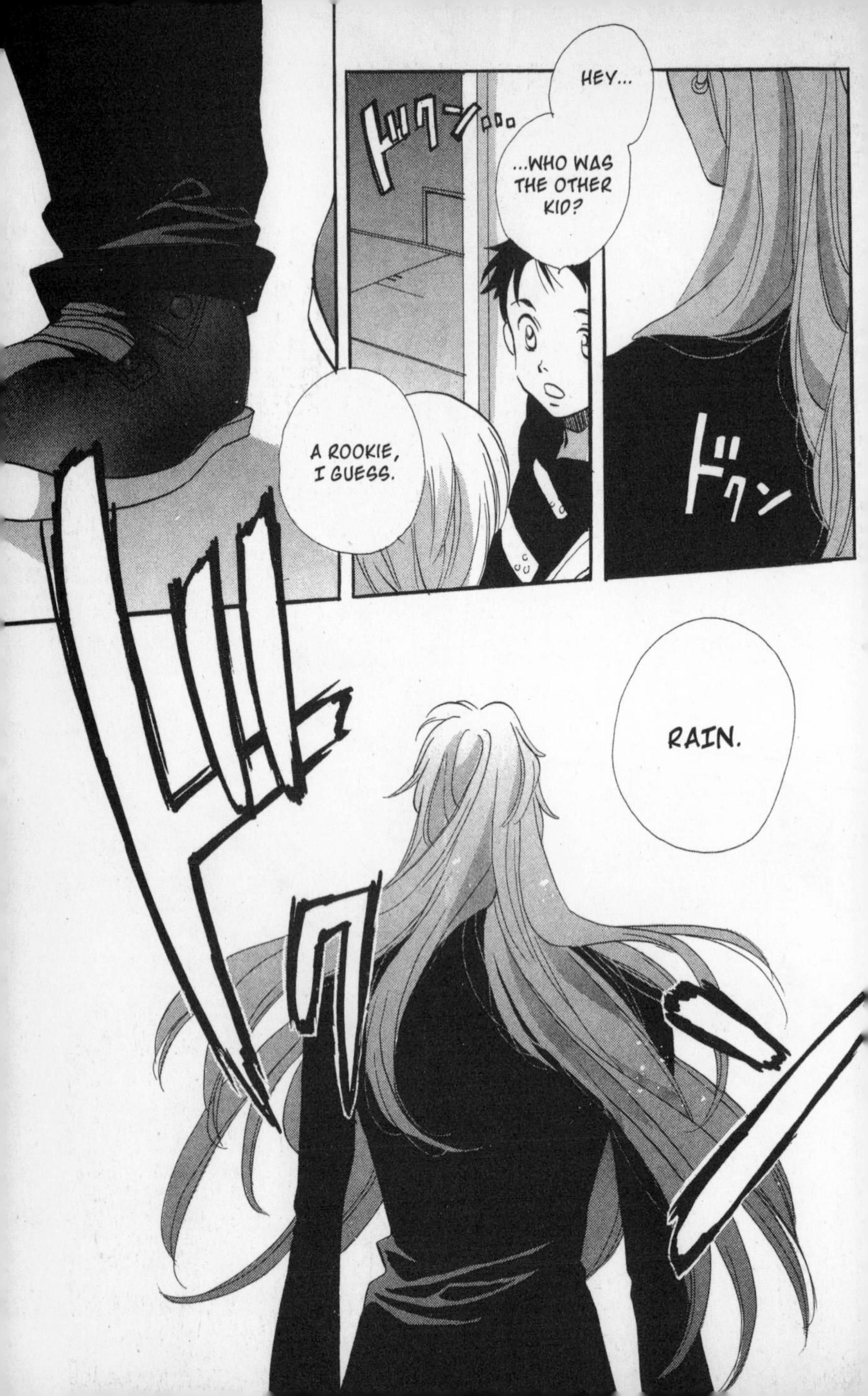
HEY...
...WHO WAS THE OTHER KID?
ドックン...
A ROOKIE, I GUESS.
ドクン
RAIN.

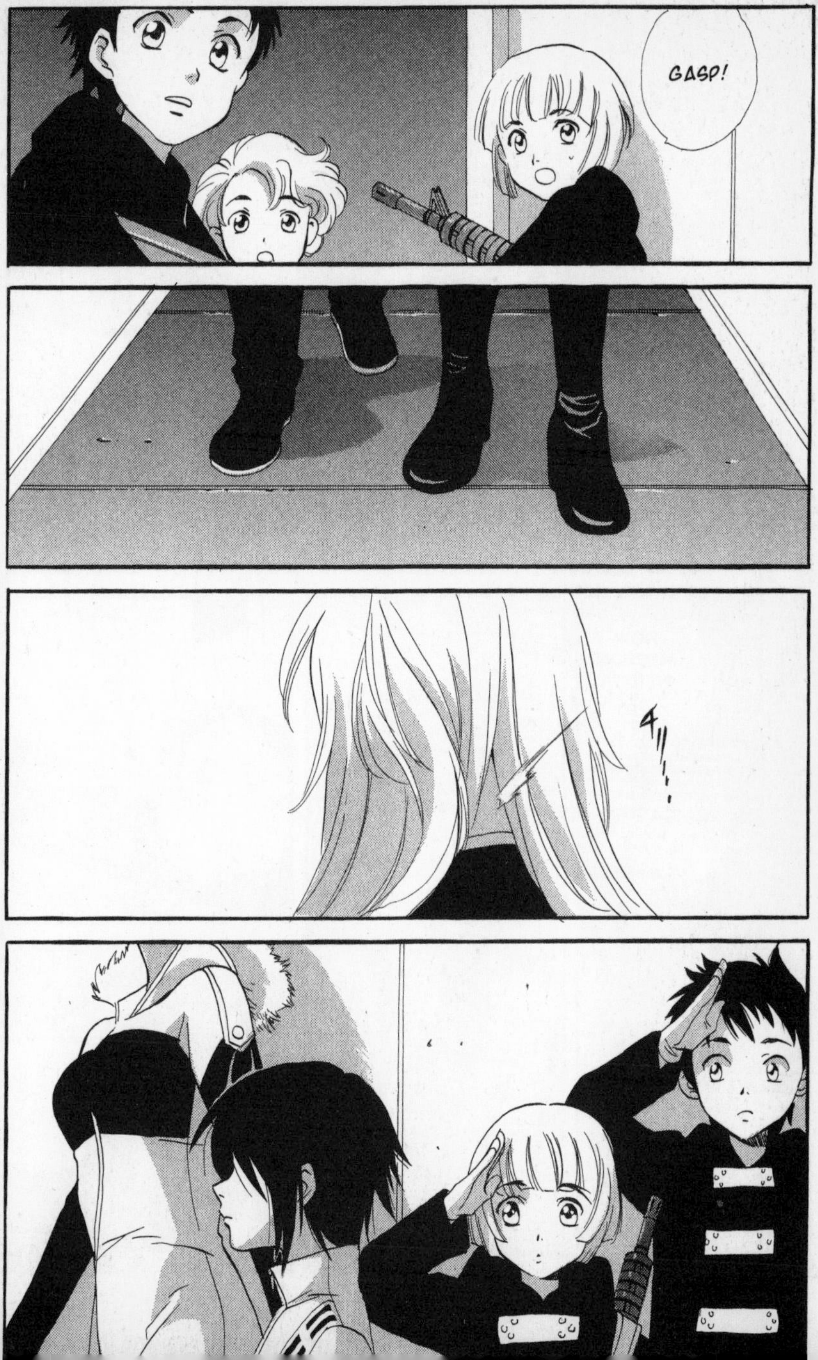
GASP!

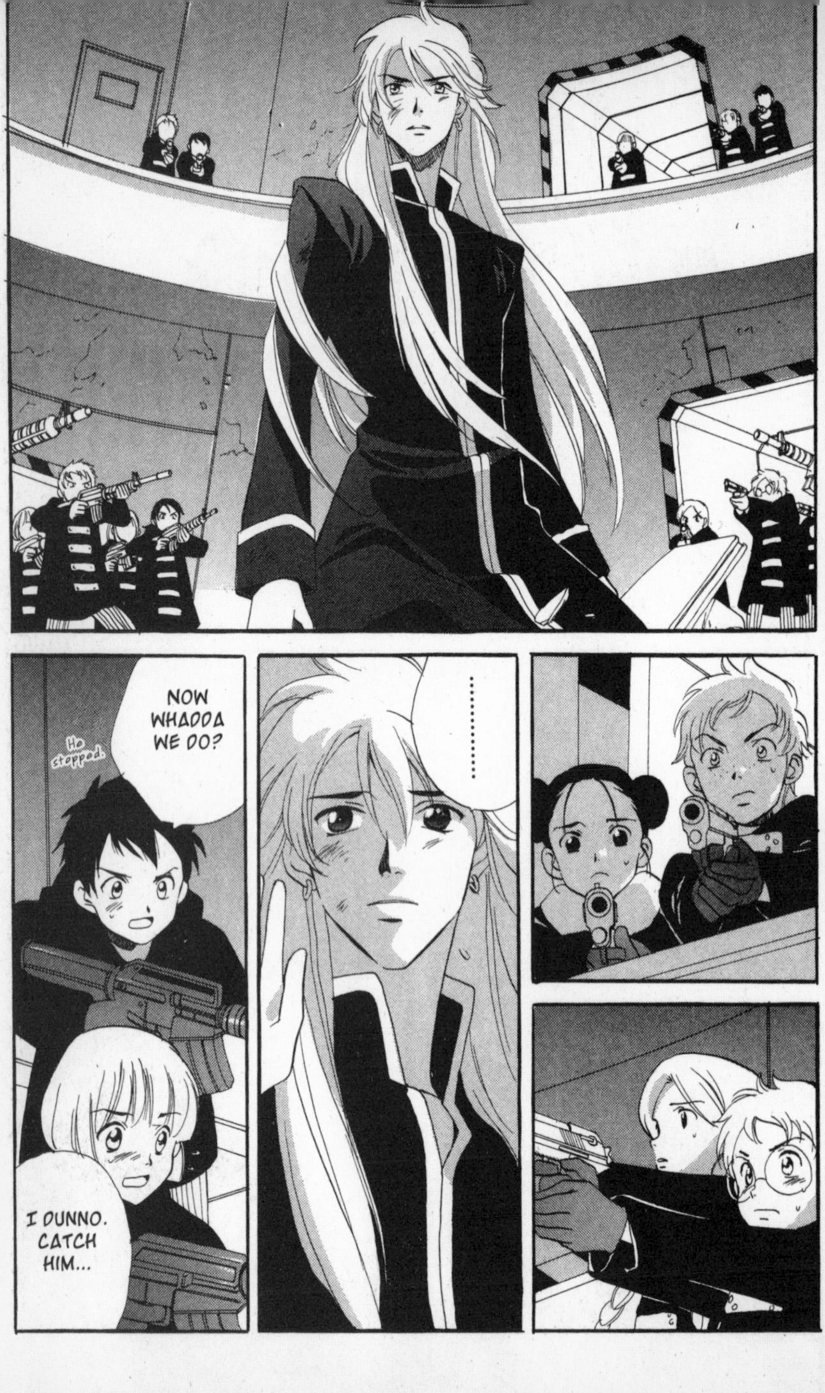
NOW WHADDA WE DO?
He stopped.
I DUNNO. CATCH HIM...
....

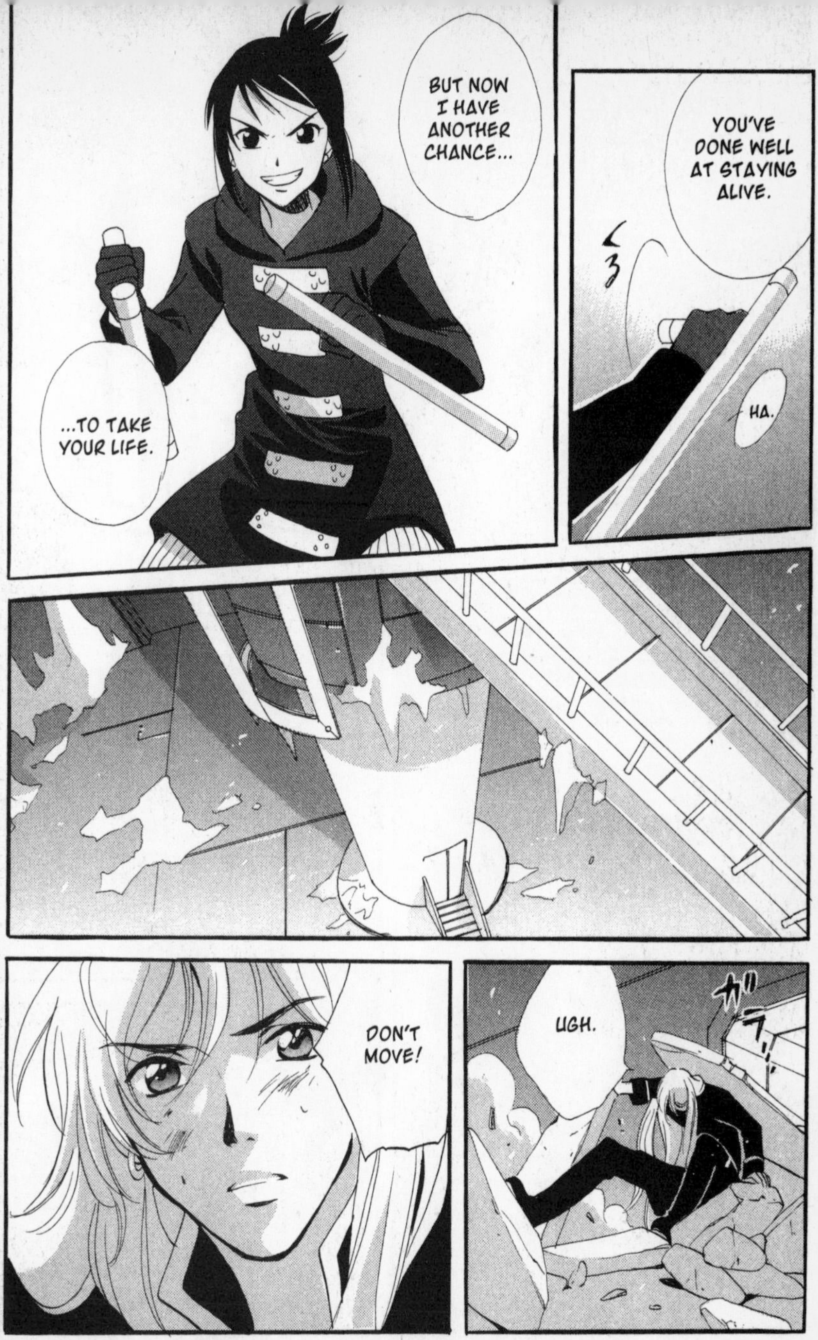
YOU'VE DONE WELL AT STAYING ALIVE.
HA.
BUT NOW I HAVE ANOTHER CHANCE...
...TO TAKE YOUR LIFE.
UGH.
DON'T MOVE!

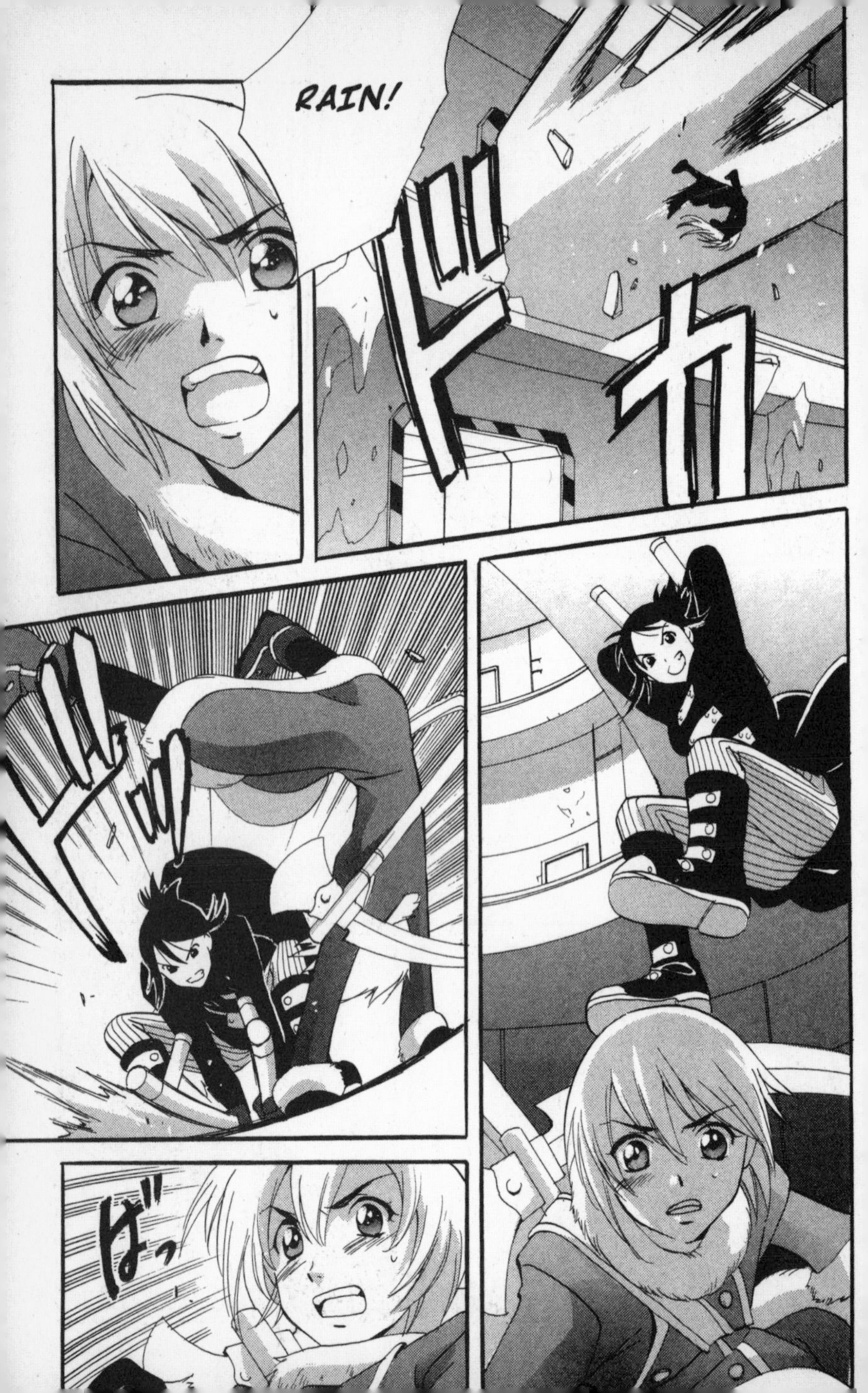
RAIN!

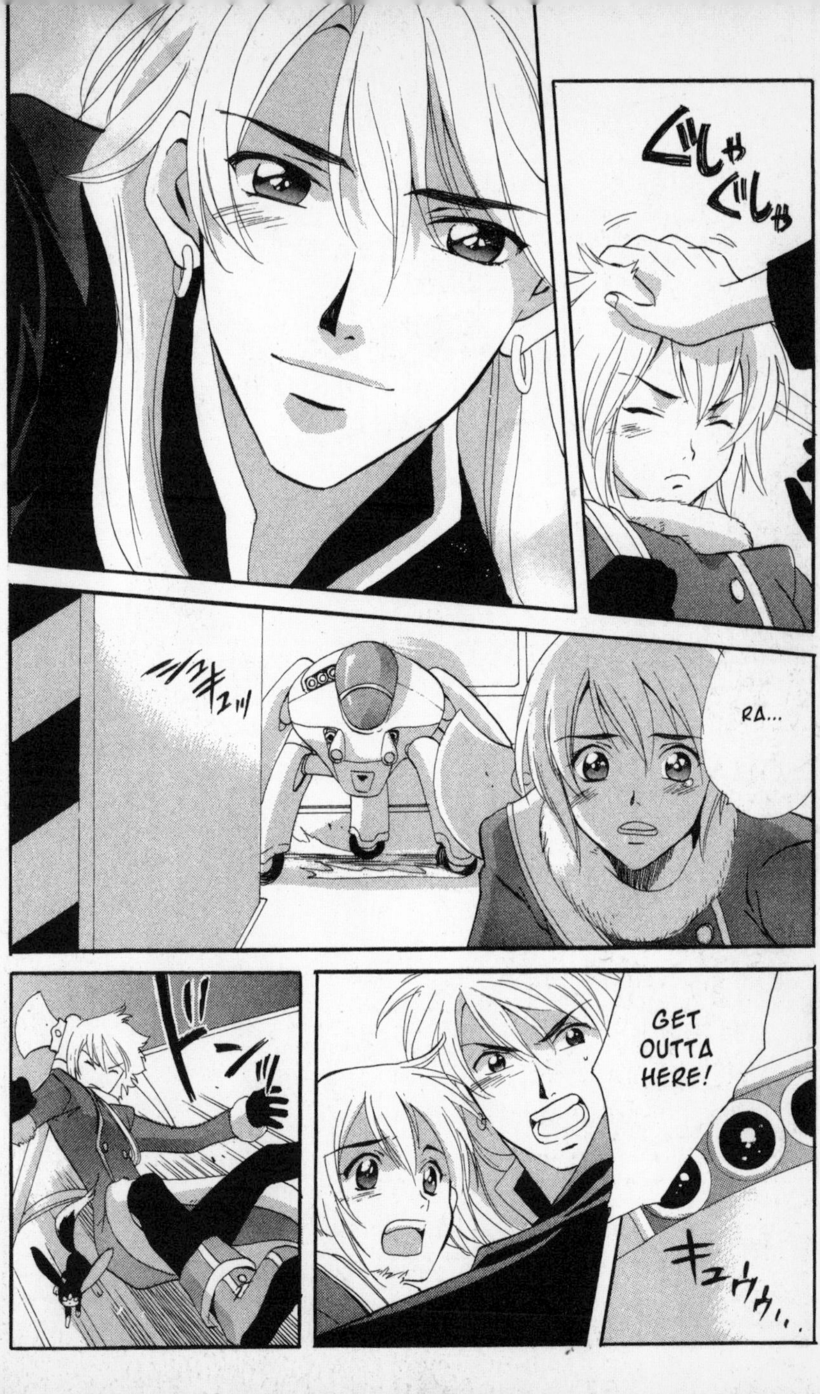
ぐしゃぐしゃ
RA...
GET OUTTA HERE!
キュウゥ...

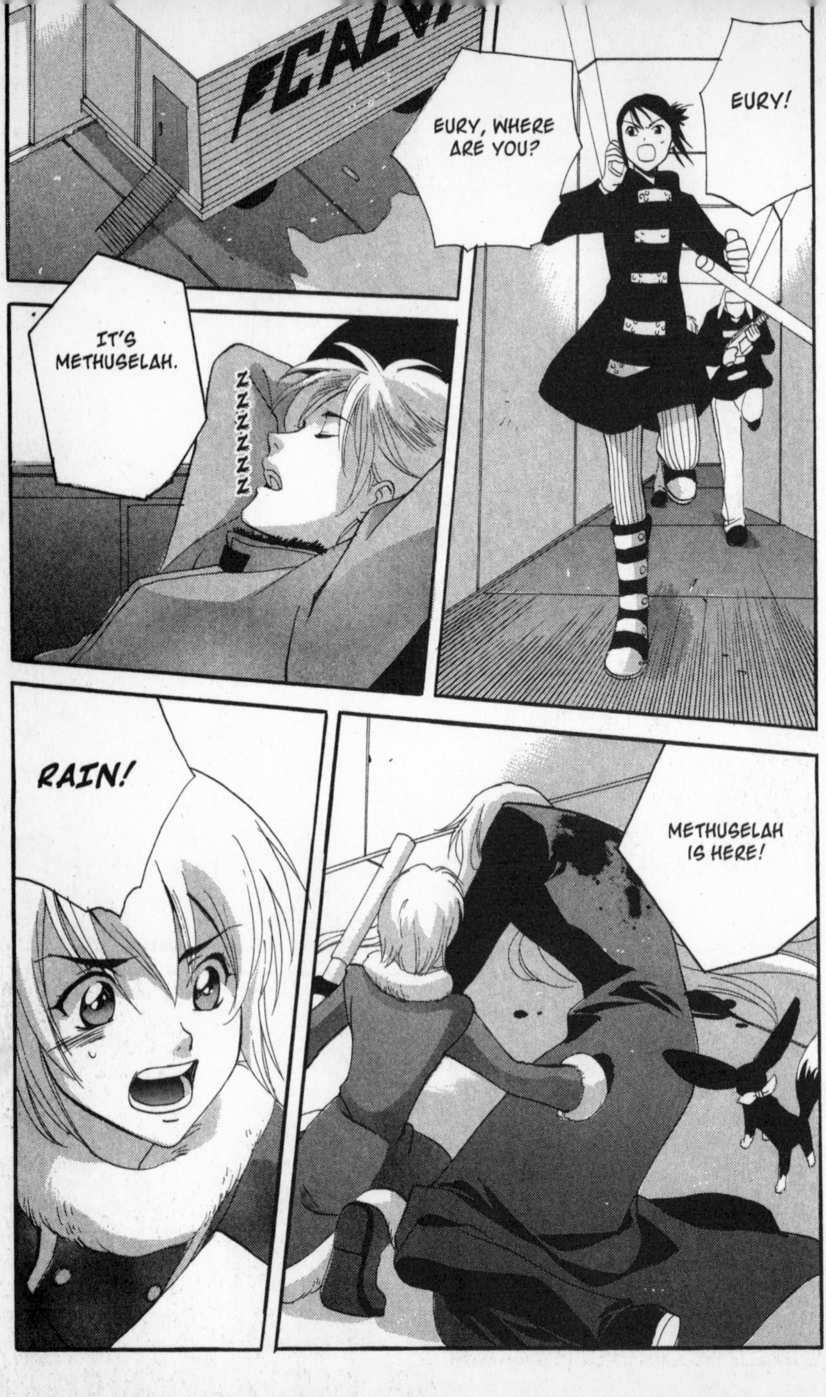
EURY!
EURY, WHERE ARE YOU?
IT'S METHUSELAH.
ZZZZZZ
METHUSELAH IS HERE!
RAIN!

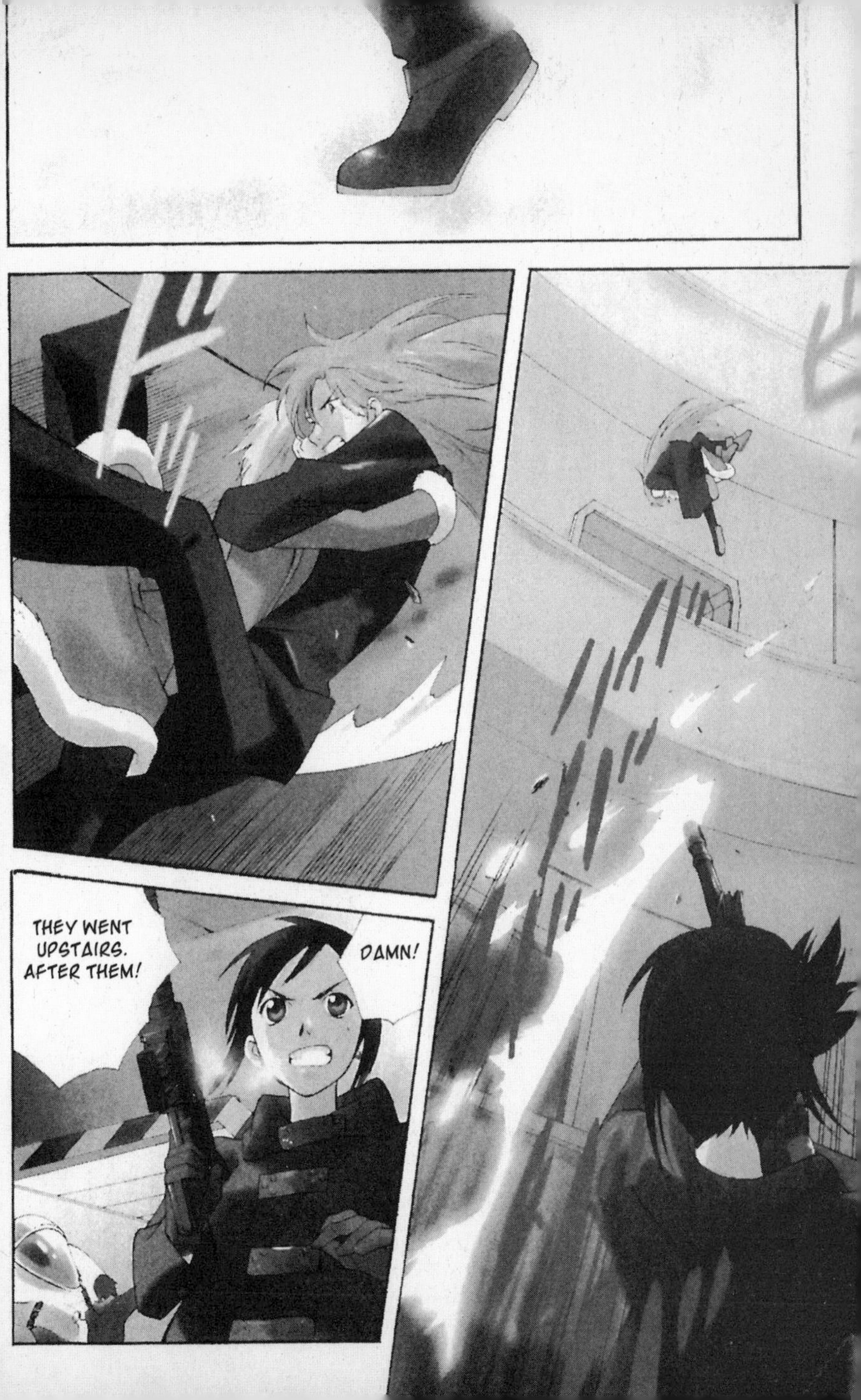
DAMN!
THEY WENT UPSTAIRS. AFTER THEM!

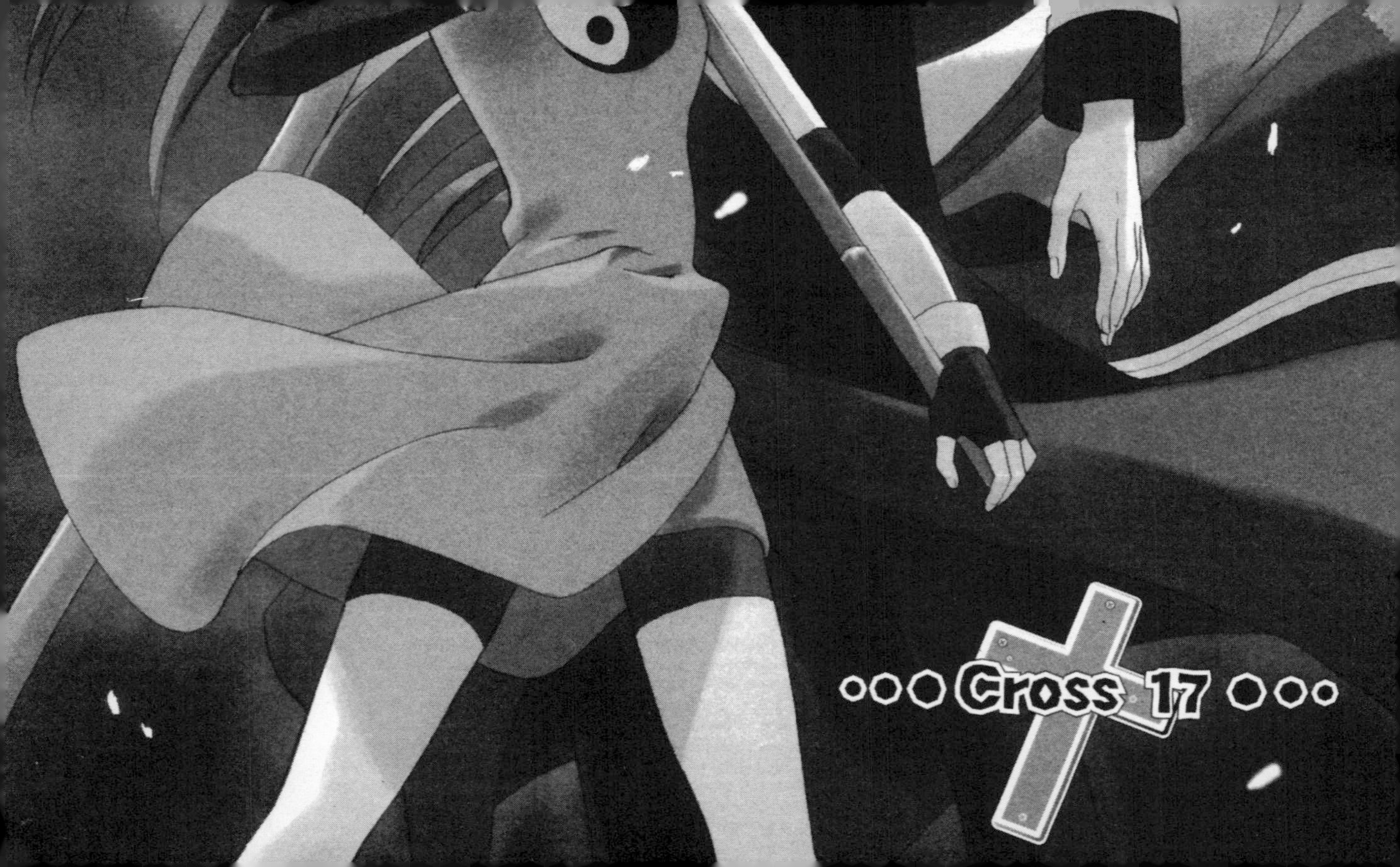
Cross 17

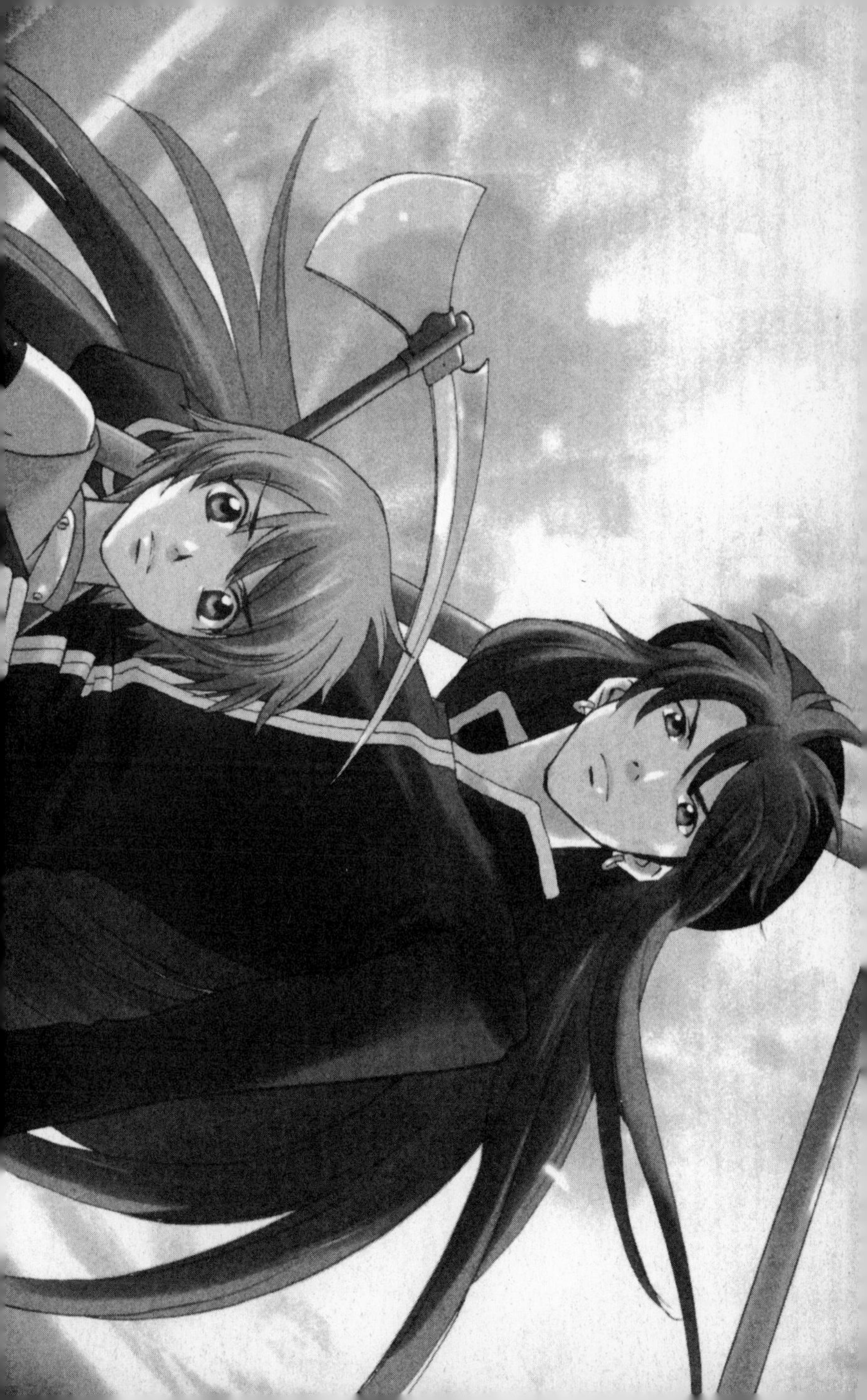

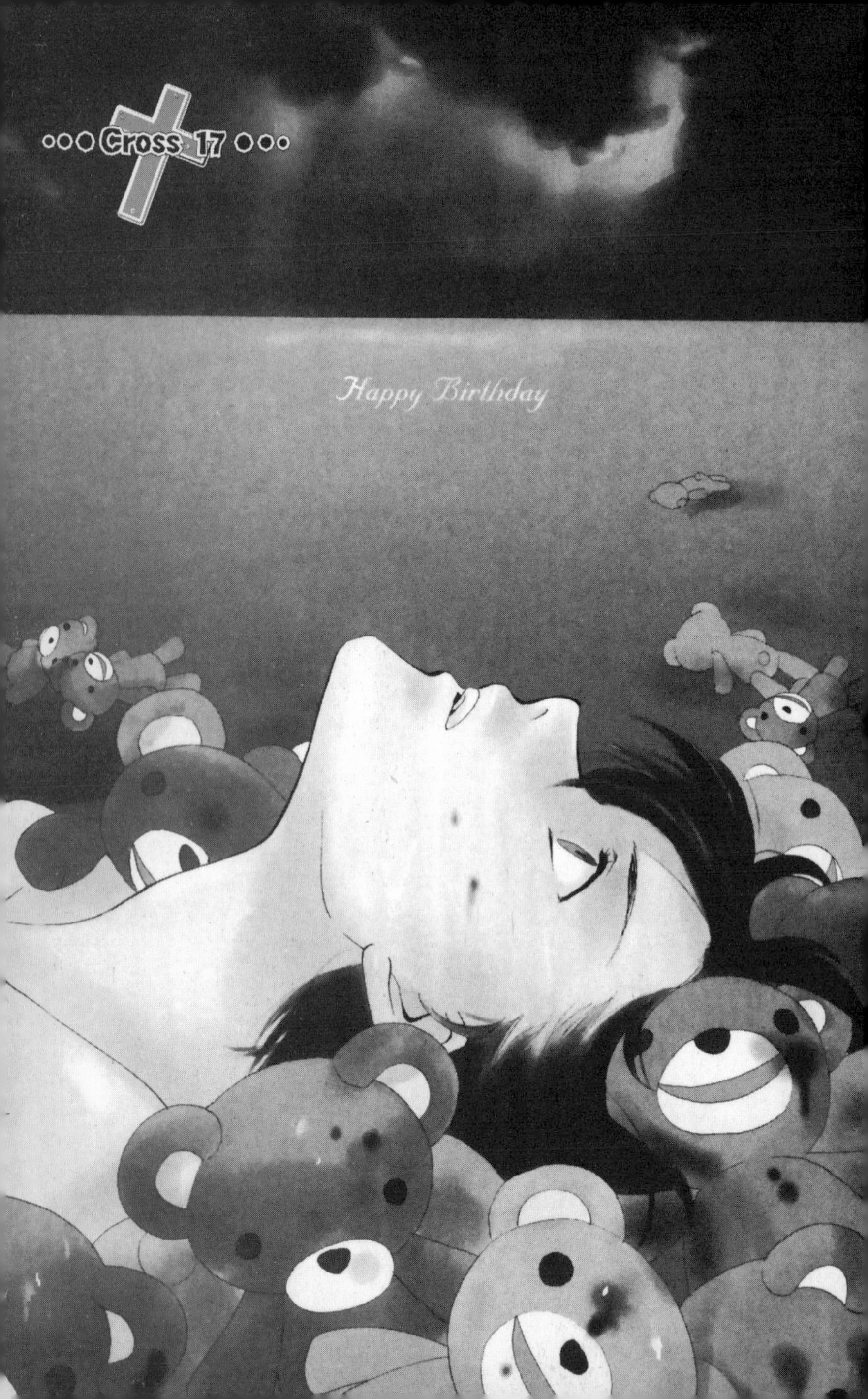
Cross 17
Happy Birthday

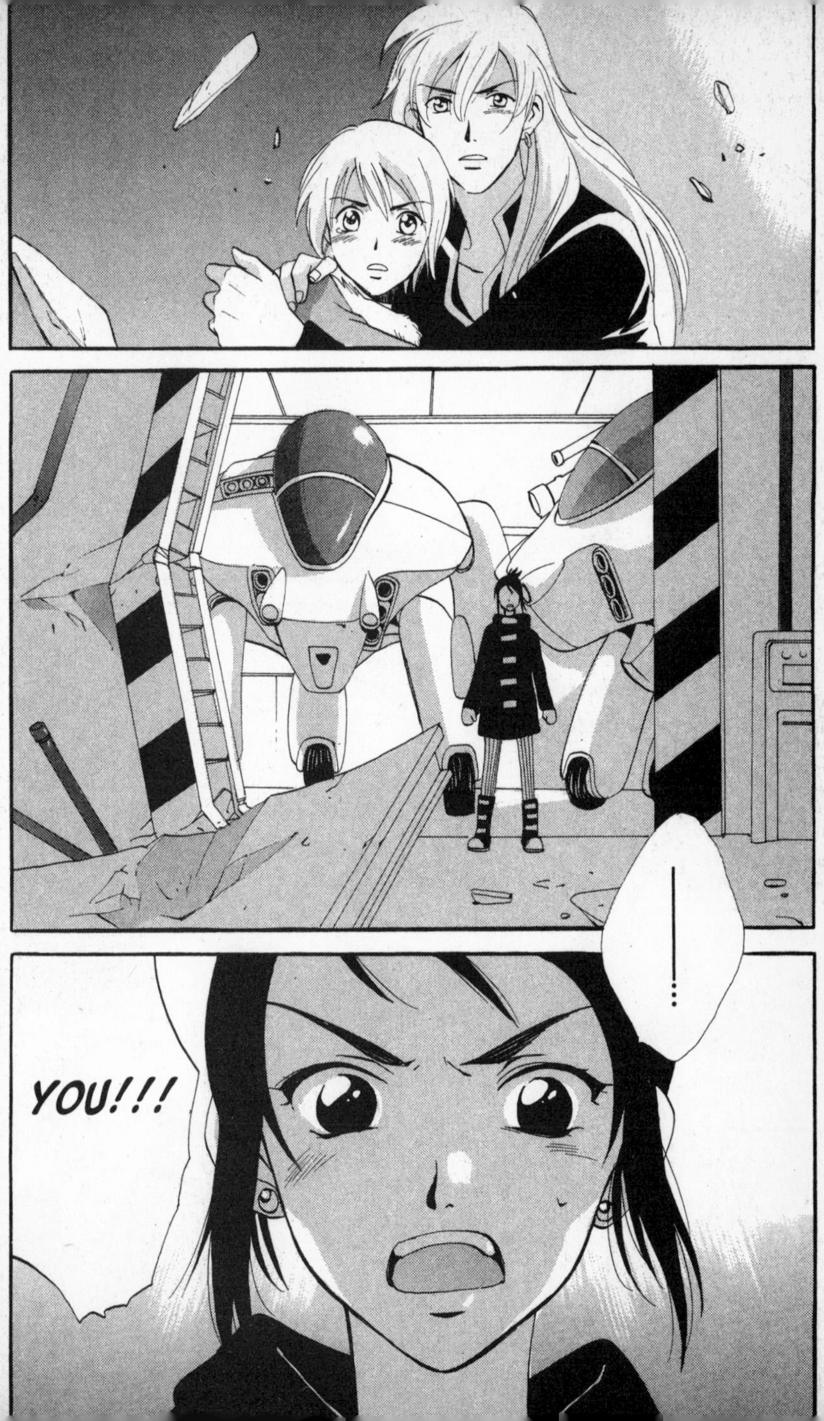

......
YOU!!!

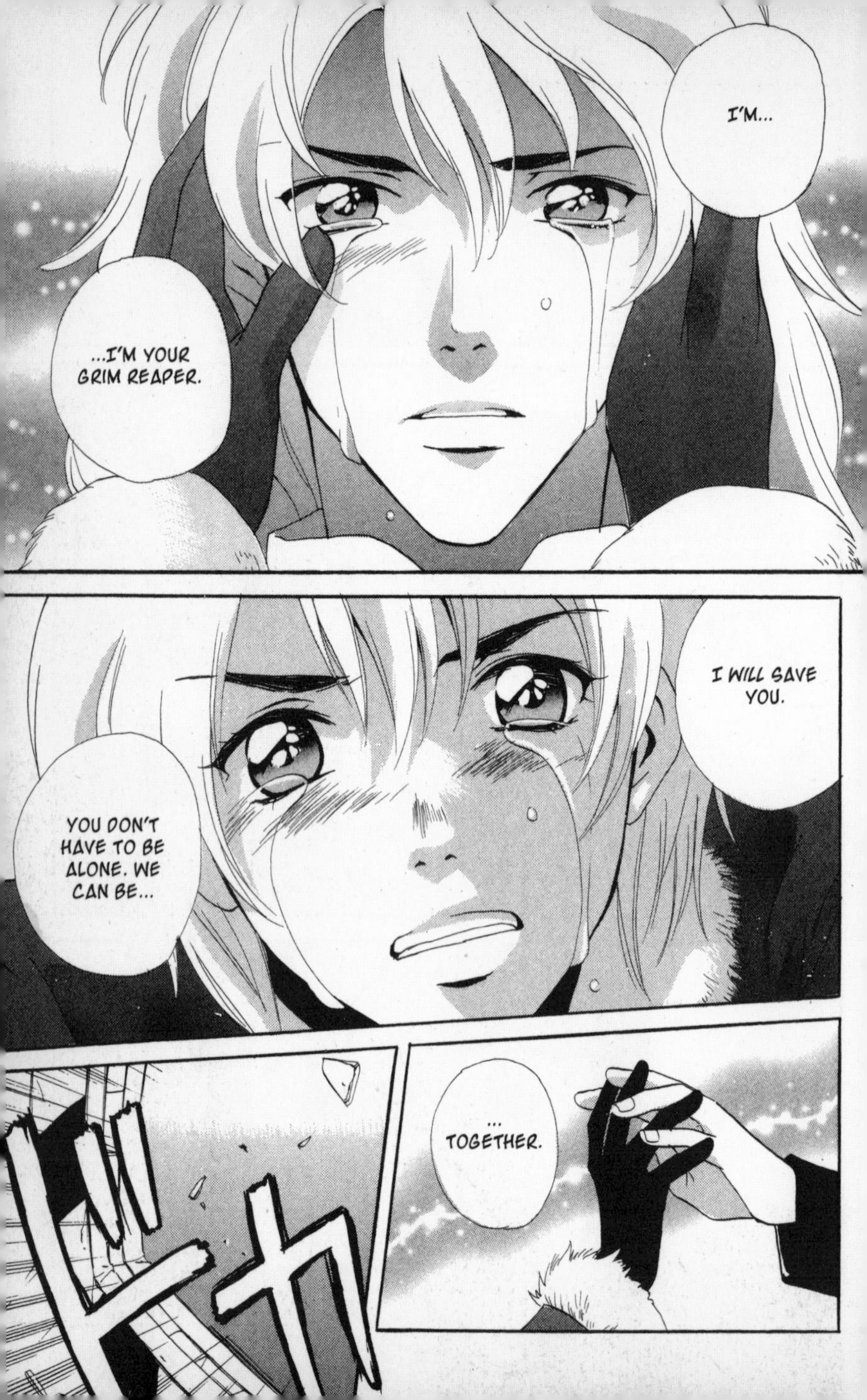

I'M...
...I'M YOUR GRIM REAPER.
I WILL SAVE YOU.
YOU DON'T HAVE TO BE ALONE. WE CAN BE...
... TOGETHER.

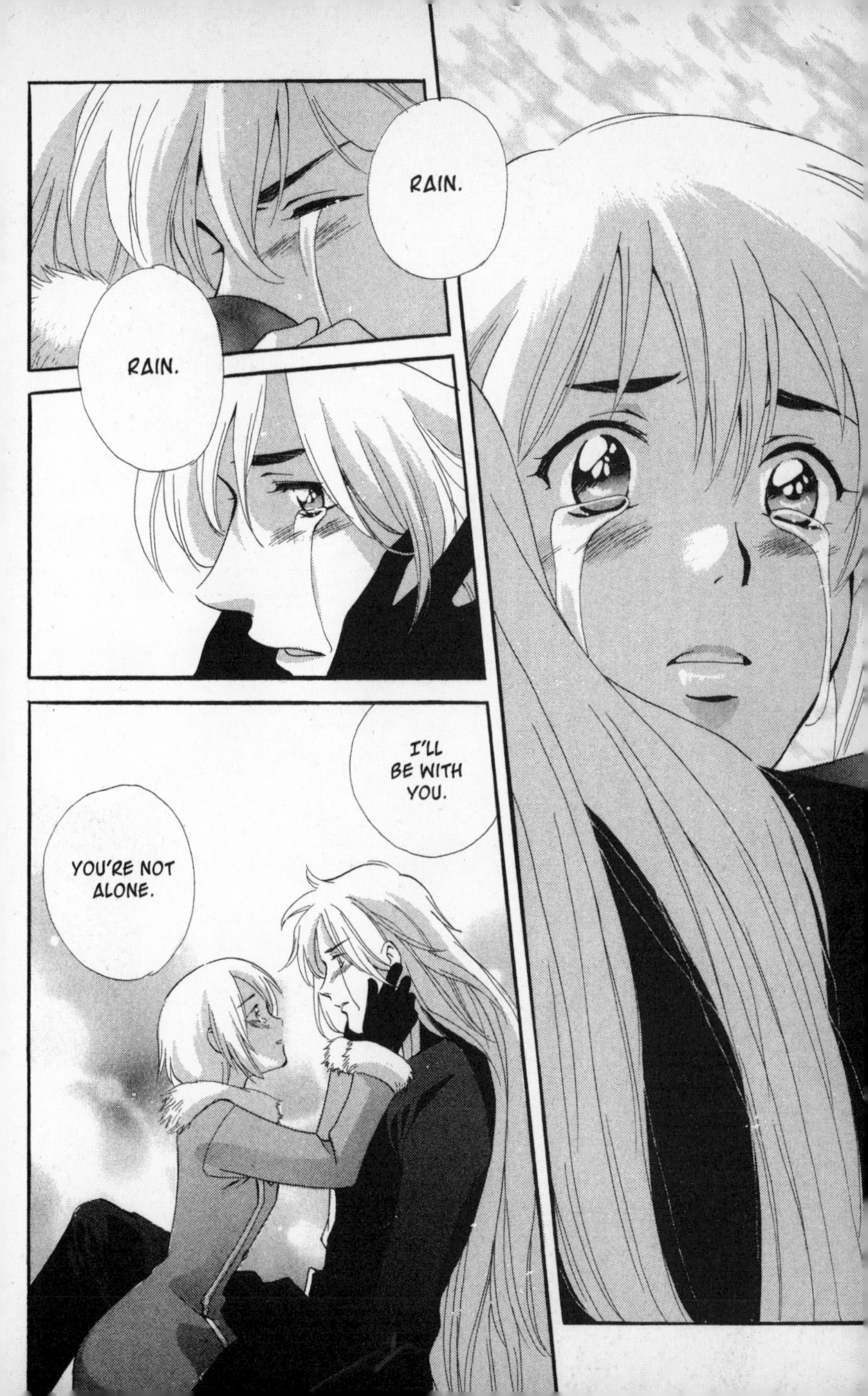
RAIN.
RAIN.
I'LL BE WITH YOU.
YOU'RE NOT ALONE.

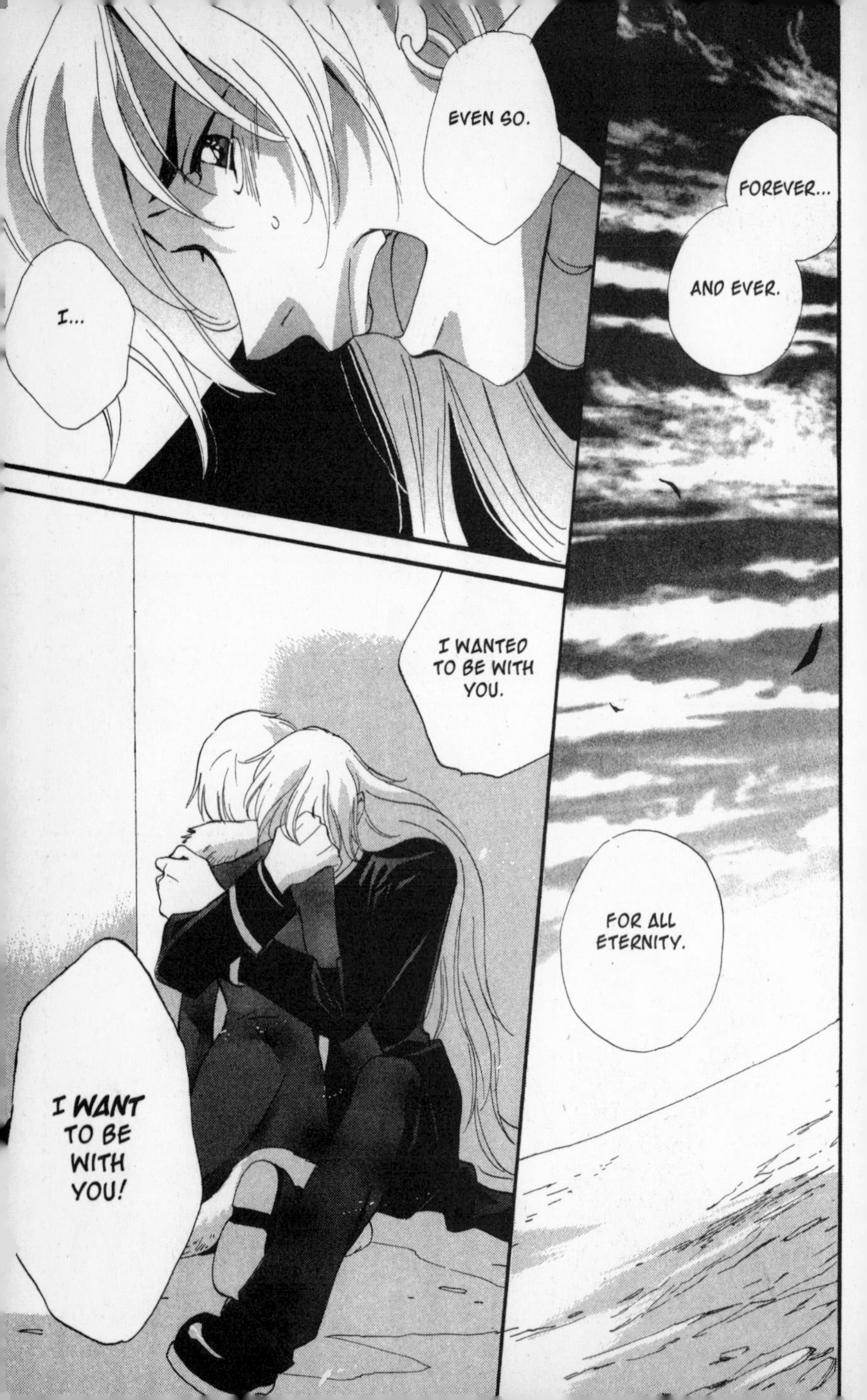
FOREVER...
AND EVER.
EVEN SO.
I...
I WANTED TO BE WITH YOU.
FOR ALL ETERNITY.
I WANT TO BE WITH YOU!

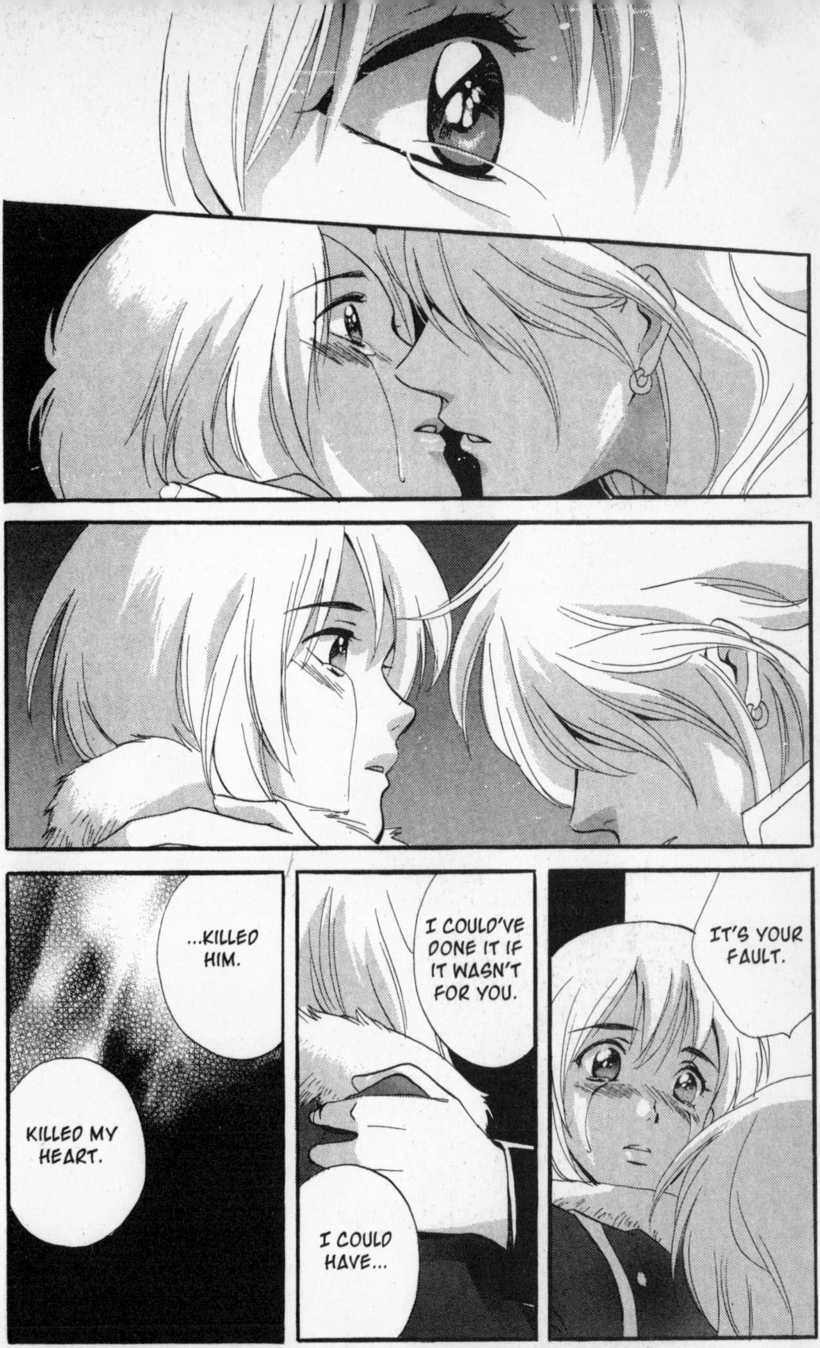
IT'S YOUR FAULT.
I COULD'VE DONE IT IF IT WASN'T FOR YOU.
I COULD HAVE...
...KILLED HIM.
KILLED MY HEART.

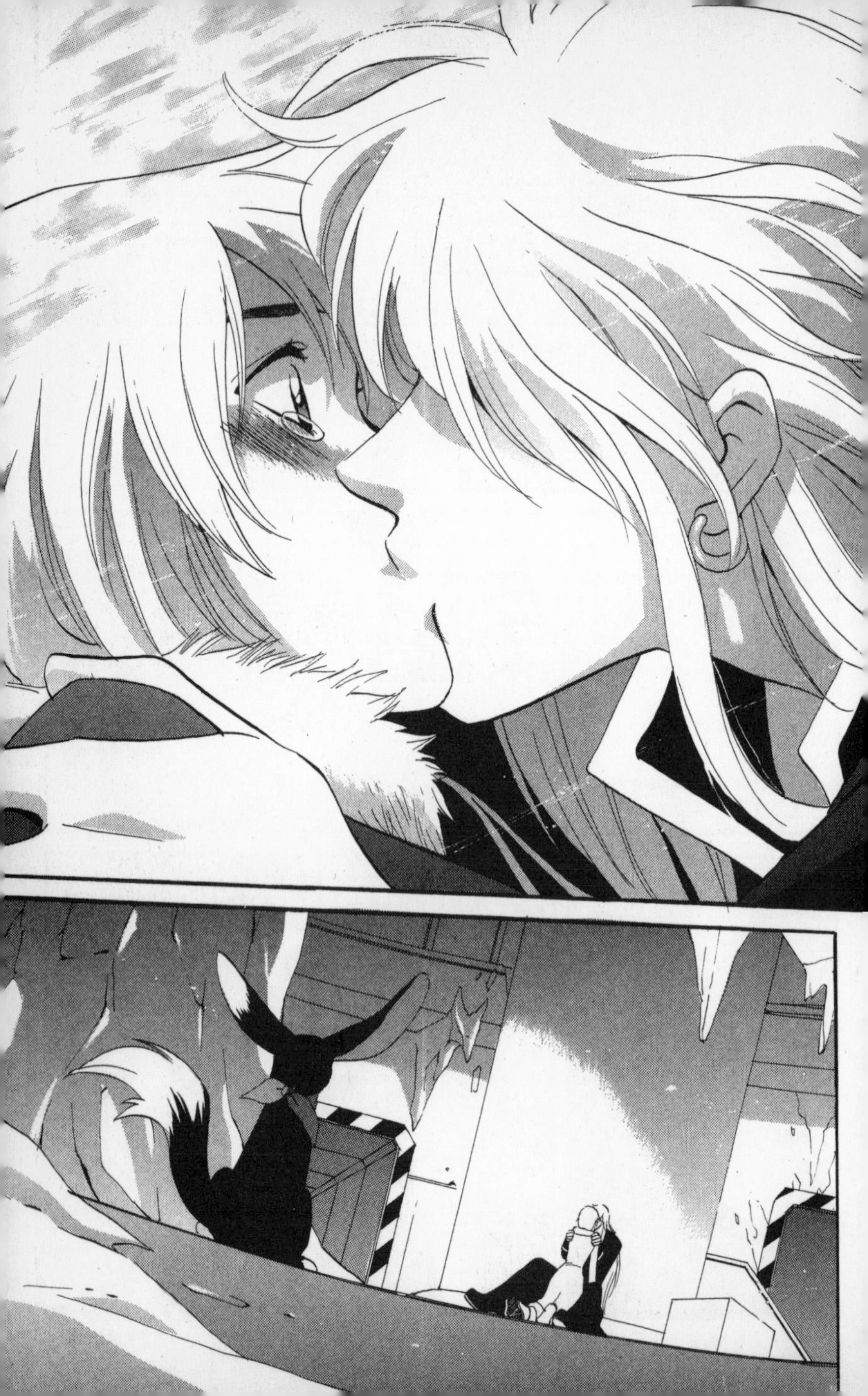

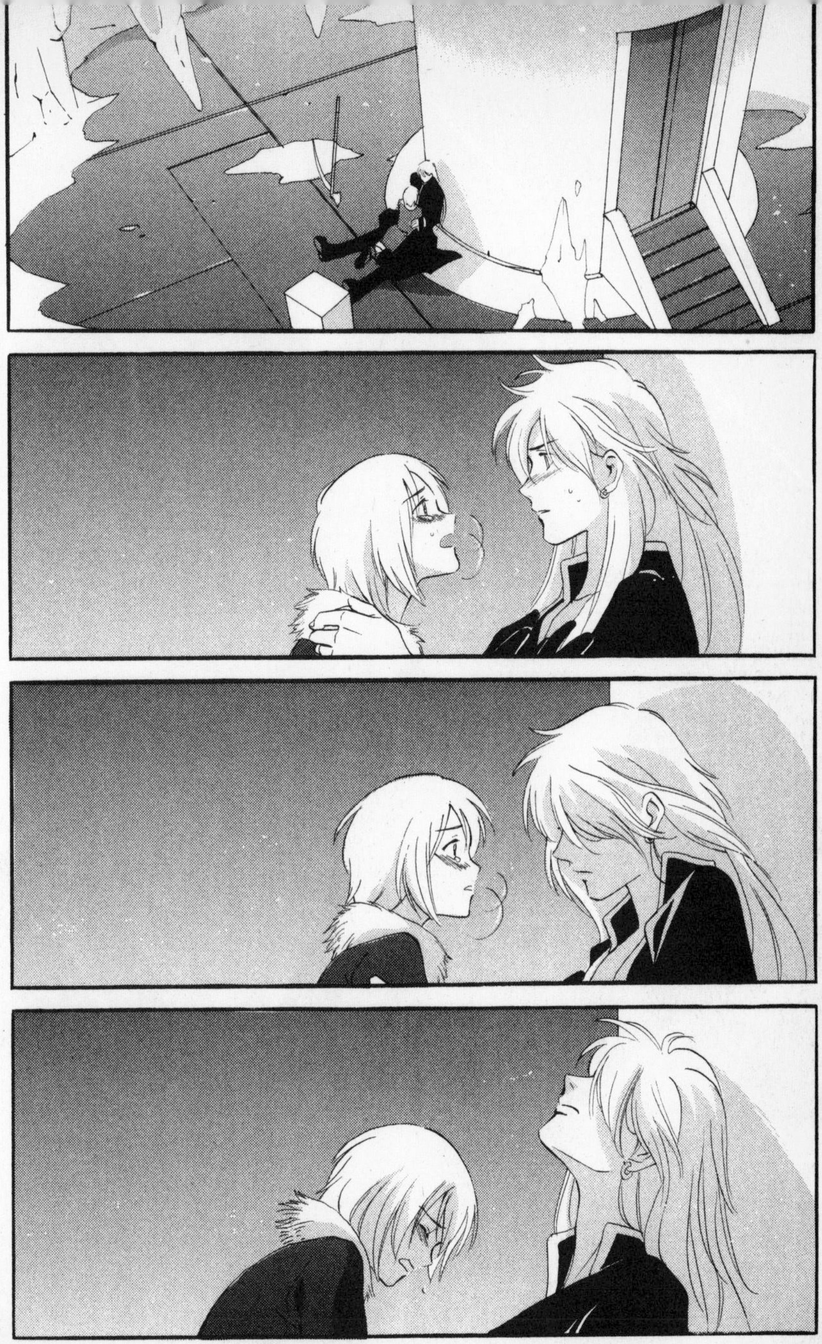

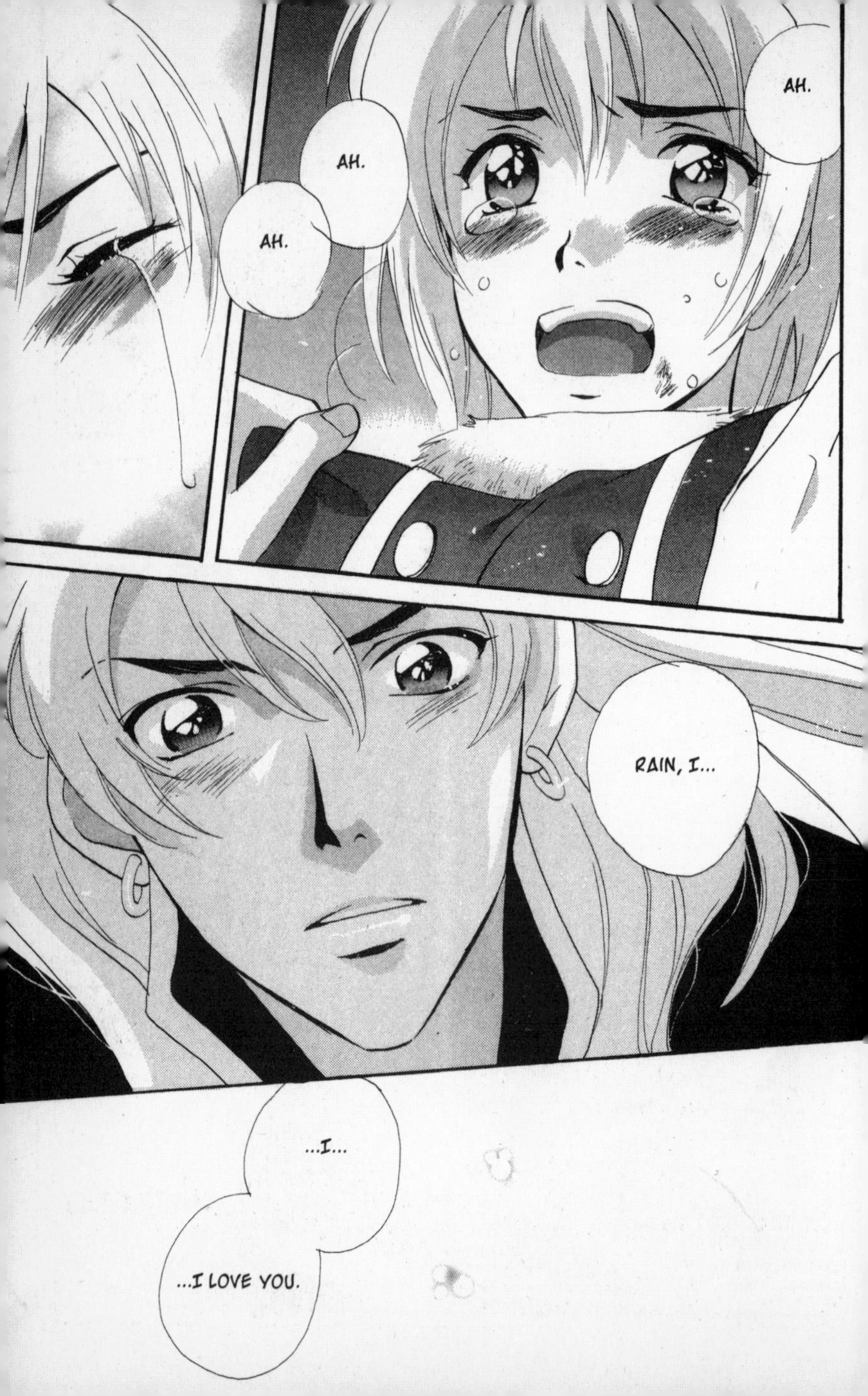
AH.
AH.
AH.
RAIN, I...
...I...
...I LOVE YOU.

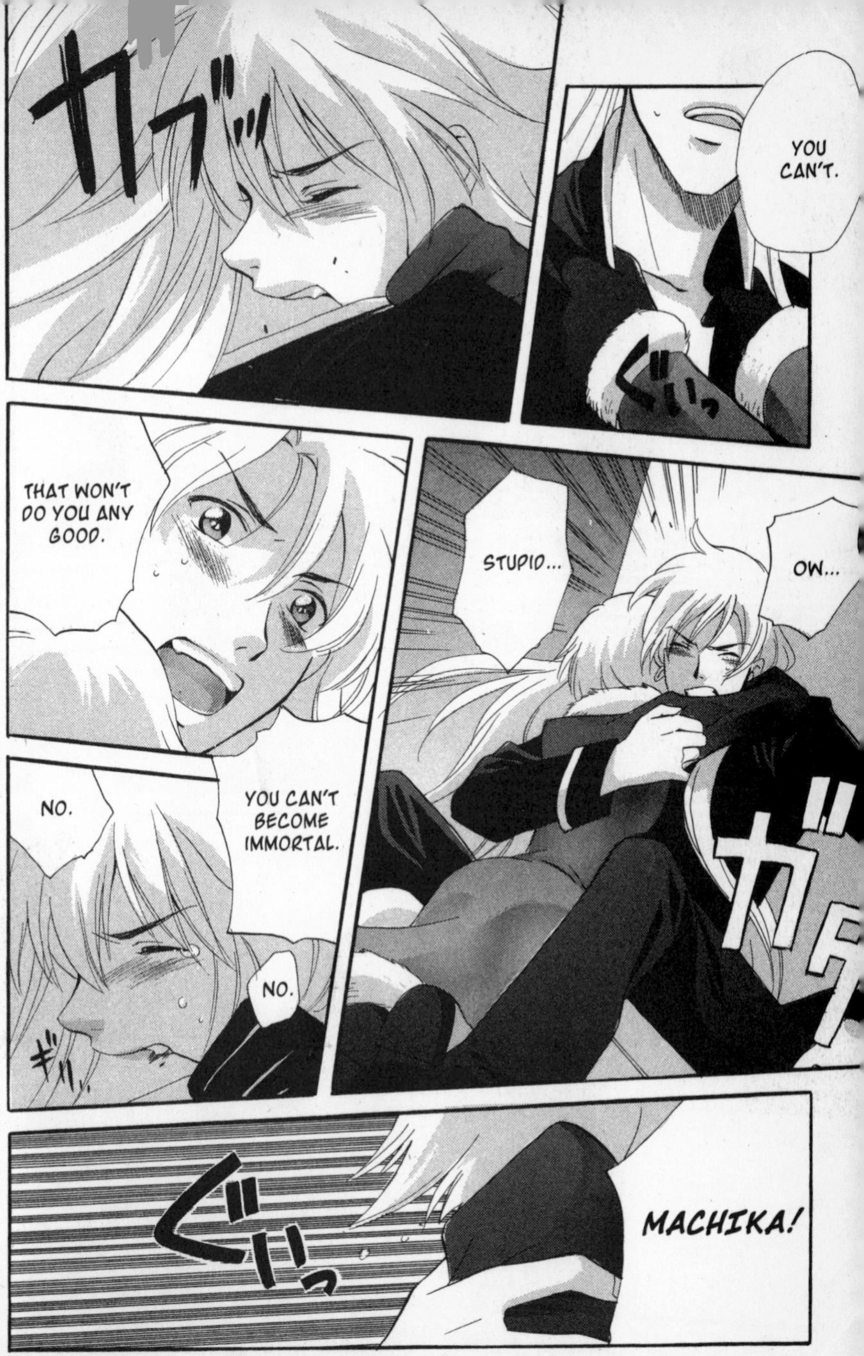
YOU CAN'T.
OW...
STUPID...
THAT WON'T DO YOU ANY GOOD.
YOU CAN'T BECOME IMMORTAL.
NO.
NO.
MACHIKA!

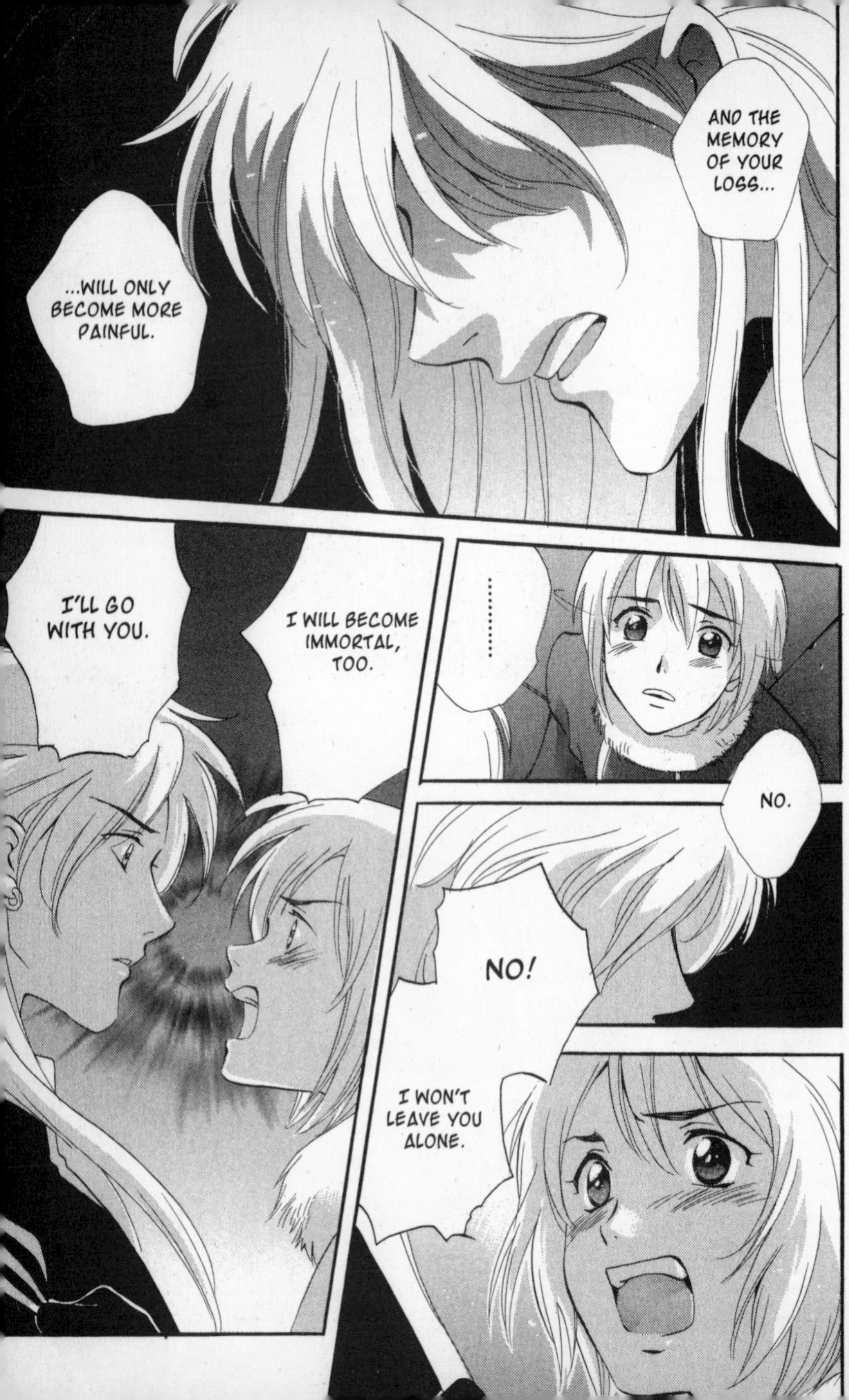
AND THE MEMORY OF YOUR LOSS...
...WILL ONLY BECOME MORE PAINFUL.
......
NO.
NO!
I WON'T LEAVE YOU ALONE.
I'LL GO WITH YOU.
I WILL BECOME IMMORTAL, TOO.

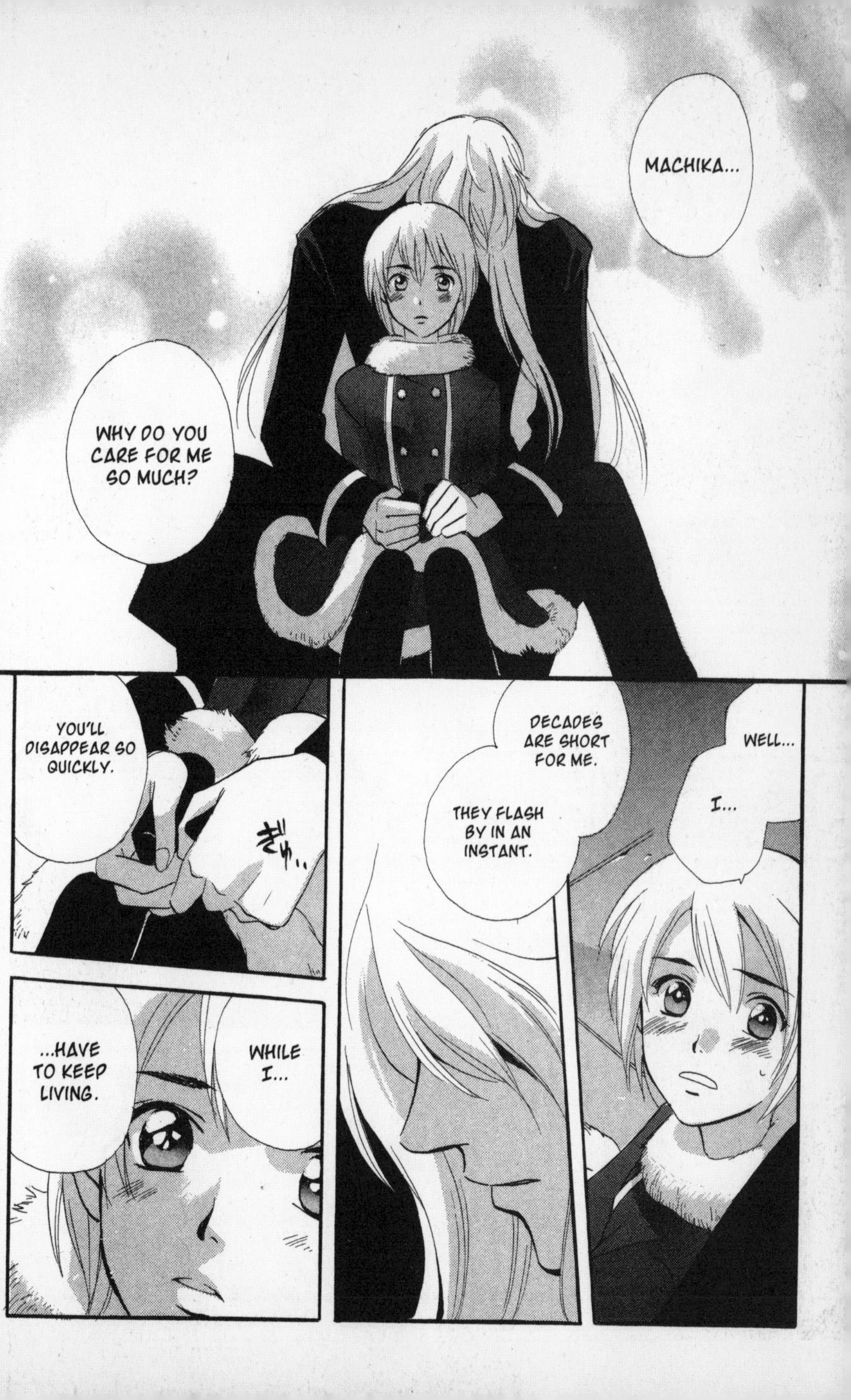
MACHIKA...
WHY DO YOU CARE FOR ME SO MUCH?
WELL...
I...
DECADES ARE SHORT FOR ME.
THEY FLASH BY IN AN INSTANT.
YOU'LL DISAPPEAR SO QUICKLY.
ぎゅ..
WHILE I...
...HAVE TO KEEP LIVING.

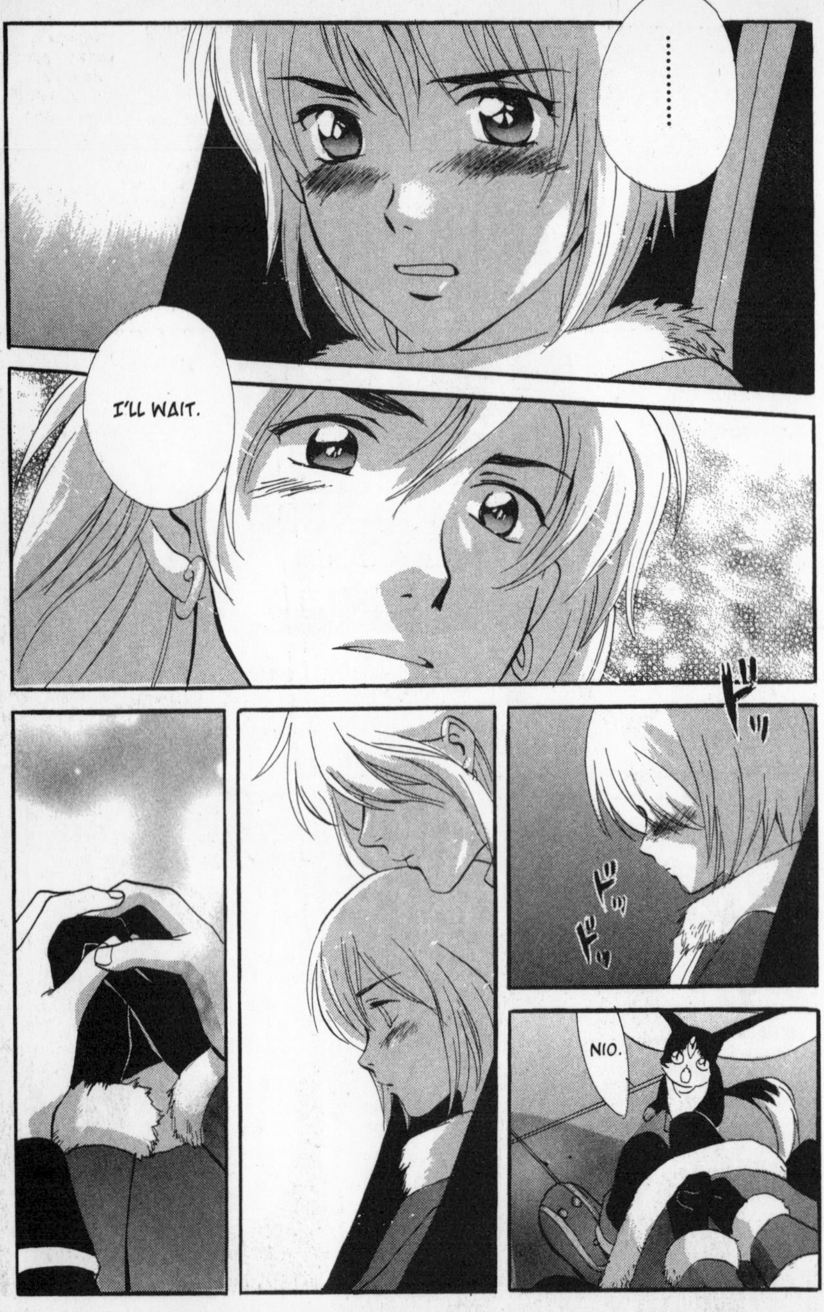
......
I'LL WAIT.
NIO.

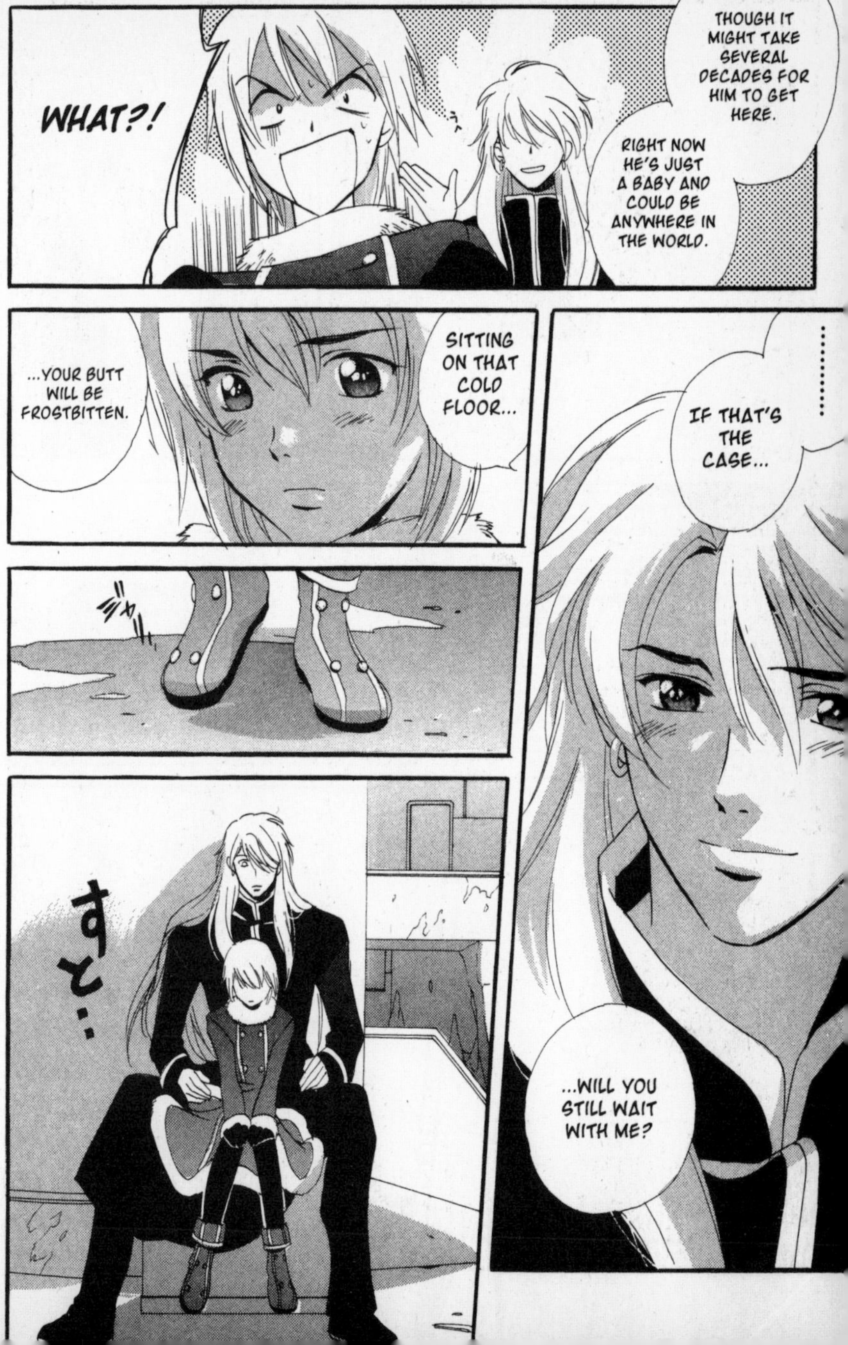
THOUGH IT MIGHT TAKE SEVERAL DECADES FOR HIM TO GET HERE.
RIGHT NOW HE'S JUST A BABY AND COULD BE ANYWHERE IN THE WORLD.
WHAT?!
......
IF THAT'S THE CASE...
...WILL YOU STILL WAIT WITH ME?
SITTING ON THAT COLD FLOOR...
...YOUR BUTT WILL BE FROSTBITTEN.
すと..

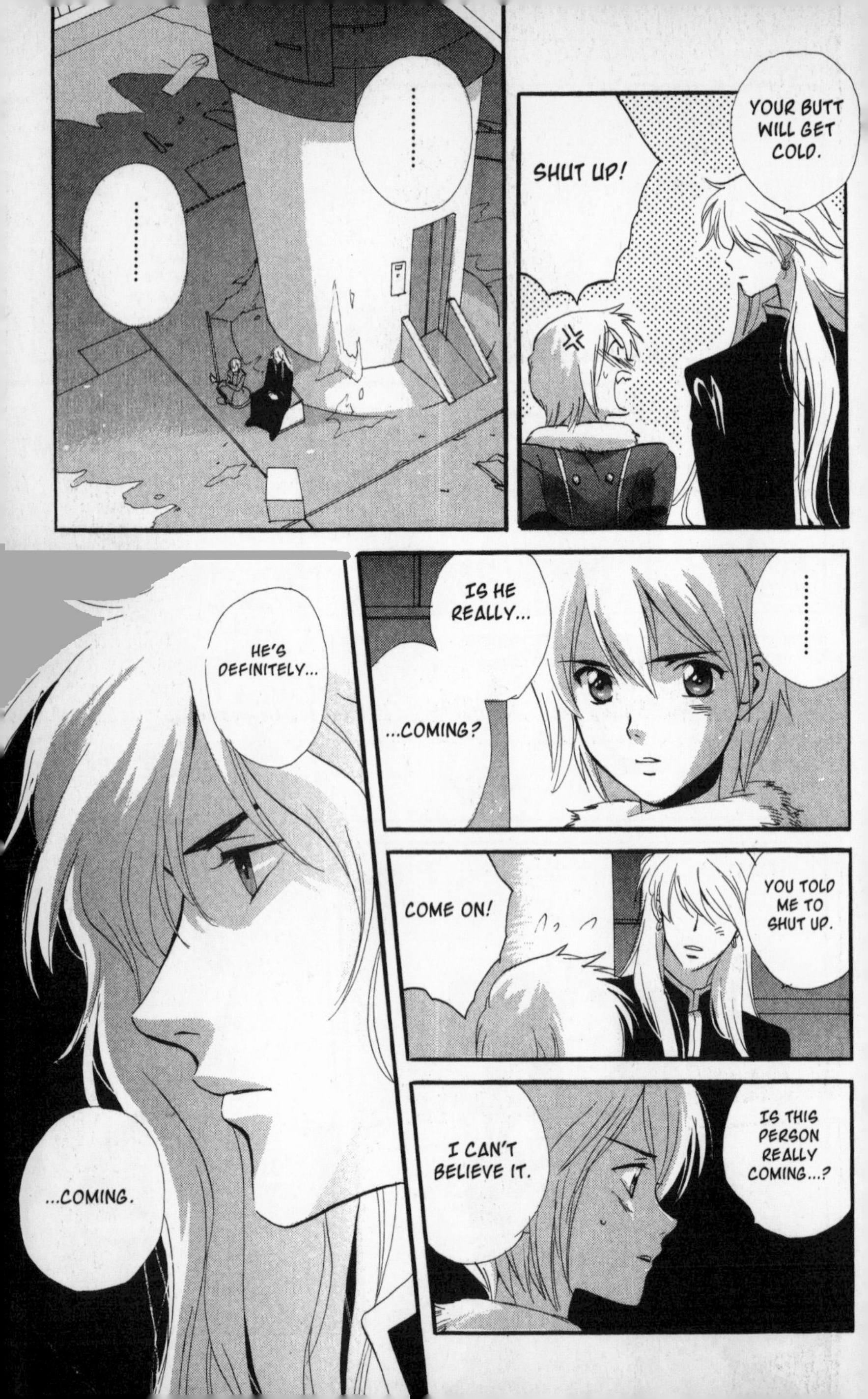
YOUR BUTT WILL GET COLD.
SHUT UP!
......
......
......
IS HE REALLY...
...COMING?
YOU TOLD ME TO SHUT UP.
COME ON!
IS THIS PERSON REALLY COMING...?
I CAN'T BELIEVE IT.
HE'S DEFINITELY...
...COMING.

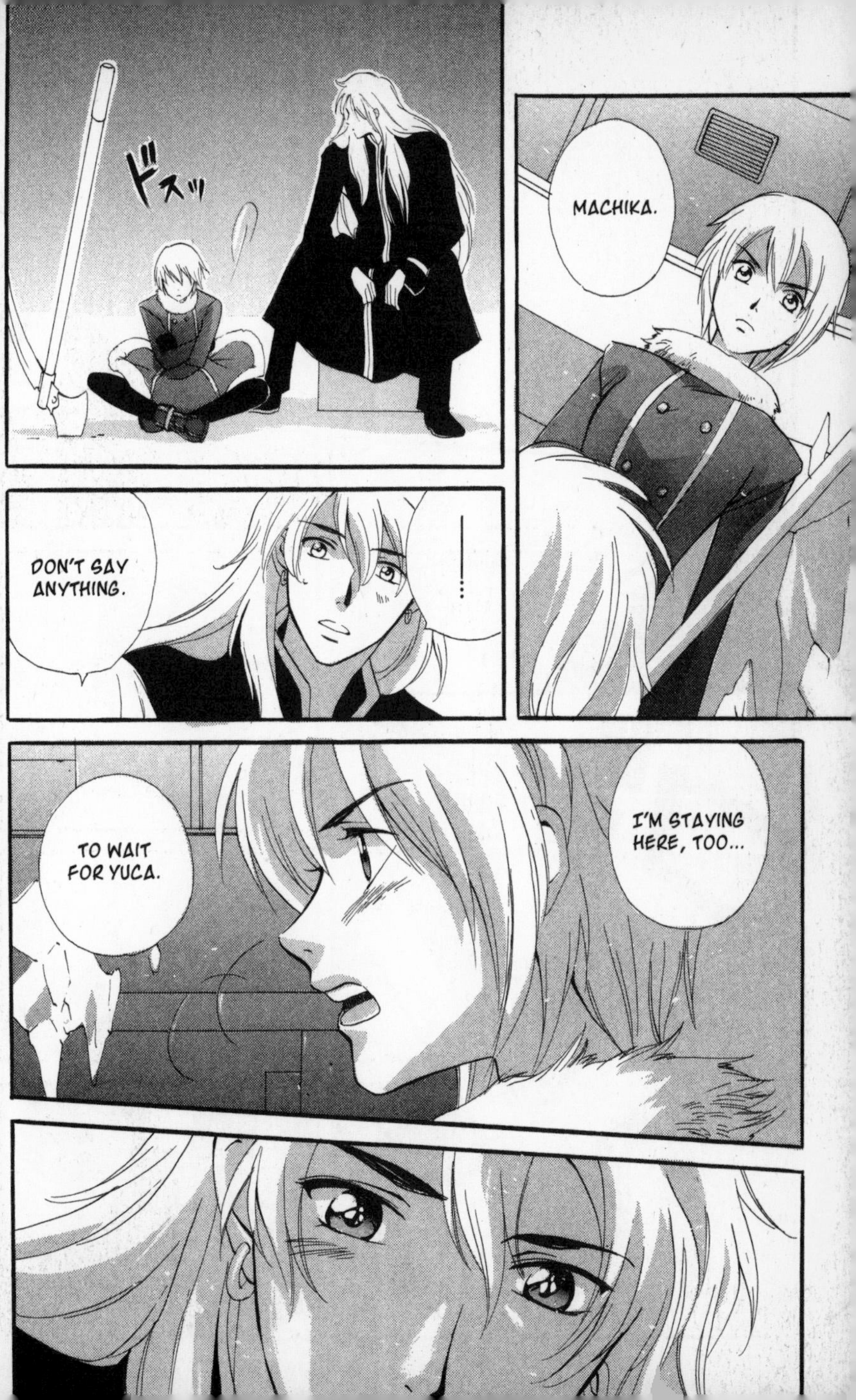
ドスッ
MACHIKA.
……!
DON'T SAY ANYTHING.
I'M STAYING HERE, TOO...
TO WAIT FOR YUCA.

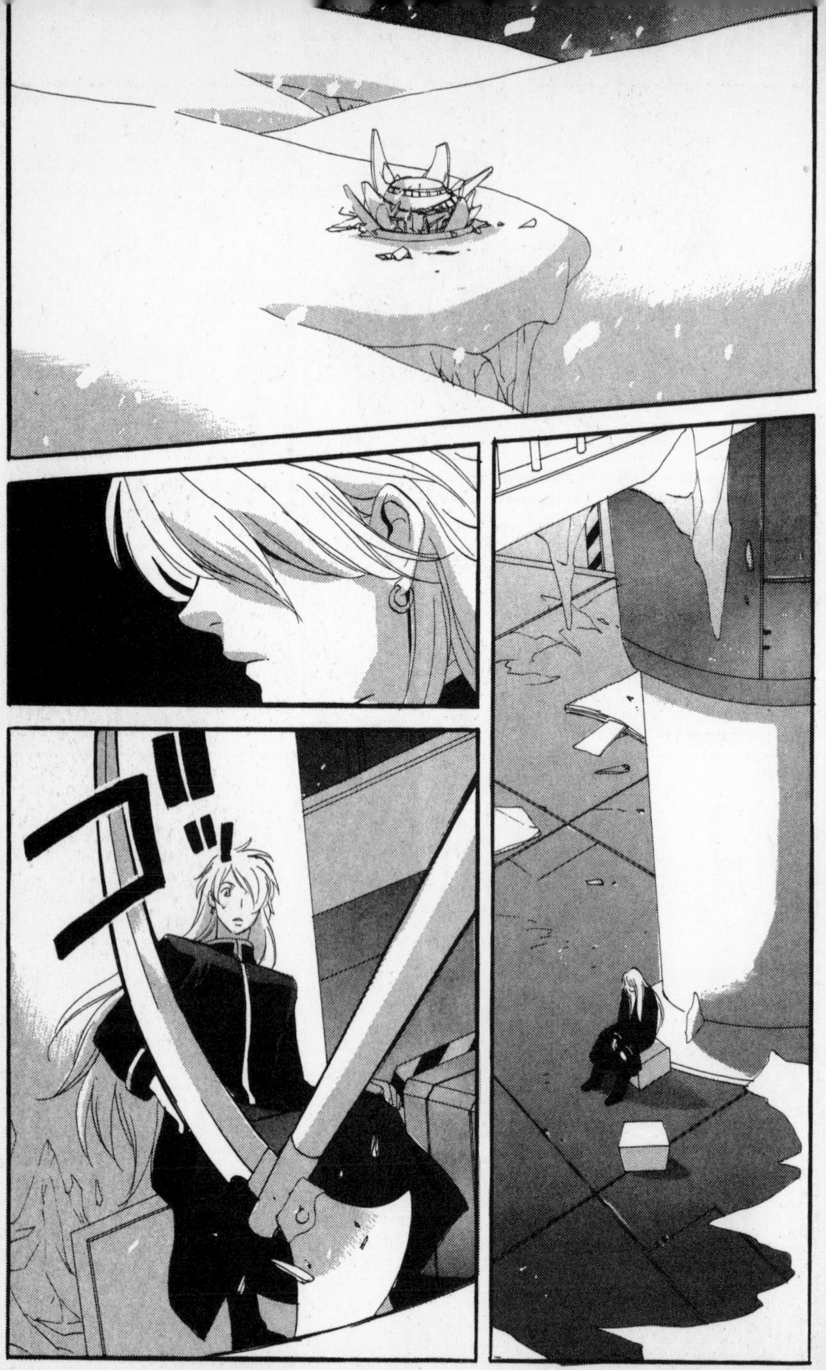

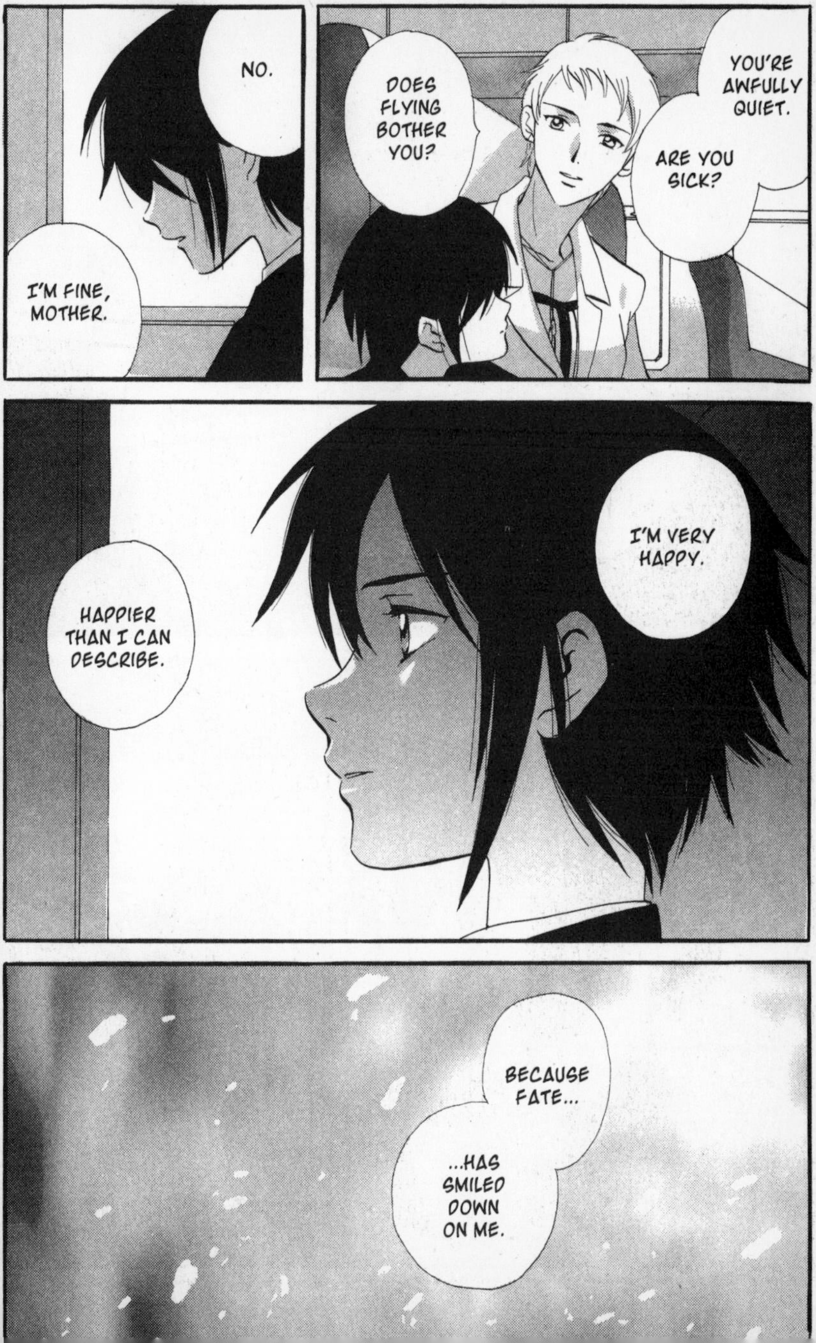
YOU'RE AWFULLY QUIET.
ARE YOU SICK?
DOES FLYING BOTHER YOU?
NO.
I'M FINE, MOTHER.
I'M VERY HAPPY.
HAPPIER THAN I CAN DESCRIBE.
BECAUSE FATE...
...HAS SMILED DOWN ON ME.

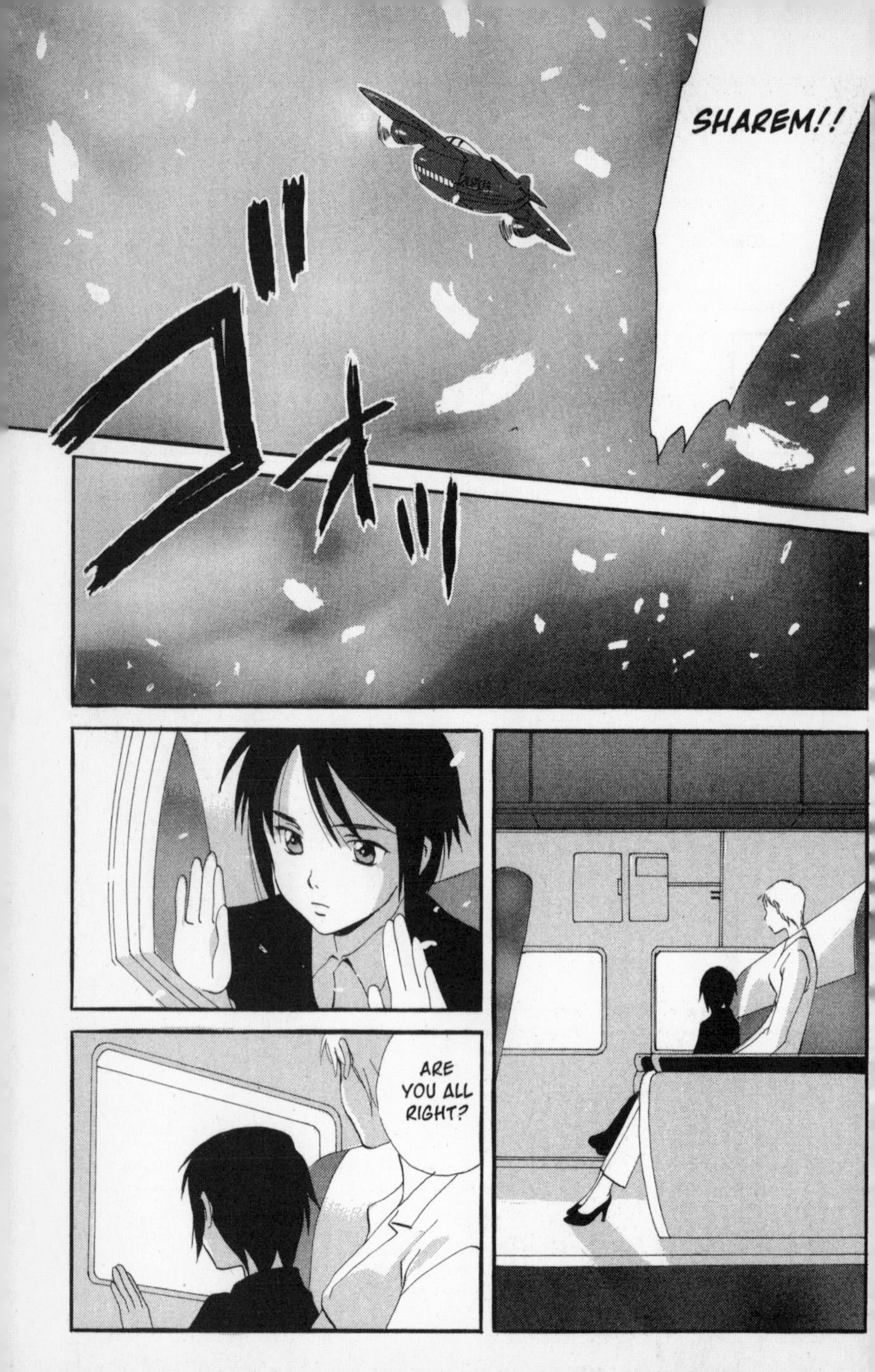

SHAREM!!
ゴオッ
ARE YOU ALL RIGHT?

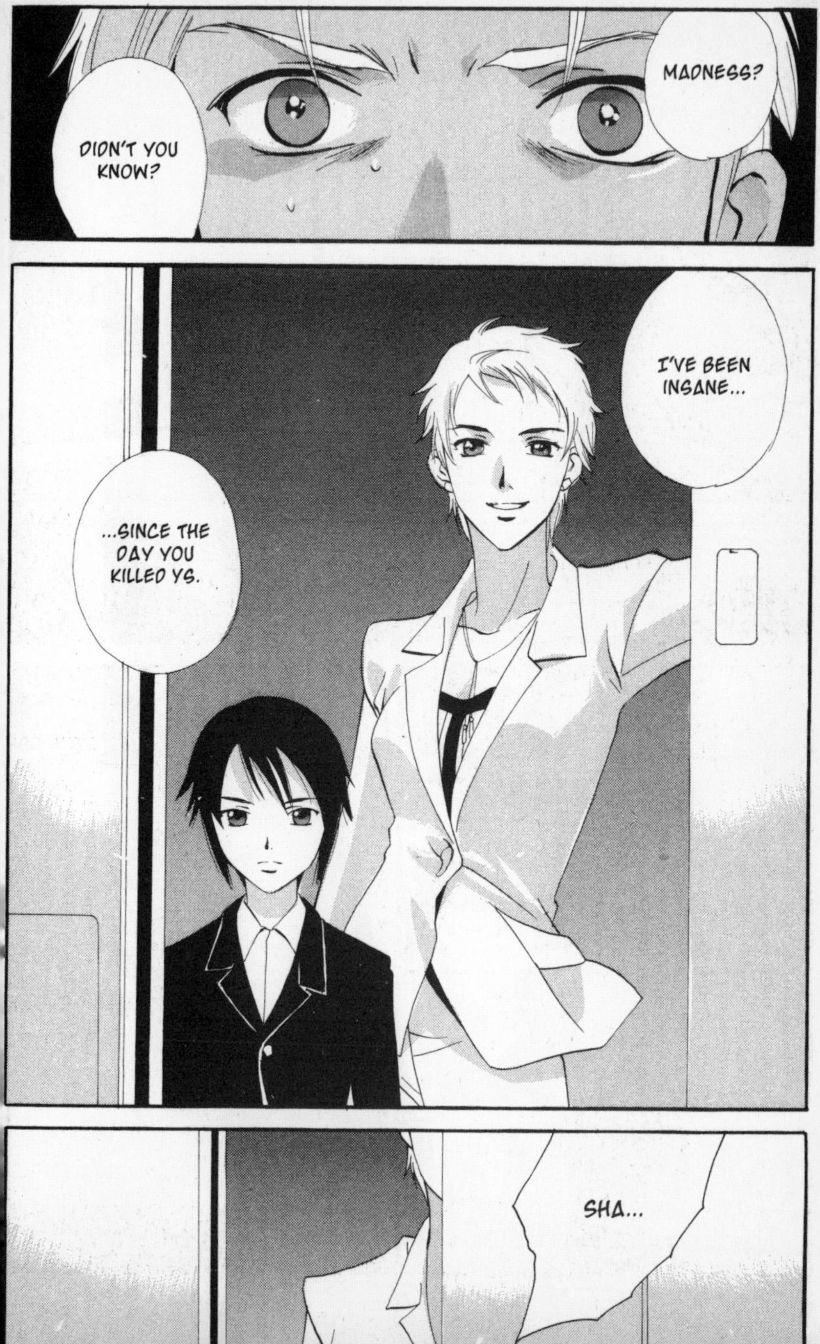
MADNESS?
DIDN'T YOU KNOW?
I'VE BEEN INSANE...
...SINCE THE DAY YOU KILLED YS.
SHA...

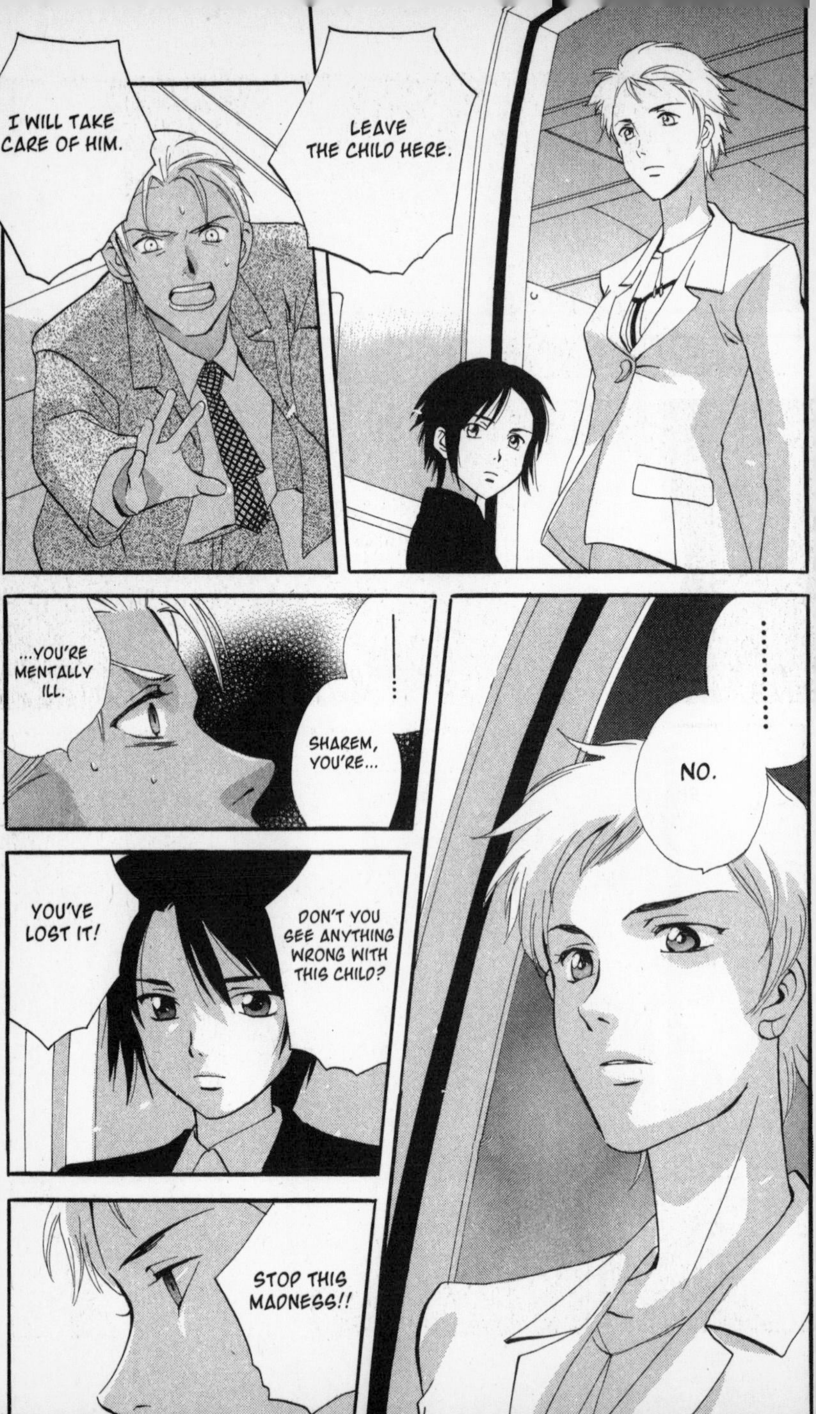
LEAVE THE CHILD HERE.
I WILL TAKE CARE OF HIM.
......
NO.
......!
SHAREM, YOU'RE...
...YOU'RE MENTALLY ILL.
DON'T YOU SEE ANYTHING WRONG WITH THIS CHILD?
YOU'VE LOST IT!
STOP THIS MADNESS!!

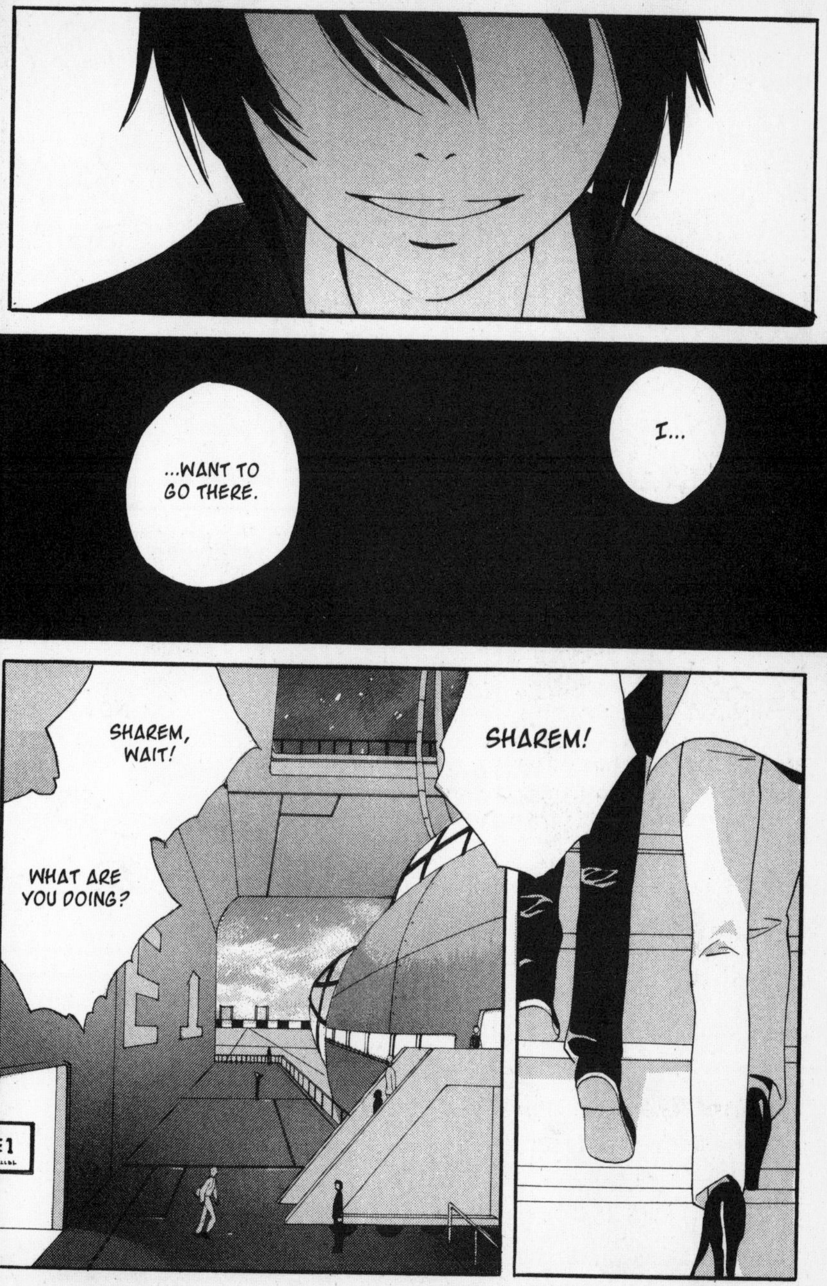
I...
...WANT TO GO THERE.
SHAREM!
SHAREM, WAIT!
WHAT ARE YOU DOING?

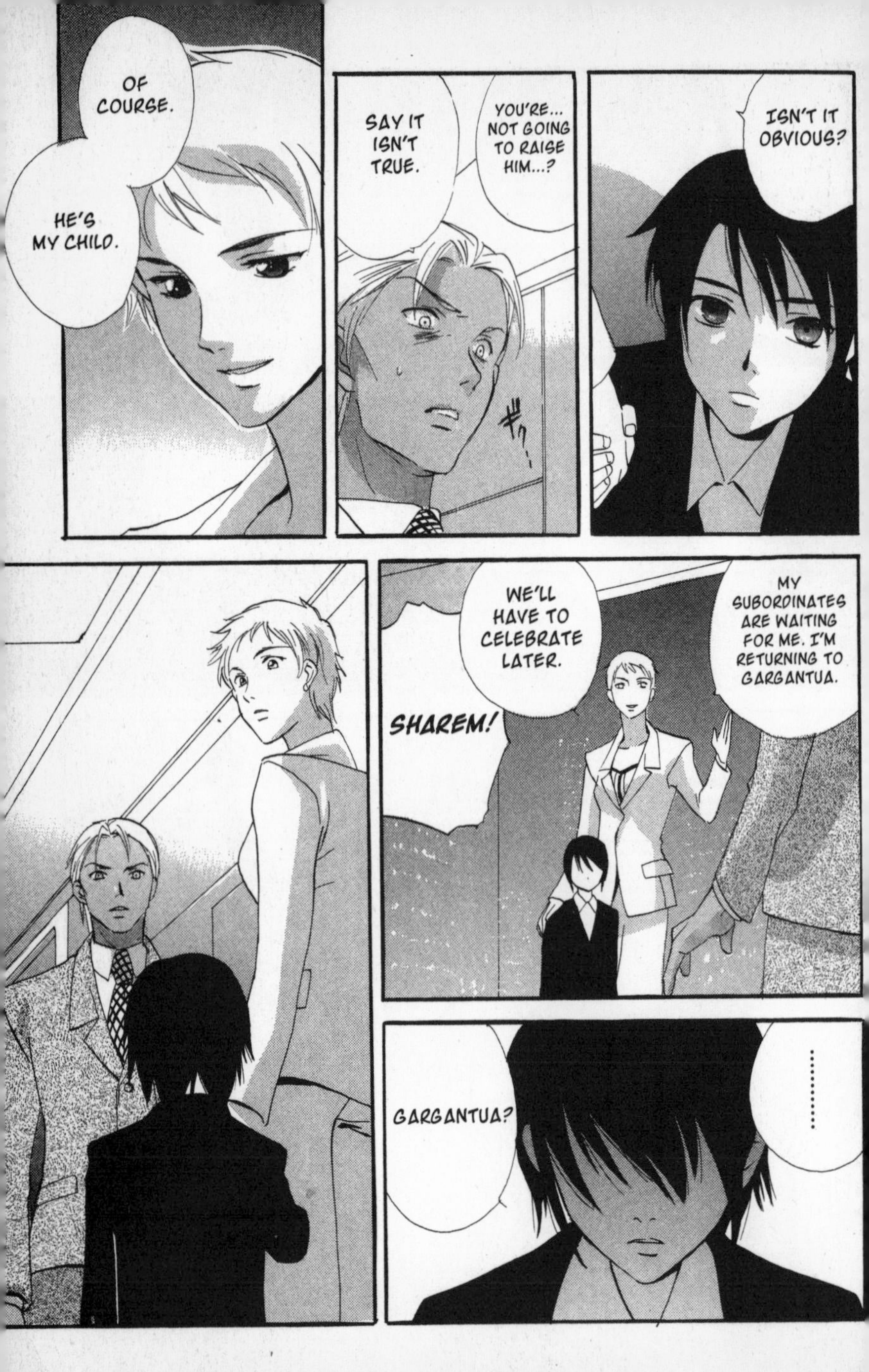
ISN'T IT OBVIOUS?
YOU'RE... NOT GOING TO RAISE HIM...?
SAY IT ISN'T TRUE.
OF COURSE.
HE'S MY CHILD.
MY SUBORDINATES ARE WAITING FOR ME. I'M RETURNING TO GARGANTUA.
WE'LL HAVE TO CELEBRATE LATER.
SHAREM!
......
GARGANTUA?

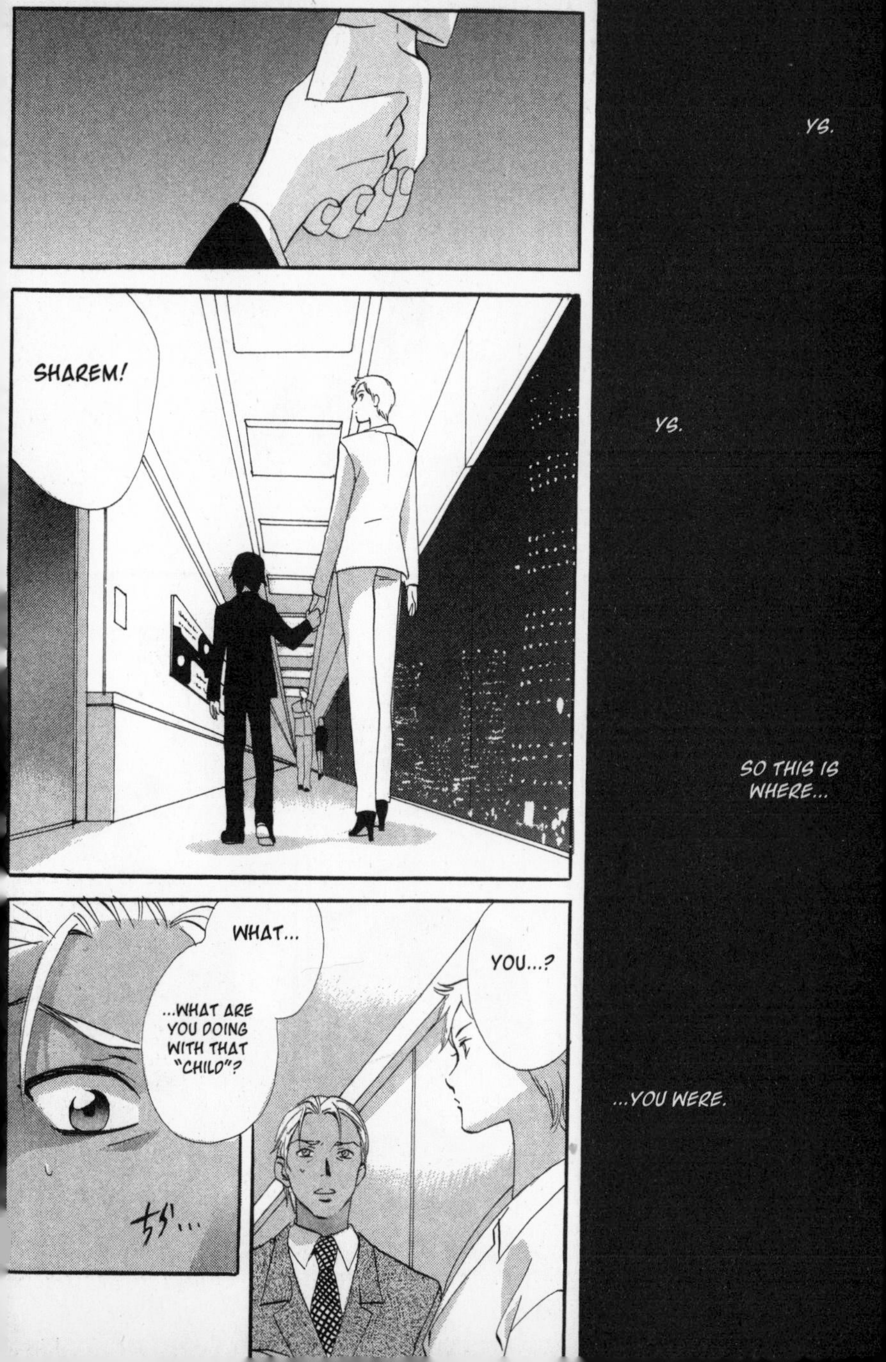
YS.
YS.
SHAREM!
SO THIS IS WHERE...
YOU...?
WHAT...
...WHAT ARE YOU DOING WITH THAT "CHILD"?
...YOU WERE.
ちが…

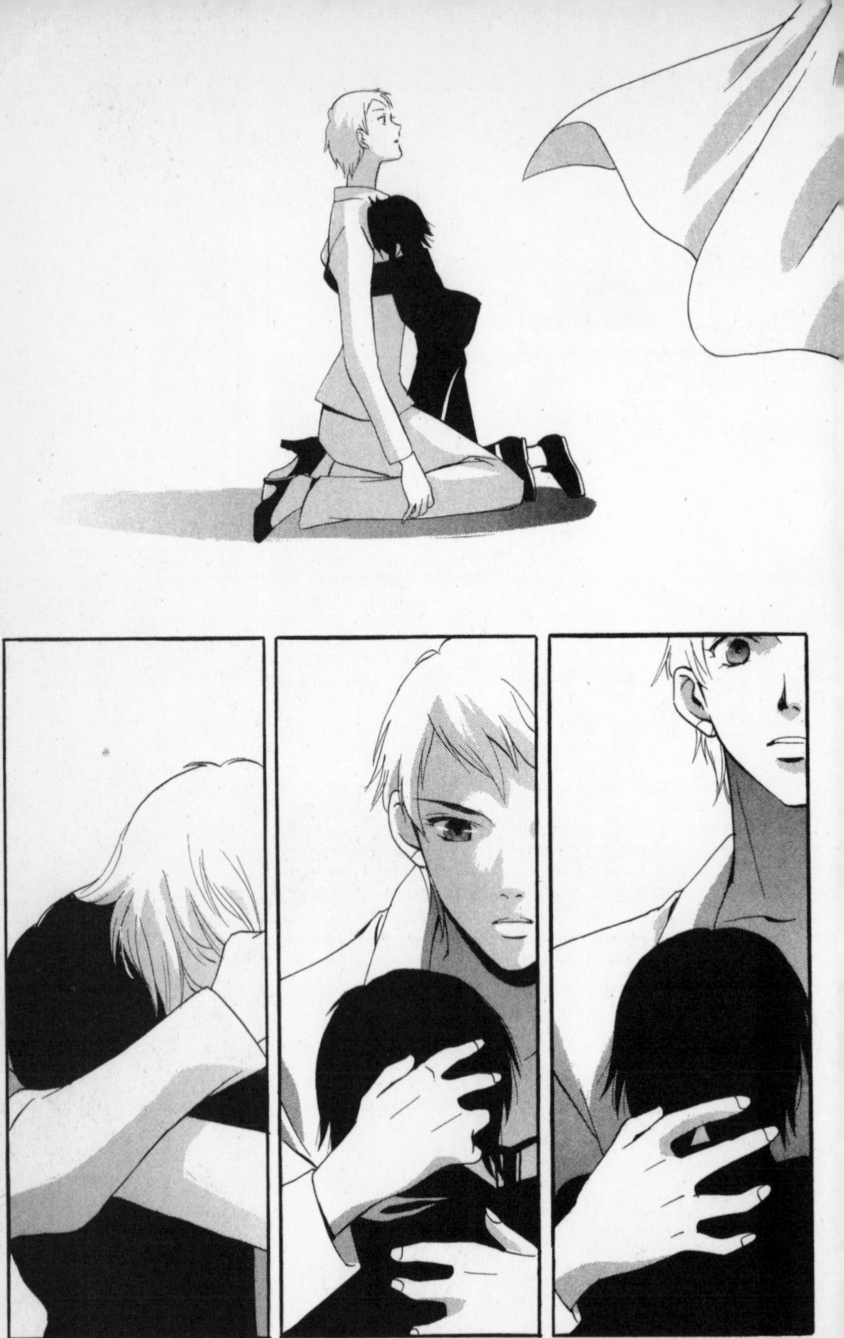

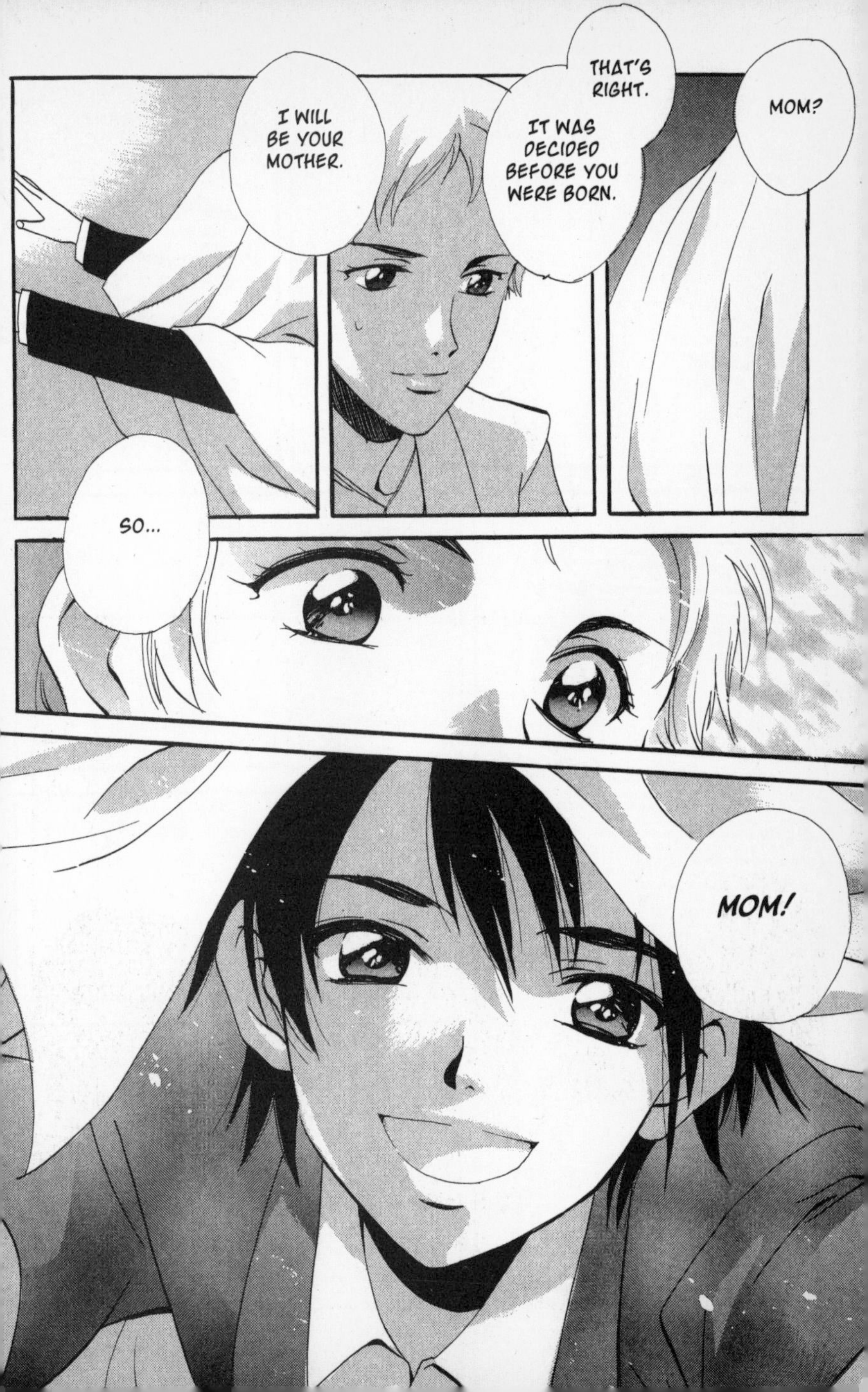
MOM?
THAT'S RIGHT.
IT WAS DECIDED BEFORE YOU WERE BORN.
I WILL BE YOUR MOTHER.
SO...
MOM!

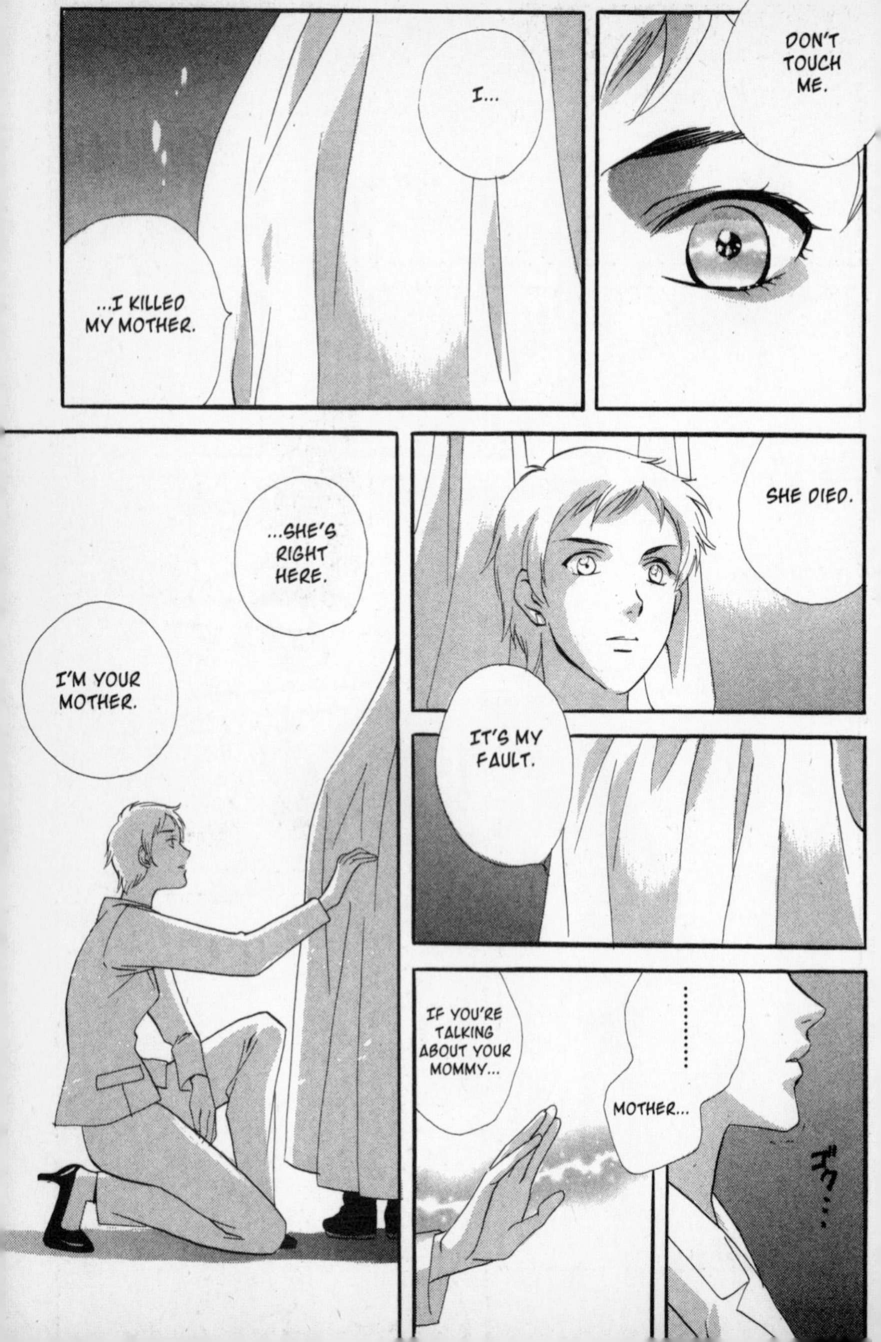
DON'T TOUCH ME.
I...
...I KILLED MY MOTHER.
SHE DIED.
IT'S MY FAULT.
....
MOTHER...
ギク…
IF YOU'RE TALKING ABOUT YOUR MOMMY...
...SHE'S RIGHT HERE.
I'M YOUR MOTHER.

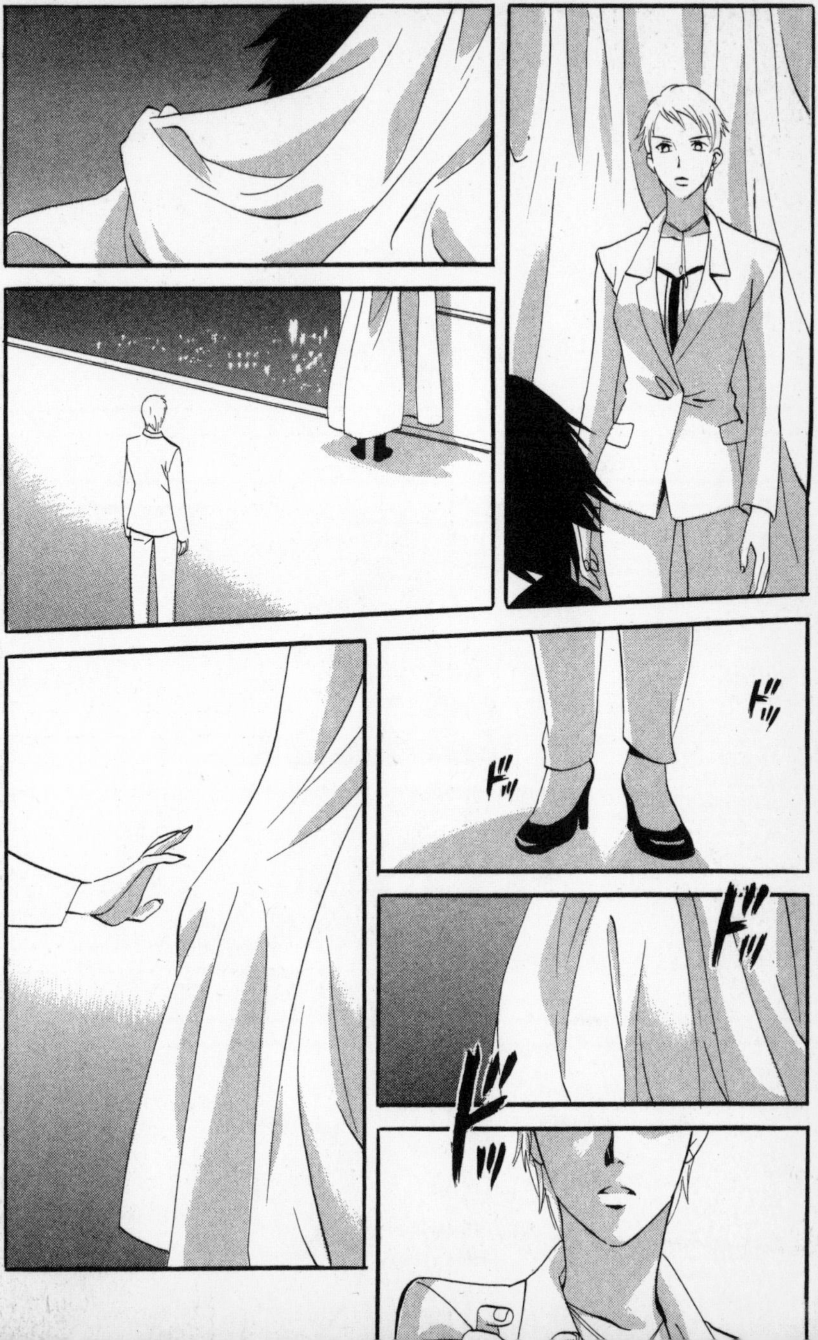
ドッ
ドッ
ドッ
ドッ

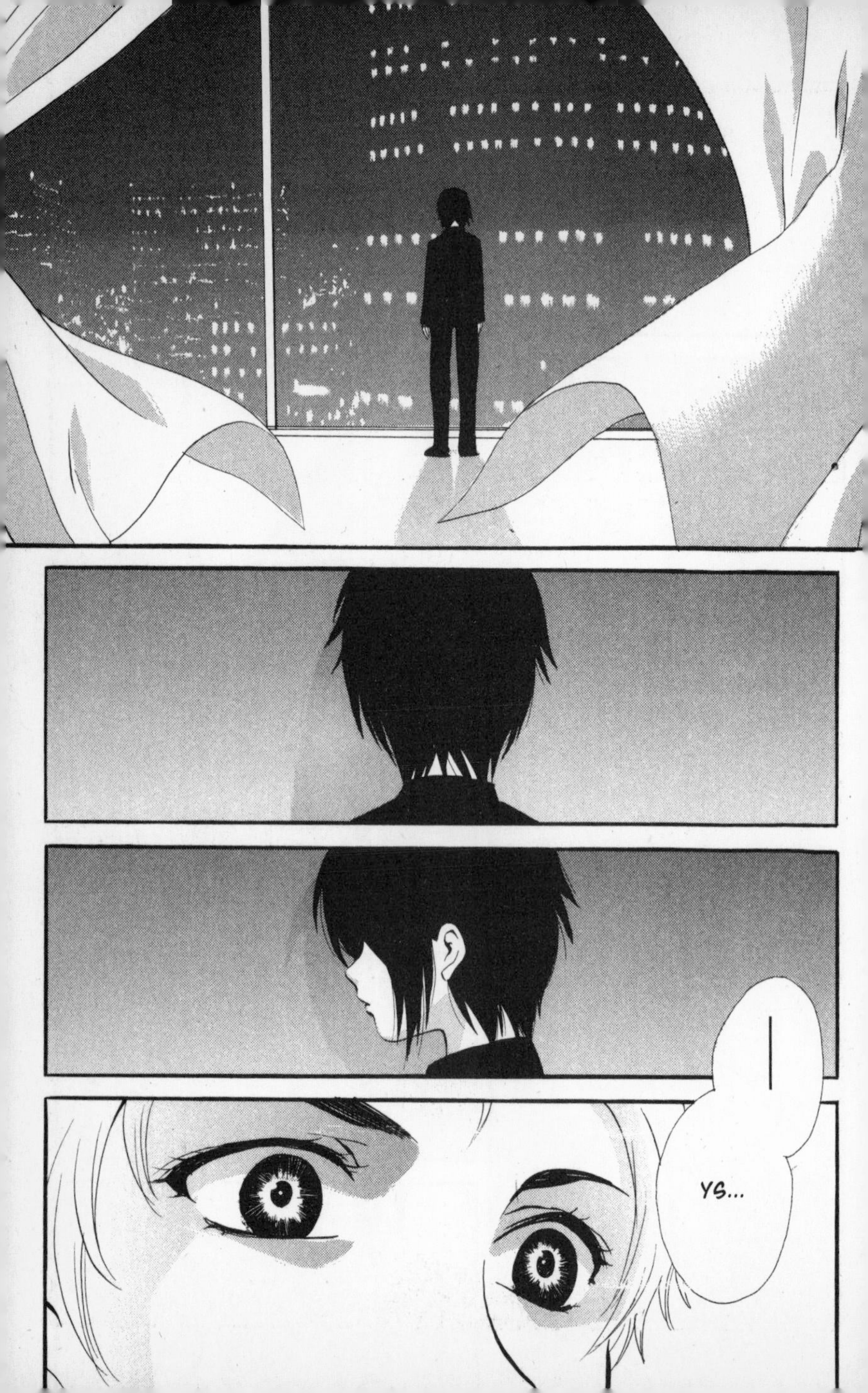
YS...

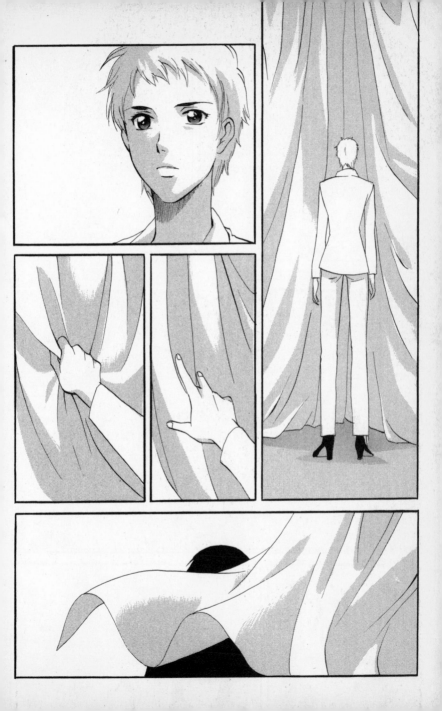

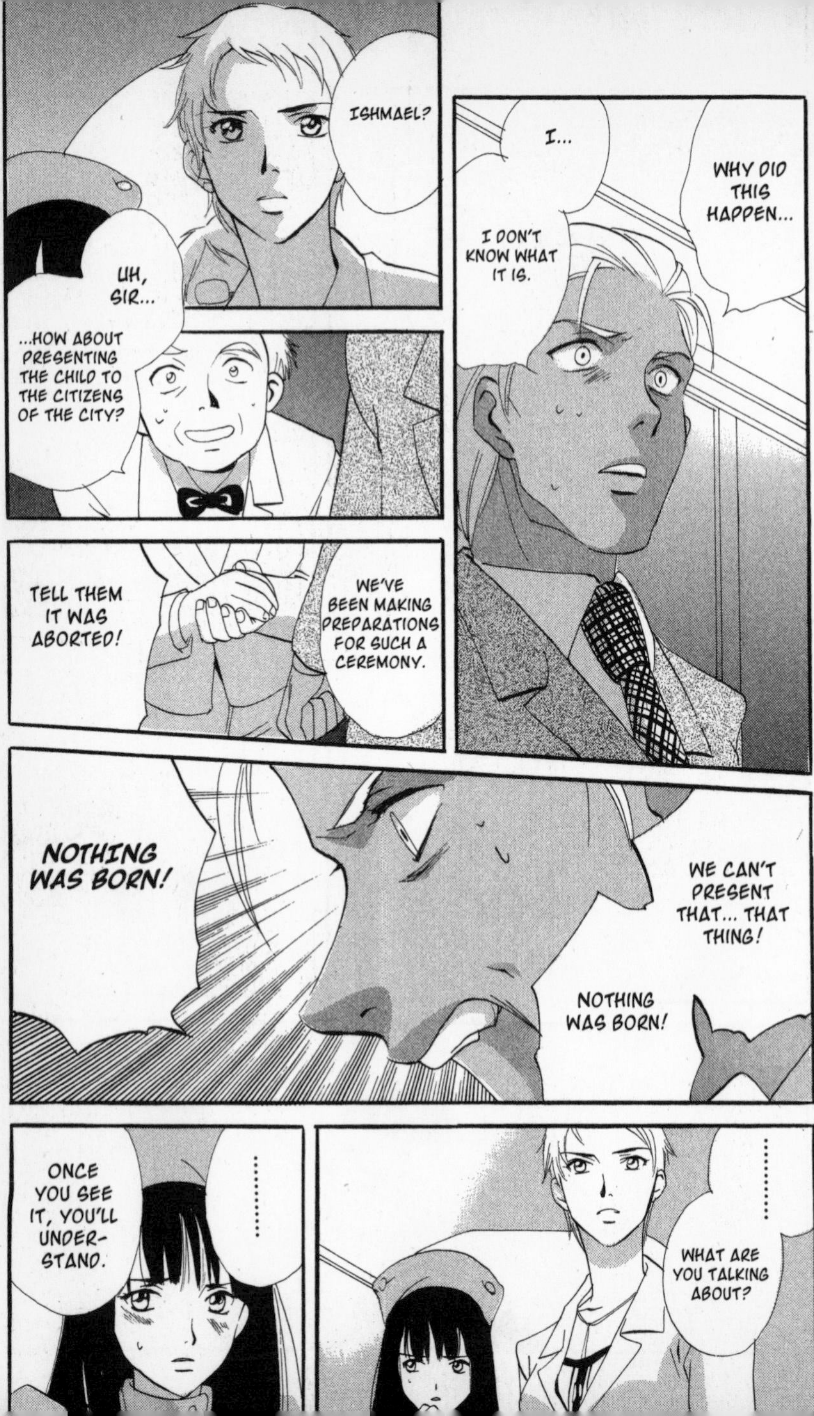
ISHMAEL?
UH, SIR...
...HOW ABOUT PRESENTING THE CHILD TO THE CITIZENS OF THE CITY?
WE'VE BEEN MAKING PREPARATIONS FOR SUCH A CEREMONY.
TELL THEM IT WAS ABORTED!
I...
I DON'T KNOW WHAT IT IS.
WHY DID THIS HAPPEN...
WE CAN'T PRESENT THAT... THAT THING!
NOTHING WAS BORN!
NOTHING WAS BORN!
......
WHAT ARE YOU TALKING ABOUT?
......
ONCE YOU SEE IT, YOU'LL UNDER-STAND.

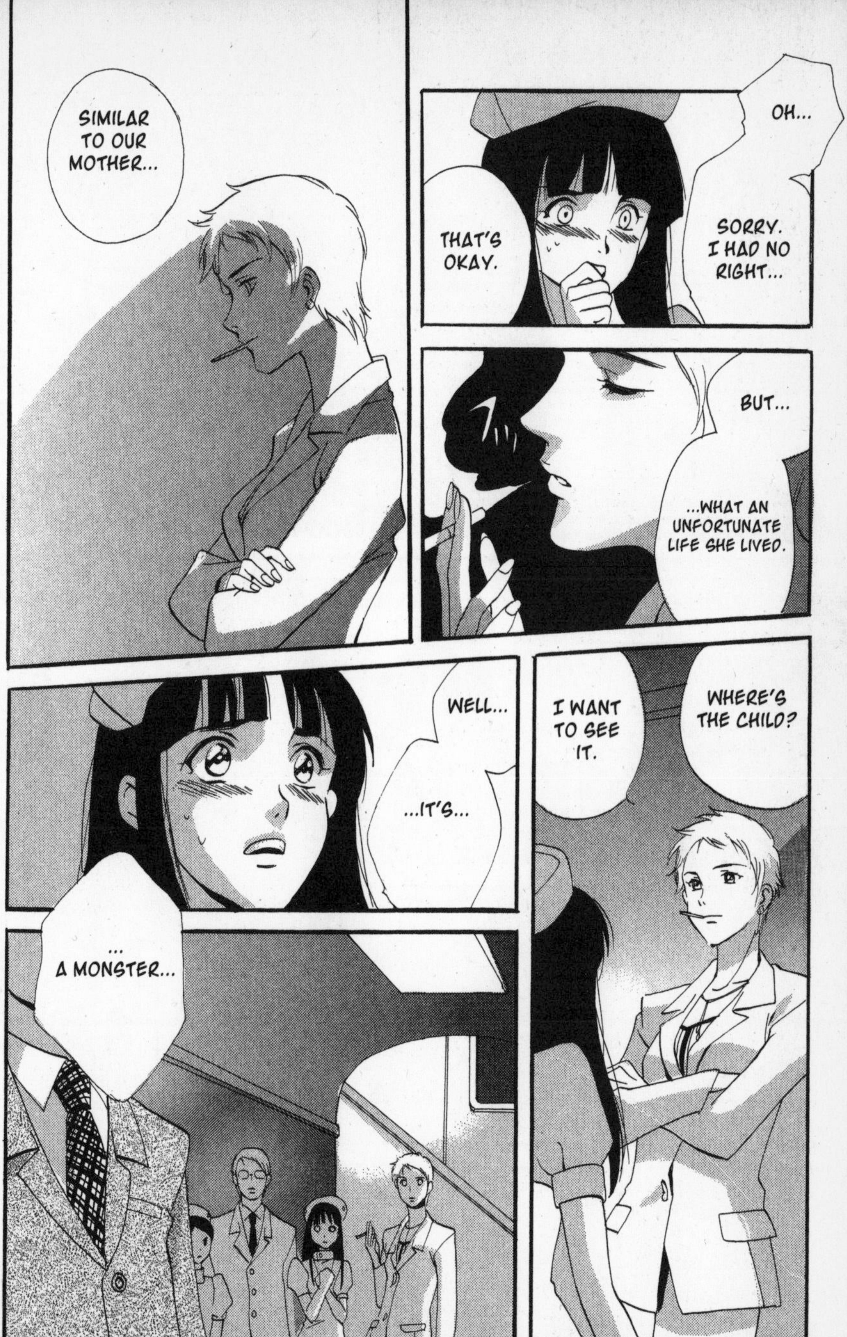
SIMILAR TO OUR MOTHER...
OH...
SORRY. I HAD NO RIGHT...
THAT'S OKAY.
BUT...
...WHAT AN UNFORTUNATE LIFE SHE LIVED.
WHERE'S THE CHILD?
I WANT TO SEE IT.
WELL...
...IT'S...
... A MONSTER...

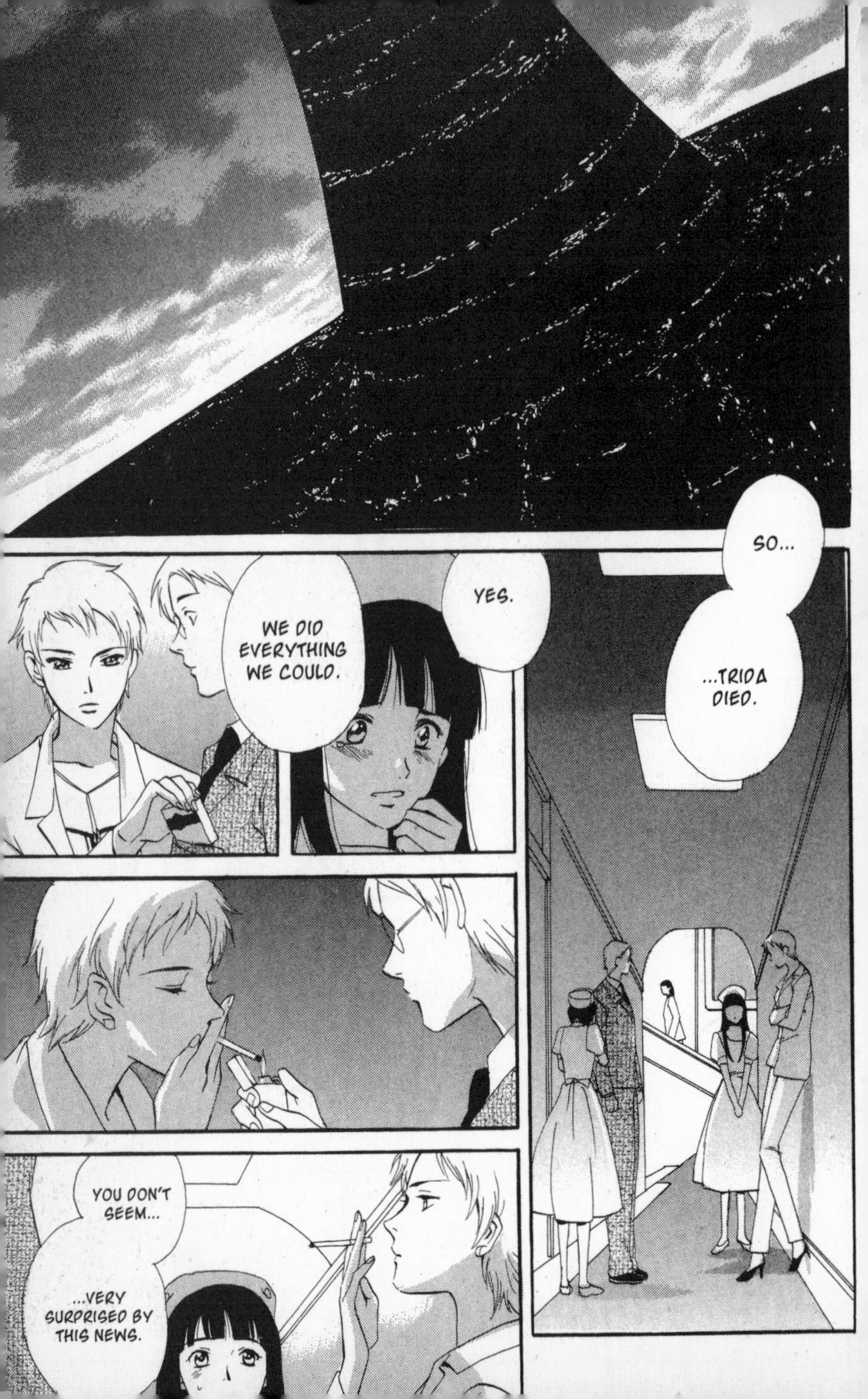
SO...
...TRIDA DIED.
YES.
WE DID EVERYTHING WE COULD.
YOU DON'T SEEM...
...VERY SURPRISED BY THIS NEWS.

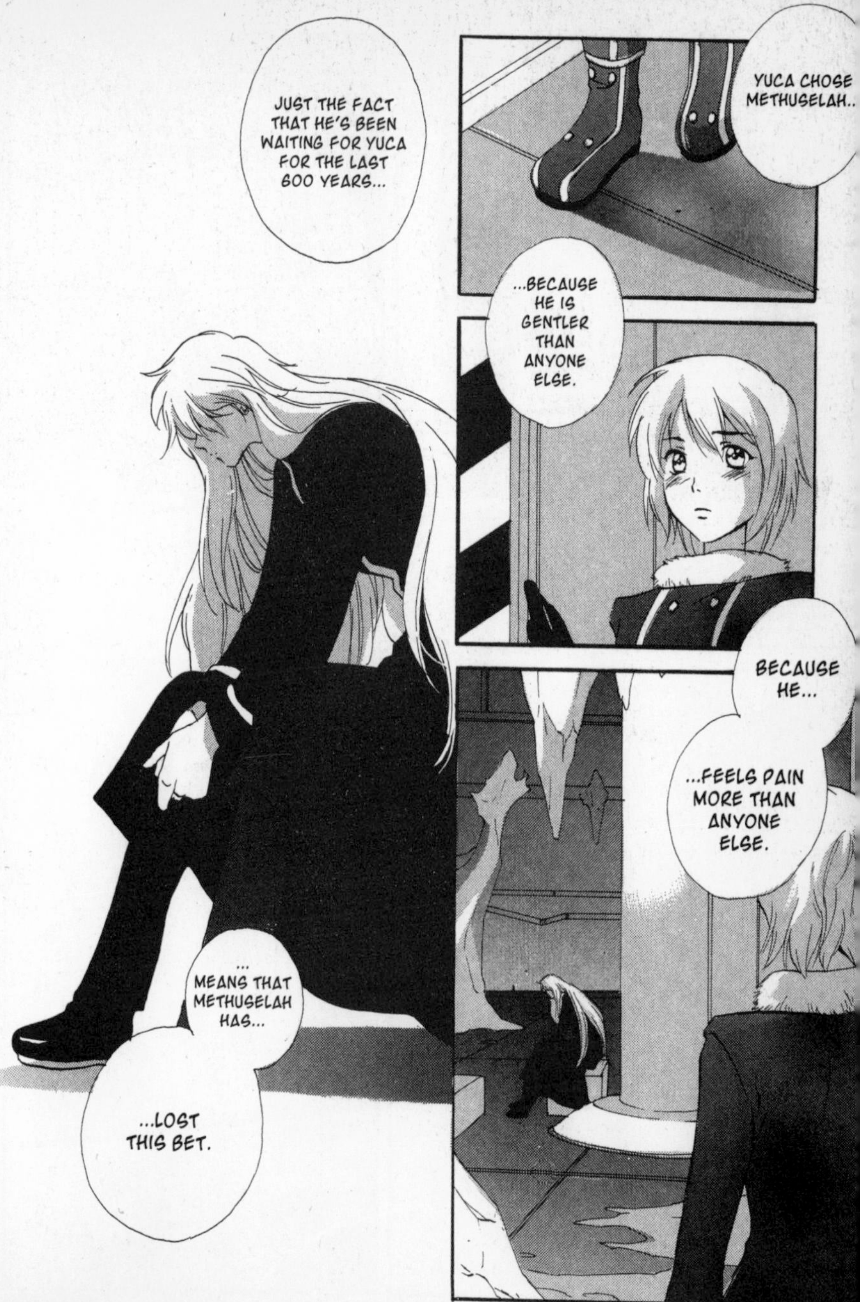
YUCA CHOSE METHUSELAH..
...BECAUSE HE IS GENTLER THAN ANYONE ELSE.
BECAUSE HE...
...FEELS PAIN MORE THAN ANYONE ELSE.
JUST THE FACT THAT HE'S BEEN WAITING FOR YUCA FOR THE LAST 600 YEARS...
... MEANS THAT METHUSELAH HAS...
...LOST THIS BET.

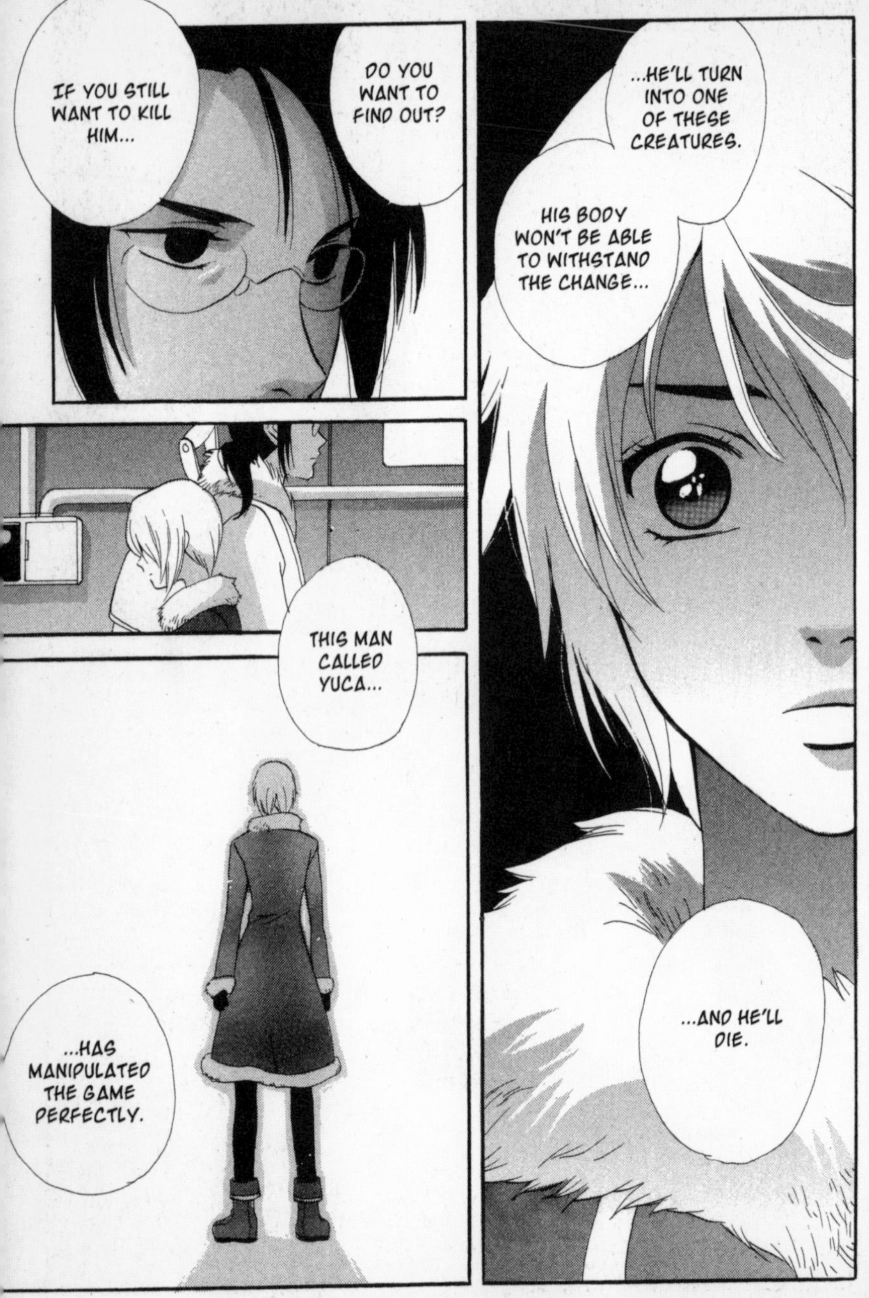
...HE'LL TURN INTO ONE OF THESE CREATURES.
HIS BODY WON'T BE ABLE TO WITHSTAND THE CHANGE...
...AND HE'LL DIE.
DO YOU WANT TO FIND OUT?
IF YOU STILL WANT TO KILL HIM...
THIS MAN CALLED YUCA...
...HAS MANIPULATED THE GAME PERFECTLY.

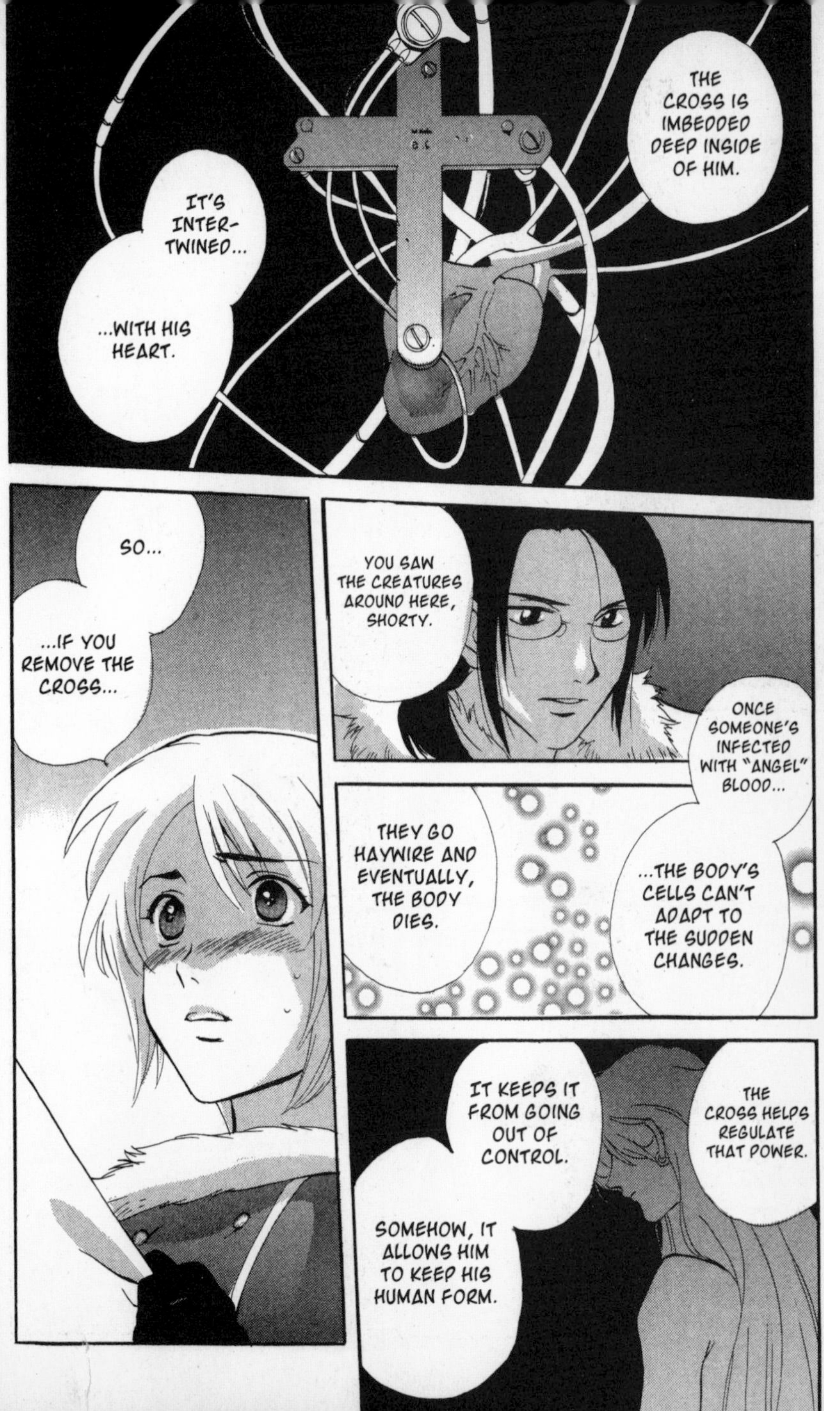
THE CROSS IS IMBEDDED DEEP INSIDE OF HIM.
IT'S INTER-TWINED...
...WITH HIS HEART.
SO...
...IF YOU REMOVE THE CROSS...
YOU SAW THE CREATURES AROUND HERE, SHORTY.
ONCE SOMEONE'S INFECTED WITH "ANGEL" BLOOD...
...THE BODY'S CELLS CAN'T ADAPT TO THE SUDDEN CHANGES.
THEY GO HAYWIRE AND EVENTUALLY, THE BODY DIES.
THE CROSS HELPS REGULATE THAT POWER.
IT KEEPS IT FROM GOING OUT OF CONTROL.
SOMEHOW, IT ALLOWS HIM TO KEEP HIS HUMAN FORM.

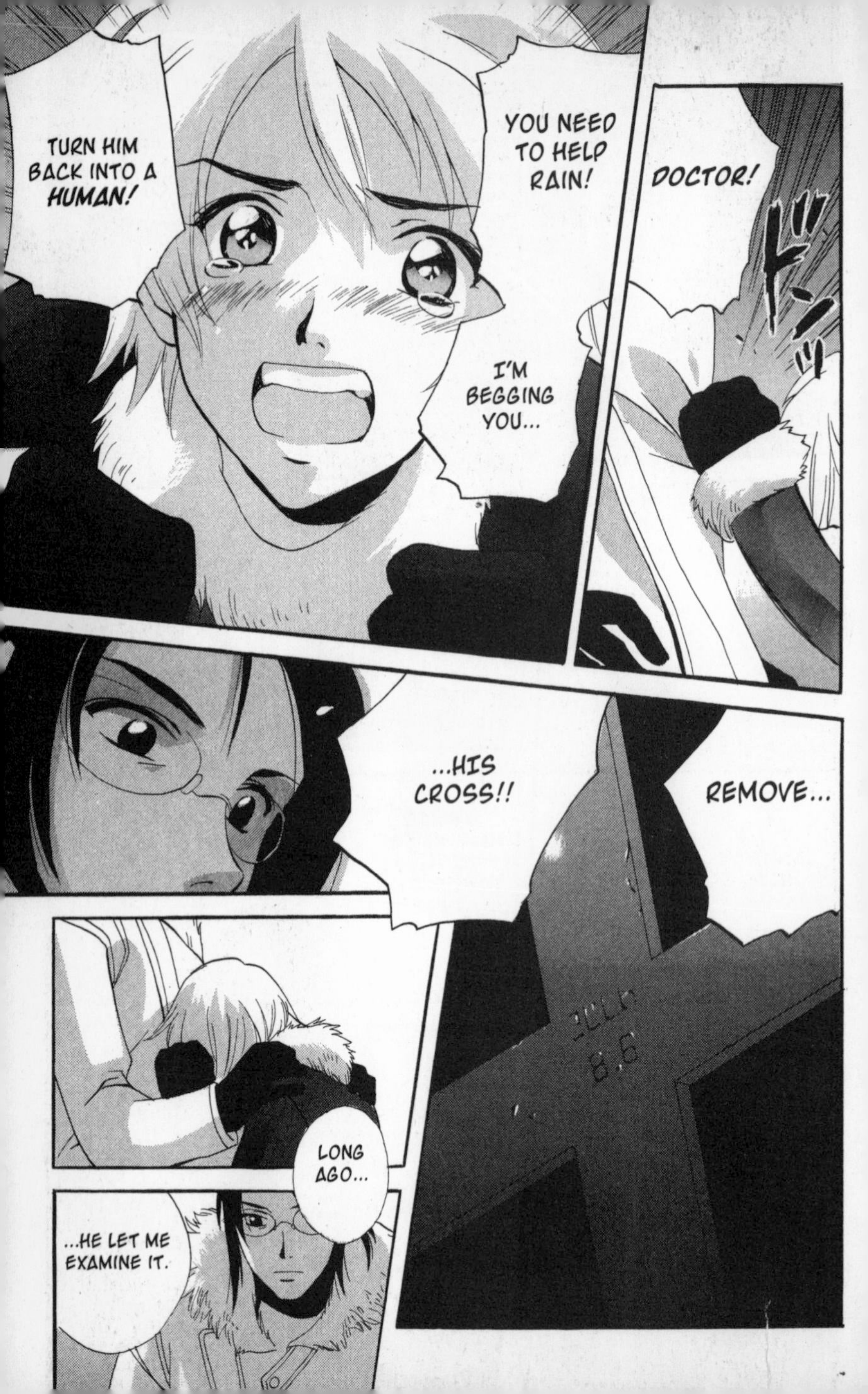
DOCTOR!
YOU NEED TO HELP RAIN!
TURN HIM BACK INTO A HUMAN!
I'M BEGGING YOU...
REMOVE...
...HIS CROSS!!
LONG AGO...
...HE LET ME EXAMINE IT.

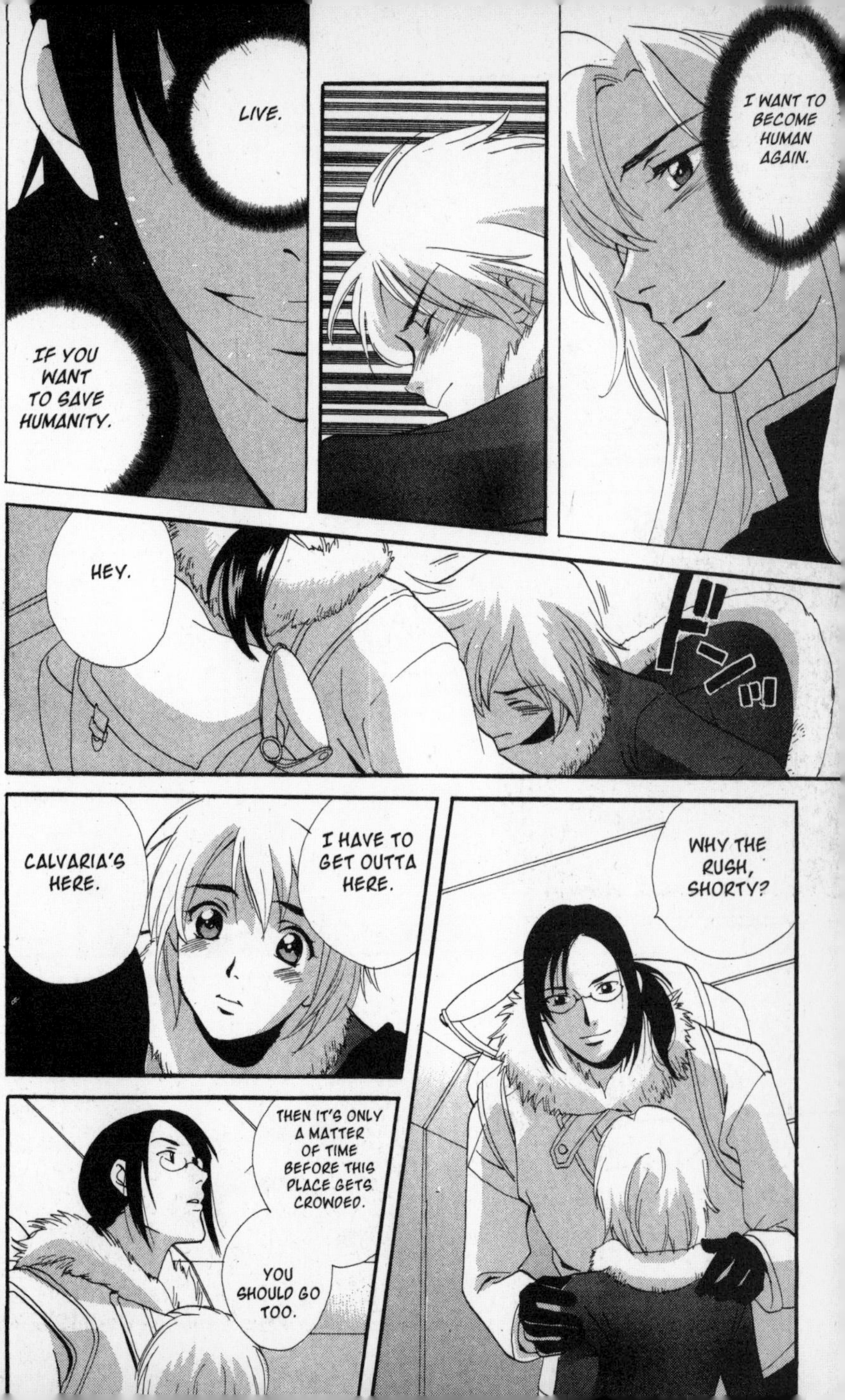

I WANT TO BECOME HUMAN AGAIN.
LIVE.
IF YOU WANT TO SAVE HUMANITY.
HEY.
I HAVE TO GET OUTTA HERE.
CALVARIA'S HERE.
WHY THE RUSH, SHORTY?
THEN IT'S ONLY A MATTER OF TIME BEFORE THIS PLACE GETS CROWDED.
YOU SHOULD GO TOO.

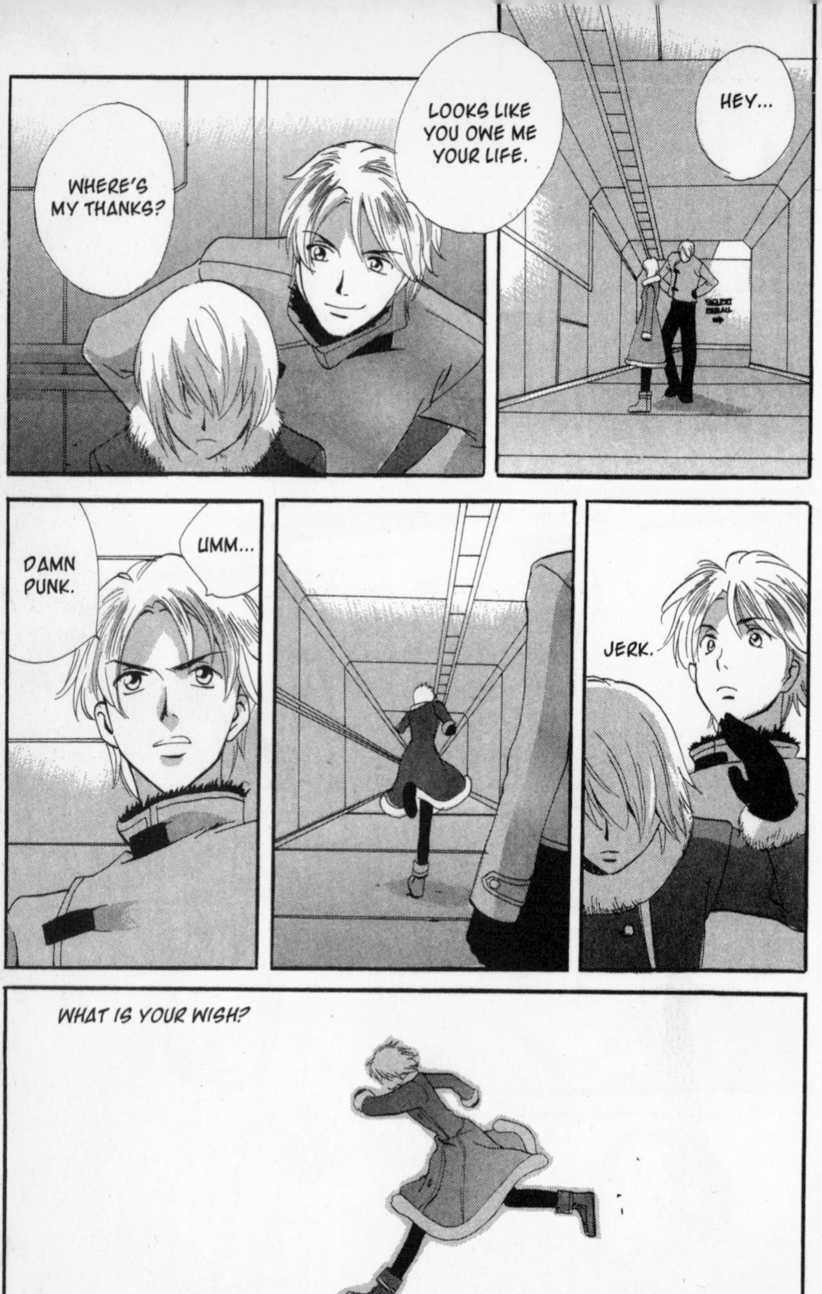
HEY...
LOOKS LIKE YOU OWE ME YOUR LIFE.
WHERE'S MY THANKS?
JERK.
UMM...
DAMN PUNK.
WHAT IS YOUR WISH?

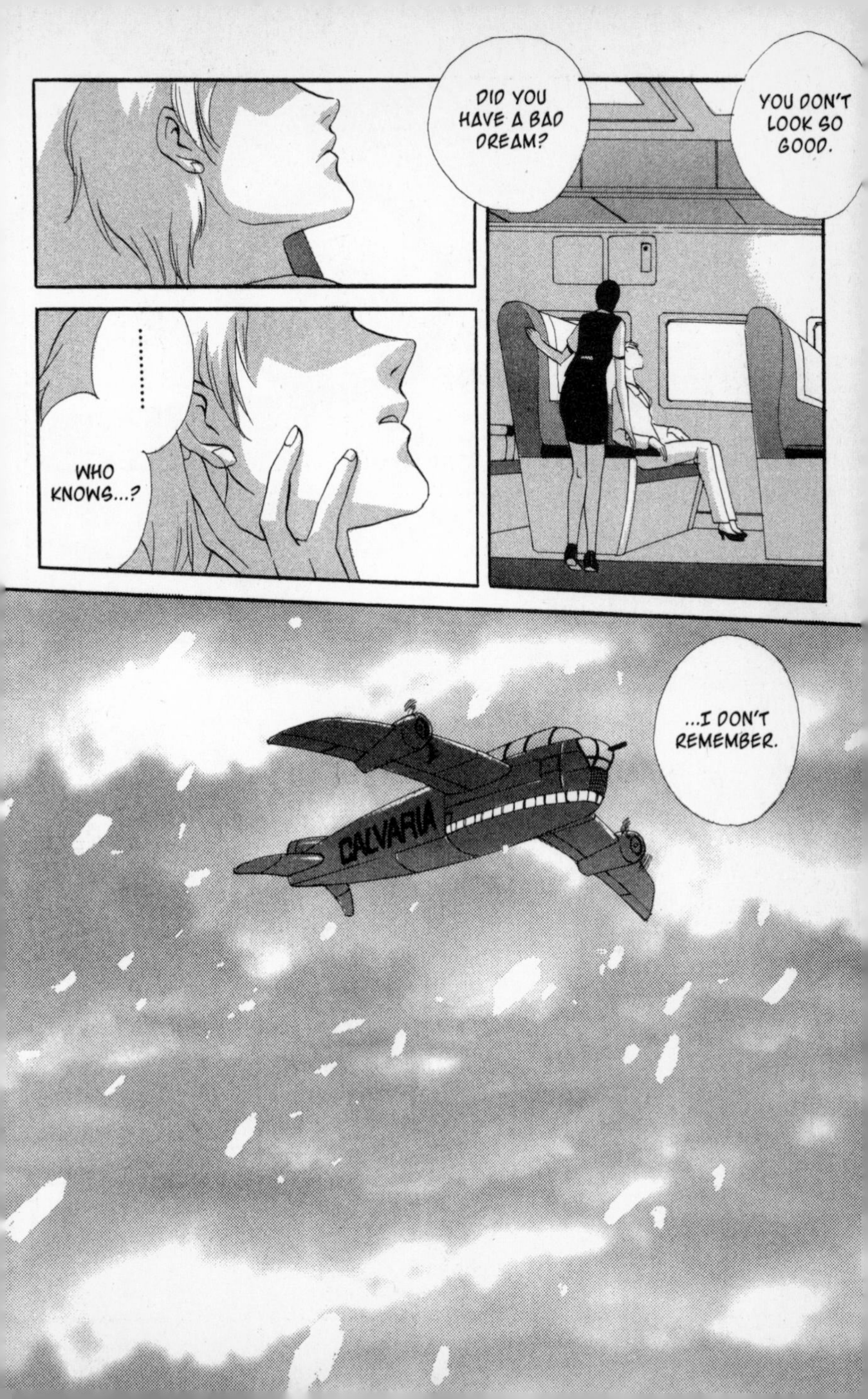

YOU DON'T LOOK SO GOOD.
DID YOU HAVE A BAD DREAM?
......
WHO KNOWS...?
...I DON'T REMEMBER.
CALVARIA

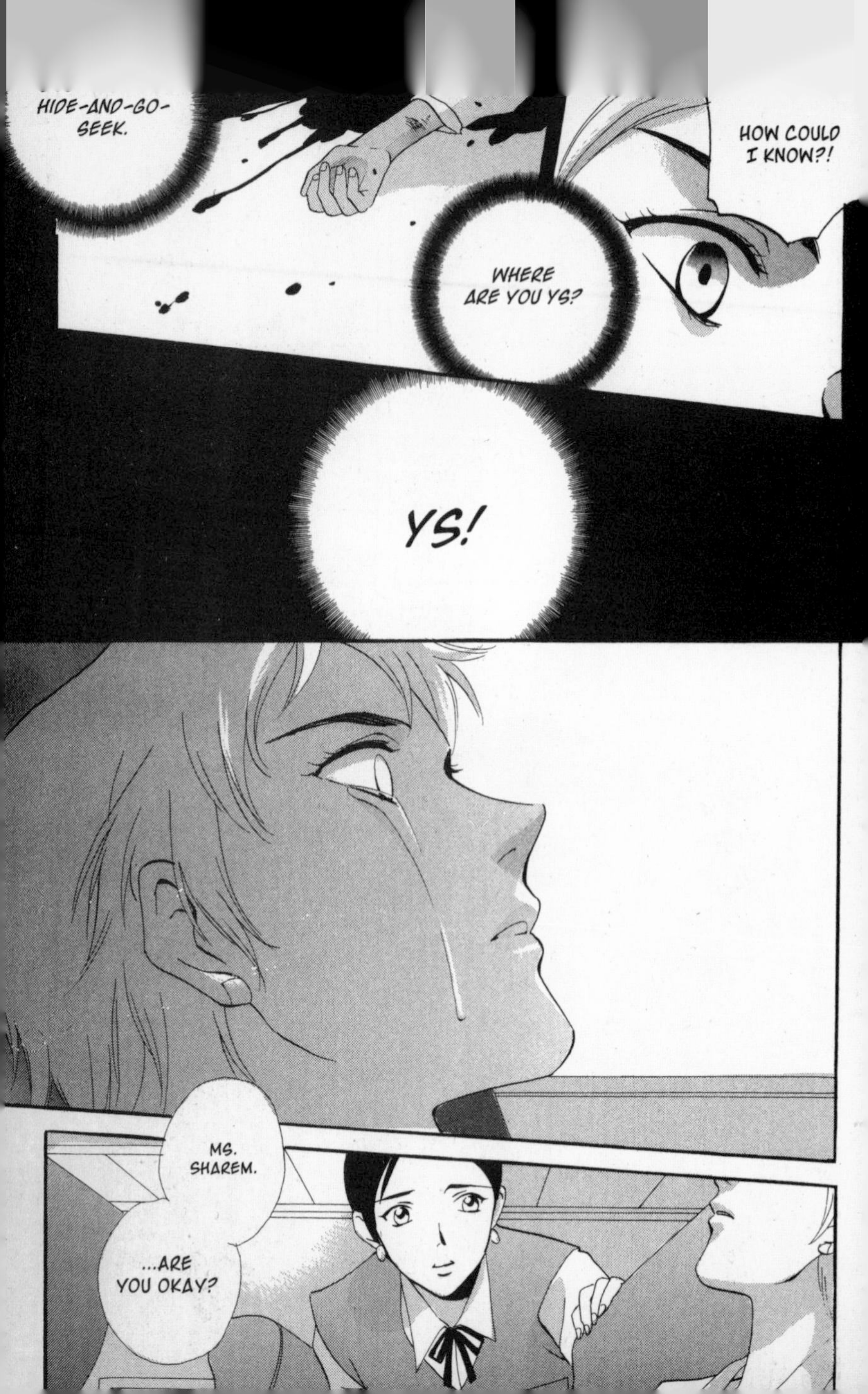
HOW COULD I KNOW?!
HIDE-AND-GO-SEEK.
WHERE ARE YOU YS?
YS!
MS. SHAREM.
...ARE YOU OKAY?

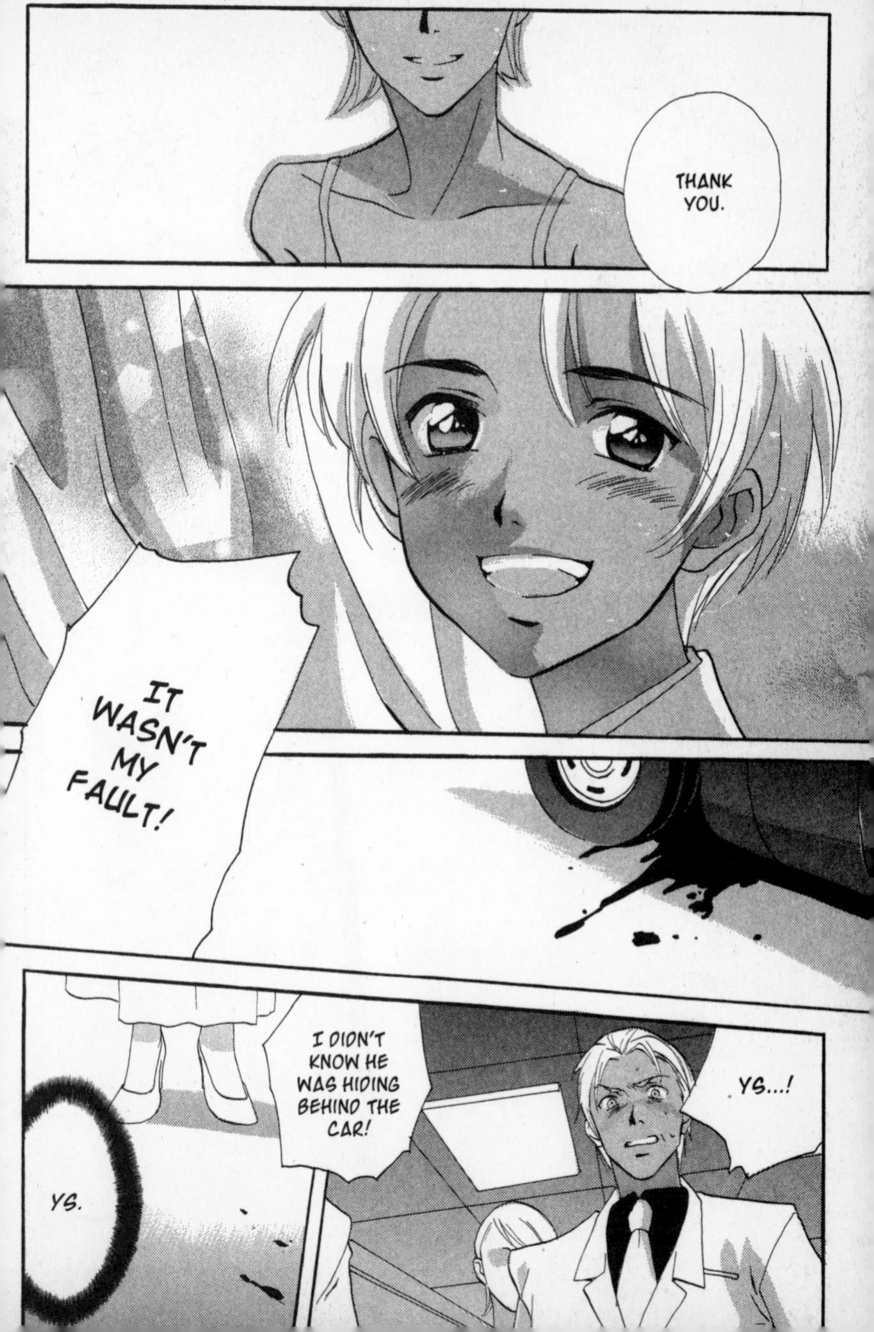
THANK YOU.
IT WASN'T MY FAULT!
YS...!
I DIDN'T KNOW HE WAS HIDING BEHIND THE CAR!
YS.

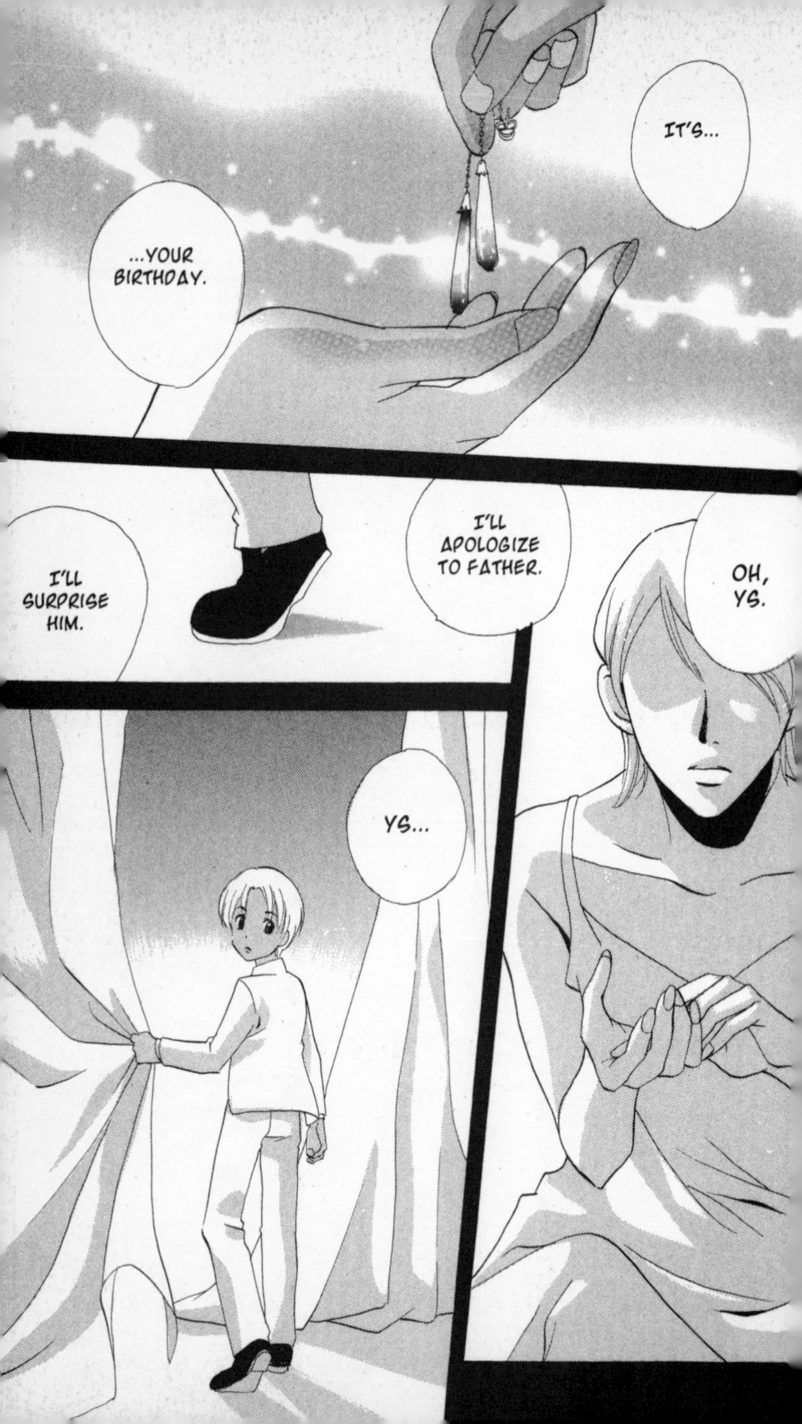
IT'S...
...YOUR BIRTHDAY.
OH, YS.
I'LL APOLOGIZE TO FATHER.
I'LL SURPRISE HIM.
YS...

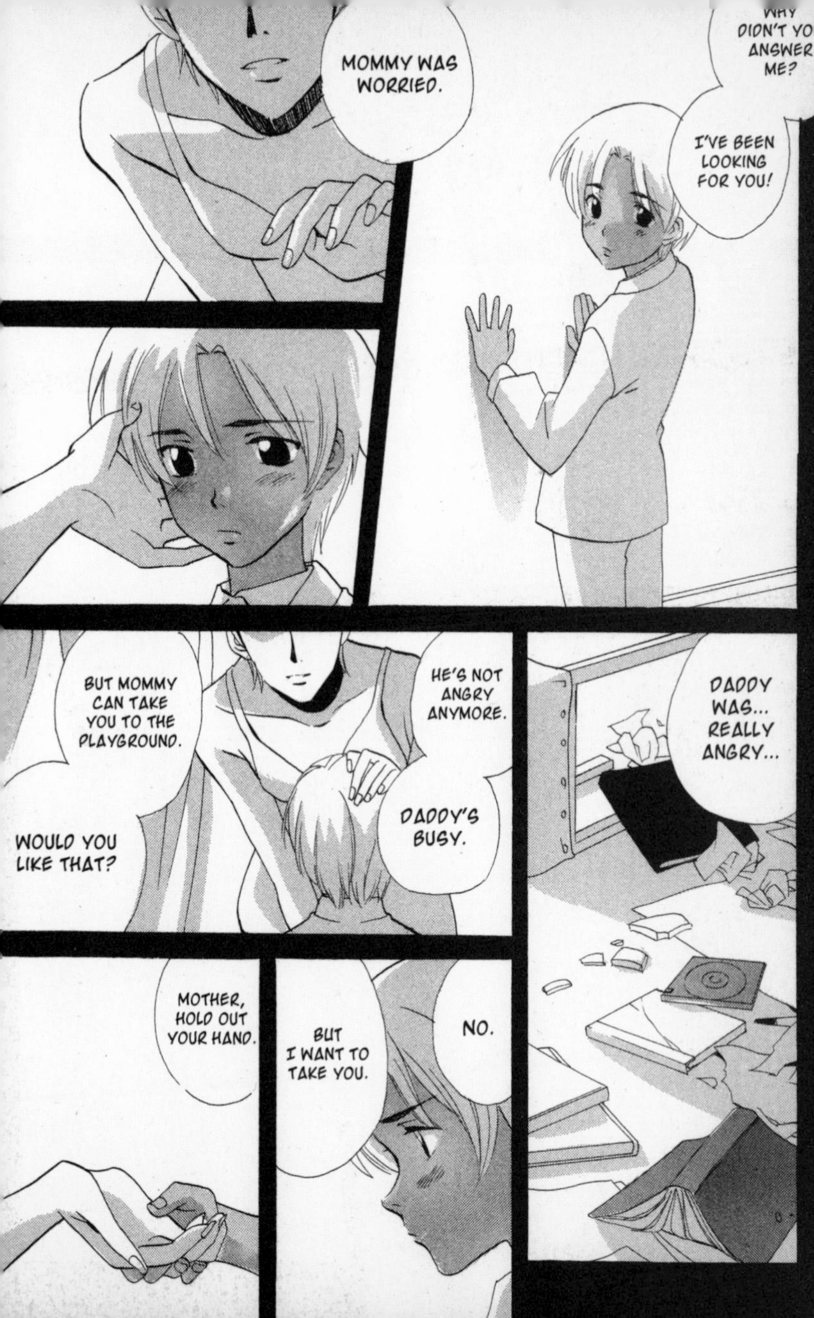

WHY DIDN'T YOU ANSWER ME?
I'VE BEEN LOOKING FOR YOU!
MOMMY WAS WORRIED.
DADDY WAS... REALLY ANGRY...
HE'S NOT ANGRY ANYMORE.
DADDY'S BUSY.
BUT MOMMY CAN TAKE YOU TO THE PLAYGROUND.
WOULD YOU LIKE THAT?
NO.
BUT I WANT TO TAKE YOU.
MOTHER, HOLD OUT YOUR HAND.

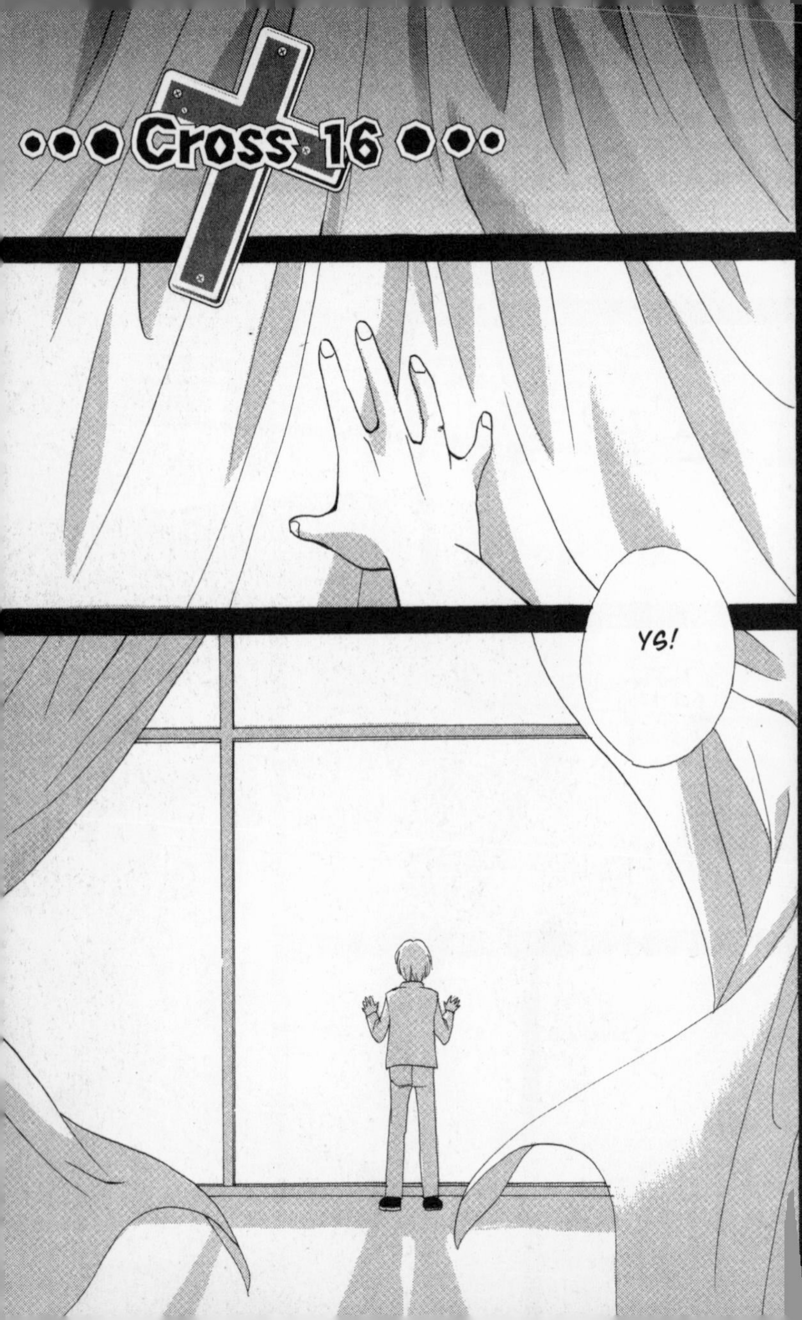
Cross 16
YS!

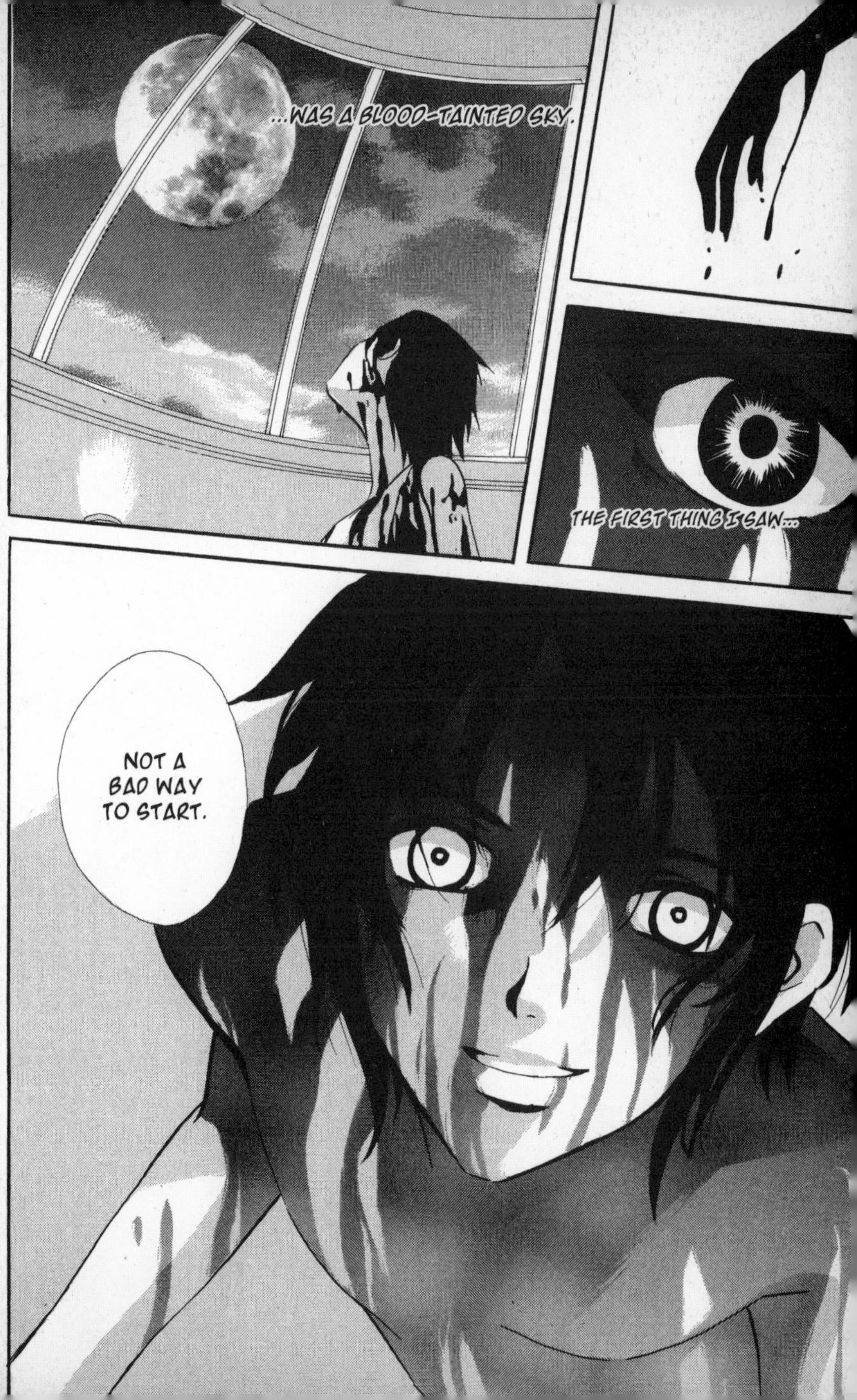
THE FIRST THING I SAW...
...WAS A BLOOD-TAINTED SKY.
NOT A BAD WAY TO START.

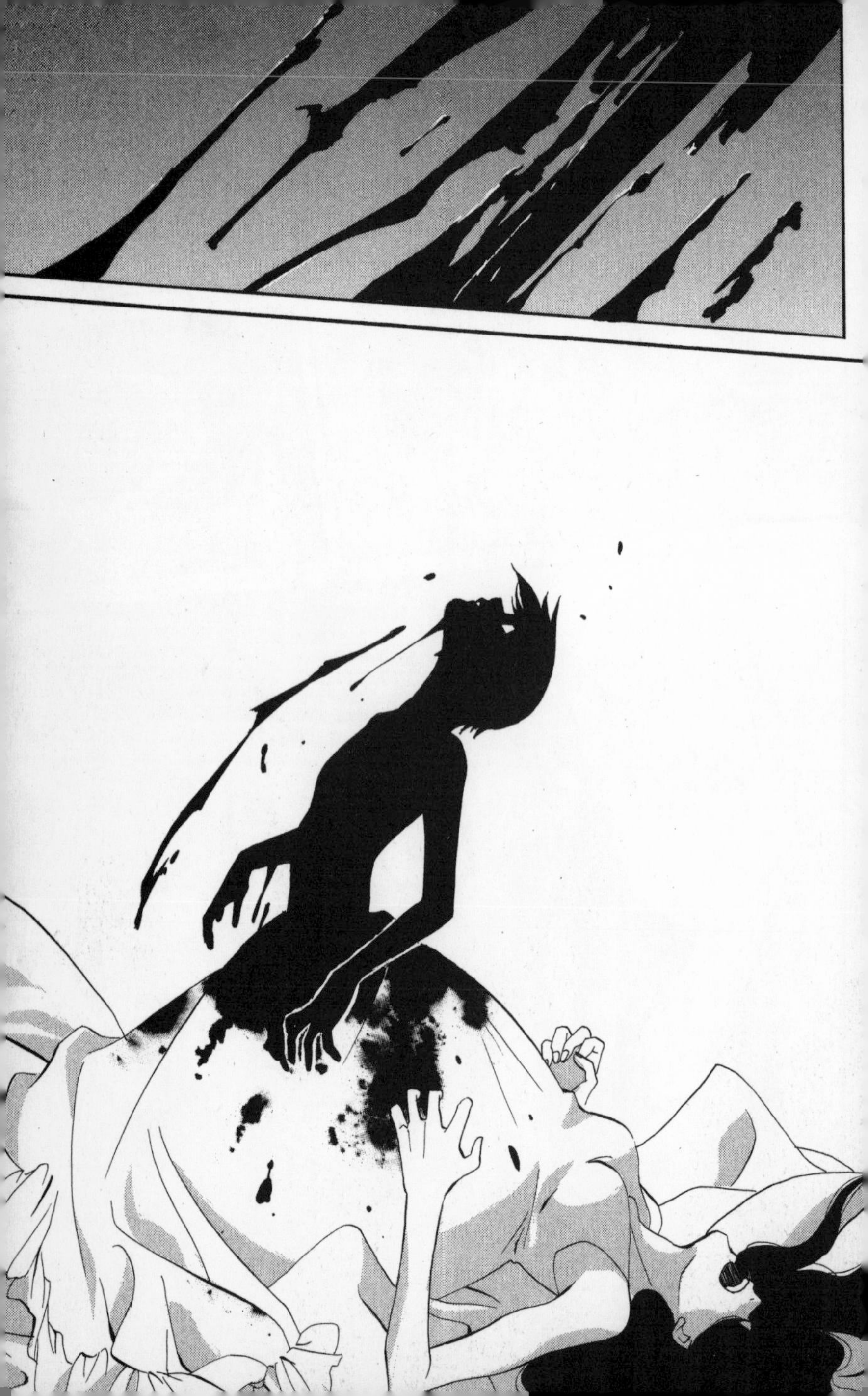

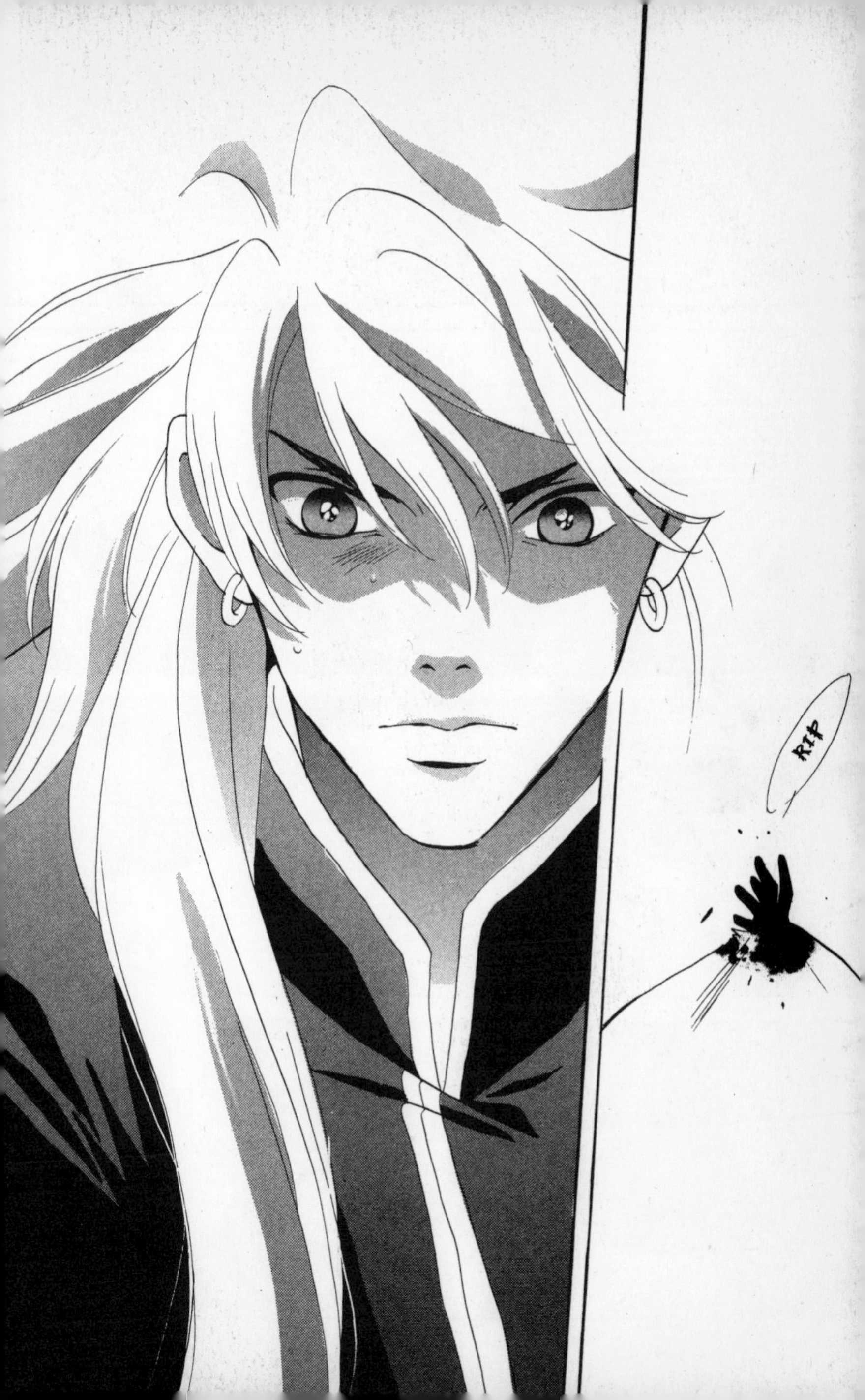
RIP

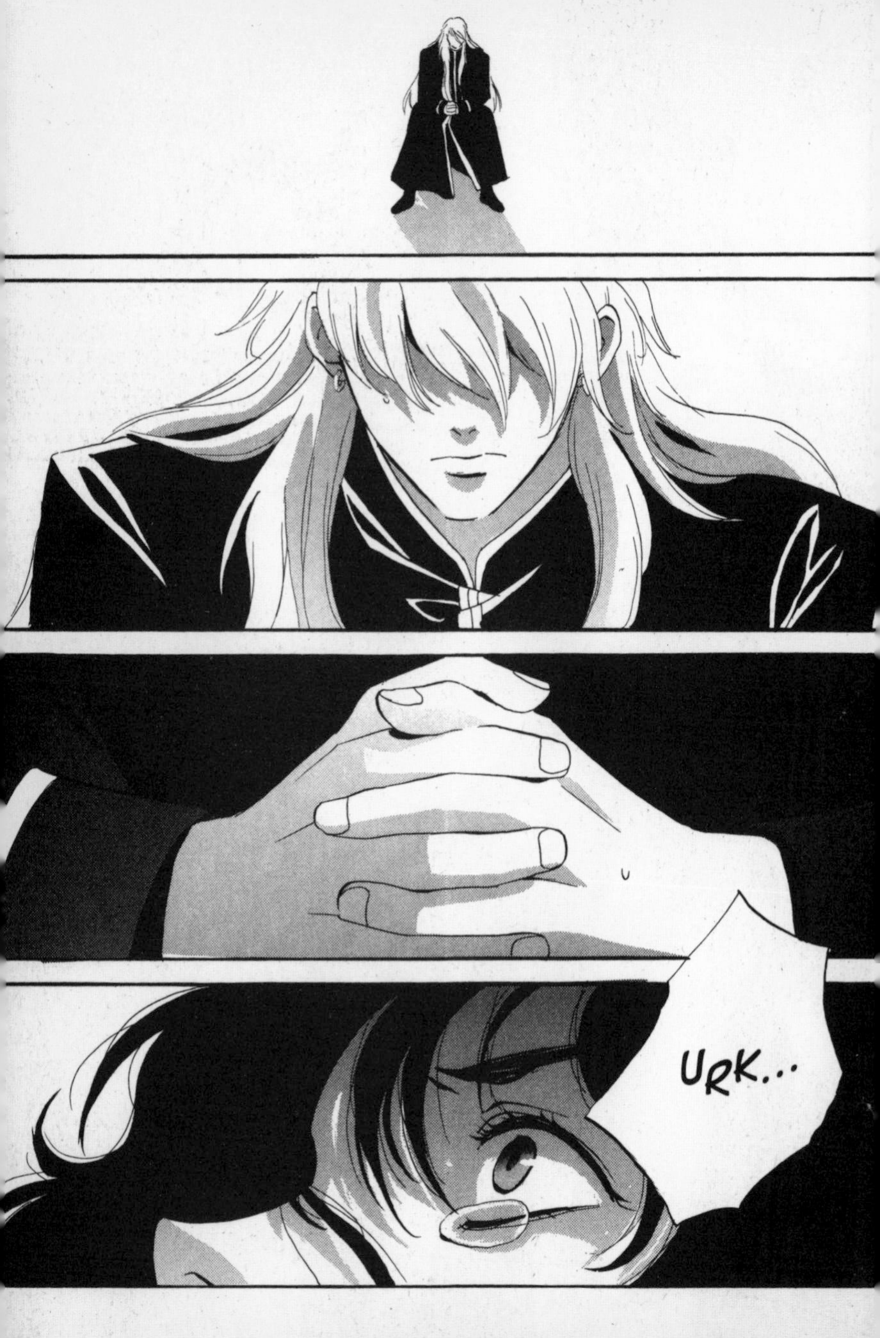
URK...

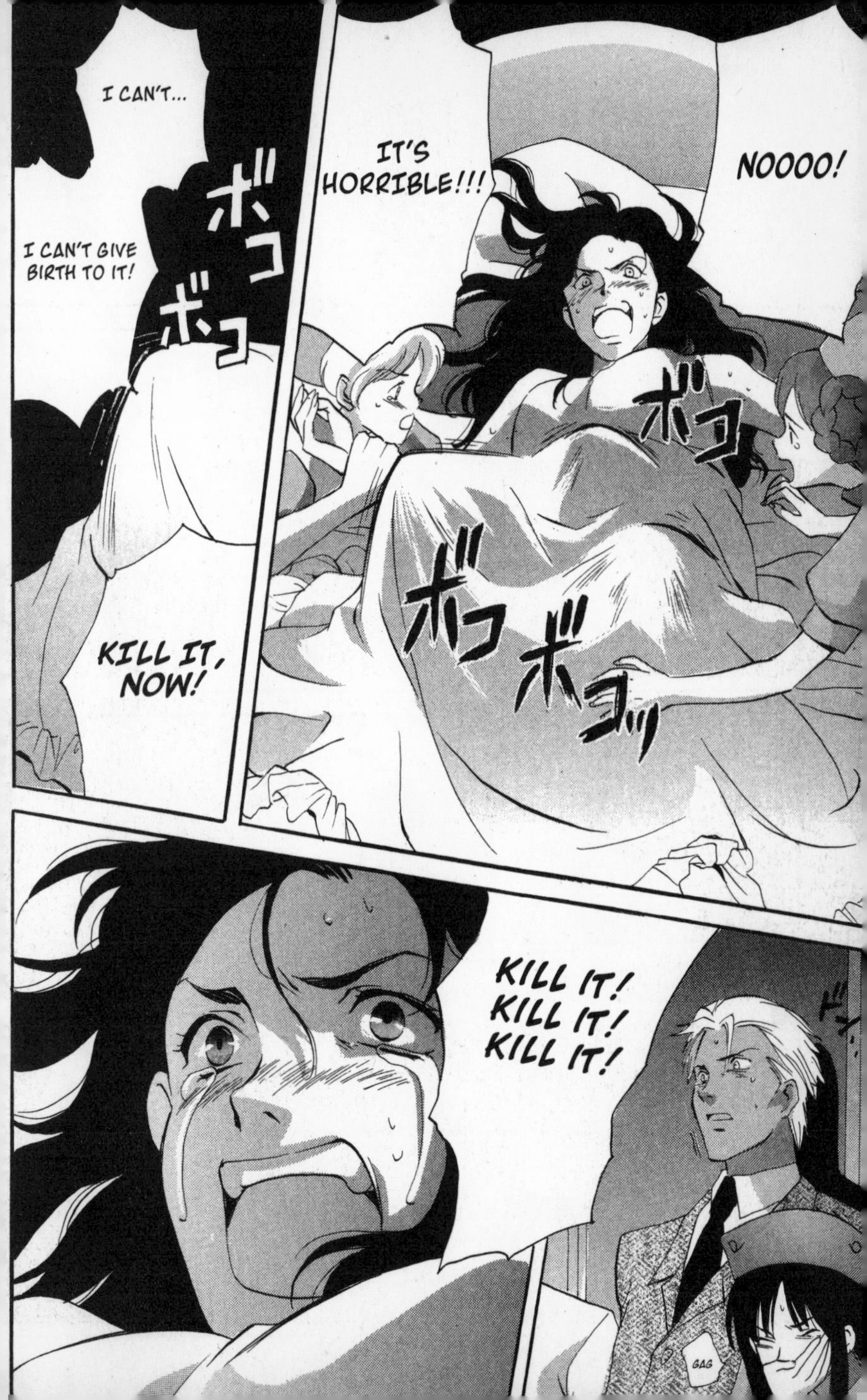

NOOOO!
IT'S HORRIBLE!!!
ボコ
ボコボコッ
I CAN'T...
ボコボコ
I CAN'T GIVE BIRTH TO IT!
KILL IT, NOW!
KILL IT! KILL IT! KILL IT!
GAG

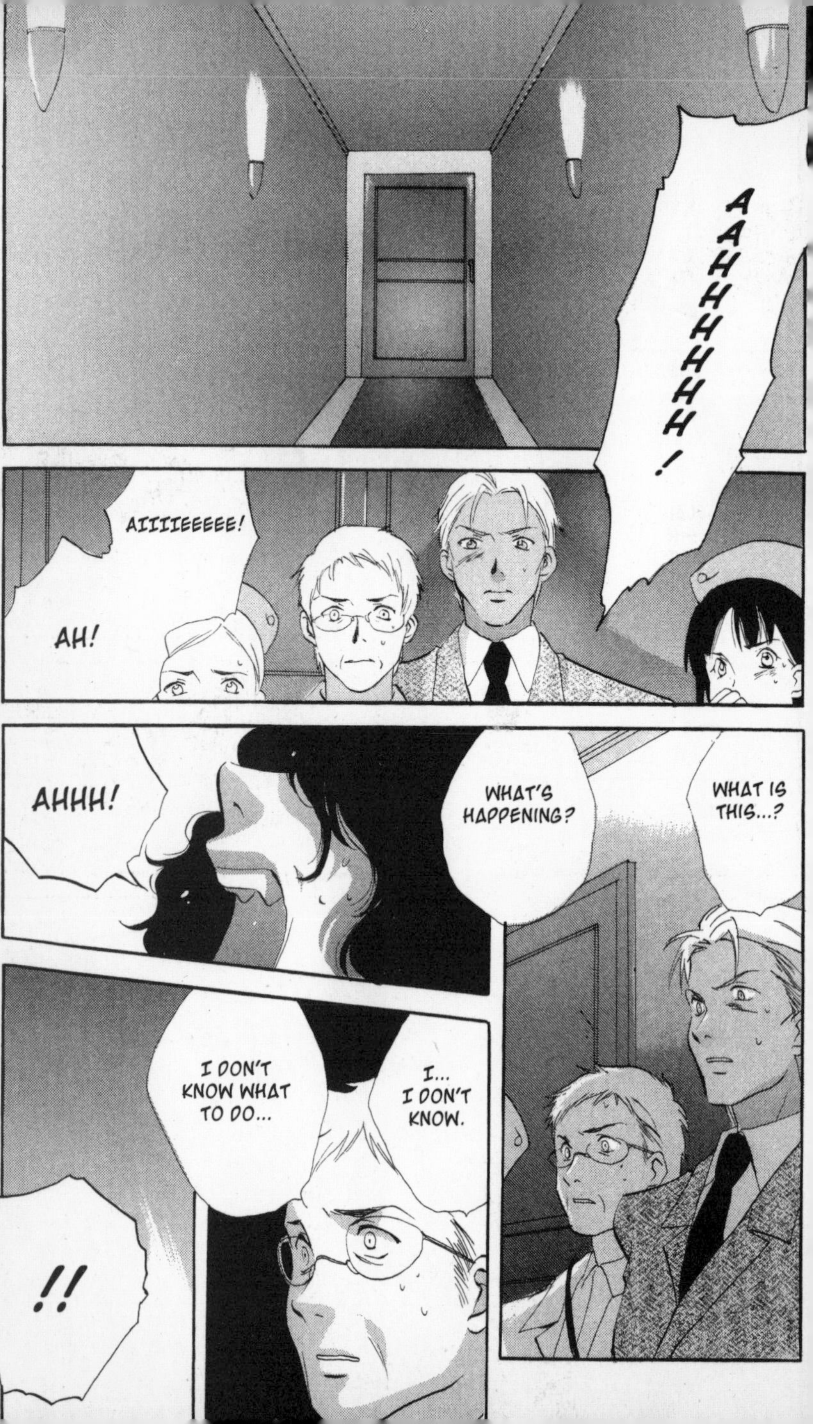
AAHHHHHHH!
AIIIIEEEEE!
AH!
AHHH!
WHAT IS THIS...?
WHAT'S HAPPENING?
I... I DON'T KNOW.
I DON'T KNOW WHAT TO DO...
!!

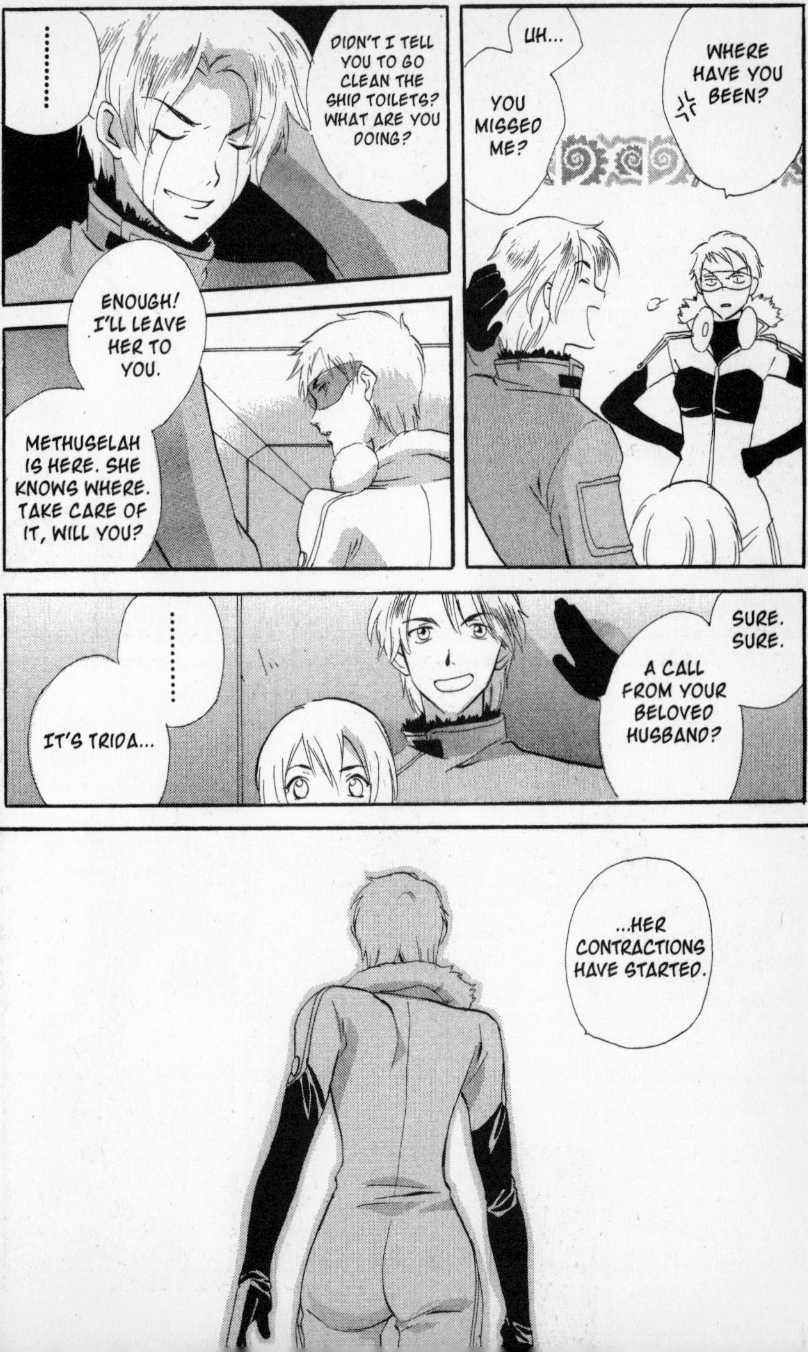
WHERE HAVE YOU BEEN?
UH...
YOU MISSED ME?
DIDN'T I TELL YOU TO GO CLEAN THE SHIP TOILETS? WHAT ARE YOU DOING?
......
ENOUGH! I'LL LEAVE HER TO YOU.
METHUSELAH IS HERE. SHE KNOWS WHERE. TAKE CARE OF IT, WILL YOU?
SURE. SURE.
A CALL FROM YOUR BELOVED HUSBAND?
......
IT'S TRIDA...
...HER CONTRACTIONS HAVE STARTED.

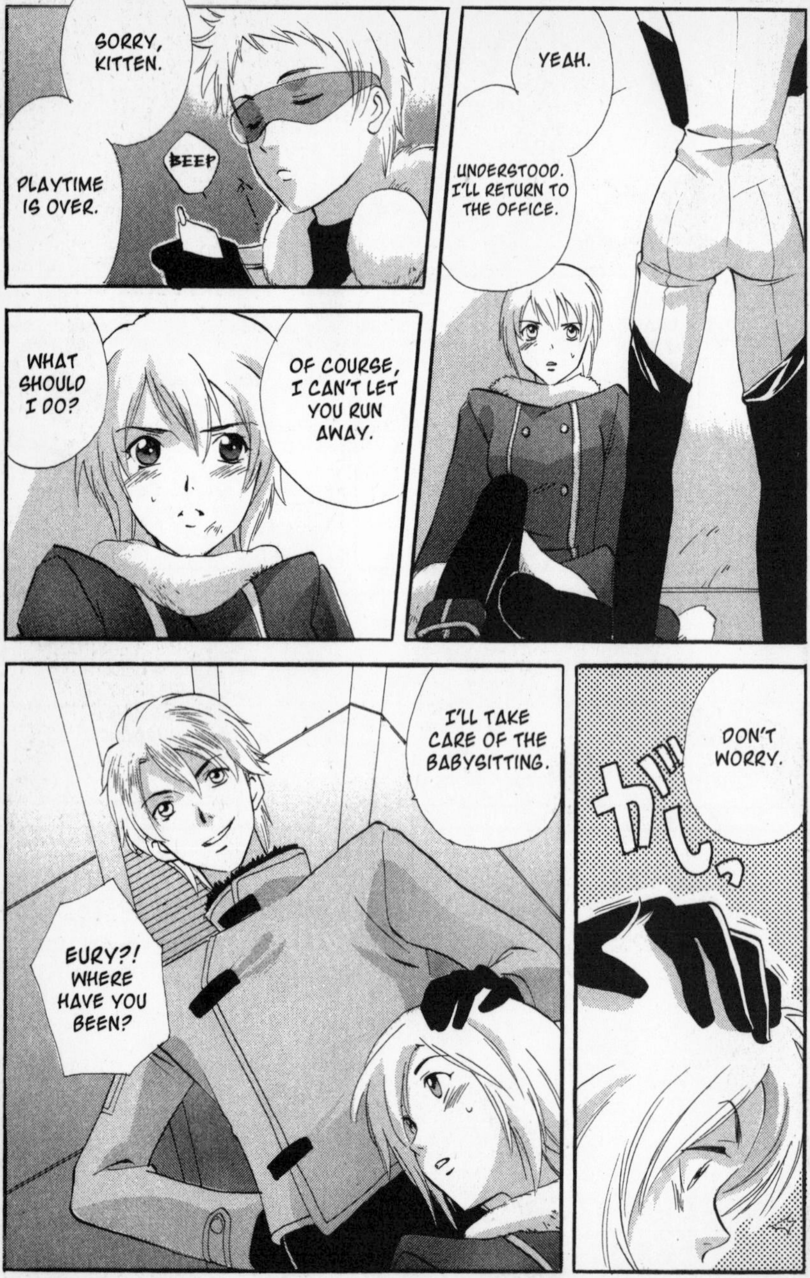
SORRY, KITTEN.
PLAYTIME IS OVER.
BEEP
YEAH.
UNDERSTOOD. I'LL RETURN TO THE OFFICE.
WHAT SHOULD I DO?
OF COURSE, I CAN'T LET YOU RUN AWAY.
DON'T WORRY.
がしっ
I'LL TAKE CARE OF THE BABYSITTING.
EURY?! WHERE HAVE YOU BEEN?

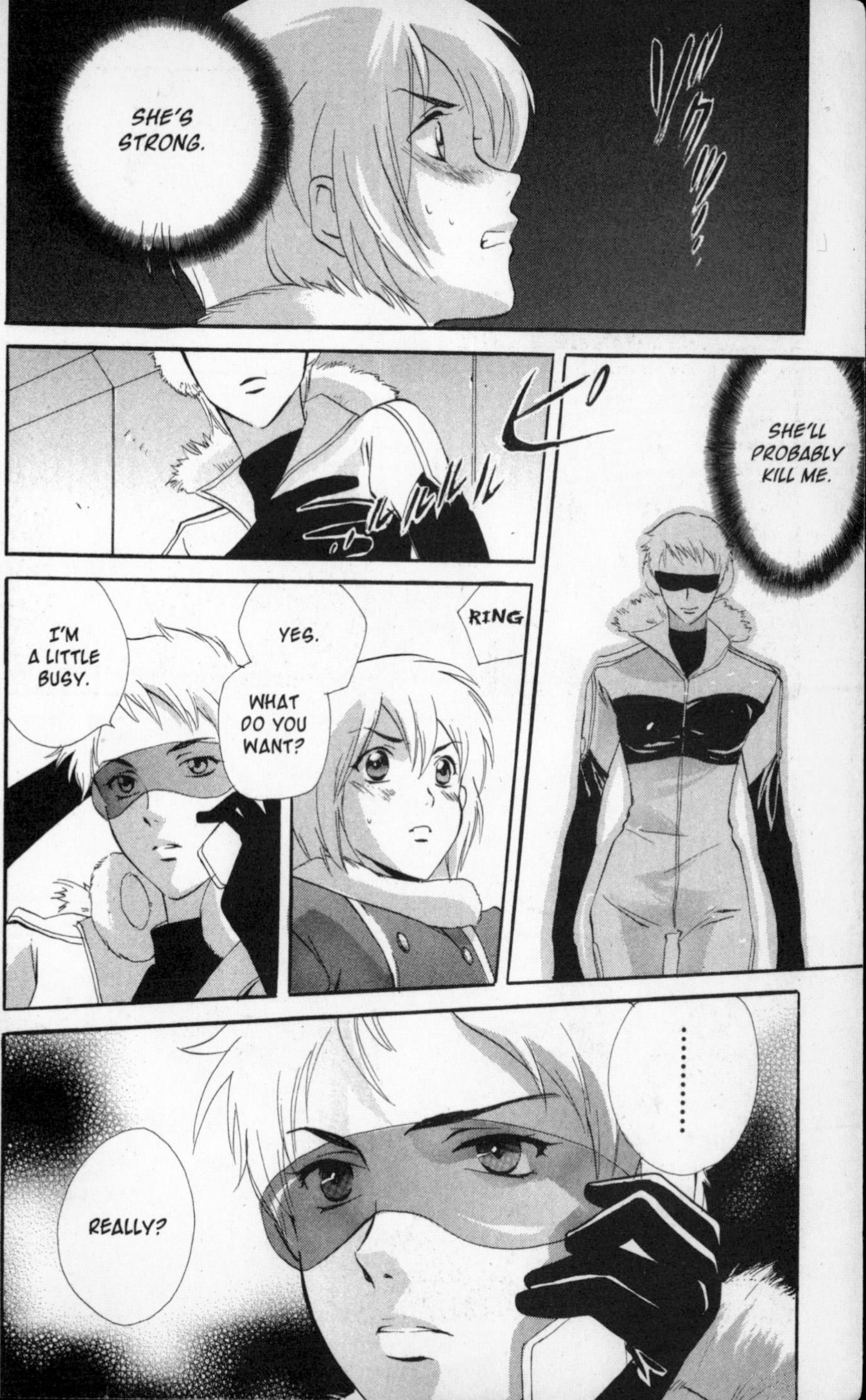
SHE'S STRONG.
SHE'LL PROBABLY KILL ME.
RING
YES.
WHAT DO YOU WANT?
I'M A LITTLE BUSY.
......
REALLY?

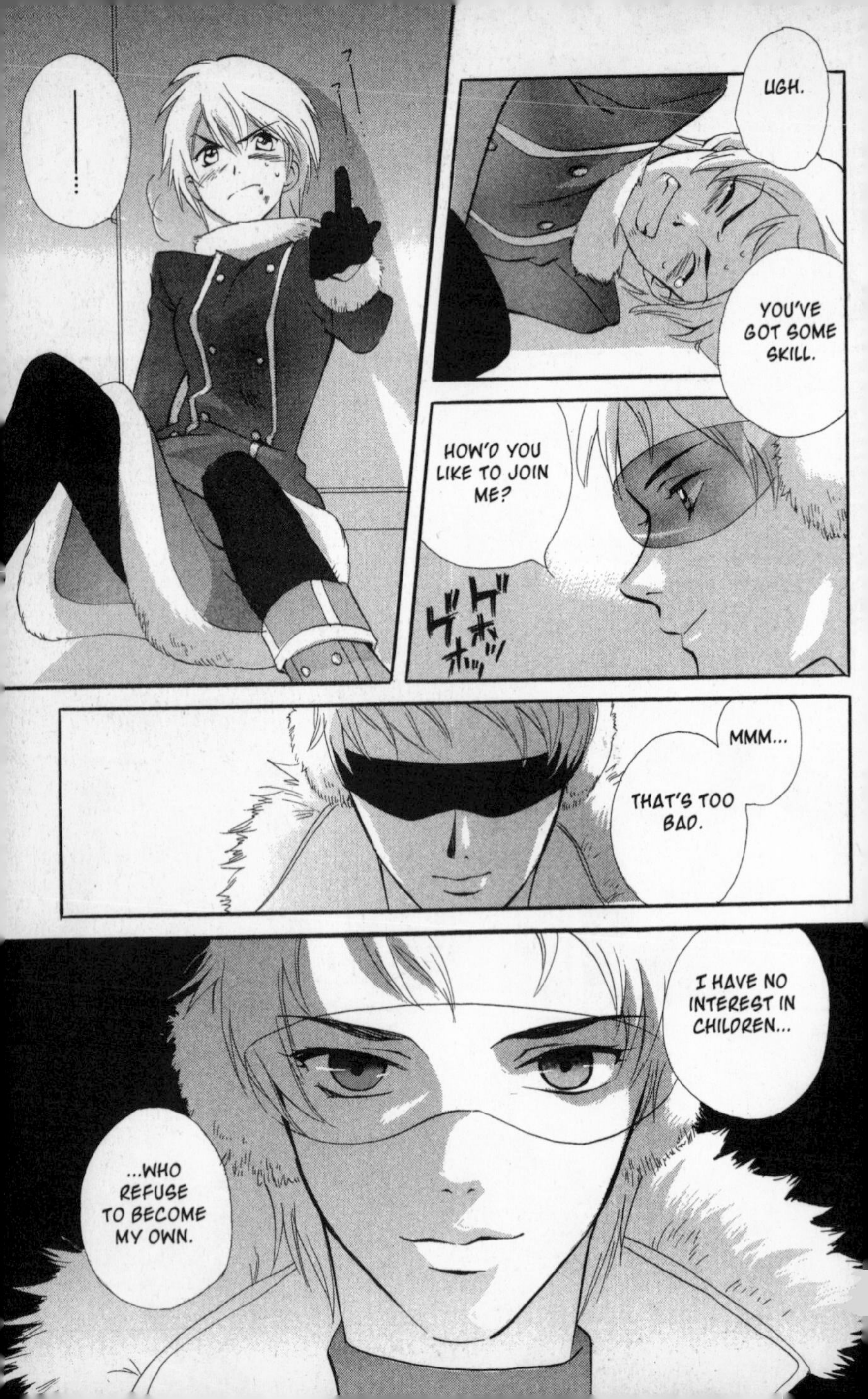
UGH.
YOU'VE GOT SOME SKILL.
HOW'D YOU LIKE TO JOIN ME?
ゲホッ
ゲホッ
......
MMM...
THAT'S TOO BAD.
I HAVE NO INTEREST IN CHILDREN...
...WHO REFUSE TO BECOME MY OWN.

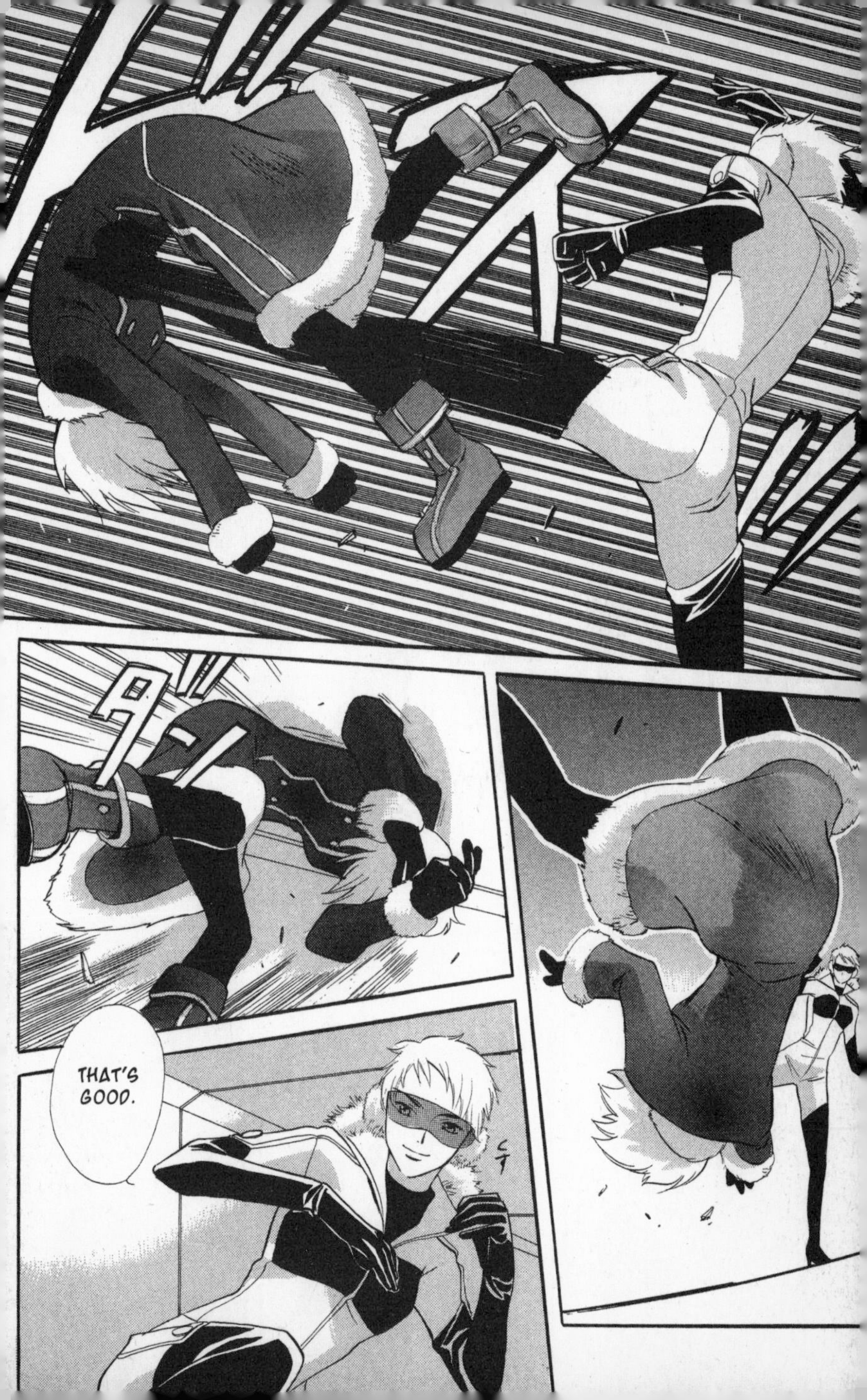
THAT'S GOOD.

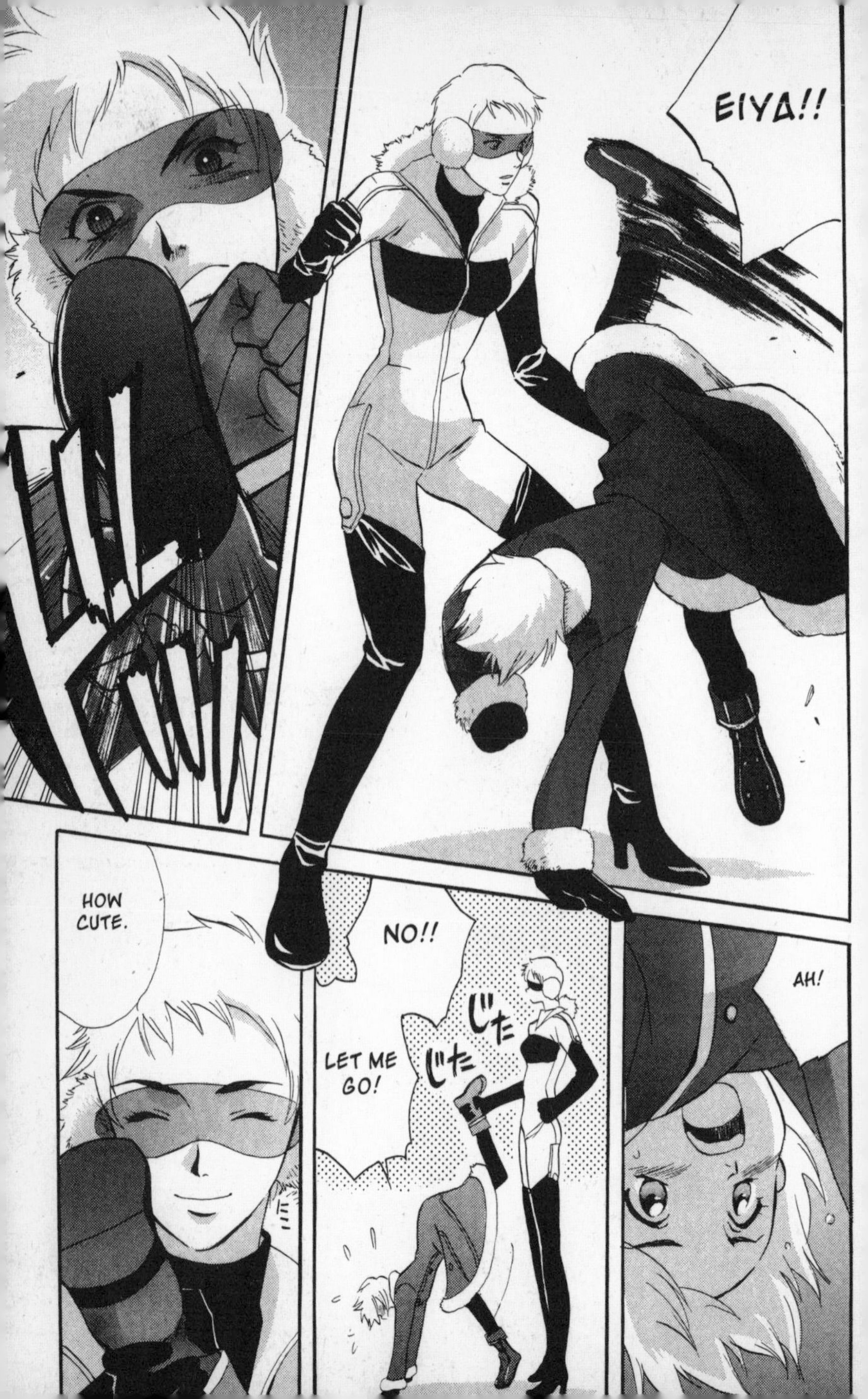
EIYA!!
AH!
NO!!
じた
じた
LET ME GO!
HOW CUTE.

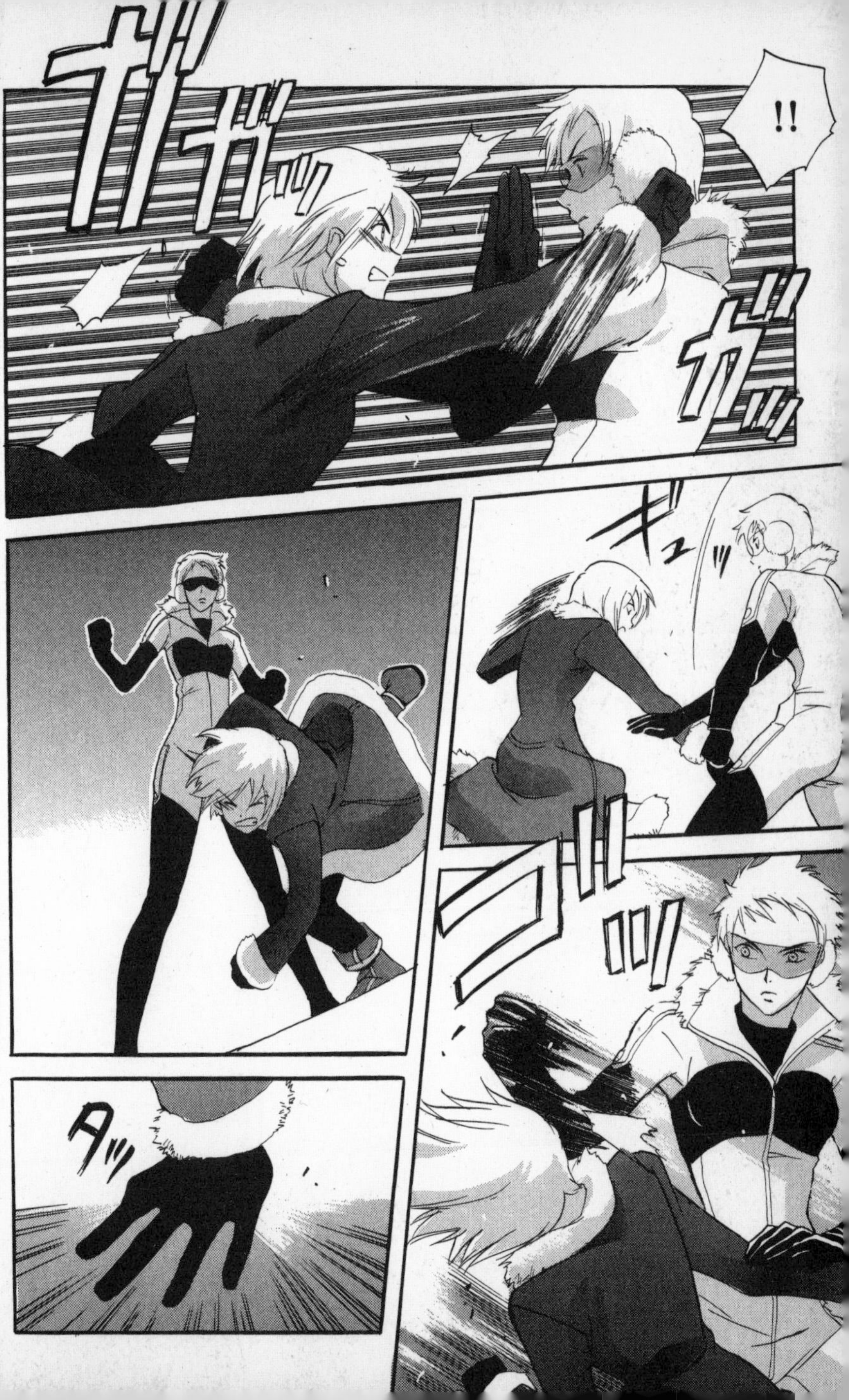
!!
ガッ
ガガッ
ギュッ
ゴッ
タッ

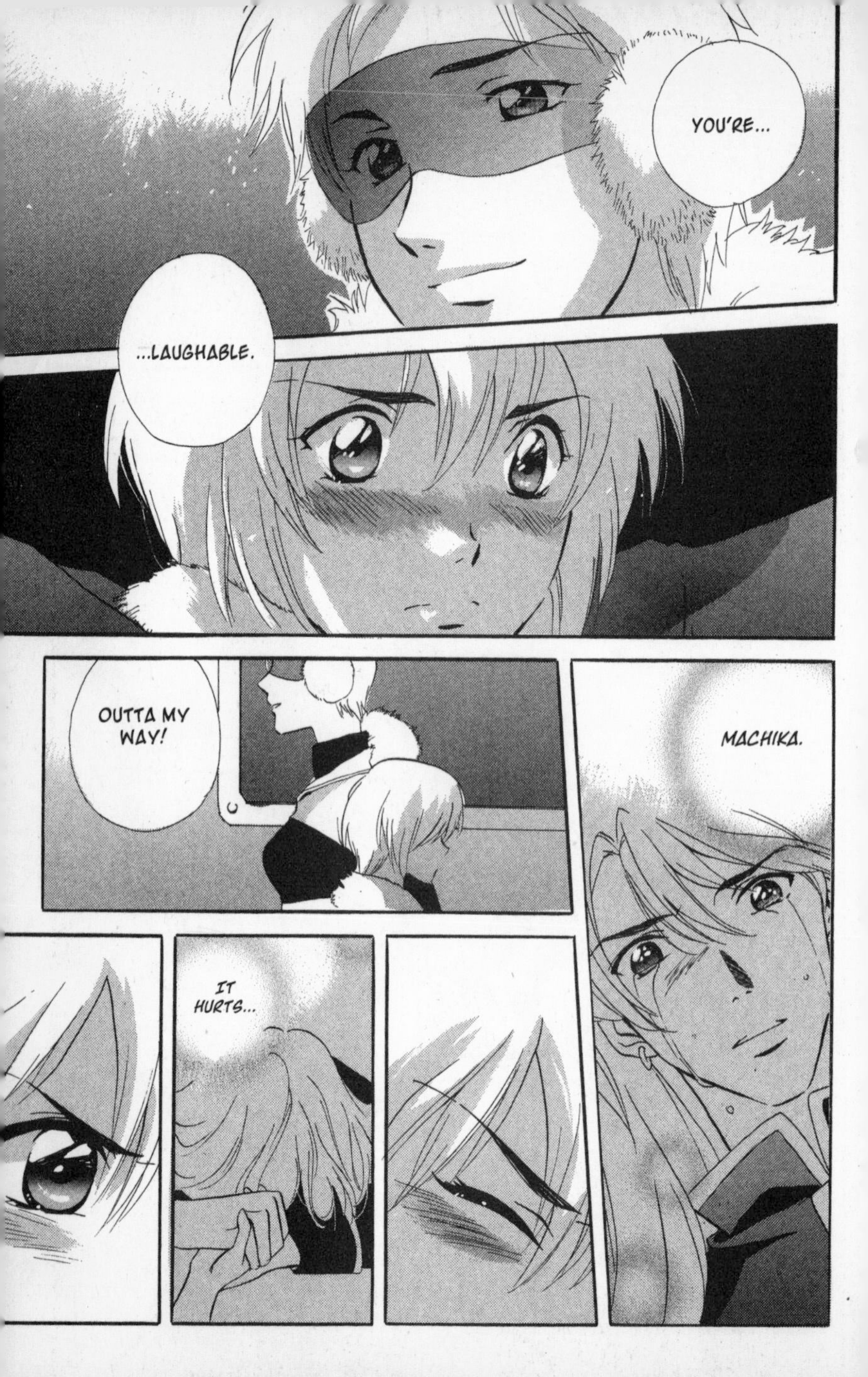
YOU'RE...
...LAUGHABLE.
MACHIKA.
OUTTA MY WAY!
IT HURTS...

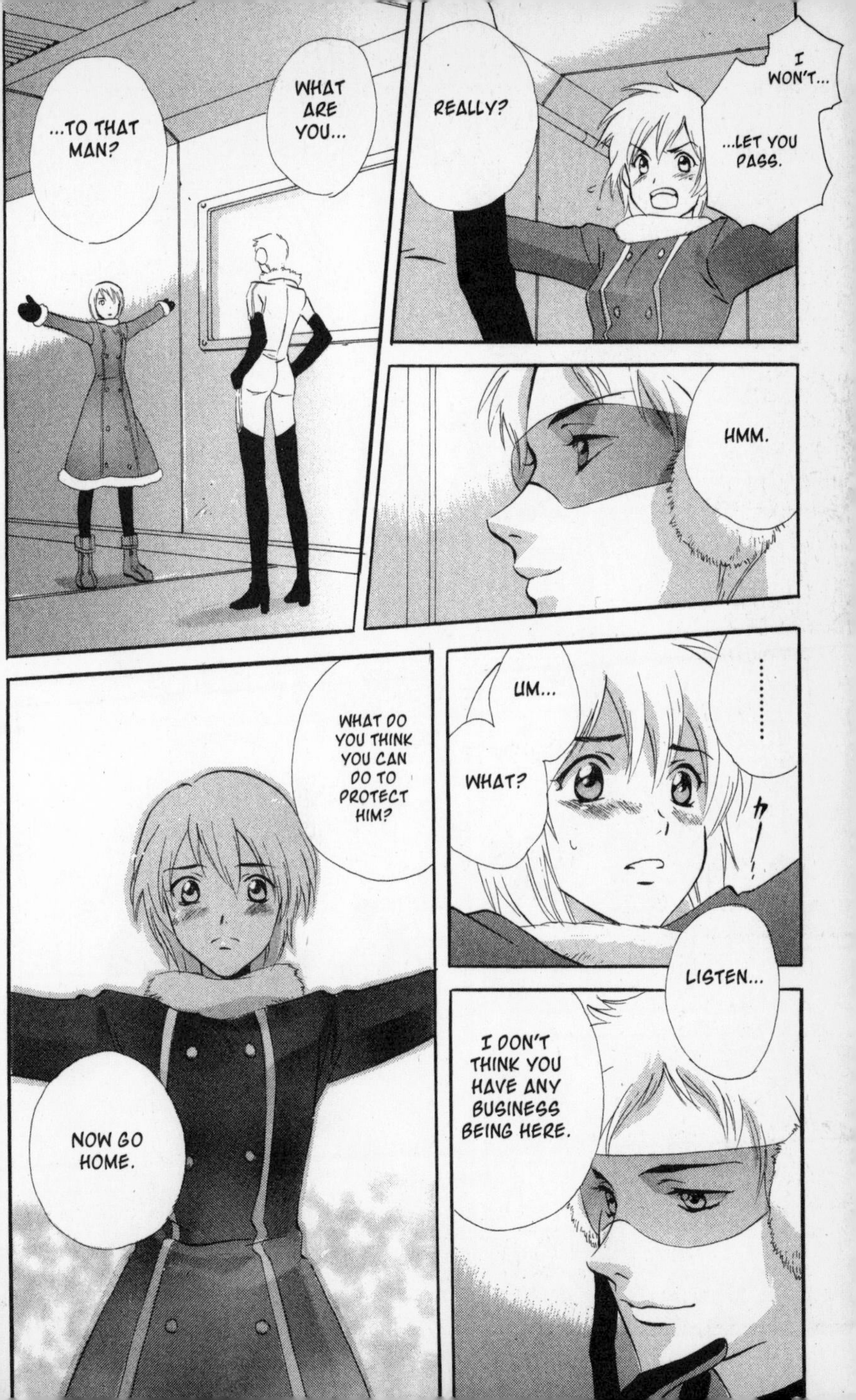
I WON'T...
...LET YOU PASS.
REALLY?
HMM.
WHAT ARE YOU...
...TO THAT MAN?
......
UM...
WHAT?
LISTEN...
I DON'T THINK YOU HAVE ANY BUSINESS BEING HERE.
WHAT DO YOU THINK YOU CAN DO TO PROTECT HIM?
NOW GO HOME.

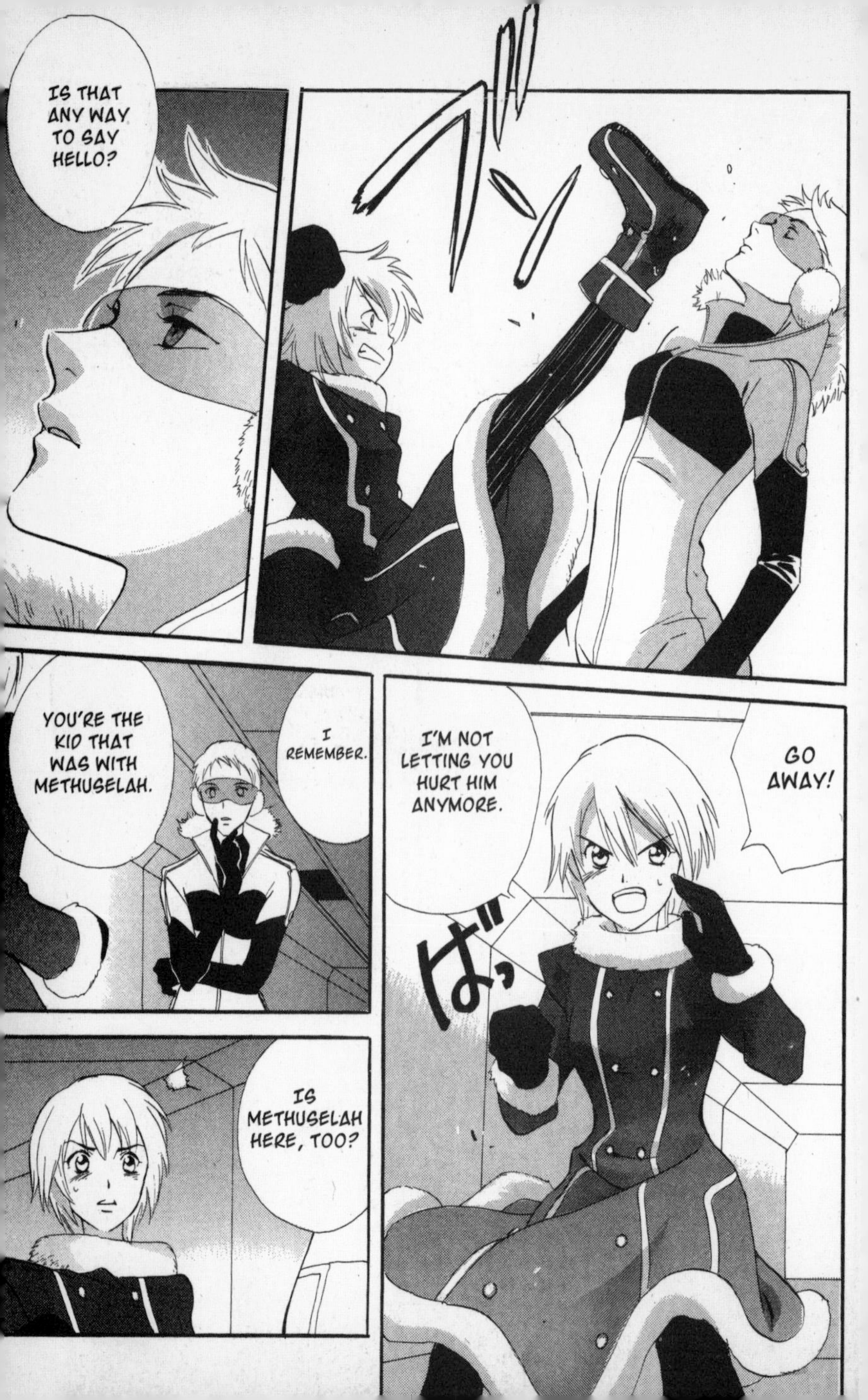
IS THAT ANY WAY TO SAY HELLO?
GO AWAY!
I'M NOT LETTING YOU HURT HIM ANYMORE.
ばっ
I REMEMBER.
YOU'RE THE KID THAT WAS WITH METHUSELAH.
IS METHUSELAH HERE, TOO?

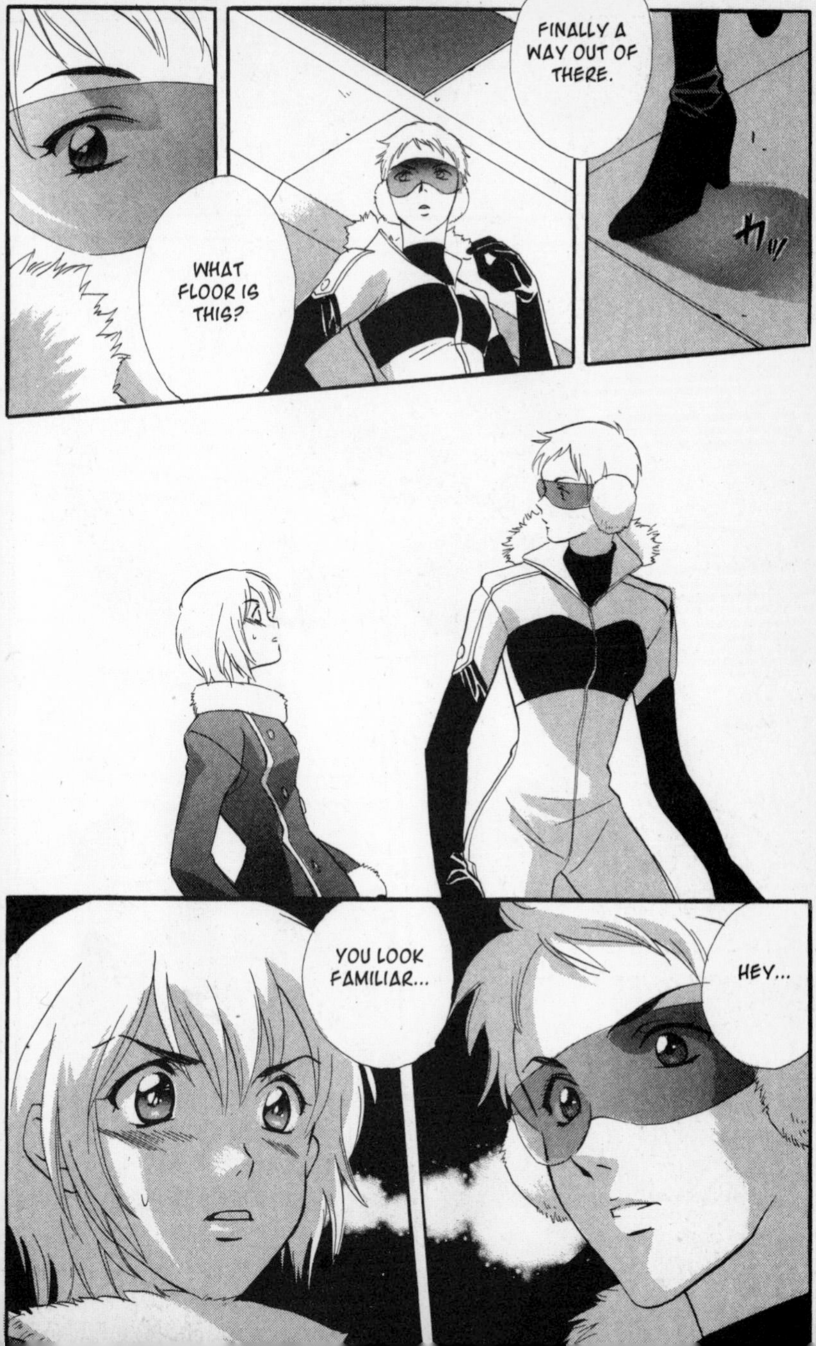
ガッ
FINALLY A WAY OUT OF THERE.
WHAT FLOOR IS THIS?
HEY...
YOU LOOK FAMILIAR...

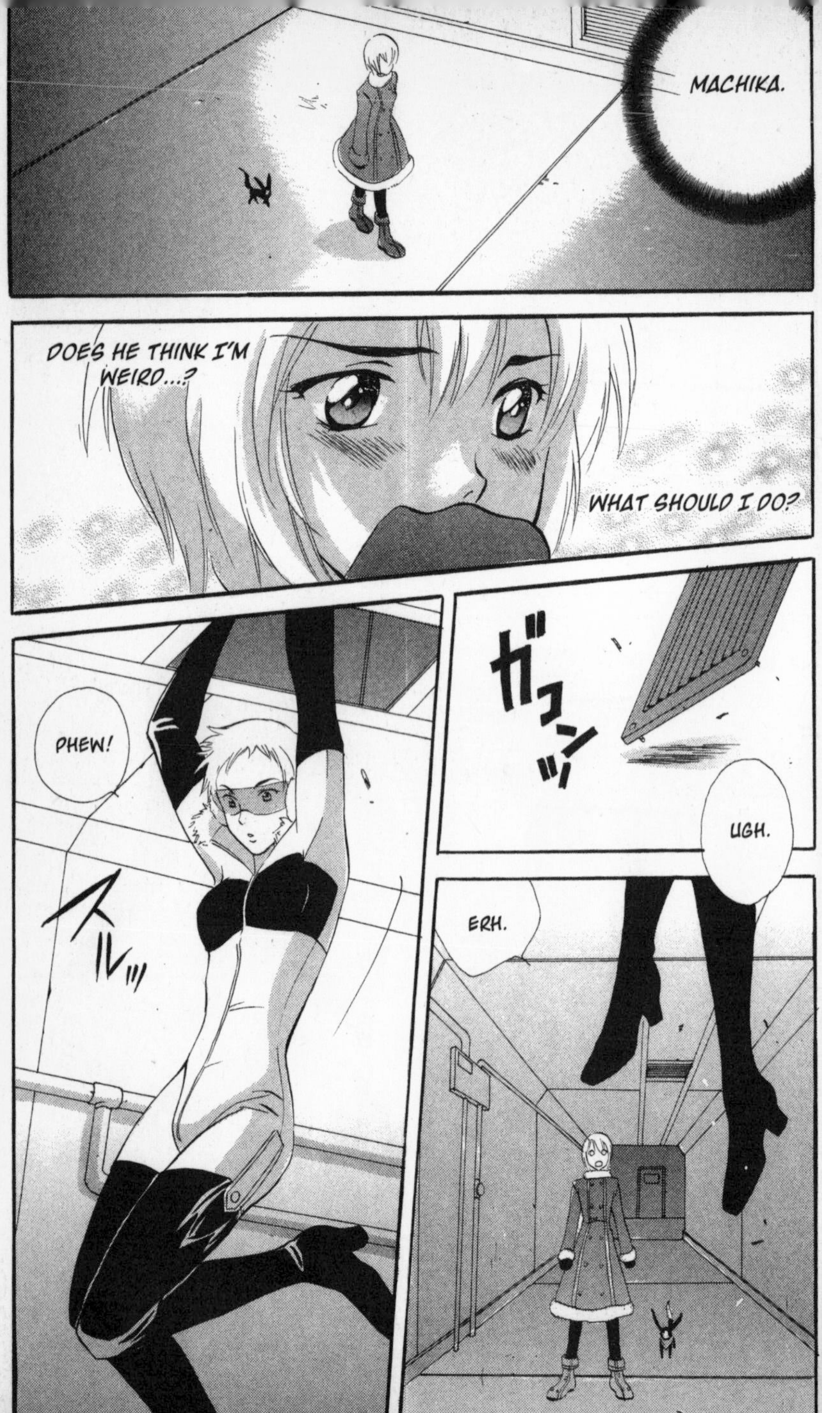
MACHIKA.
WHAT SHOULD I DO?
DOES HE THINK I'M WEIRD...?
ガコンッ
UGH.
ERH.
スルッ
PHEW!

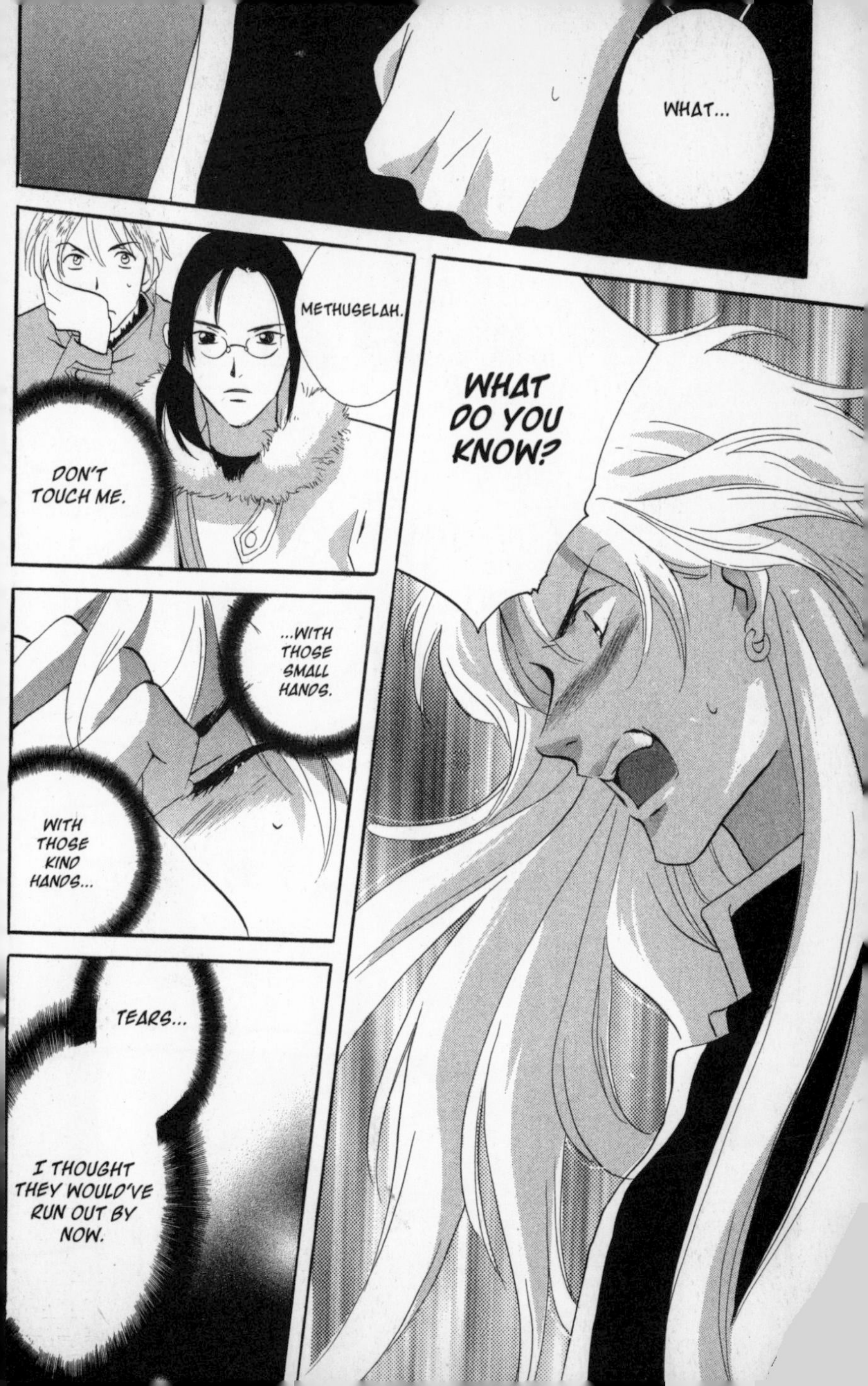
WHAT...
WHAT DO YOU KNOW?
METHUSELAH.
DON'T TOUCH ME.
...WITH THOSE SMALL HANDS.
WITH THOSE KIND HANDS...
TEARS...
I THOUGHT THEY WOULD'VE RUN OUT BY NOW.

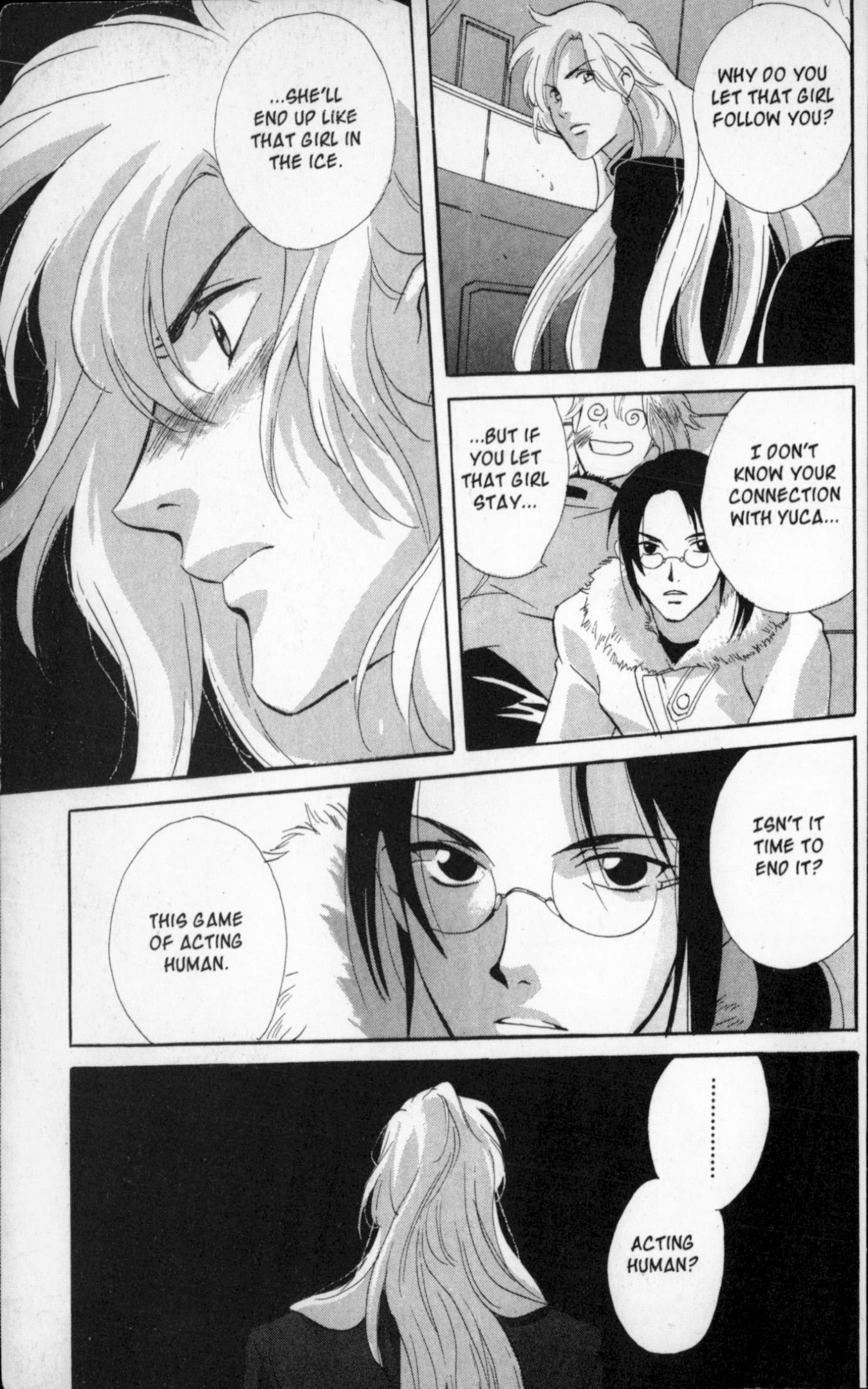
WHY DO YOU LET THAT GIRL FOLLOW YOU?
I DON'T KNOW YOUR CONNECTION WITH YUCA...
...BUT IF YOU LET THAT GIRL STAY...
...SHE'LL END UP LIKE THAT GIRL IN THE ICE.
ISN'T IT TIME TO END IT?
THIS GAME OF ACTING HUMAN.
......
ACTING HUMAN?

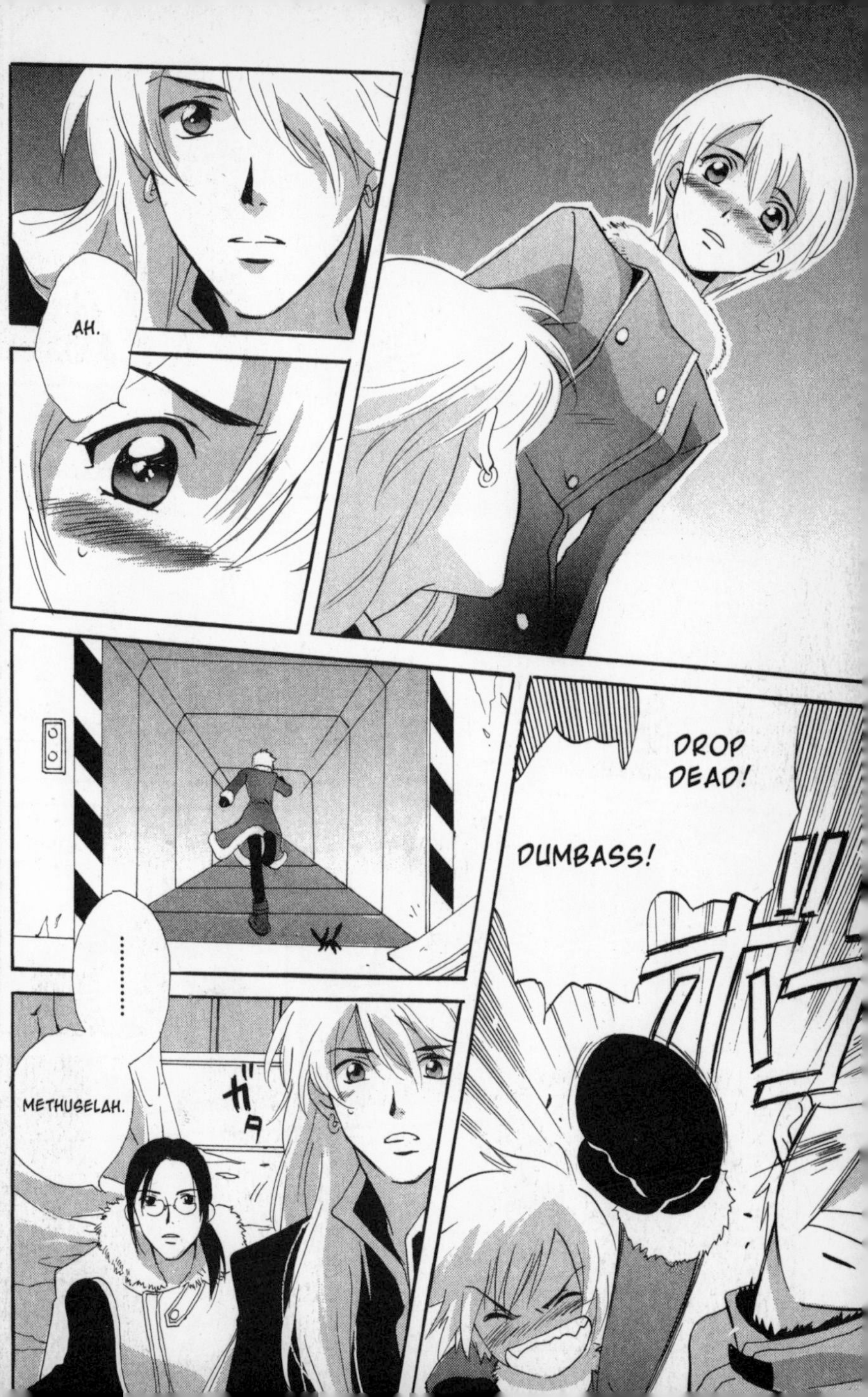
AH.
DROP DEAD!
DUMBASS!
......
METHUSELAH.

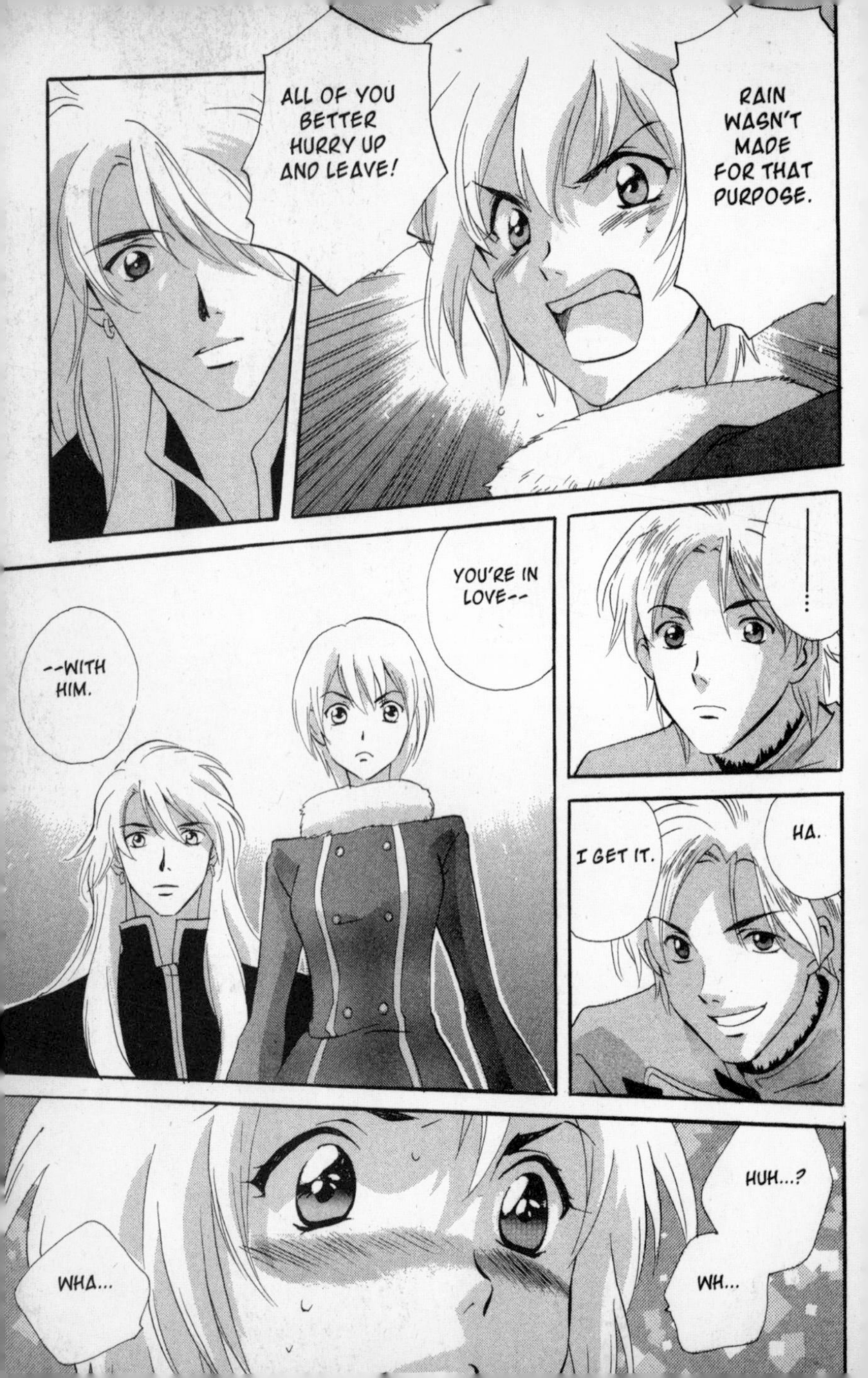
RAIN WASN'T MADE FOR THAT PURPOSE.
ALL OF YOU BETTER HURRY UP AND LEAVE!
!
YOU'RE IN LOVE--
--WITH HIM.
HA.
I GET IT.
HUH...?
WH...
WHA...

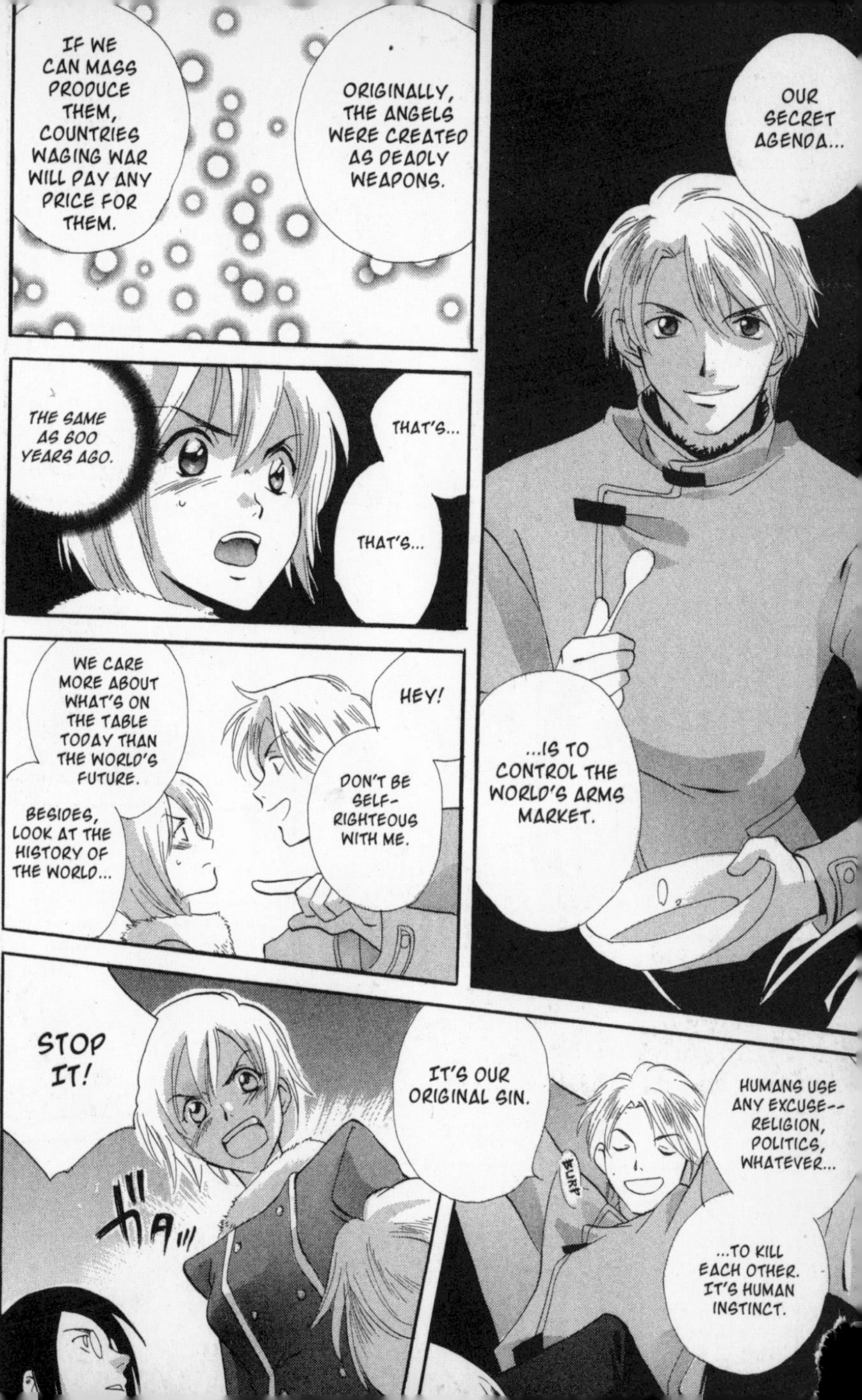
OUR SECRET AGENDA...
...IS TO CONTROL THE WORLD'S ARMS MARKET.
ORIGINALLY, THE ANGELS WERE CREATED AS DEADLY WEAPONS.
IF WE CAN MASS PRODUCE THEM, COUNTRIES WAGING WAR WILL PAY ANY PRICE FOR THEM.
THAT'S...
THAT'S...
THE SAME AS 600 YEARS AGO.
HEY!
DON'T BE SELF-RIGHTEOUS WITH ME.
WE CARE MORE ABOUT WHAT'S ON THE TABLE TODAY THAN THE WORLD'S FUTURE.
BESIDES, LOOK AT THE HISTORY OF THE WORLD...
HUMANS USE ANY EXCUSE--RELIGION, POLITICS, WHATEVER...
...TO KILL EACH OTHER. IT'S HUMAN INSTINCT.
BURP
IT'S OUR ORIGINAL SIN.
STOP IT!
ガタ

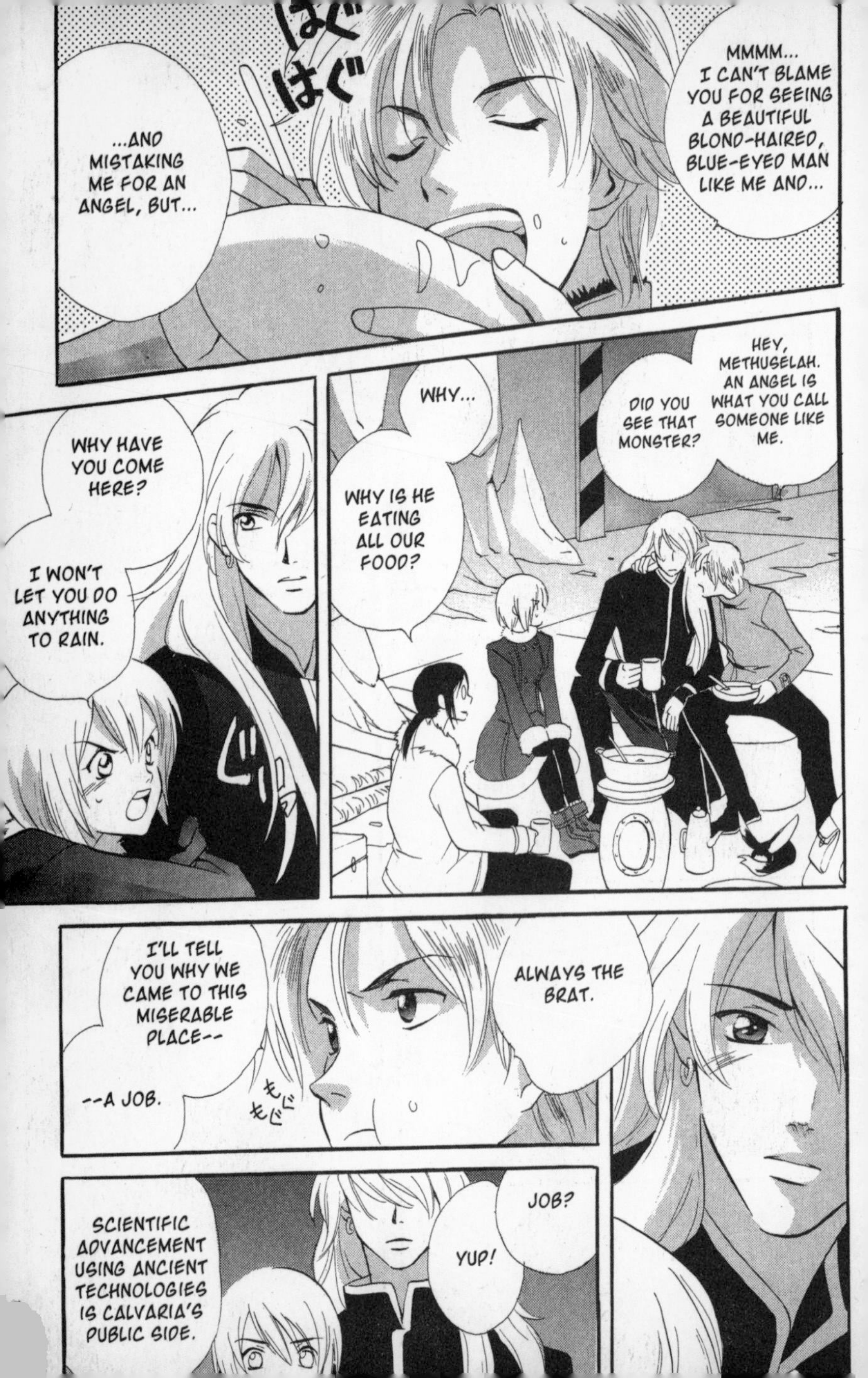
はぐはぐ
MMMM... I CAN'T BLAME YOU FOR SEEING A BEAUTIFUL BLOND-HAIRED, BLUE-EYED MAN LIKE ME AND...
...AND MISTAKING ME FOR AN ANGEL, BUT...
HEY, METHUSELAH. AN ANGEL IS WHAT YOU CALL SOMEONE LIKE ME.
DID YOU SEE THAT MONSTER?
WHY...
WHY IS HE EATING ALL OUR FOOD?
WHY HAVE YOU COME HERE?
I WON'T LET YOU DO ANYTHING TO RAIN.
ALWAYS THE BRAT.
もぐもぐ
I'LL TELL YOU WHY WE CAME TO THIS MISERABLE PLACE--
--A JOB.
JOB?
YUP!
SCIENTIFIC ADVANCEMENT USING ANCIENT TECHNOLOGIES IS CALVARIA'S PUBLIC SIDE.

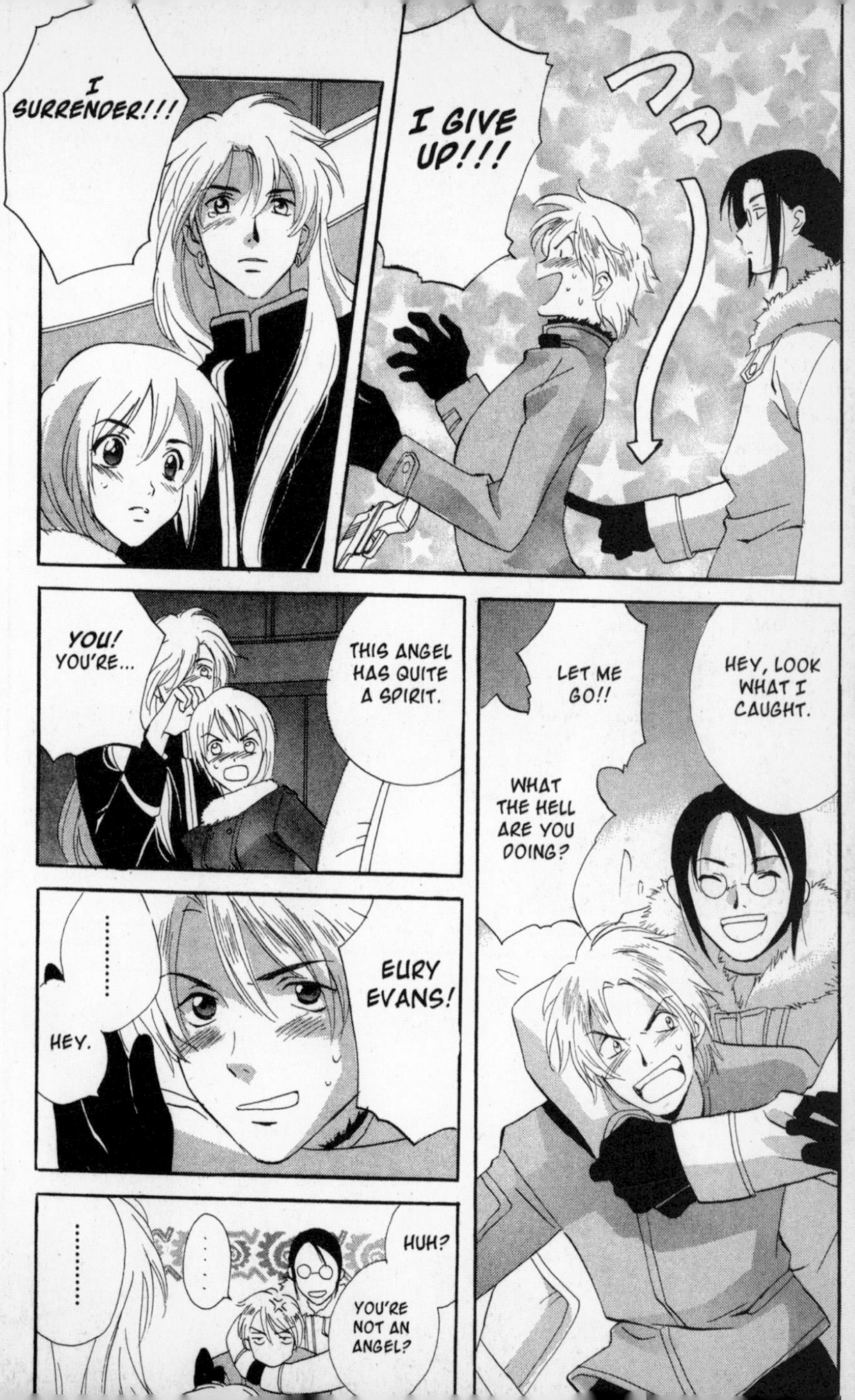
I GIVE UP!!!
I SURRENDER!!!
HEY, LOOK WHAT I CAUGHT.
LET ME GO!!
WHAT THE HELL ARE YOU DOING?
THIS ANGEL HAS QUITE A SPIRIT.
YOU! YOU'RE...
EURY EVANS!
......
HEY.
HUH?
YOU'RE NOT AN ANGEL?
. . . . .
......

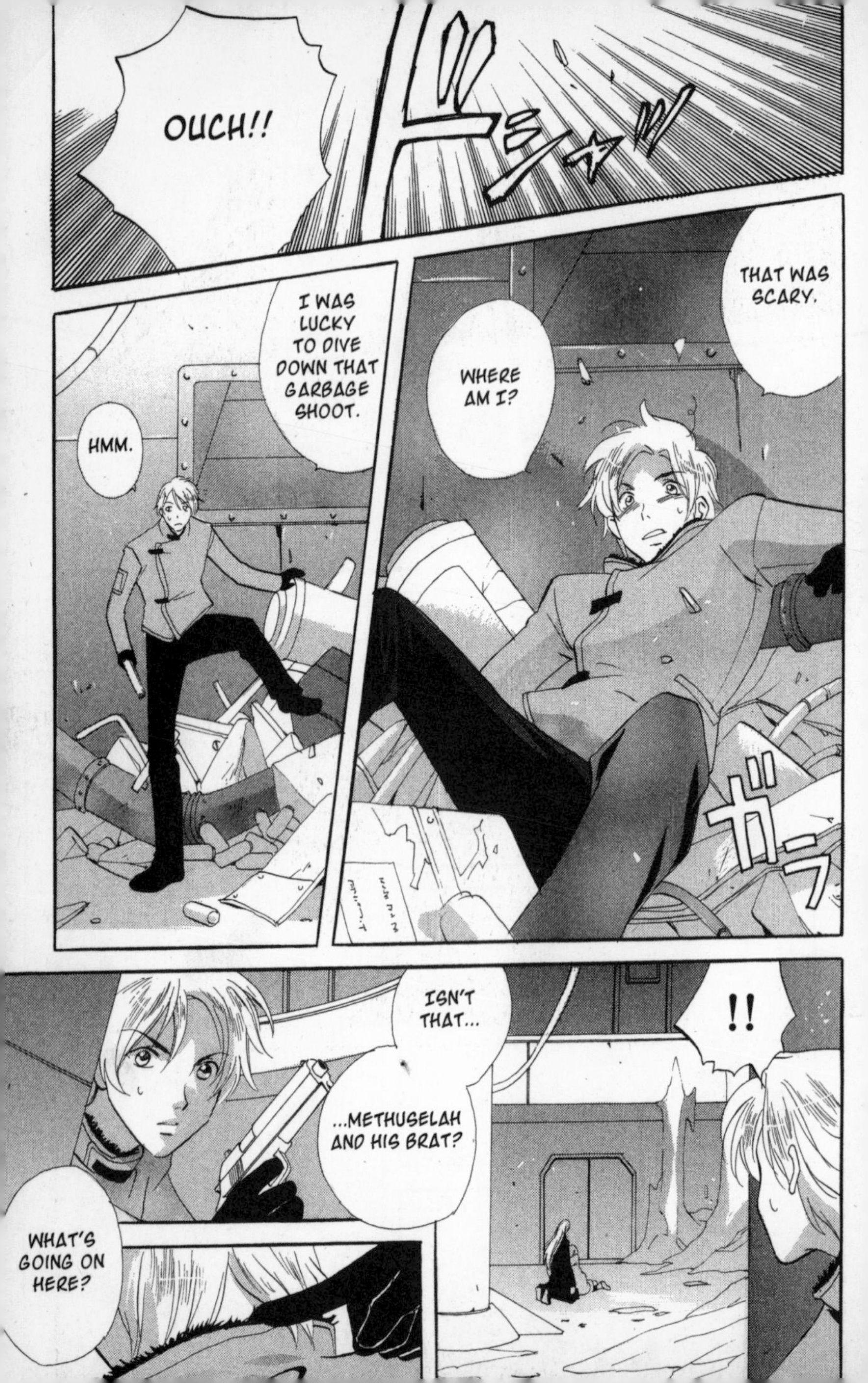
OUCH!!
ドシャッ
THAT WAS SCARY.
WHERE AM I?
ガラ
I WAS LUCKY TO DIVE DOWN THAT GARBAGE SHOOT.
HMM.
!!
ISN'T THAT...
...METHUSELAH AND HIS BRAT?
WHAT'S GOING ON HERE?

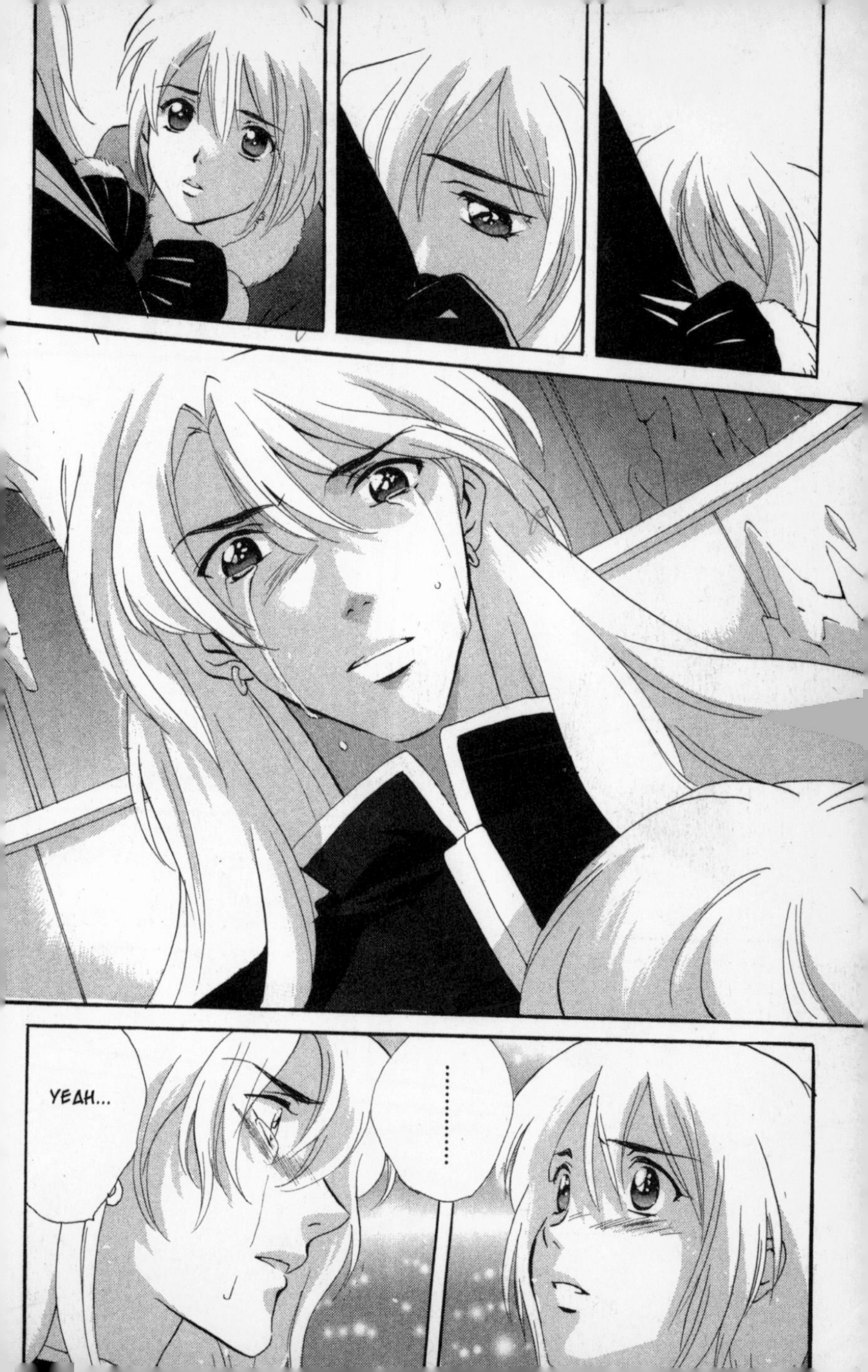

......
YEAH...

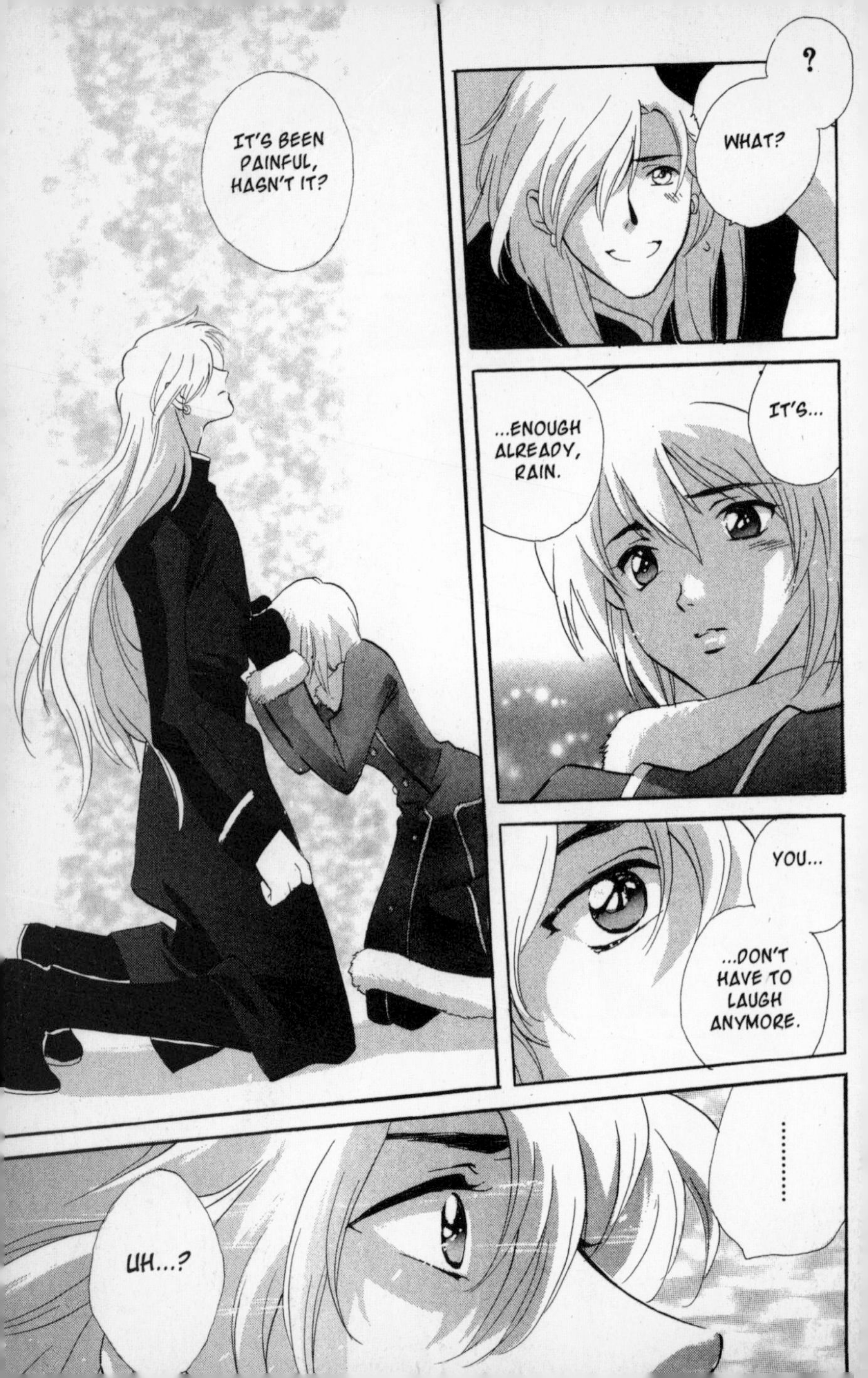
?
WHAT?
IT'S...
...ENOUGH ALREADY, RAIN.
YOU...
...DON'T HAVE TO LAUGH ANYMORE.
IT'S BEEN PAINFUL, HASN'T IT?
......
UH...?

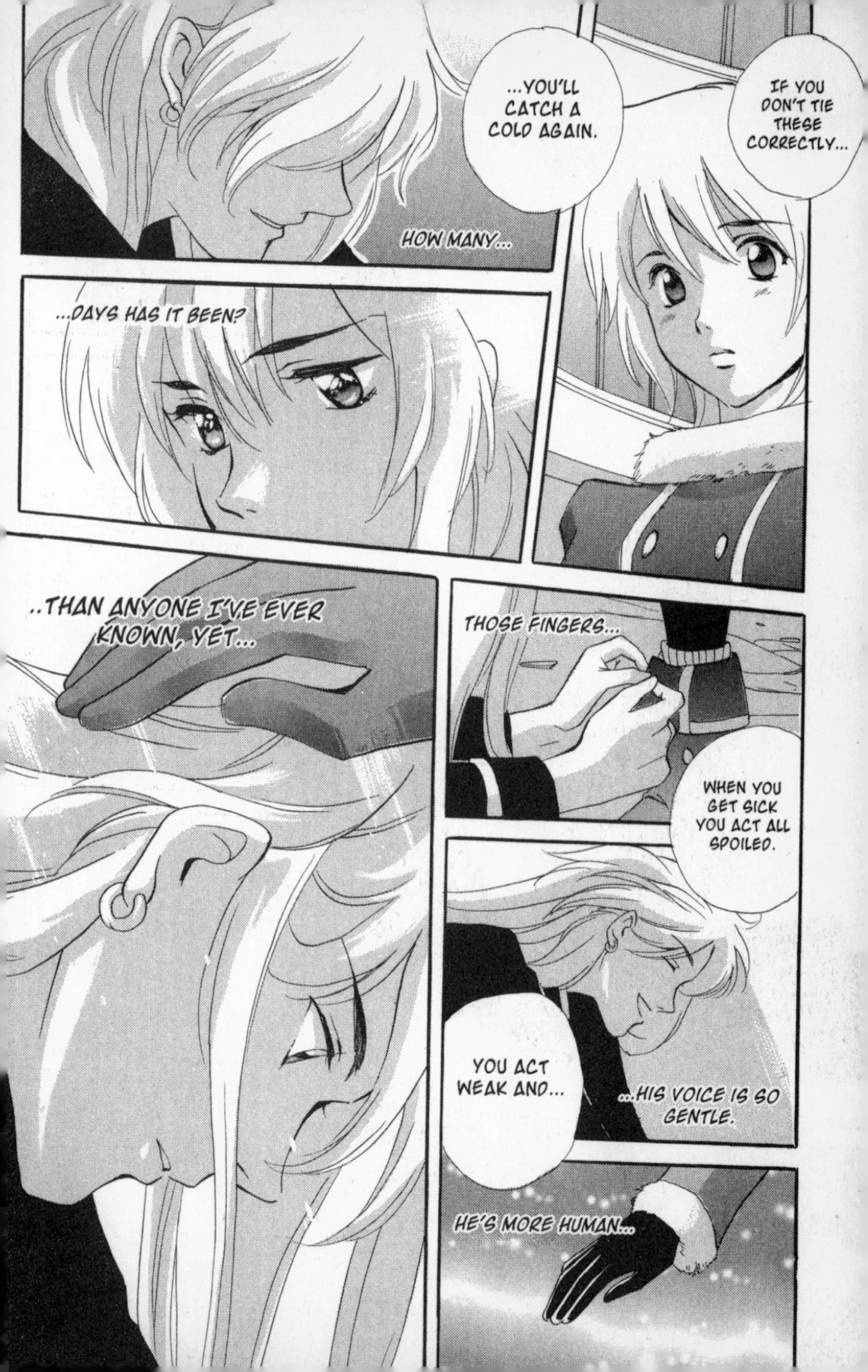
IF YOU DON'T TIE THESE CORRECTLY...
...YOU'LL CATCH A COLD AGAIN.
HOW MANY...
...DAYS HAS IT BEEN?
THOSE FINGERS...
WHEN YOU GET SICK YOU ACT ALL SPOILED.
YOU ACT WEAK AND...
...HIS VOICE IS SO GENTLE.
HE'S MORE HUMAN...
..THAN ANYONE I'VE EVER KNOWN, YET...

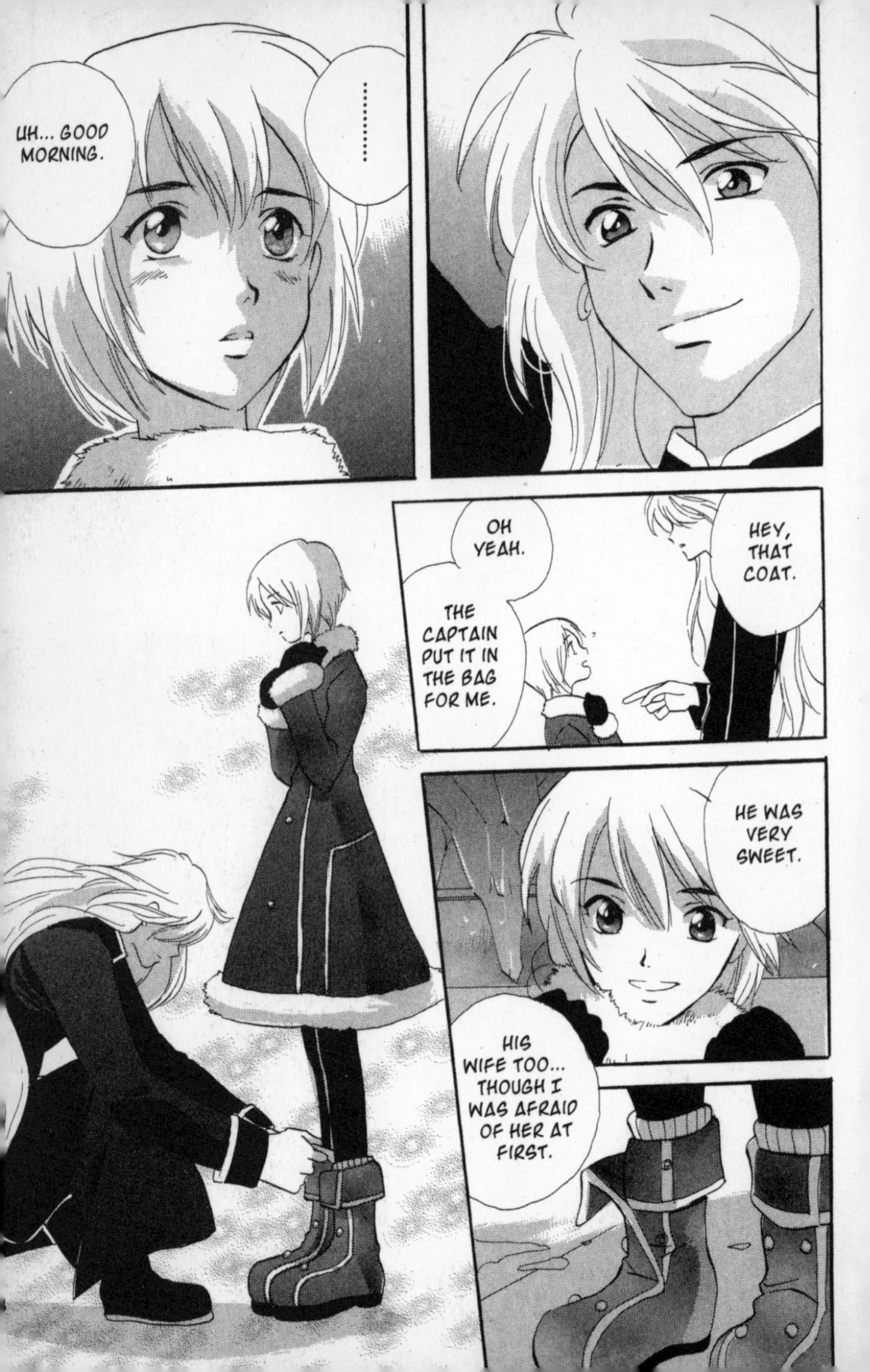
......
UH... GOOD MORNING.
HEY, THAT COAT.
OH YEAH.
THE CAPTAIN PUT IT IN THE BAG FOR ME.
HE WAS VERY SWEET.
HIS WIFE TOO... THOUGH I WAS AFRAID OF HER AT FIRST.

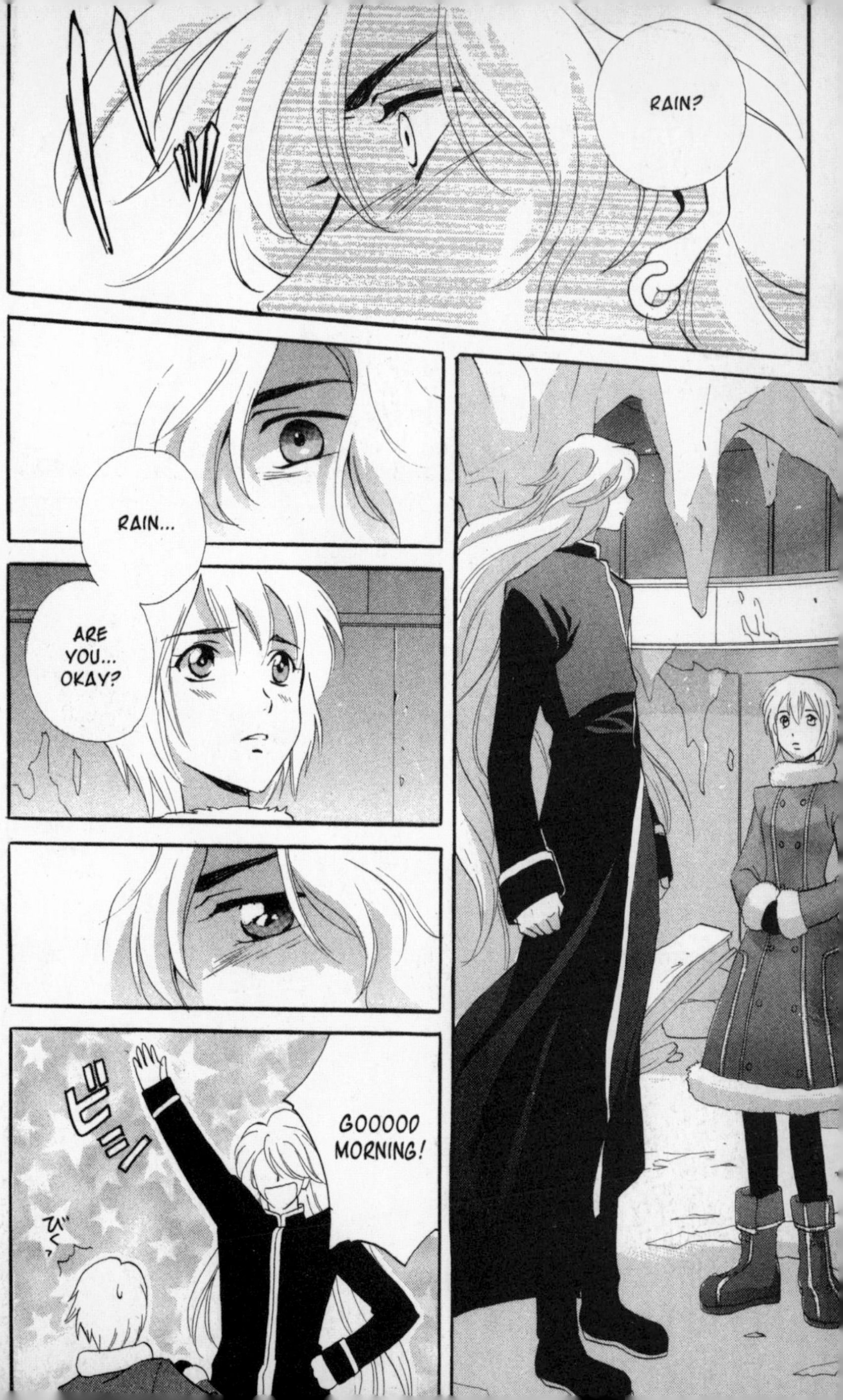
RAIN?
RAIN...
ARE YOU... OKAY?
GOOOOD MORNING!

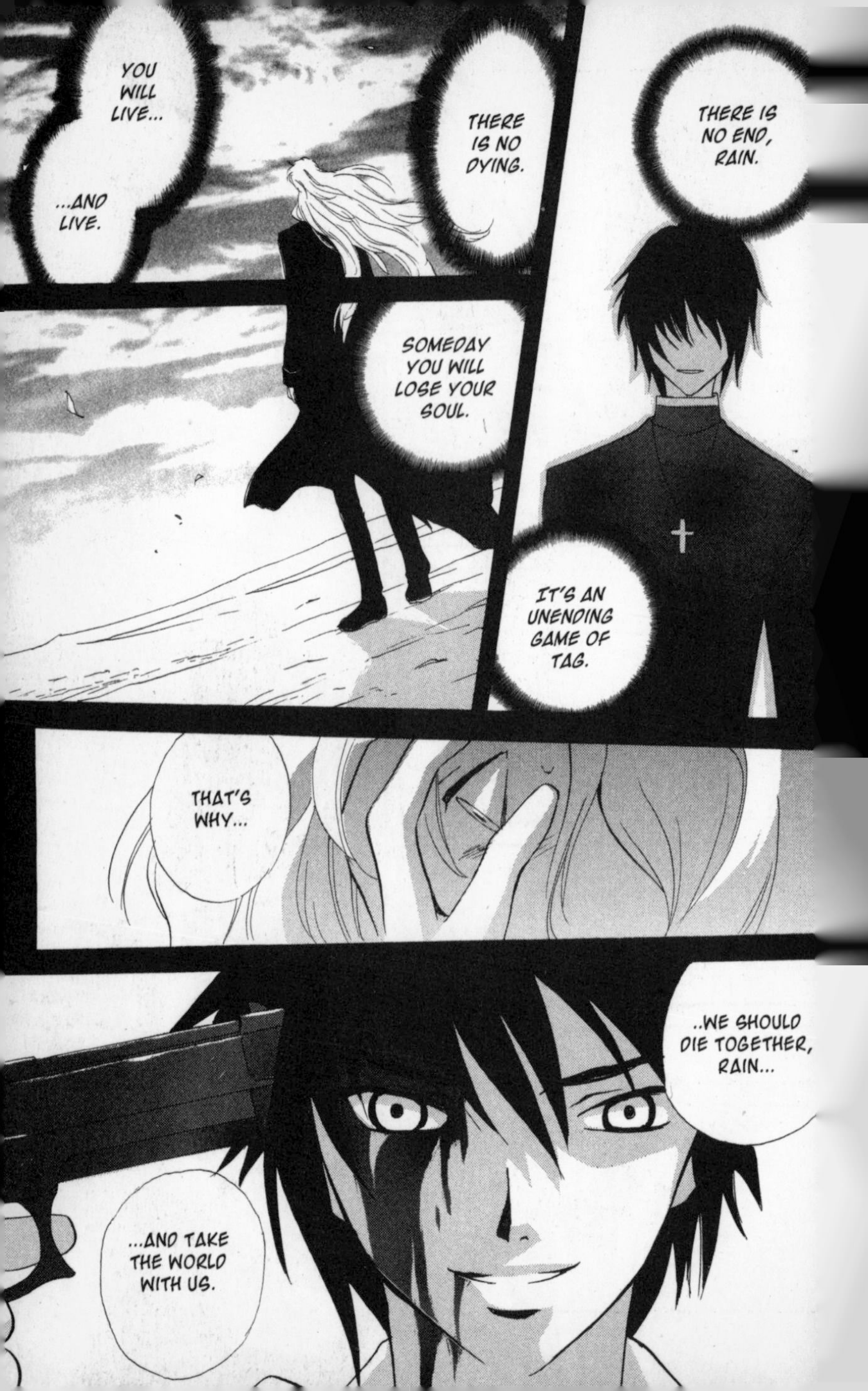
THERE IS NO END, RAIN.
THERE IS NO DYING.
YOU WILL LIVE...
...AND LIVE.
SOMEDAY YOU WILL LOSE YOUR SOUL.
IT'S AN UNENDING GAME OF TAG.
THAT'S WHY...
..WE SHOULD DIE TOGETHER, RAIN...
...AND TAKE THE WORLD WITH US.

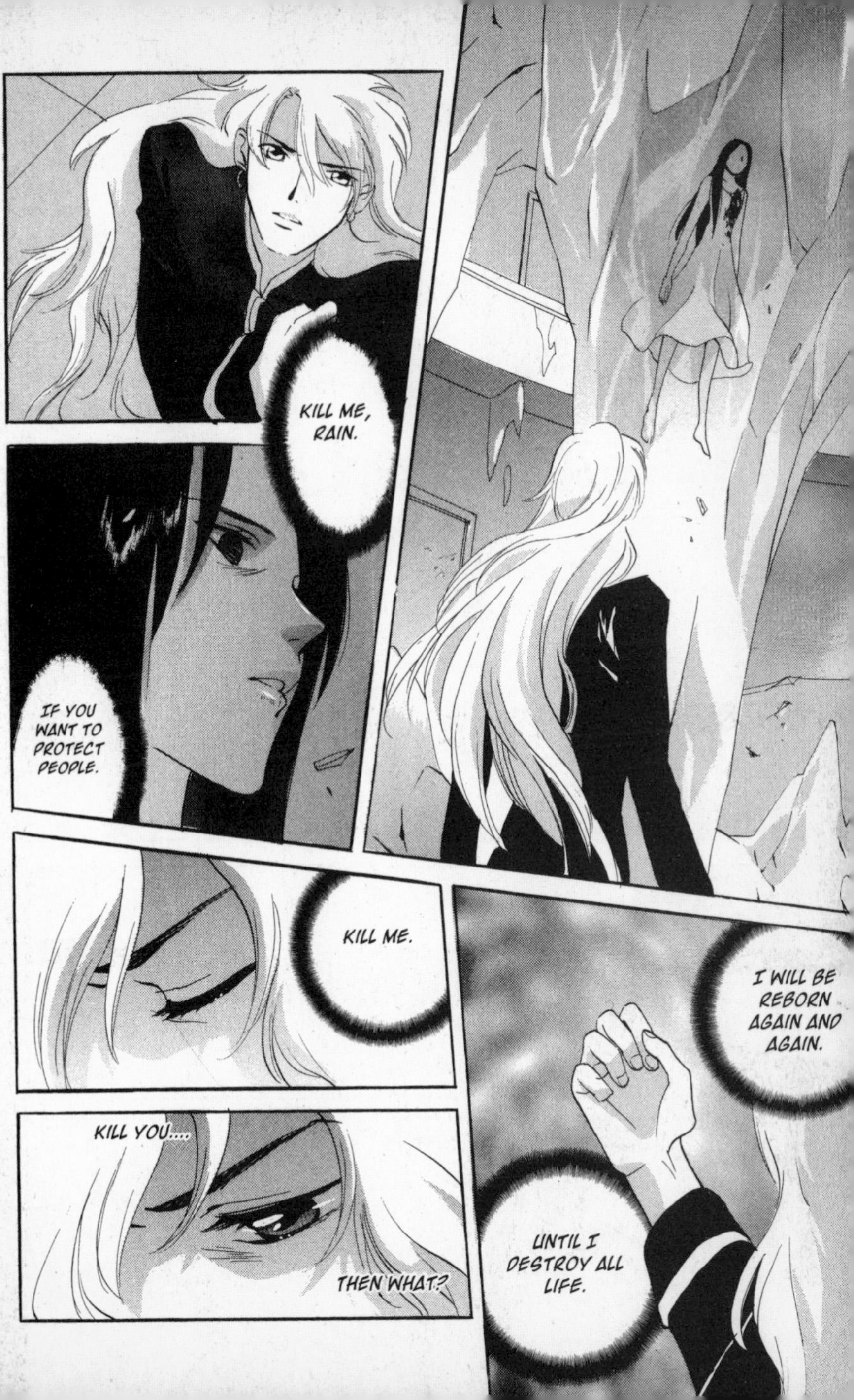

KILL ME, RAIN.
IF YOU WANT TO PROTECT PEOPLE.
I WILL BE REBORN AGAIN AND AGAIN.
UNTIL I DESTROY ALL LIFE.
KILL ME.
KILL YOU....
THEN WHAT?

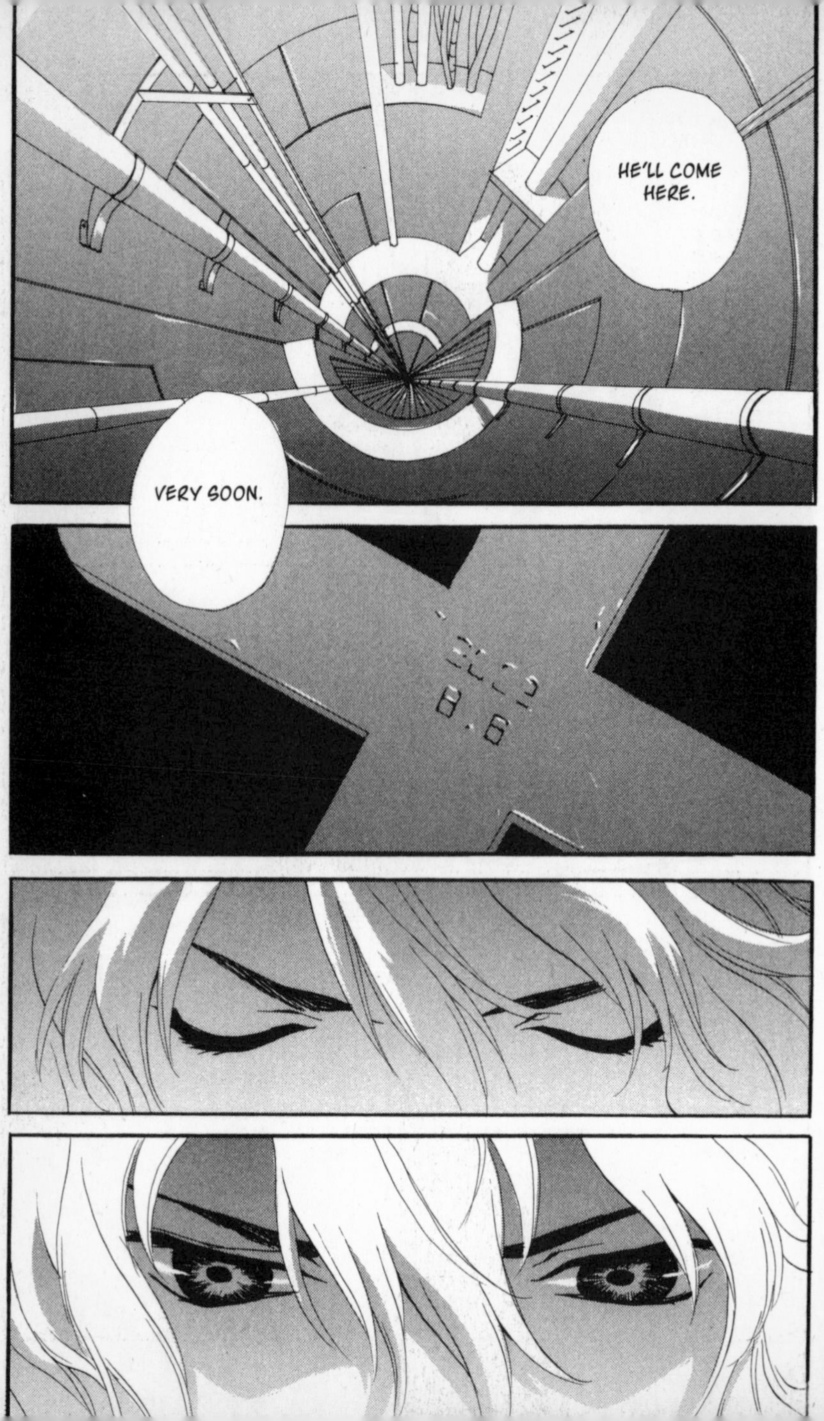
HE'LL COME HERE.
VERY SOON.

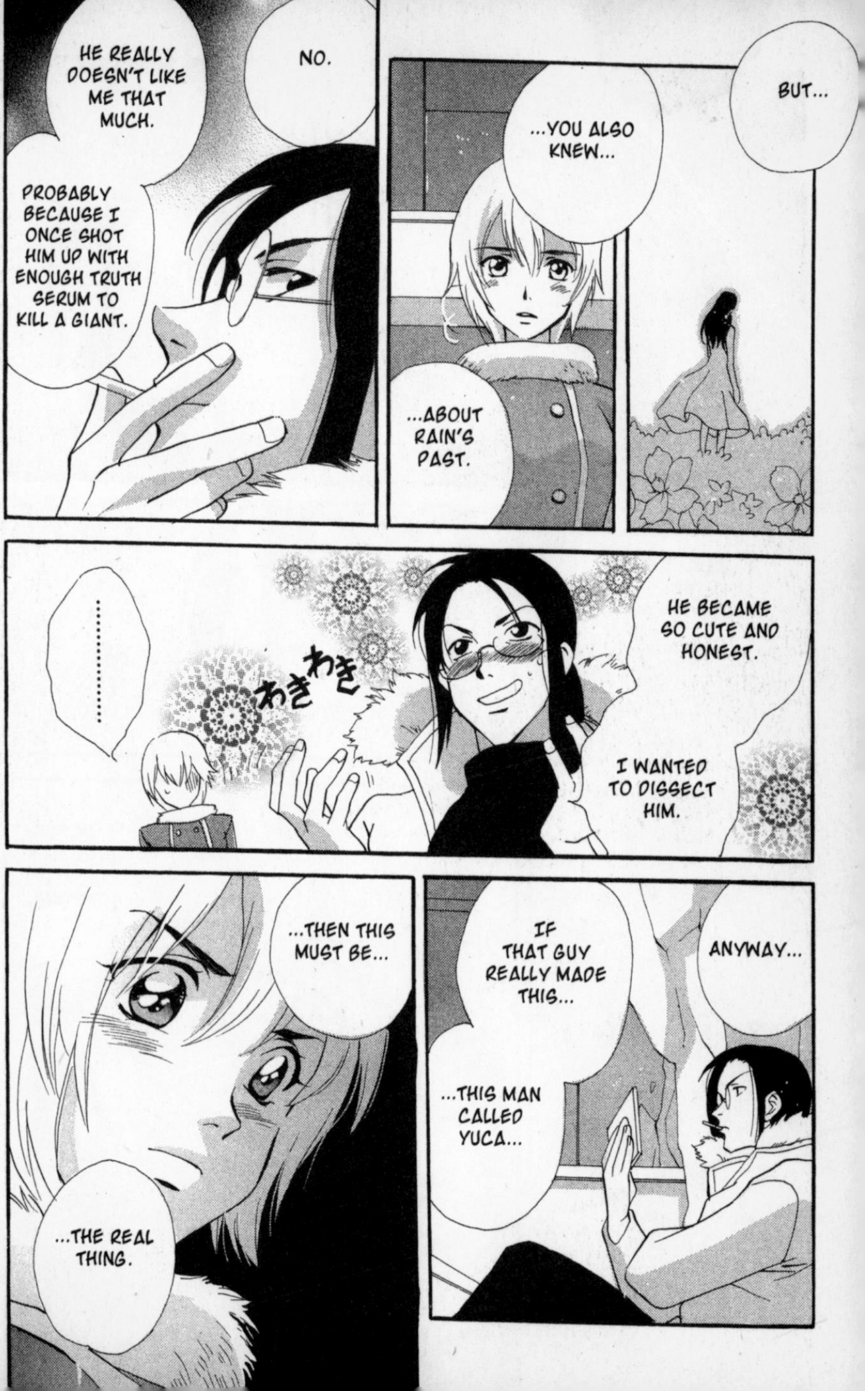
BUT...
...YOU ALSO KNEW...
...ABOUT RAIN'S PAST.
NO.
HE REALLY DOESN'T LIKE ME THAT MUCH.
PROBABLY BECAUSE I ONCE SHOT HIM UP WITH ENOUGH TRUTH SERUM TO KILL A GIANT.
HE BECAME SO CUTE AND HONEST.
I WANTED TO DISSECT HIM.
わきわき
....
ANYWAY...
IF THAT GUY REALLY MADE THIS...
...THIS MAN CALLED YUCA...
...THEN THIS MUST BE...
...THE REAL THING.

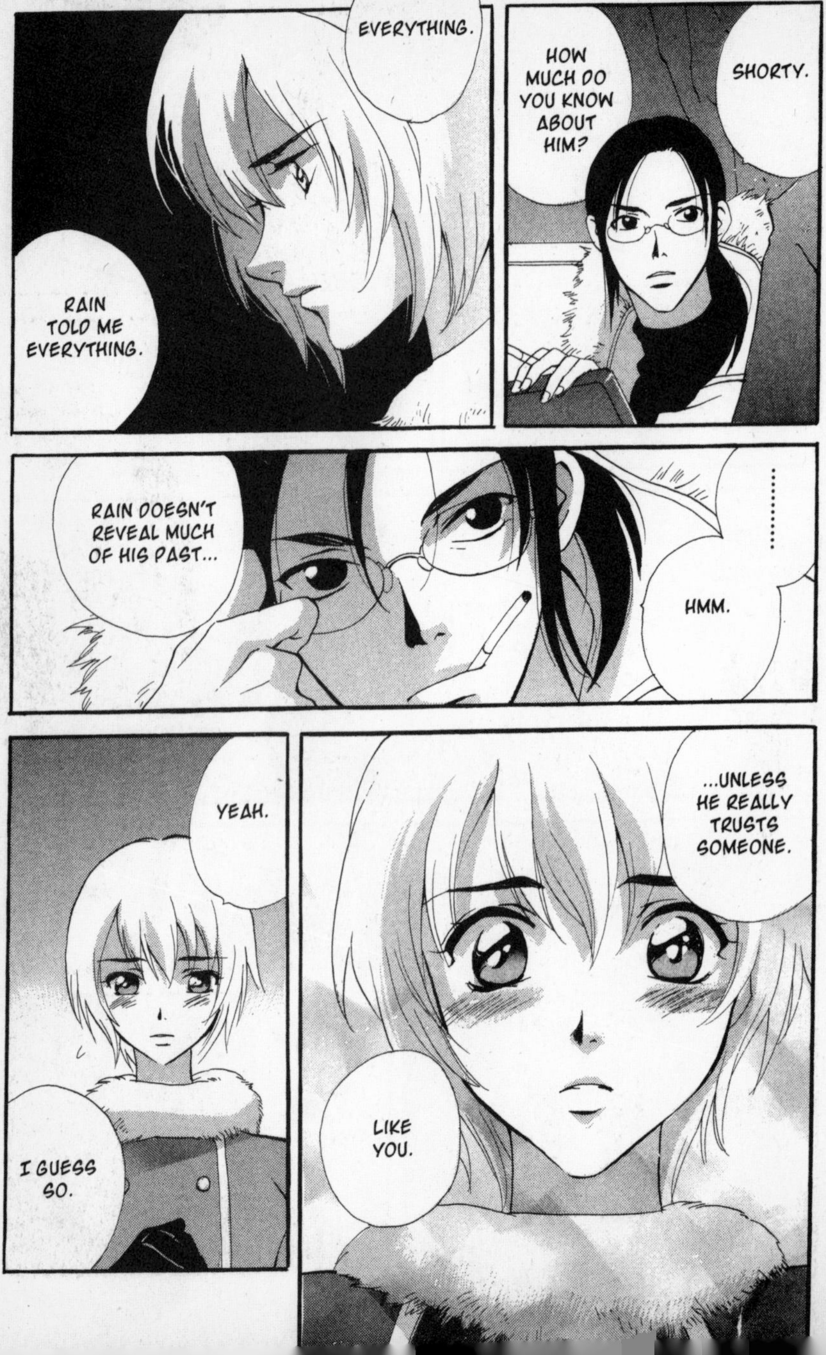
SHORTY.
HOW MUCH DO YOU KNOW ABOUT HIM?
EVERYTHING.
RAIN TOLD ME EVERYTHING.
......
HMM.
RAIN DOESN'T REVEAL MUCH OF HIS PAST...
...UNLESS HE REALLY TRUSTS SOMEONE.
LIKE YOU.
YEAH.
I GUESS SO.

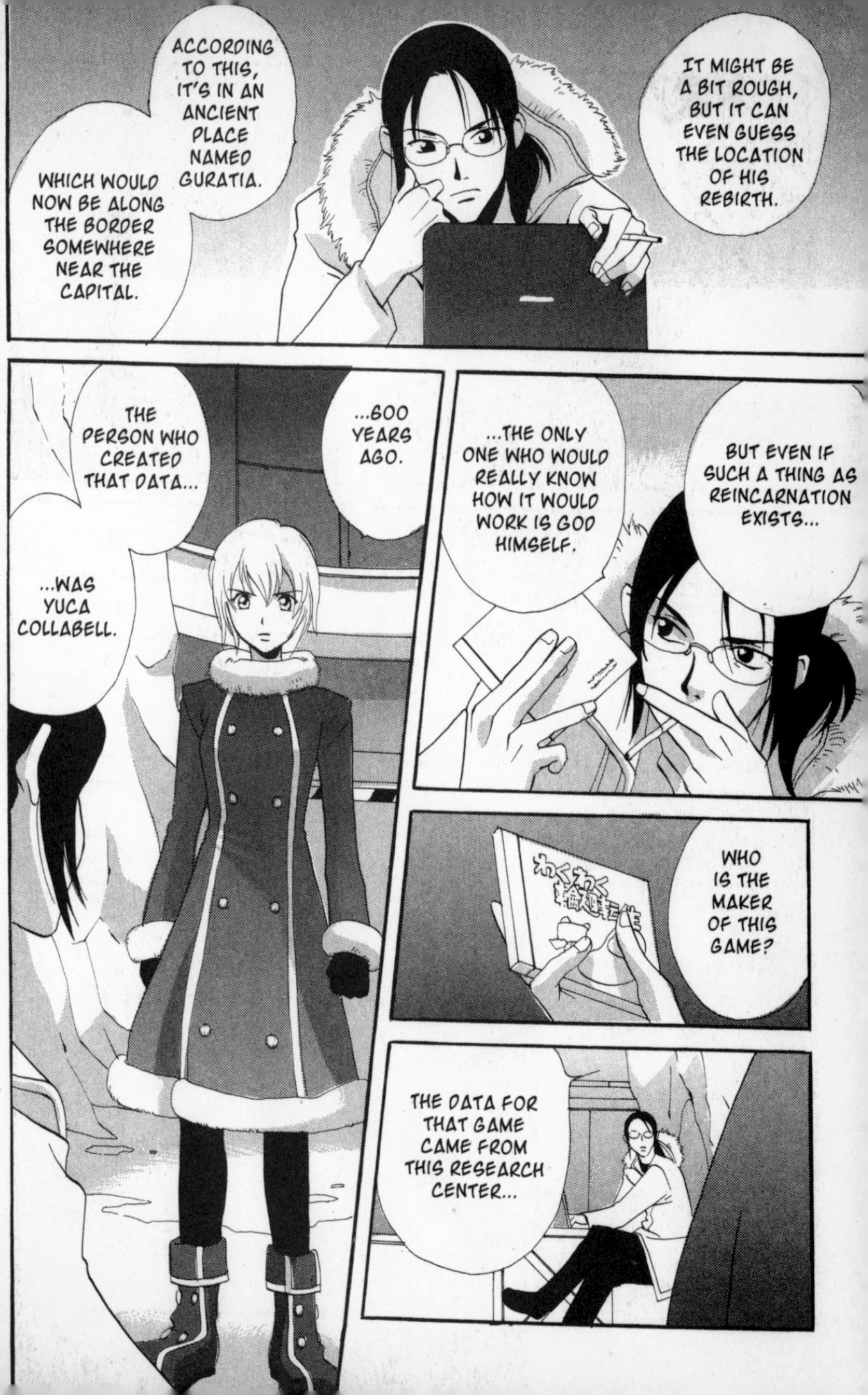
IT MIGHT BE A BIT ROUGH, BUT IT CAN EVEN GUESS THE LOCATION OF HIS REBIRTH.
ACCORDING TO THIS, IT'S IN AN ANCIENT PLACE NAMED GURATIA.
WHICH WOULD NOW BE ALONG THE BORDER SOMEWHERE NEAR THE CAPITAL.
BUT EVEN IF SUCH A THING AS REINCARNATION EXISTS...
...THE ONLY ONE WHO WOULD REALLY KNOW HOW IT WOULD WORK IS GOD HIMSELF.
わくわく輪廻転生
WHO IS THE MAKER OF THIS GAME?
THE DATA FOR THAT GAME CAME FROM THIS RESEARCH CENTER...
...600 YEARS AGO.
THE PERSON WHO CREATED THAT DATA...
...WAS YUCA COLLABELL.

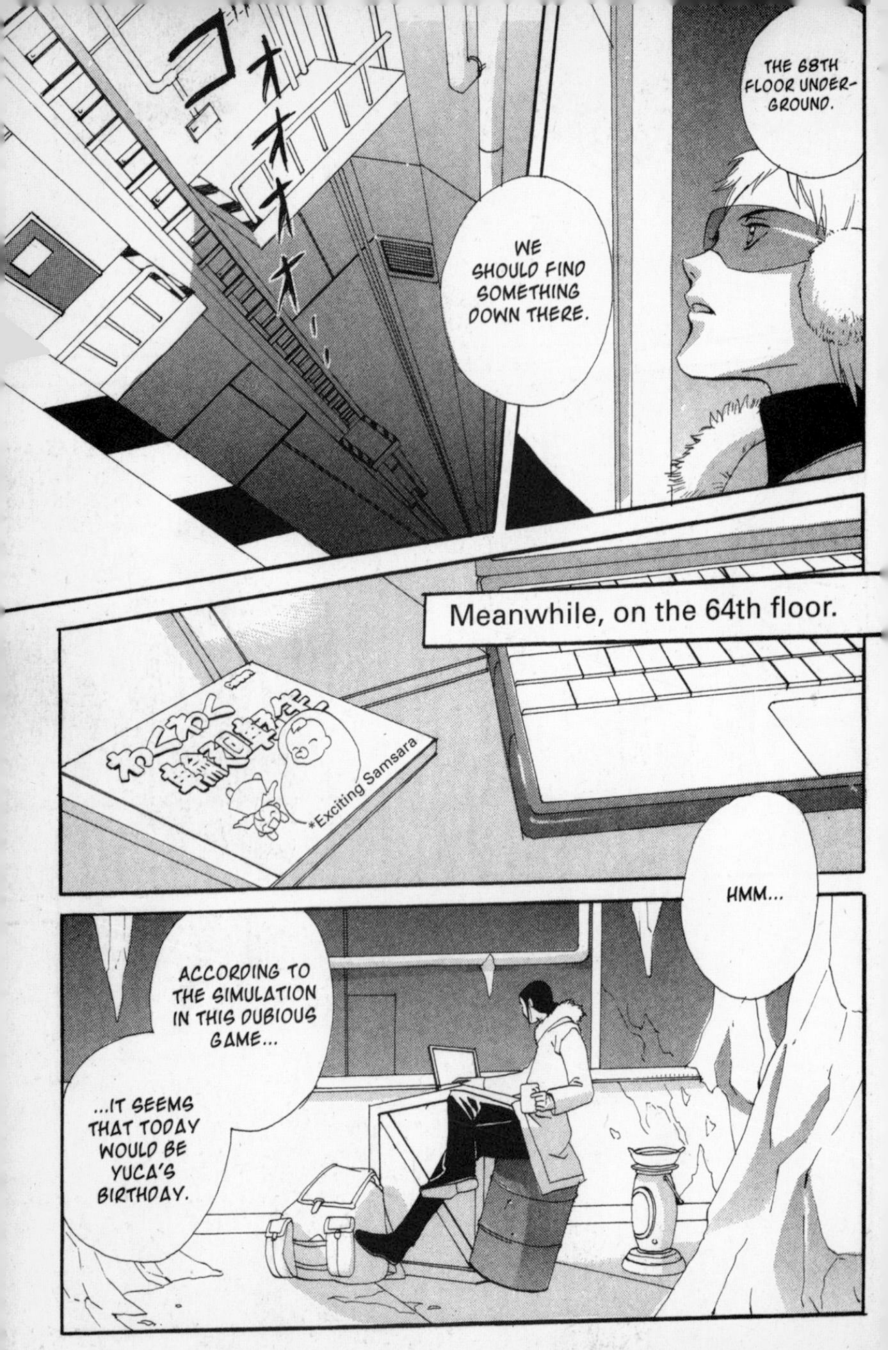

THE 68TH FLOOR UNDER-GROUND.
WE SHOULD FIND SOMETHING DOWN THERE.
Meanwhile, on the 64th floor.
わくわく輪廻転生
*Exciting Samsara
HMM...
ACCORDING TO THE SIMULATION IN THIS DUBIOUS GAME...
...IT SEEMS THAT TODAY WOULD BE YUCA'S BIRTHDAY.

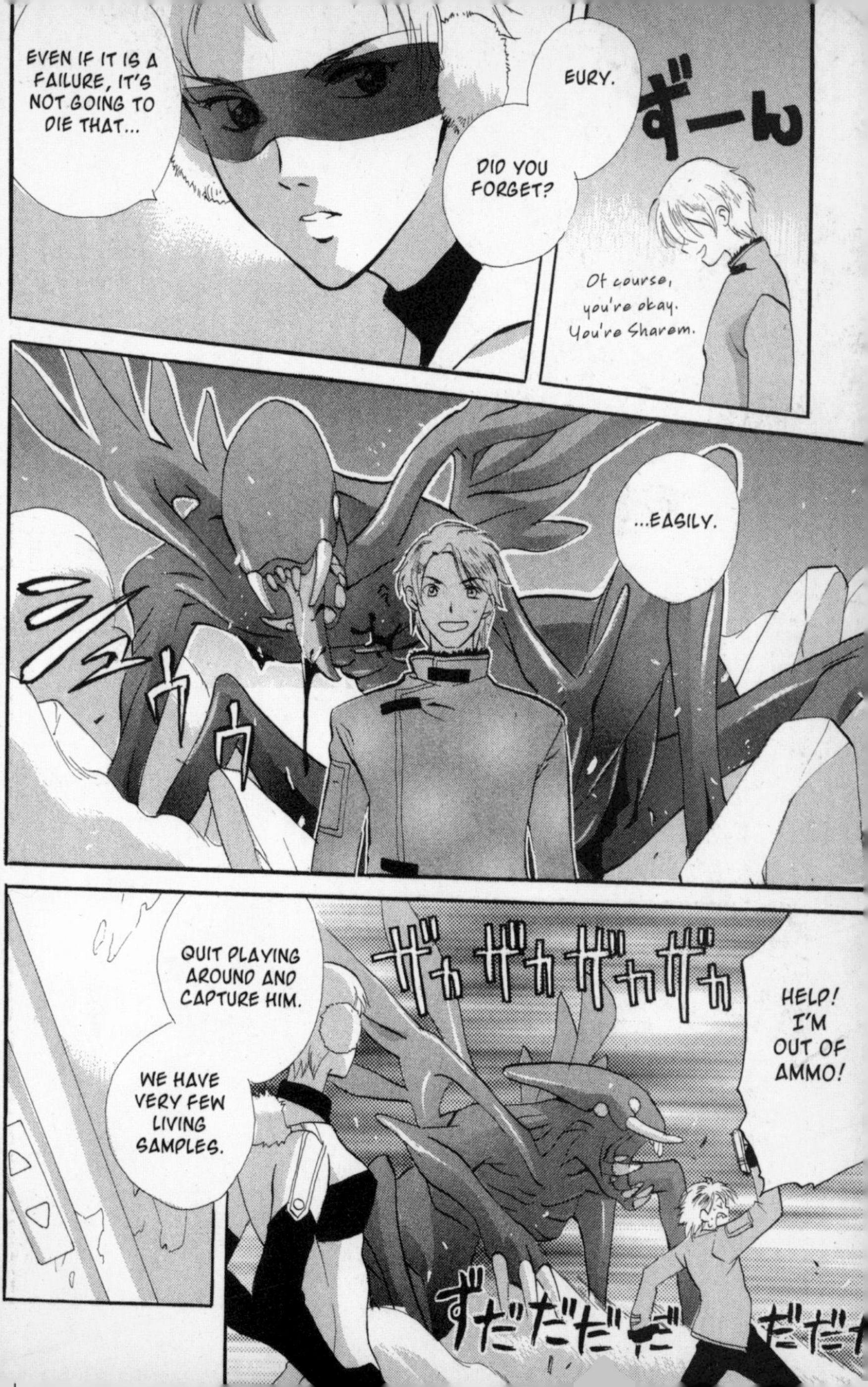

EURY.
DID YOU FORGET?
ずーん
Of course, you're okay. You're Sharem.
EVEN IF IT IS A FAILURE, IT'S NOT GOING TO DIE THAT...
...EASILY.
HELP! I'M OUT OF AMMO!
ザヵザヵザヵザヵ
QUIT PLAYING AROUND AND CAPTURE HIM.
WE HAVE VERY FEW LIVING SAMPLES.

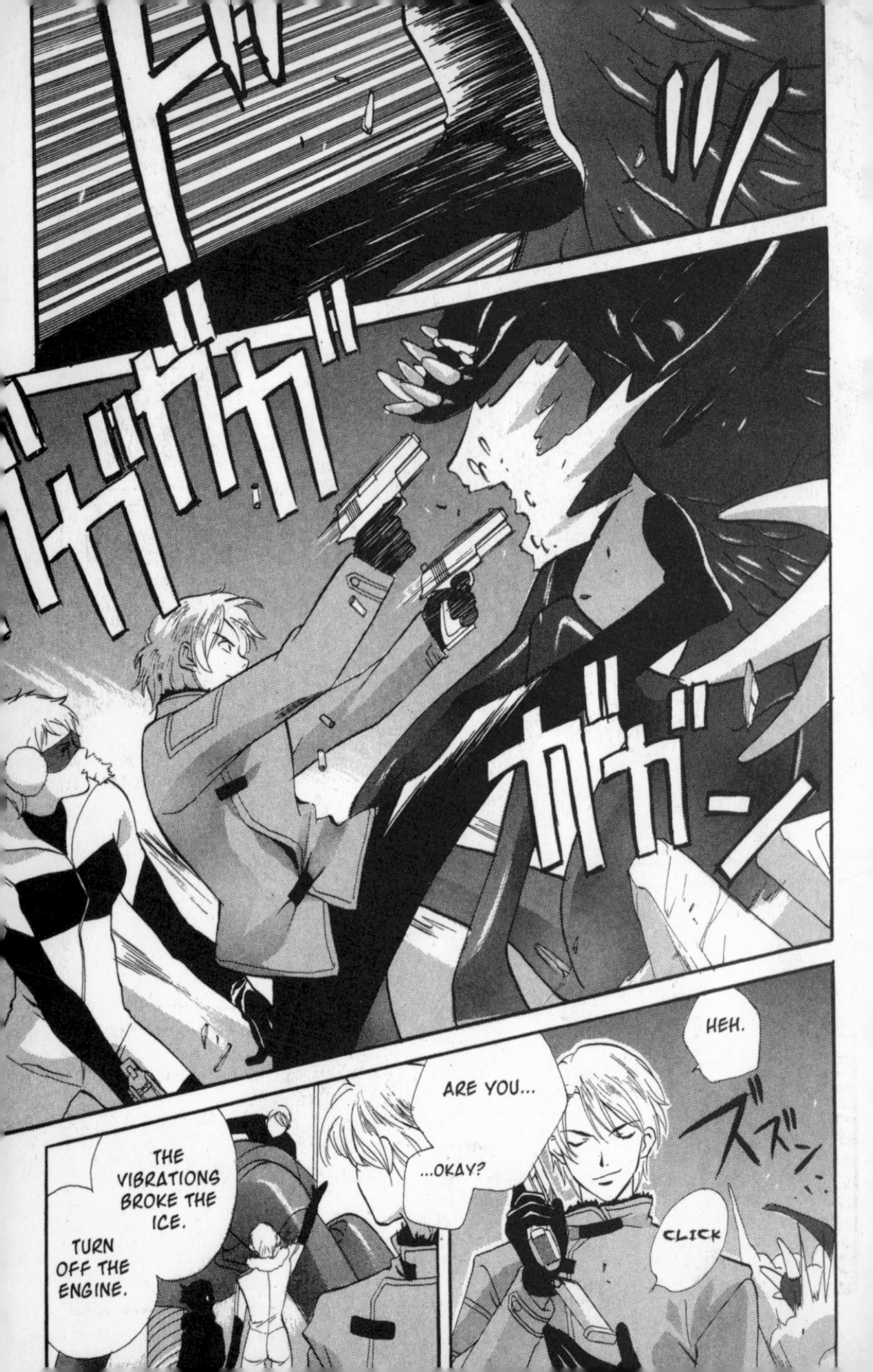
HEH.
ARE YOU...
...OKAY?
CLICK
THE VIBRATIONS BROKE THE ICE.
TURN OFF THE ENGINE.

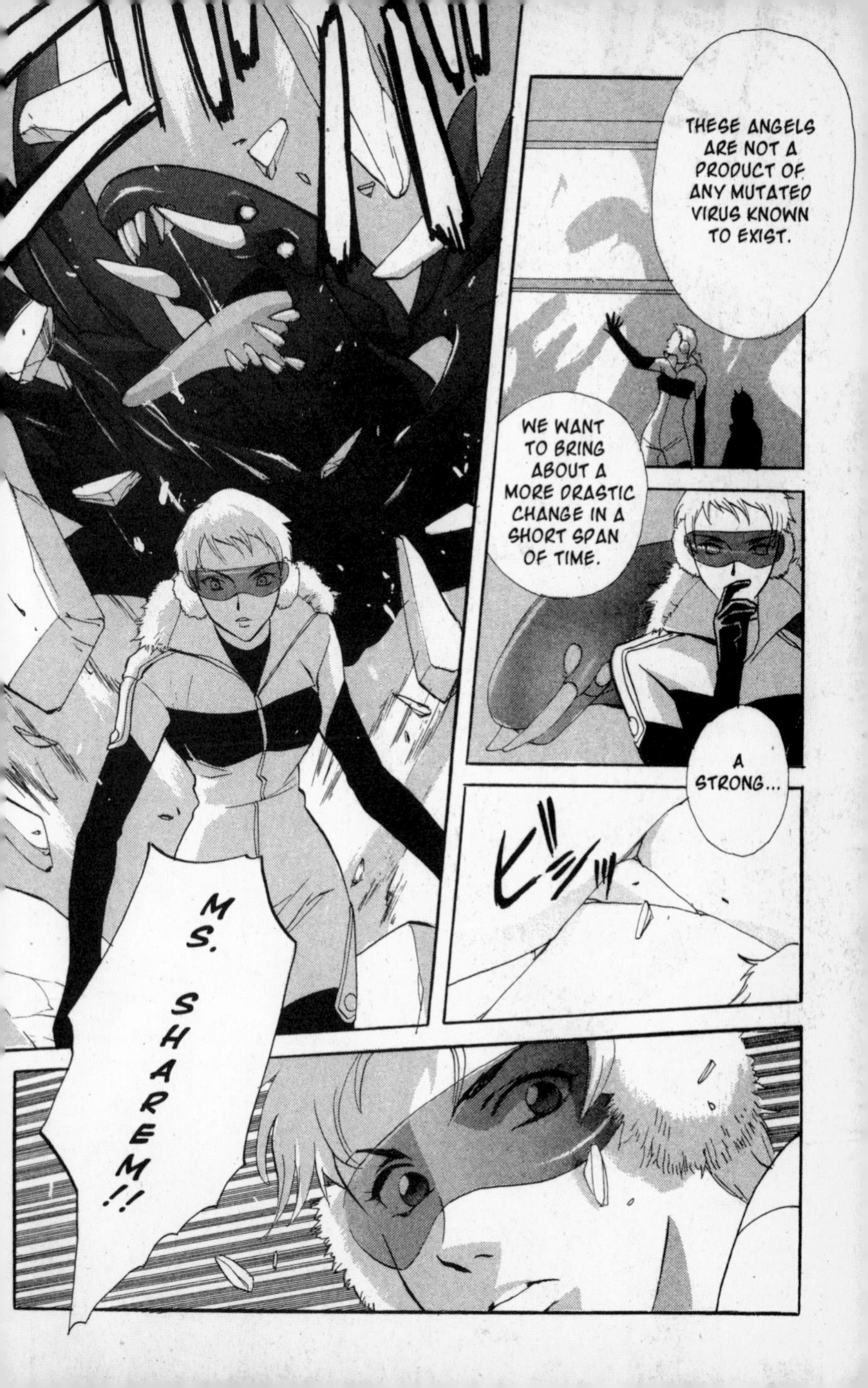
THESE ANGELS ARE NOT A PRODUCT OF ANY MUTATED VIRUS KNOWN TO EXIST.
WE WANT TO BRING ABOUT A MORE DRASTIC CHANGE IN A SHORT SPAN OF TIME.
A STRONG...
ビシッ
MS. SHAREM!!

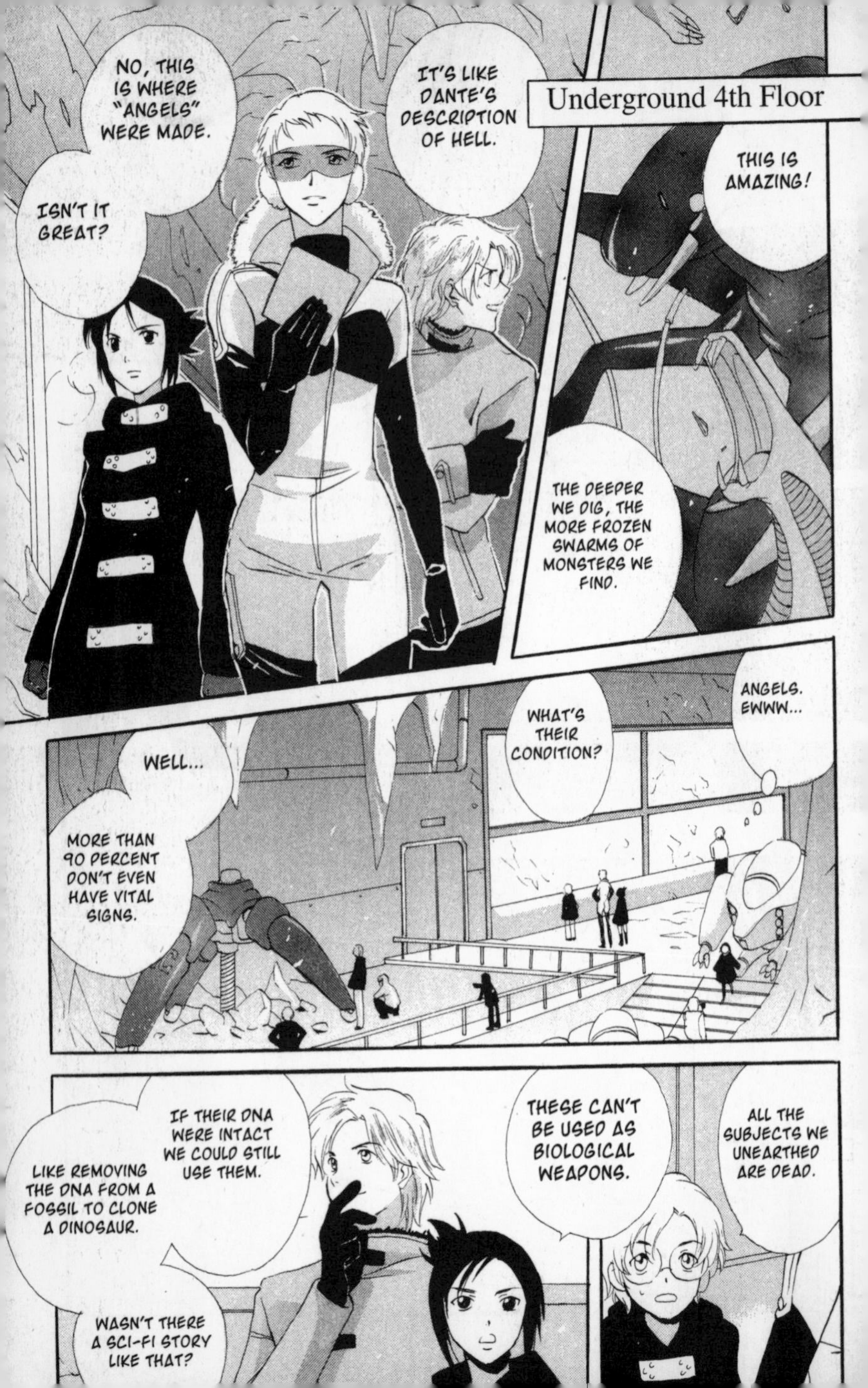
Underground 4th Floor
THIS IS AMAZING!
THE DEEPER WE DIG, THE MORE FROZEN SWARMS OF MONSTERS WE FIND.
IT'S LIKE DANTE'S DESCRIPTION OF HELL.
NO, THIS IS WHERE "ANGELS" WERE MADE.
ISN'T IT GREAT?
ANGELS. EWWW...
WHAT'S THEIR CONDITION?
WELL...
MORE THAN 90 PERCENT DON'T EVEN HAVE VITAL SIGNS.
ALL THE SUBJECTS WE UNEARTHED ARE DEAD.
THESE CAN'T BE USED AS BIOLOGICAL WEAPONS.
IF THEIR DNA WERE INTACT WE COULD STILL USE THEM.
LIKE REMOVING THE DNA FROM A FOSSIL TO CLONE A DINOSAUR.
WASN'T THERE A SCI-FI STORY LIKE THAT?

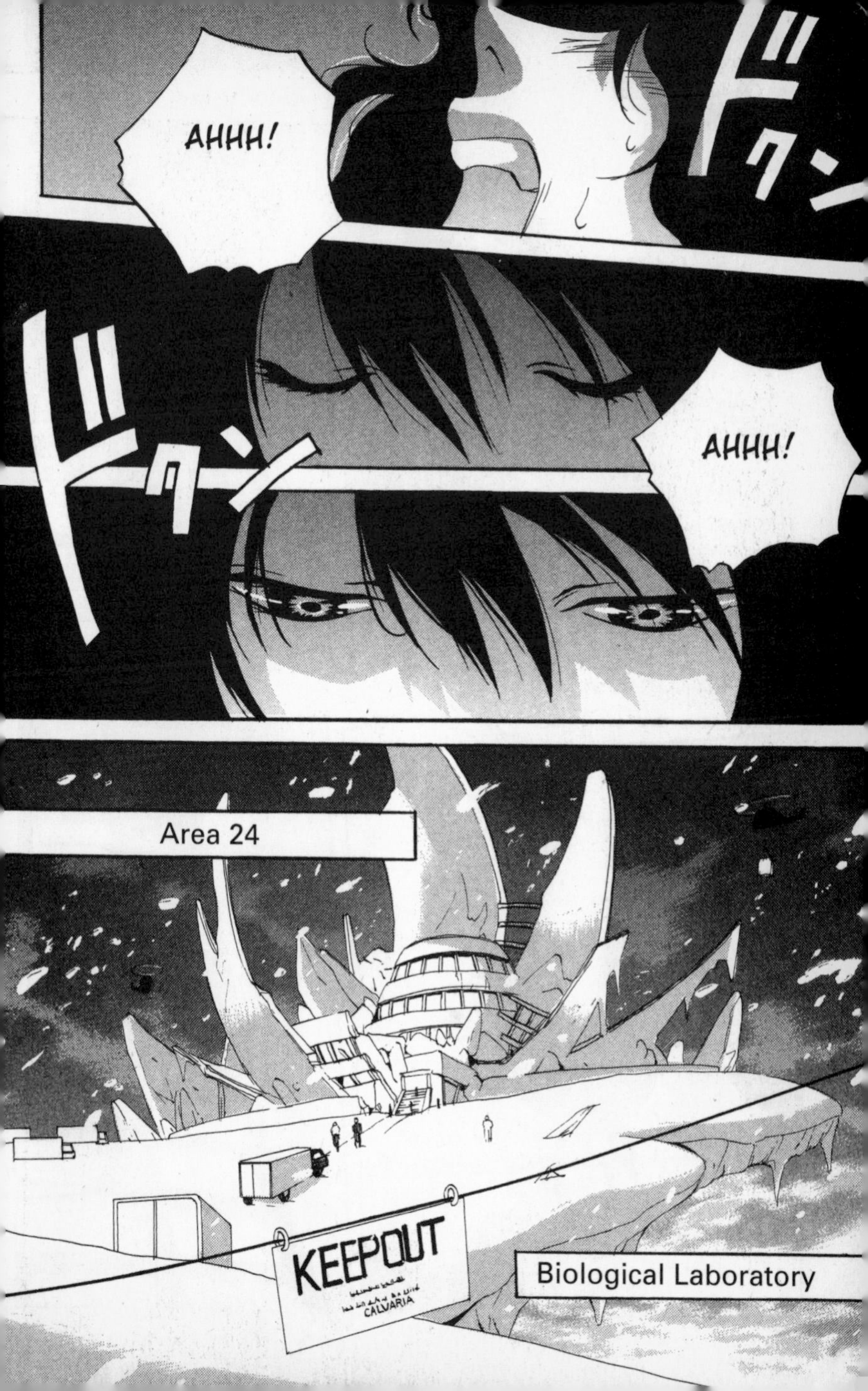
ドクン
AHHH!
AHHH!
ドクン
Area 24
KEEPOUT
CALVARIA
Biological Laboratory

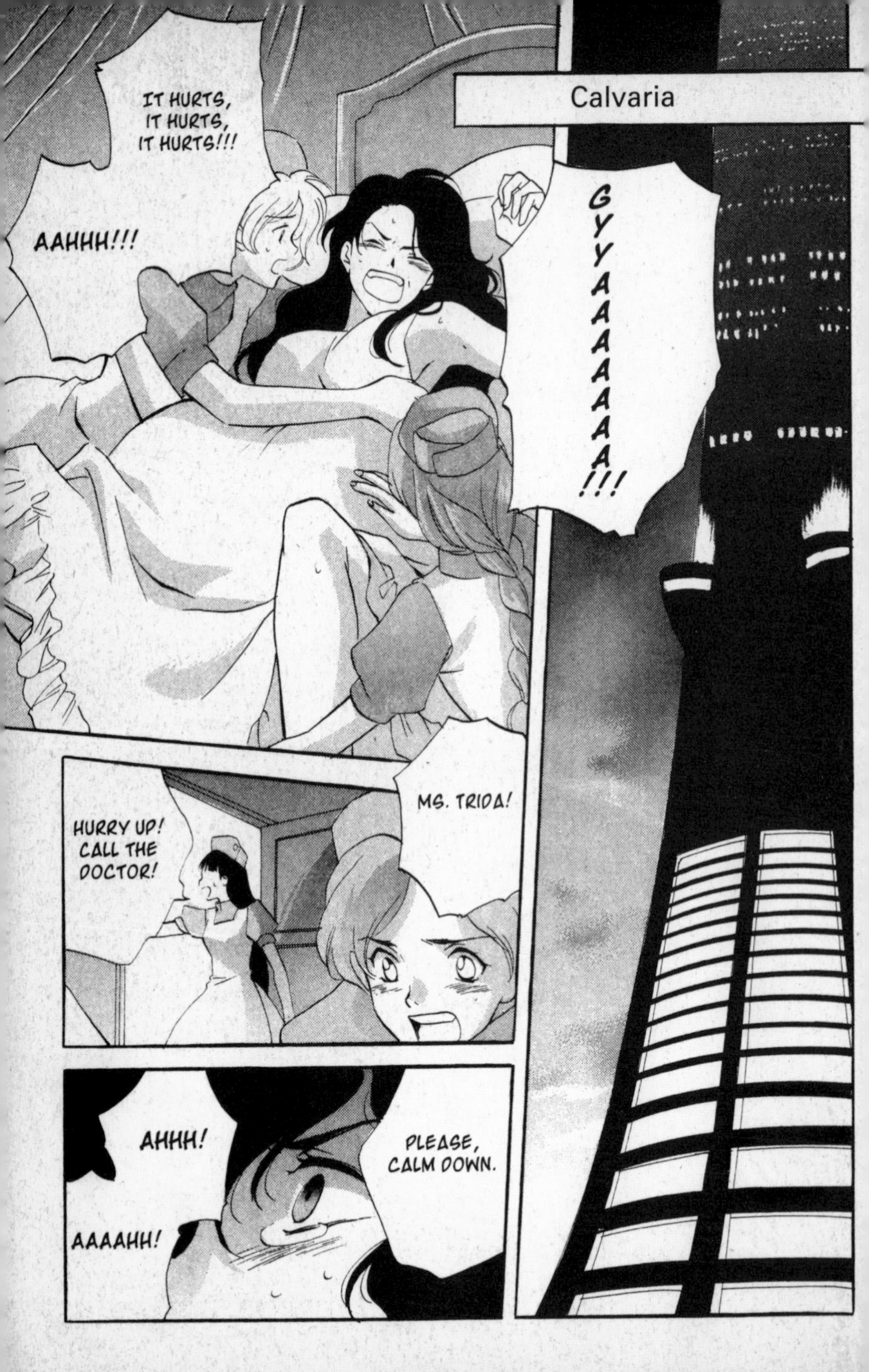
Calvaria
GYYAAAAAAA!!!
IT HURTS, IT HURTS, IT HURTS!!!
AAHHH!!!
MS. TRIDA!
HURRY UP! CALL THE DOCTOR!
PLEASE, CALM DOWN.
AHHH!
AAAAHH!

August 6th–

Cross 15

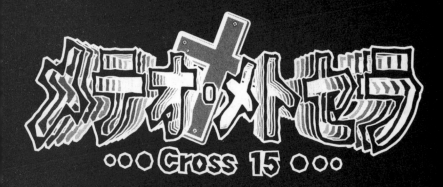

GOD SAID,

"LIVE"
"LOVE"
"FIGHT"
"KILL"
"EAT"
"GIVE BIRTH"
"REPEAT"

WE WERE BOUND IN CHAINS.

THE WORLD WAS MADE BY PEOPLE
AND IT OVERFLOWED
TILL WE COULD NO LONGER
BREATHE.

WE DIDN'T KNOW.

THAT GOD LEFT US HERE.

YET WE CONTINUE TO DANCE
THIS ENDLESS DANCE.

EVEN WHEN BOTH OF OUR LEGS
ARE COVERED IN BLOOD.

••• Cross 15 •••

IMMORTAL RAIN

CONTENTS

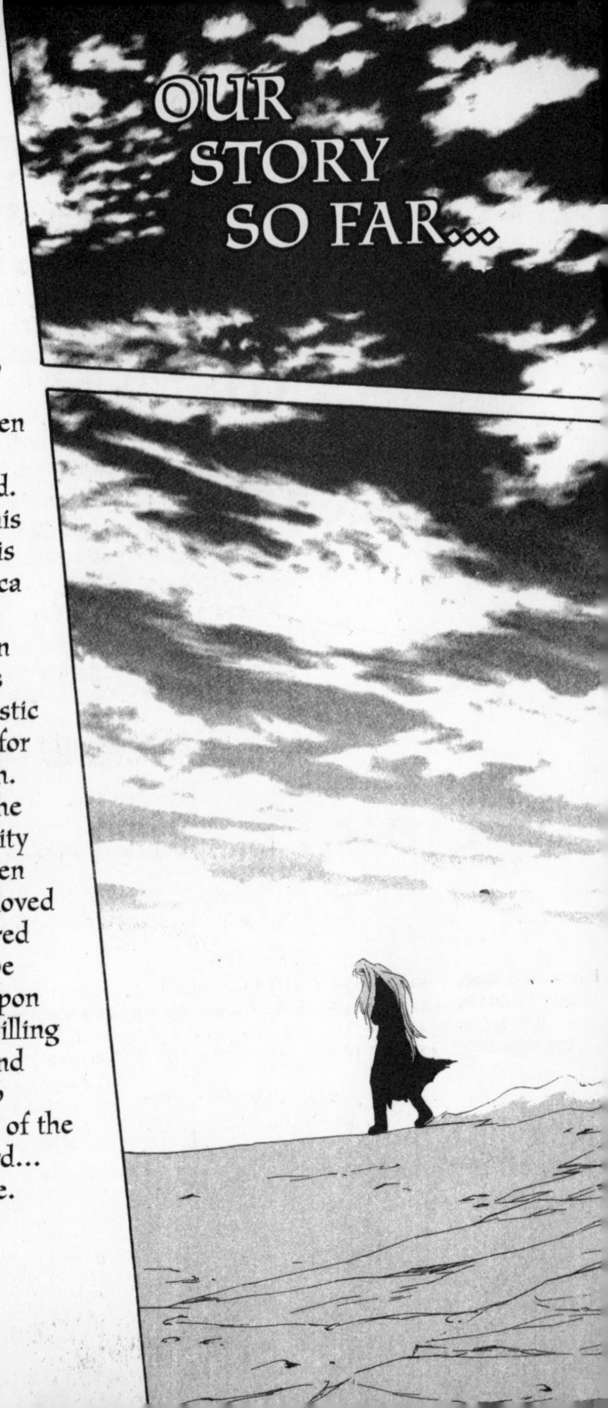
OUR STORY SO FAR...

Hunted by the insidious Calvaria Corporation, Rain and his young companion, Machika, take shelter in the frozen confines of the Angel's Graveyard. There he relates his tragic past, and his relationship to Yuca Collabell, the man who betrayed Rain hundreds of years ago. Yuca, a nihilistic immortal, longed for the peace of death. And by passing the curse of immortality on to Rain and then murdering his beloved Freya, Yuca ensured that Rain would be waiting for him upon his rebirth, and willing to kill him once and for all. Now, deep within the bowels of the Angel's Graveyard... that day has come.

Immortal Rain Vol. 4
Created by Kaori Ozaki

Translation - Michael Wert
English Adaptation - Sam Stormcrow Hayes
Copy Editors - Suzanne Waldman and Aaron Sparrow
Retouch and Lettering - SSI Production Support Team
Production Artist - James Dashiell
Cover Design - Kyle Plummer

Editor - Bryce P. Coleman
Digital Imaging Manager - Chris Buford
Pre-Press Manager - Antonio DePietro
Production Managers - Jennifer Miller and Mutsumi Miyazaki
Art Director - Matt Alford
Managing Editor - Jill Freshney
VP of Production - Ron Klamert
Editor-in-Chief - Mike Kiley
President and C.O.O. - John Parker
Publisher and C.E.O. - Stuart Levy

A **TOKYOPOP** ® Manga

TOKYOPOP Inc.
5900 Wilshire Blvd. Suite 2000
Los Angeles, CA 90036

E-mail: info@TOKYOPOP.com
Come visit us online at www.TOKYOPOP.com

ISBN: 1-59182-990-9

First TOKYOPOP printing: January 2005
10 9 8 7 6 5 4 3 2 1
Printed in the USA

IMMORTAL RAIN

VOLUME 4

BY
KAORI OZAKI

HAMBURG // LONDON // LOS ANGELES // TOKYO